Daniel Seelhofer

INTERPERSONAL LEADERSHIP
AN APPLIED GUIDE

Daniel Seelhofer

INTERPERSONAL LEADERSHIP
AN APPLIED GUIDE

ACADEMIC EDITION

ogma

OGMA EDUCATION
We work with international experts
to develop easy-to-understand,
application-focused materials for
graduate students and executives,
providing you with current,
advanced thinking and practice.

Interpersonal Leadership: An Applied Guide
Daniel Seelhofer

First edition

Published by OGMA Education
An imprint of OGMA Publishing GmbH, Switzerland

Copyright © 2017 OGMA Publishing GmbH, Switzerland

Cover design: dase
Cover photo: ShutterStock
Editing: misi

Printed in the U.S.A.
ISBN 978-3-9523944-9-6

TO MY TEAM
AND TO MY STUDENTS

CONTENT OVERVIEW

DETAILED CONTENTS

Tables

Figures

Illustrations

Exercises

Forms and Templates

FOREWORD

Entering the term *leadership* into Google elicits more than 600 million search results. Clearly, the topic is highly relevant. However, even today few companies seem to consider the traits and behaviors that leaders need to be effective in their jobs and to serve their organizations' goals and people. In this context, leadership and its study and practice have become more important than ever. Interpersonal leadership skills that are able to channel attention and motivation from the individual to the collective are crucial to building teams of strong individuals with a sense of shared purpose for a company's success. Leadership has a tremendous effect on an organization: Good leaders can get outstanding performance even from inexperienced teams, while bad leaders can demoralize even the most experienced and highly motivated people. Selecting and developing leaders is thus a key task for any organization.

Leadership is a journey. Dr. Seelhofer's extensive professional and academic experience and knowledge and his impressive track record as a leader has enabled him to describe and explain the factors that define good leadership in a clear and easily accessible way. This excellently researched and very insightful book will guide you through that journey and will help you achieve success in your leadership duties.

Gianni Valeri
Leadership consultant & former
CEO Staffinder/Coople (Switzerland)

PREFACE

Dear Reader,

Thank you for buying this book. In it, you will find a number of practical tips and tools as well as a lot of reliable, empirically validated information about leading. Its contents, although based on a very thorough review of the extant literature, are also strongly influenced by my own leadership experience, which by now spans more than thirty years in the military and the private and public sectors. Additionally, they reflect my extensive interactions with executives around the globe, both during projects and while teaching on various Executive MBA and Master of Science programs. Despite the many differences in their work settings, one thing these practicing or aspiring leaders all have in common is a perpetual lack of time. And although you will find a plethora of books on leadership, my experience over the years has left me convinced that there is still a clear need for an easy-to-understand, application-focused and most of all holistic introduction to important concepts of leadership.

The book you hold in your hand is my attempt to fill part of that niche. It is the first of three books about leadership at the interpersonal, organizational, and strategic levels and is intended for administrators and graduate or executive students who have some leadership experience but lack formal training and knowledge in this subject. Its aim is to provide you with a solid understanding of fundamentals and the corresponding tools that will help you in your organizational work. It is by no means a complete account of everything there would be to know nor is it likely to answer every single question you might have. But it will provide you with an efficient introduction to things you have to know as a leader—and that is what it sets out to achieve. Enjoy!

Daniel Seelhofer
Zurich, July 2017

1 INTRODUCTION TO LEADERSHIP

LEARNING OUTCOMES

After this chapter, you should be able to

- explain the three levels of leadership,
- define 'leadership',
- discuss the nature and contingent importance of leadership, and
- analyze a leadership problem using the Four Factors of Leadership framework.

1.1 Levels of Leadership

A lot has already been written about leadership. However, the literature often confuses aspiring leaders by using contradictory terms and varying definitions. This is partly because, often without saying so explicitly, the various authors are not actually discussing the same thing. In fact, there are three distinct levels of leadership, and each requires a different skill set:

- interpersonal,
- tactical, and
- strategic. *(together: organizational)*

This book is concerned with the first of these, interpersonal or direct leadership. Unless otherwise specified, the term 'leadership' is used throughout to refer to this level.

Interpersonal leadership is concerned with leading small units and teams, normally no more than five to eight direct reports, the leader's immediate subordinates. This type of leadership is characterized by frequent interaction between leader and followers, including regular face-to-face contact. In fact, even the heads of huge organizations only lead a handful of people directly. For example, in 2017 less than a dozen people reported directly to the CEO of ABB[1]. The number of direct reports is called the *leadership span*. It is an important number, because higher leadership span has been empirically linked to higher group member fluctuation (Dorian et al., 2004): people leave for greener pastures. More people means less face-to-face time with each, until the leader spends too much time doing personnel management and not enough actually leading. This can lead to subordinates feeling neglected, and then in turn to faltering motivation, decreased performance, and eventually higher team turnover. Consequently, in most organizations, basic team size tends to be less than ten. Examples of skills and traits required for this level of leadership include self-awareness, situational awareness, decisiveness, and empathy. These aspects are discussed in Chapters 3.1 and 5.3.

Tactical leadership deals with entire organizational units, which normally consist of several teams and/or functional areas. The size of such units is not clearly defined. Although often less than 100 employees, they may also be much larger. For example, in some companies, the typical tactical business unit, a department, may be up to 250 employees, and in many armies a battalion consists of up to 1,000 soldiers. In contrast to strategic units, tactical units do not develop their own long-term strategies, but they do develop and implement tactical (i.e. medium-term) and operational (i.e. short-term) plans when implementing the strategies of a superior level. In addition to solid interpersonal leadership skills, this level calls for mastery of organizational leadership methodology, good cross-cultural communication abilities, and the effective use of leadership support to master complexity.

---

[1] ABB (ASEA Brown Boveri) is a Swedish-Swiss high-tech engineering multinational corporation with a 2016 headcount of about 132,000.

Finally, strategic leadership refers to the long-term direction of strategic units. These may be whole companies but could also be individual divisions if they have strategic responsibility. Whether an SME of 50 people or a multinational's strategic business unit of 10,000 people or more, the distinguishing characteristic of this level is that its decisions ultimately affect the very survival of the organization. In addition to interpersonal and tactical leadership skills, this level requires excellent analytical skills, foresight, and sound strategic thinking.

Tactical and strategic leadership are often amalgamated under the terms organizational or indirect leadership. The skill sets mentioned above are cumulative; higher-level leadership always also needs the lower-level leadership skills. Therefore, it is difficult for organizational leaders to succeed without interpersonal skills. Figure 1 summarizes these deliberations.

Figure 1: The Three Levels of Leadership

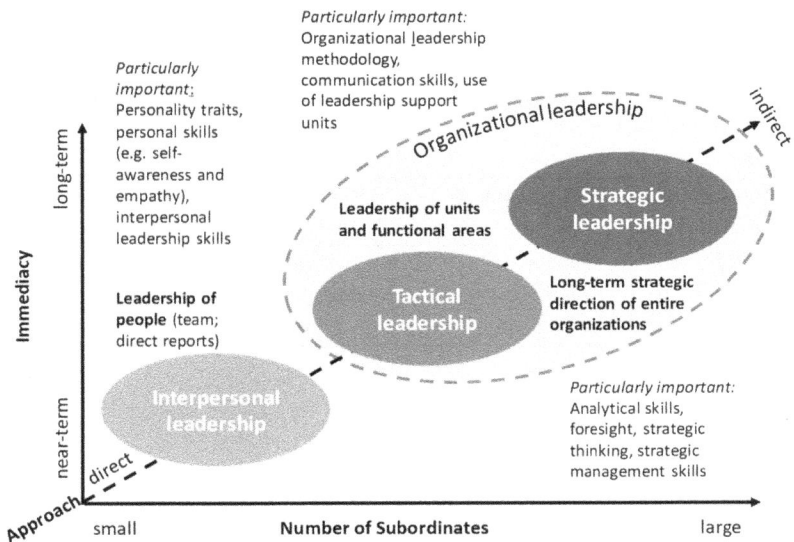

Source: author.

Each level differs in how many people are directly and indirectly led, how subordinates should be approached, their purpose, and their leadership task and time focus. However, the ideal direct leadership span at any level remains at a recommended maximum of about eight subordinates. Table 1, below, shows how each level differs from the other two.

Table 1:   The Three Levels of Leadership

Aspect	Type of Leadership		
	Interpersonal	Organizational	
		Tactical	Strategic
Purpose	Implementing the mission	Implementing the mission	Setting the mission
Leadership task focus	Enabling and motivating people to do their jobs	Creating the right circumstances for success	Ensuring survival of the organization
Number of subordinates	Small groups or teams	Medium to large groups (departments, business units), normally consisting of several teams and hierarchical levels	Entire organizations (companies or strategic business units)
Leadership span	Max. 8 direct reports (recommendation)		
Approach to subordinates	Mostly direct	Semi-direct	Mostly indirect
Time focus	Tends to be immediate or short-term	Tends to be near- to medium-term	Medium- to long-term

Source: author.

1.2   Definitions of Leadership

Even if we focus only on the interpersonal level, the term 'leadership' still means many things to many people, and no universally agreed definition exists. As mentioned before, this may partly be because different authors talk about different levels of leadership. However, the concept is also inherently subjective. People have specific, culturally influenced expectations of leaders which are reflected in the varying definitions of leadership. Nonetheless, most of these include common themes and terms, such as

- people orientation—'influence', 'motivate', 'enable', 'leaders and followers', 'trust',
- goal orientation—'mission', 'vision', 'achieve', 'purpose', 'direction', 'success',
- change orientation—'changes', 'future',
- process orientation—'action', 'effectiveness', 'flexible', 'anticipate', and
- time orientation—'timely'.

The definitions of leadership in Table 2 attest to this.

Table 2:   Definitions of Leadership

Definition	Source
"Leadership is the ability of an individual to influence, motivate, and enable others to contribute toward the effectiveness and success of the organizations of which they are members."	House et al. (2004)
"Leadership is an influence relationship among leaders and followers who intend real changes that reflect their shared purposes."	Rost (1993)
"Leadership is a function of knowing yourself, having a vision that is well communicated, building trust among colleagues, and taking effective action to realize your own leadership potential."	Bennis and Nanus (1985)
"Excellent organizations have leaders who shape the future and make it happen, acting as role models for its values and ethics and inspiring trust at all times. They are flexible, enabling the organization to anticipate and react in a timely manner to ensure its on-going success of the organization."	EFQM (2013)
"Leadership is the process of influencing others to accomplish the mission by providing purpose, direction, and motivation."	U.S: Army (1990)

Another highly important aspect of leadership, though often neglected in its definition, is making decisions. Leaders regularly need to make decisions about a host of issues, even if this is only the small decision to include the team in making a much bigger decision. A leader who is unable or unwilling to make decisions when they are needed is a poor leader. Based on these considerations, the following definitions of leadership will be used in this book:

> **Generic definition of leadership:** *leadership is aligning and focusing the leader's and the subordinates' thoughts and actions to serve a common purpose or reach a common goal.*
>
> **Definition of interpersonal leadership:** *leadership is making timely decisions, developing workable solutions, motivating and enabling followers to implement them, monitoring the implementation, ensuring the circumstances for success, taking responsibility for direct consequences, and sharing recognition and rewards.*

This definition highlights major aspects of leadership:

- Decisions have to be made in time; if not, they may be worthless.
- Solutions do not need to be perfect, but they need to work.
- Followers need to be both motivated and given the resources and competences necessary to perform their assigned tasks.
- Before and while solutions are implemented, the leader has to ensure the right circumstances for success, for instance by using his or her network to find additional resources, protecting the team from office politics, and so on.
- When implementing solutions, the leader needs to take an active interest in the work of the team to recognize problems early on.
- In case of problems, the leader accepts responsibility.
- And if things turn out well, the leader shares rewards and recognition with the team members involved.

That is what leaders do.

1.3   The Nature of Leadership

To paraphrase British author and dramatist W. Somerset Maugham (1874–1965), there are three rules for creating good leaders. Unfortunately, no one knows what they are."

The nature of leadership is elusive, yet leadership is found in many places: families, schools, clubs, politics, sports, and the armed forces, as well as management. Basically, some form of leadership arises wherever people congregate. This raises a number of questions. How universal is leadership? When is a leader seen as good? When is he or she objectively effective? Why do people follow one person but not another?

To some extent, leadership is in the eye of the beholder. Implicit Leadership Theory (ILT), as developed by Robert Lord and others, suggests that followers have implicit assumptions and expectations about what constitutes good leadership and what personal traits, qualities, and behaviors a leader should display[1]. These assumptions influence followers' perception of, reception of, and responses to a new leader, because they implicitly generalize from ingrained values and past experiences to this new situation. Consequently, a leader who was very successful in one context is not necessarily equally good in another.

Leadership is also complex. The consequences of decisions and actions are often not fully foreseeable, and leadership situations tend to be fluid. The uncertainty that characterizes most leadership problems stems from three principal sources: the leader, his or her followers, and the situation itself. For most leaders, uncertainty leads to stress. This is partly moderated by cultural forces; some cultures tend to deal with uncertainty much better than others.[2] Nonetheless,

---

[1] This point is further explored in Chapter 5 on page 253f.

[2] For example, Germany is a culture that exhibits strong uncertainty avoidance. This is reflected in the formalized, codified law system and in the preference for deductive rather than inductive work styles. In contrast, Ireland is a culture in which uncertainty avoidance is less evident, with a reliance on pragmatism and creativity and a preference for inductive work styles.

reducing uncertainty, for instance through good business intelligence, solid fact-checking, or reliable reporting by subordinates, is an important aspect of leadership in any setting. Uncertainty can be caused by incomplete information, by organizational factors such as ongoing change processes, group dynamics among followers, or by factors related to the leader's person, such as cognitive style, inside-the-box thinking, ego, ambition, or an inherent resistance to change. Other aspects, such as time pressure or media scrutiny, can increase stress further, which in turn can lead to problems like the illusion of control—feeling on top of the situation, even if that is objectively not the case—or a loss of perspective that may impede the leader's decision-making capability.

Illustration 1 provides further perspectives on the nature of leadership through quotes from famous leaders.

1.4   The Impact of Leadership

Leadership is commonly considered to have a significant impact on the performance of teams and organizations. However, this notion is not universally shared. A stream of studies in the 1970s aimed to show empirically that leadership, contrary to popular opinion, had little to no impact. So, who is right? One problem is that the impact of leadership is hard to measure directly. To examine it scientifically, researchers have often found it more practicable to study leadership succession instead. They reason that if noticeable improvements in performance occur after a leader has been replaced, then that effect must be due to the influence of the new leader, and thus of leadership. This logic has led to the emergence of three competing theories[1] that try to explain why leaders are replaced.

The *ritual scapegoating theory* (RST) postulates that succession, and thus leadership, has no effect on organizational outcomes.

---

[1] For more details on these perspectives, see Seelhofer (2007).

Illustration 1:   The Nature of Leadership in Quotes

"Treat your men as you would your own beloved sons.
And they will follow you into the deepest valley."
Sun Tzu (~544-496 BC), Chinese general, strategist, and philosopher

"I am not afraid of an Army of lions led by a sheep.
I am afraid of an Army of sheep led by a lion."
Alexander the Great (356-323 BC), King of Macedon and
creator of one of the ancient world's largest empires

"A leader leads by example, whether he intends to or not."
John Quincy Adams (1767–1848), 6ᵗʰ President of the United States

"A leader is a dealer in hope."
Napoleon Bonaparte (1769-1821), French general and emperor

"Example is not the main thing in influencing others. It is the only thing."
Albert Schweitzer (1875–1965), French-German theologist, philosopher, and physician

"You must be the change you wish to see in the world."
Mahatma Gandhi (1869-1948), leader of the Indian
independence movement in British-ruled India

"Success is not final, failure is not fatal: it is the courage to continue that counts."
Sir Winston Leonard Spencer-Churchill, (1874–1965), British politician and statesman
and Prime Minister of the United Kingdom 1940–1945 and 1951–1955.

"You don't lead by hitting people over the head. That's assault, not leadership."
Dwight D. Eisenhower (1890-1969), 34th President of the United States and
Supreme Commander Allied Forces in Europe during World War II.

"Management is doing things right. Leadership is doing the right things."
Peter F. Drucker (1909–2005), management scholar and thinker

"The only real training for leadership is leadership."
Antony Jay (born 1930), English writer, broadcaster, and director

"Before you're a leader, success is all about growing yourself.
When you become a leader, success is all about growing others."
John Francis "Jack" Welch, Jr. (born 1935), former Chairman and
CEO of General Electric and leadership author.

"Business is not war, but leadership is leadership."
William A. Cohen (born 1938), former U.S. Air Force Major General,
leadership scholar, marketing professor, and author

"A leader is one who knows the way, goes the way, and shows the way."
John C. Maxwell (born 1947), American leadership author and speaker

Instead, leaders are replaced because this pacifies a public which falsely believes that the leader's influence has led to periods of poor performance.

The *common sense theory* (CST) holds that successions occur primarily after spells of bad performance, and that these increase performance as a result of a positive shift in the organization's environmental fit[1]. Thus, leadership matters, and bad performance leads to the replacement of bad leaders with better ones.

The *vicious cycle theory* (VCT) suggests that low performance caused by bad leadership and insufficient organizational efficiency leads to the replacement of the leader. This further disrupts the organization and leads to even worse performance. Thus, leadership matters, but succession is disruptive, and the effect of a new leader is not strong enough to offset this.

All three perspectives enjoy some empirical support. So how can their apparent incompatibility be resolved? Friedman and Singh (1989: 722) state that the real question should not be whether leaders matter but rather under what conditions they do. In a study of top managers in 531 companies from 42 industries, Wasserman, Nohria, and Anand (2001) found that the impact of leadership differs considerably between industries. Furthermore, industry concentration and exchange constraints such as difficulties in obtaining funding affect a leader's influence (Salancik and Pfeffer, 1977). The higher industry concentration is, and thus the higher exchange constraints are, the higher the impact of the leader tends to be. Consequently, the impact of a leader is higher when opportunities are scarce or there is a corporate crisis, because it is in such a situation that missing an opportunity could do the most damage.

In summary, the more dynamically a situation develops, the more important leadership tends to become.

---

[1] The idea of 'environmental fit' is a key postulate of contingency theory. In a nutshell, it holds that an organization's strategy and structure must be able to deal with the challenges posed by the organization's environment. Therefore, if the environment changes significantly, the strategy and, possibly, structure need to be changed as well.

Figure 2: The Contingent Importance of Leadership

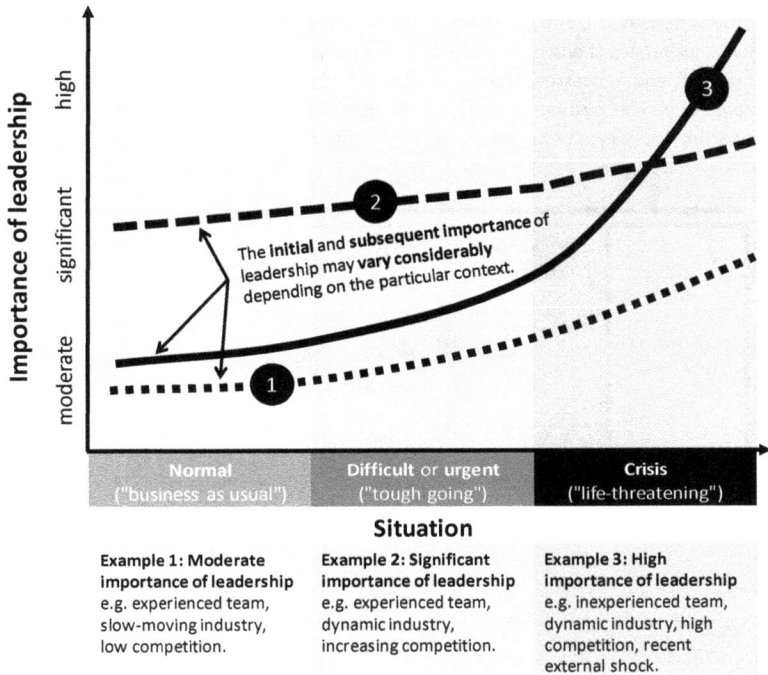

Example 1: Moderate importance of leadership e.g. experienced team, slow-moving industry, low competition.

Example 2: Significant importance of leadership e.g. experienced team, dynamic industry, increasing competition.

Example 3: High importance of leadership e.g. inexperienced team, dynamic industry, high competition, recent external shock.

Source: author.

Depending on an organization's particular situation, leadership may have a very noticeable or rather limited effect under normal conditions, but its impact will inevitably grow when a situation becomes more difficult. Note, though, that the scale in Figure 2 starts at 'moderate', not 'zero'. This reflects the stance taken in this book that, while its specific impact may vary, leadership is always an important contributor to team and organizational results. In other words, leadership is not always equally important, but it is never negligible. Excellence models like that of the European Foundation for Quality Management (EFQM) reflect this, as shown in Illustration 2.

Illustration 2:   Leadership in the EFQM Model

In the widely used European Foundation for Quality Management (EFQM) Excellence Model, leadership is one of five enablers, alongside 'people', 'strategy', 'partnerships & resources', and 'processes, products & services'. These enablers then influence results related to people, customers, society, and busines. This underscores the importance of leadership in the eyes of this influential accreditation body.

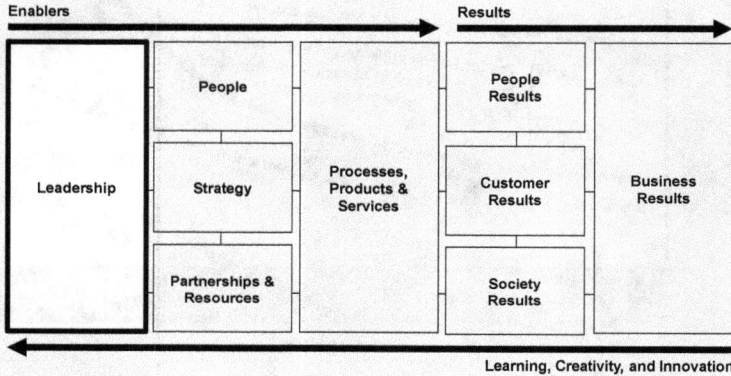

Enablers   Results

Leadership	People		People Results	
	Strategy	Processes, Products & Services	Customer Results	Business Results
	Partnerships & Resources		Society Results	

Learning, Creativity, and Innovation

Source: EFQM (2012:4)

1.5   The Leadership Development Dilemma

The well-known nature versus nurture[1] debate arises in the context of leadership as the question of whether leaders are born or made. The Great Man Theory[2] of the 19th century claims that leadership cannot be learned. However, if that were the case, then all leadership development programs would be useless, all the companies and people that undertake them stupid, and the only sensible leadership-related activity of companies would be to select the right leaders for

---

[1] This long-running debate is about whether a person's behavior is inherited (i.e. genetic) or determined by the environment, (i.e. through a person's upbringing, social circumstances, and training). The phrase was coined by British polymath Francis Galton in 1874.

[2] See Chapter 2.1, page 24.

the right jobs—a daunting task in any case, of course. Although the field has advanced considerably beyond this archaic view, the question of whether some people are born with great leadership abilities and others are not still needs an answer. In a 2003 review of the extant literature on the Big Five personality factors, Thomas Bouchard and Matt McGue found that these factors, which are to a large extent responsible for a person's leadership potential, are all inheritable, albeit to various degrees:

- openness to experience: 57%
- conscientiousness: 49%
- extraversion: 54%
- agreeableness: 42%
- neuroticism: 48%

In other words, while some people may be born with much higher leadership potential than others and thus should become effective leaders more readily, a person's upbringing and training also play an important role. Therefore, although certain personality aspects, such as an ingrained resistance to change or a lack of empathy, may make it much harder for someone with limited potential to become an effective leader, leadership can clearly be learned.

But even though leadership may be formally learned, and therefore taught, there is no substitute for experience. Excellent leadership takes long practice, and ample experience of both successes and failures are important contributors to leader effectiveness, although, as Indian IT industrialist Narayana Murthy observed, it is often harder to learn from success than failure.

Leadership development is covered in more detail in Chapter **7**.

1.6   The Four Factors of Leadership

So, if leadership matters and can be learned, what are its components? The Four Factors of Leadership[1] framework is a convenient and simple—but not simplistic—way of thinking about leadership problems. It postulates that, in essence, these all comprise four distinct, interrelated factors:

- the leader,
- the followers,
- the communication used, and
- the situation.

The *leader* directly influences the leadership situation through his or her personality, competencies, and decisions. Consequently, the leader must have good self-awareness and an honest understanding of his or her own capabilities and limitations, strengths and weaknesses, and available leadership styles. The leader must also strive continuously to develop and improve.

The *followers* differ in experience, confidence, personality, and quite likely cultural and demographic background. Consequently, they require a leadership approach suitably adapted to each individual as well as a common, appropriate leadership approach to the group as a whole. The leader must understand each team member's personality, capabilities, limitations, strengths, and weaknesses individually. The leader must also know their relevant individual histories and be able to anticipate their responses to particular leadership and communication styles. The leader must understand the dynamics at work in the group and the team's group history, rituals, and symbols.

---

[1] Note that this is not identical to Bower's and Seashore's Four Factors of Effective Leadership. Rather, the idea of leadership problems having four factors that all need to be considered goes back to a U.S. Army manual that was in use in the 1990s.

Table 3: Leader Insights, Traits, and Skills for the Four Factors

Factor	What the leader must understand (examples)	Types and sources of knowledge (examples)	Required leader traits and skills (examples)
Leader	▪ Personality ▪ Capabilities and limitations ▪ Strengths & weaknesses ▪ Available leadership styles	▪ Personality assessment tools (e.g. MBTI, 16 pf, EQ, NEO…) ▪ Knowledge of leadership theory ▪ Experience and outside feedback	▪ Self-knowledge ▪ Self-discipline ▪ A realistic understanding of own strengths and weaknesses
Followers	*Individually* ▪ Personalities ▪ Individual histories ▪ Strengths/weaknesses ▪ Response to a particular leadership and communication style *As a group* ▪ Group dynamic ▪ Group history, rituals, and symbols	▪ Personality assessment tools (where appropriate) ▪ Observations and discussions ▪ Knowledge of follower personalities, backgrounds, and circumstances ▪ Knowledge of motivators and demotivators ▪ Knowledge of follower's work	▪ Empathy ▪ Analytical skills ▪ Work-related skills
Communication	▪ Available channels (e.g. phone, face-to-face, email) ▪ Required frequency ▪ Appropriate style	▪ Knowledge of situation and its urgency and resonance ▪ Knowledge of followers and their reactions	▪ Communication skills
Situation	▪ Major drivers and aspects ▪ Possible development paths (scenarios) ▪ Available decisions and their consequences	▪ Analytical tools ▪ Leadership methodologies ▪ Decision-making tools ▪ Experience	▪ Decisiveness ▪ Analytical skills ▪ Professional skills

Source: author.

Communication facilitates the exchange of information and ideas from one person to another. It is effective only if each side understands completely what the other wants, which may be influenced by differing personalities as well as by the choice of transmission channel and cultural and linguistic differences. The leader must also understand the required frequency and style of communication.

Finally, good leadership depends on a solid understanding of the *situation*, which constantly shifts and always differs in some aspect or another from previous situations, even if they seem exactly the same. Staying on top of the situation is a key skill of excellent leaders. The leader must understand not just the situation's major drivers and key aspects but also its possible development paths or scenarios and the corresponding decisions and their consequences.

These four factors together pose a number of demands on a leader, and they are summarized in Table 3.

1.7   Chapter Recap

TAKEAWAYS

What you should take away from this chapter:

1. There are three levels of leadership: interpersonal, tactical, and strategic. The first is also referred to as direct leadership, the latter two together as organizational leadership.

2. The leadership span refers to the number of direct reports of a leader. The recommended leadership span is normally around 5-8 people.

3. Leadership is defined as making timely decisions, developing workable solutions, motivating and enabling followers to implement them, monitoring the implementation, ensuring the circumstances for success, taking responsibility for direct consequences, and sharing recognition and rewards.

4. Leadership is complex. Uncertainty leads to stress, so leaders should take measures to reduce uncertainty.

5. Leadership is always important, but its importance is contingent on circumstances and rises with the urgency of a situation.

6. Some people are born with better chances of becoming good leaders than others, but leadership can be taught and learned.

7. When analyzing a leadership problem, four factors must be considered: the leader, those following (i.e. the team), communication, and the specific situation.

CHECK QUESTIONS

Try to answer the questions below. If you need help, check the sample answers in the annex.

1. Which skills are particularly important for interpersonal leadership?

2. What is the number of direct reports called, what is the recommended optimal number, why, and on what does this depend?

3. What is the definition of leadership?

4. What causes uncertainty about a leadership situation?

5. What are the Four Factors of Leadership?

6. What must a leader understand about his team?

1.8   Exercises

On the following pages, you will find exercises related to the content of this chapter. If you need help, check the sample solutions in the annex.

Exercise 1   Seeking Solomon

Liz, the CEO of a mid-sized producer of parts for the automotive industry, is pondering a problem. It's really the same thing every time, over and over: her two senior department heads fight constantly. Budgets, events, recognition—they cannot agree on virtually anything. Aware of this, Liz is already wary of the skirmish that'll inevitably occur during next week's meeting.

Part of the problem is the competitive nature of the two managers' relationship. Peter, who is head of production and at 52 years the older of the two, progressed quite slowly through the ranks and is physically small. He has a reputation as a bit of a recluse. Krish, the Canadian-born 43-year old head of marketing with Indian roots, is the opposite: physically big and strong, he is outspoken and popular. He was always promoted rapidly in the past, but he has gotten a bit stuck recently. Consequently, both managers constantly try to assert themselves. Peter feels superior thanks to his more advanced age, longer tenure, and more prestigious education, but inferior due to his slower progress in the past and his smaller physical stature. For Krish, it's the other way around.

The two tend to be jealous of whatever recognition the other receives. And when budgets need to be set, the fight's usually about who gets the bigger piece of the pie, even if Liz has always taken special pains to fund all projects adequately. Even when discussing innocuous, non-work-related stuff like restaurants or sports, the two can hardly ever agree on anything.

In the past, Liz has tried threats and reasoning, to no avail. She has frequently expounded how the constant tension and fighting takes its toll on the team harmony. She's tried to bribe them with fringe benefits and used emotion to appeal to their loyalty. Nothing has worked.

Now the company is about to initiate two major strategic initiatives. Liz wants each of the two squabblers to head one of these important projects. But she's not sure how to assign them. The projects are not exactly equal in size and scope, so they'll probably need to be funded differently. Exacerbating the problem is the fact that Bolin, the chairman of the board and one of Liz's oldest work friends as well as her role model, is expected to attend the kick-off this coming Friday. Liz fears the inevitable fight will reflect badly on her as a leader: that she'll feel terribly embarrassed as a result and lose face in front of Bolin. She turns to you for advice.

Questions and Assignments

- List four realistic options how Liz could proceed, with advantages and disadvantages.
- Is there a 'fair' way of assigning projects and distributing budgets?
- What is your advice to Liz? How can/should she handle this issue?

Exercise 2   Analyzing the Four Factors of Leadership

Sometimes, it can be helpful to think systematically about a given leadership problem, even going as far as writing down the key points for each of the four factors. The table below summarizes the four factors for a dysfunctional project team in a world-leading Swiss company:

Situation		
General situation: A large Swiss elevator manufacturer has won the contract to install hypermodern elevators in the bottom and top stations of a large Japanese ski resort. The project team consists of members located in three countries (Switzerland, Germany, Japan). Only after the elevators had already been installed was it noticed that they use touchscreen panels that cannot be operated using gloves, which has caused a large number of complaints. The client has threatened to sue the company.		
Specific situation (now): The former project leader has been fired, and a new project leader brought in from outside the firm. He has just started his job and, so far, has only spoken to the three leaders of the subprojects and a few project team members on the phone. The subproject leaders do not work full-time for the project and do not report to him.		
Leader	**Followers (Team)**	**Communications**
Experienced project manager with a reputation for completing challenging multi-million projects. New to the company. Swiss, male, middle-aged.	Three leaders of subprojects (one Swiss, middle-aged, based in Zurich; one German, older, based in Stuttgart; and one German, young, based in Tokyo) who have all worked on the project from the beginning (marketing, development/engineering, fulfilment). No shared understanding of where the project went wrong and what needs to be done. Engineering blames marketing, marketing blames fulfilment, and fulfilment blames engineering.	Mainly written (email), sometimes via video call, rarely face-to-face (group and individual meetings).

Imagine you are the new head of this project. Using your real background (and, where necessary, reasonable assumptions), fill in the table below.

Situation
Possible development paths or scenarios: How could the situation conceivably progress? What is the worst case, what the best?

Leader	Followers	Communications
Immediate measures to be taken regarding the leader (you)?	*Immediate measures (what needs to be done right now) with regard to followers?*	*Appropriate mix of channels/media, with frequency?*
Your leadership development needs?	*Additional measures (for later implementation?)*	

2 THE EVOLUTION OF LEADERSHIP THEORY

LEARNING OUTCOMES

After this chapter, you should be able to

- explain the evolution of leadership research and theory, and
- name and explain major concepts and tools that have emerged over the course of it.

Note: this chapter traces the evolution of modern leadership theory and provides an overview. Particularly important models and frameworks are examined in more detail in subsequent chapters.

2.1 Great Man Theory

Although man's interest in leadership is likely as old as mankind itself, modern systematic inquiry into the nature of leadership is comparatively new. It originated in the mid-1800s with Scottish historian Thomas Carlyle's assertion that "the history of the world is but the biography of great men". This reflected his conviction that history is shaped by heroes, both through their personal attributes, such as charisma, intelligence, or sheer will, and through divine inspiration. Following this logic, learning about leadership would be accomplished by studying the biographies of such 'great men'. Other well-known contemporaries supported this view, which came to be known as the *Great Man Theory*. For example, Nietzsche wrote in *Untimely Meditations* (1876) that "the goal of humanity lies in its highest specimens". However, some other writers of the period, such as Herbert Spencer and William James, criticized this view as a fantasy and insisted that these great men were merely a product of their environment, thereby seeding one of the core concepts of the situational, or contingency, leadership theories that emerged a hundred years later. Indeed, in 1869's *War and Peace*, Russian literary giant Leo Tolstoy referred to such men as "history's slaves". A product of its time, the Great Man Theory fell out of favor among serious leadership scholars after World War II, but it still appears in everyday life and even scholarly thought in many parts of the world.

2.2   Trait Theories

Interest in the biographies of great men also sparked an interest in what makes someone a good leader: which personal characteristics good leaders possess. The *Trait School*, which was dominant in leadership research during the 1930s and 1940s and re-emerged in the 1980s, is concerned with the mental, physical, and social characteristics of good leaders, in other words with leaders' personalities. Scholars like W. H. Cowley (1931) examined such questions as "which traits distinguish a leader from a non-leader?" or "what is the extent of differences between leaders and other people?"

While early scholars generally viewed traits quite narrowly as those immutable aspects of personality that are present at birth, this view has shifted to considering all the relatively enduring qualities that distinguish leaders from non-leaders (Kirckpatrick and Locke, 1991). For example, Stogdill (1948) lists decisiveness, fluency in speech, interpersonal skills, and administrative abilities as important leader traits.

The original Trait School was heavily criticized, for three main reasons. Firstly, it failed to reliably identify traits that predicted leader emergence and effectiveness. Secondly, it could not account for situation-specific differences in leader behavior. Finally, it tended to rely on follower interpretations of leader effectiveness rather than objective measures.

Using greater conceptual sophistication and more rigorous methodologies, the new Trait School that emerged in the 1980s has regained attention and prominence. For example, although Dean Barnlund found no reliable predictor of leadership emergence in a 1962 study, David Kenny of the University of Connecticut and Stephen Zaccaro of Virginia Tech re-examined Barnlund's results using more advanced methodology[1] and concluded in a 1983 paper that a substantial portion of observed leadership variance could indeed be attributed to a few stable characteristics that involved perceiving group needs and goals and adjusting one's personal approach accordingly.

In a 2002 review of more recent Trait School literature and meta-analysis of its empirical results, Timothy Judge and colleagues used the well-established *Big Five* personality factors[2] as a framework to organize the results of previous trait-based studies. They found substantial support for the trait perspective by organizing traits in this way. For example, they found that traits associated with extraversion, openness, and to a lesser extent conscientiousness were all conducive to both leader emergence and leader effectiveness, while agreeableness contributed to leader effectiveness but was negative for leader emergence[3], and neuroticism tended to contribute to neither.

In 2004, Zaccaro, Kemp, and Bader published their *Leader Attributes and Leader Performance Model*. This offers an explanation of how two types of leader attributes, *distal* (consisting of cognitive abilities, personality, and motives/values) and *proximal* (consisting of social appraisal skills, problem-solving skills, and expertise or

---

[1] Barnlund used a rotation design in which both the task and group members were repeatedly changed and the correlation between leadership rank in one group with the average leadership ranks received in all others groups calculated. In contrast, Kenny and Zaccaro used the so-called Social Relations Model.

[2] The Big Five are openness, conscientiousness, extraversion, agreeableness, and neuroticism.

[3] See Table 5 on page 52 for more details.

tacit knowledge), influence the leader processes which then, albeit moderated by the leader's environment, predict leader emergence, leader effectiveness, and leader advancement. The model is based on the premise that leadership emerges from the combined influence of multiple traits. In the annual meeting of the Society for Industrial and Organizational Psychology that same year, Kemp, Zaccaro, and two colleagues reported the findings of a study about the performance of military officers in a three-day decision-making exercise. The study assessed metacognition, tolerance for ambiguity, and social intelligence. It found that performance ratings were significantly stronger for participants who exhibited high levels of all three attributes than for those in whom this was not the case, while there were no differences among the rest (Kemp et al., 2004).

Trait research gave rise to a number of frameworks and instruments that are still in use today, most prominent among them a number of personality assessment tools such as the *Myers-Briggs Type Indicator* (MBTI), the *16 Personality Factors* framework, the Big Five personality traits framework mentioned above, the *NEO Personality Inventory*, and many more.

2.3　Behavioral Theories

Following the initial interest in leader traits, the 1940s saw the emergence of the *Behavioral School* of leadership. Moving beyond personality factors, these researchers were interested in which kinds of behaviors successful leaders exhibit, what type of leadership styles they can and actually do employ, and what kind of behavioral modification successful leaders undergo during their development. Questions examined included "which behaviors do leaders display?", "is leader behavior hard or soft?", "is leader behavior task or relationship oriented?", and "which behavior is most effective?" Many, though by no means all, of these studies were conducted in a management setting, and there was usually no distinction made between leaders and managers, as has sometimes been the case in later research literature.

One of the earliest systematic studies of leadership styles, although these were referred to as 'work climates', was conducted by German-born American sociologist Kurt Lewin, together with colleagues Ronald Lippitt and Ralph White. They identified three archetypical leadership styles (Lewin, Lippitt, and White, 1939):

- authoritarian,
- democratic, and
- laissez-faire.

In their experiment, *authoritarian* (later also called autocratic) leaders, who took decisions without consulting others, caused high levels of discontent.

In contrast, *democratic* (later also called participative) leaders involved their followers in the decision-making process. Fully democratic leaders facilitated a group consensus, while participative leaders listened to the various opinions in the group but reserved the right to make the decision themselves. This style was found to be appreciated the most by followers in these experiments, although reaching a good decision may be problematic if the leader is indecisive and there is a wide range of opinions.

Finally, a *laissez-faire* style minimized the leader's involvement in the decision-making process, allowing followers to make their own decisions. This style has subsequently been found to work well in teams of highly motivated and skilled experts without the need for central coordination. In general, however, teams led in this way were found not to invest the same energy and not to be as coherent in their work as when they were more actively led.

Lewin's framework is still one of the most commonly used classifications of leadership styles. More details are provided in Chapter 3.21[1].

In 1960, American management professor Douglas McGregor published *The Human Side of Enterprise*, in which he described two commonly found management styles that he referred to as Theory X and Theory Y. McGregor's work, which became highly influential, emerged from the Human Relations approach of organizational studies but, in essence, linked Maslow's Hierarchy of Needs with Taylor's Scientific Management.

Theory X describes a work environment in which workers are considered to be cogs in a machine. They are inherently lazy and try to avoid work whenever they can. They have no ambition and consequently prefer routine tasks. They pursue security and balk at responsibility. Because of this, however, they are also highly receptive to both positive and negative incentives. They must usually be forced to work and have to be offered rewards for above-average performance. They also need to be supervised very closely and threatened with punishment for misbehavior and underperformance. The assembly line factories of the early 20th century's automotive industry provide an example of this approach, with close supervision, challenging work quotas, high bonuses if those quotas were surpassed, and steep penalties for underperformance.

Theory Y, in contrast, sees workers as inherently self-motivated and ambitious, optimistic, dynamic, and flexible. They are perceived as enjoying their mental and physical labor, and the leader's main job is therefore to provide them with a stimulating work environment. An example of this approach is Google, whose workplaces, called campuses, include a number of play and relaxation areas, including so-called nap pods. The company also offers free meals, health and dental insurance, and even dry-cleaning, so that its employees can focus on their best work.

---

[1] See page 43f.

From a leadership perspective, putting a leader with a Theory X worldview in charge of teams that require a Theory Y approach (and vice versa) often leads to problems. The chances are quite strong that you have already experienced this.

A few years later, in 1964, American management theorists Robert Blake and Jane Mouton published the *Managerial Grid* model of leadership, which introduced the idea that managers normally exhibit concern for both production and people but that one of these two will usually be dominant. Based on this insight, they identified four archetypal management styles:

- In the *impoverished* (later called *indifferent*) style, managers show low concern for both production and people.
- In the *country-club management* (later called *accommodating*) style, managers show high concern for people but low concern for production.
- In the *middle-of-the-road* (later called *status quo*) style, managers with limited capabilities try to accommodate both production and people's needs but, as this is a trade-off for them, are only able to do so at medium levels.
- In the *authority-compliance* (also called *dictatorial* and, previously, *produce or perish*) style, managers show high concern for production but low concern for people, providing them with money and expecting performance in return.
- In the *team management style*, managers show high concern for both people and production, encouraging commitment and teamwork while mastering all aspects of production.

The optimal leadership style in this model, team management, is based on Theory Y. For more information on Blake-Mouton's model, see Chapter 3.23 on page 73f.

Research on *emotional intelligence*, although originally mainly trait-focused, can also be considered part of the Behavioral School, because it frequently considers abilities[1],which are behavior-based, in addition to traits. For instance, Goleman, Boyatzis, and McKee (2002) propose a 'mixed model' of emotional intelligence. This construct consists of self-awareness, self-management, social awareness, and relationship management. Self-awareness consists of emotional self-awareness, accurate self-assessment, and self-confidence, and is described as the leader's ability to read his or her own emotions and recognize their impact while using gut feelings to guide decisions. Self-management refers to controlling one's emotions and impulses and adapting to changing circumstances, and includes good self-control, adaptability, achievement orientation, initiative, and optimism. The chief component of social awareness, meaning the ability to sense, understand, and react to other's emotions while comprehending social networks, is empathy. Organizational awareness and a service mentality are also seen as important. Finally, relationship management requires inspiration, influence, and the abilities to help others develop, to manage conflict, to facilitate teamwork, and to act as a change catalyst.

In this line of research, Goleman (2000) identified several leadership styles commonly found in organizations:

- visionary,
- coaching,
- affiliative,
- democratic,
- pace-setting, and
- commanding.

These styles partly resemble those described by other authors but integrate elements from emotional intelligence research. According to Goleman, effective leaders use all of them in any given workweek. A detailed overview of them is provided in Chapter 3.27[2].

---

[1] In some leadership theory overviews, these ability, or skill, theories are considered a separate school of leadership.

[2] See page 80f.

2.4   Power and Influence Theories

Following the phenomenal success of Dale Carnegie's 1936 self-help megaseller *How to Win Friends and Influence People*, leadership research also turned its attention to this topic. Representing a particular interest in the nature, sources, and forms of power and influence, French and Raven's *Five Points of Power*, published in 1959, is the best known of the *power and influence theories*. It postulates that a leader's influence over his or her followers stems from two types of power, positional and personal. Positional power consists of legitimate power (i.e. being the boss), reward power (e.g. being able to issue raises and bonuses or grant time off), and coercive power (i.e. the ability to punish). Personal power stems from expert knowledge (acquired through education and experience) and what the authors call 'referent' power: the force of the leader's personality or charisma. The more of these powers that are present and the more each is developed, the more the leader can influence his or her followers.

Another important contribution to this body of literature is Robert Cialdini's 1980 book *Influence: The Psychology of Persuasion*. His basic premise is that people rely on generalizations when making decisions because they are overloaded with information, and this approach helps them to make mainly optimal decisions with a reasonable investment of time and thought. Understanding these generalizations enables an individual to exploit them to influence others. Cialdini uses a number of empirical examples to demonstrate that people have a tendency to reciprocate favors or what they consider to be favors[1]) done for them. In addition, someone who makes an initial, often small, commitment tends to honor that commitment[2] even if it grows, because they want to appear consistent in their behavior, just as they value consistency in others. Observing similar people, such as peers at work, provides 'social proof', which makes

---

[1] This is the basis for e.g. the omnipresence of free samples in marketing.

[2] This is the basis for e.g. try-before-you-buy offers.

people subconsciously want to act in a similar manner. People also tend to obey authority figures[1], and they are more easily persuaded by people they like[2]. Finally, people react instinctively to the information that something is scarce, for instance because it is limited in availability [3].

Although Cialdini was originally only interested in how customers make buying decisions, the six principles he identified can also be considered general factors that may influence a decision—including the decision to follow someone:

1. reciprocity,
2. commitment and consistency,
3. social proof,
4. authority,
5. liking, and
6. scarcity.

Although scholarly interest in this topic waned after its original heyday, it is still clearly relevant for leaders.

2.5   Situational and Contingency Theories

The *Situational and Contingency School*, which developed from the late 1950s onwards, was based on the notion of environmental 'fit': the need to match leaders, or at least their style, with situational demands. Important contributions include Tannenbaum and Schmidt's Leadership Continuum, Fiedler's Contingency Theory, Hersey and

---

[1] This is the basis for e.g. the use of medical doctors in pharmaceutical advertisements.

[2] This is the basis for e.g. the use of attractive actors in commercials, because people tend to believe that people who are physically appealing also possess other socially desirable characteristics (in psychology, this is called the *physical attractiveness stereotype*).

[3] This is e.g. part of the sales tactic employed by Spanish fashion chain Zara, which consciously produces less of each item than forecast demand to convey a sense of exclusivity and pressure customers to instantly buy at full price. This in turn largely eliminates the need to sell off remaining stock at discount prices or to write it off.

Blanchard's Situational Leadership, House's Path-Goal Theory, and the Vroom-Yetton-Jago Normative Decision Model.

In 1958, Robert Tannenbaum and Warren Schmidt published their *Leadership Continuum* in an article in the *Harvard Business Review*. In essence based on Lewin's leadership styles, the authors considered leadership to be a continuum between what they call "boss-centered" (i.e. authoritarian) and "subordinate-centered" (i.e. laissez-faire) leadership, with seven distinct "leadership patterns" (or leader behaviors) along this continuum[1]:

- *Authoritarian*: the leader makes the decision alone and then informs the team.
- *Paternalistic*: the leader makes the decision and then convinces subordinates of its value.
- *Consultative I*: the leader presents ideas and invites questions before making the decision.
- *Consultative II*: the leader presents a tentative decision that is subject to change.
- *Participative*: the leader presents the problem to the team and gathers suggestions but retains the final decision.
- *Democratic*: the leader defines the limits but delegates the decision to the team.
- *Laissez-faire*: the leader allows the subordinates to function within limits defined by a higher instance.

According to Tannenbaum and Schmidt, a leader should consider the following when deciding which of these styles to employ:

- forces in the leader,
- forces in the subordinates, and
- forces in the situation.

---

[1] Tannenbaum and Schmidt did not actually name these in their original article. Instead, they described each, as in the following example of their first style: "Manager makes decision and announces it" (Tannenbaum and Schmidt, 1958: 4).

Forces in the leader are considered by the authors to be the leader's value system, confidence in subordinates, leadership inclination (naturally more directive or more participative), and feelings of security in uncertain situations. Forces in the subordinates are their own personalities and the leader behaviors that they expect[1]. According to Tannenbaum and Schmidt, the amount of freedom that should be given to subordinates depends on their need for independence, readiness to assume responsibility, tolerance for ambiguity, interest in the problem, identification with the goals of the organization, knowledge and experience, and expectations of sharing in decision-making. Finally, forces in the situation are the type[2] of organization, the group's effectiveness, the problem itself, and the time pressure. In this model, effective leaders are those who accurately assess these forces and are able to adapt their leadership behavior accordingly.

Although highly influential, particularly in North America, Tannenbaum and Schmidt's model has also been criticized. Issues raised include the facts that the model assumes an organizational environment without power games and politics, that the leader is supposed to have sufficient information to make the choice of leadership style, and that the model only considers the first step in task allocation (i.e. the initiating structure), not the complete process that will eventually determine its actual effectiveness. In a 1973 comment on their own article, Tannenbaum and Schmidt updated their model by including the organizational and societal environment, changing the term 'subordinate' to 'non-manager', and introducing the notion of a regularly redefined total area of freedom shared between "managers" and "non-managers". For more information, see Chapter 3.22.

The *Contingency Model*, which American management psychologist Fred Fiedler introduced in 1958 and updated in 1967, postulates that group performance depends on leadership style (task or

---

[1] This is in line with *Implicit Leadership Theory*. Also see Chapter 5.3 on page 274f.

[2] By 'type' they really meant organizational culture, consisting of values and traditions, and embodied in the type of behaviors that are acceptable or unacceptable in that particular organization.

relationship orientation) and situational favorableness (determined by leader-member relations, task structure, and power) but is moderated by the stress levels of both the leader and the followers. In fact, stress is seen as a key determinant of leader effectiveness and may stem from three sources: the leader's superior(s), the leader's subordinates, and the situation.

Fiedler also examined the role of experience and found, surprisingly, that experience did not increase performance in all circumstances. Instead, he found that experience can impair performance under low-stress conditions but normally contributes to better performance in high-stress situations. The ability to control the group situation is therefore crucial for a leader, and because Fiedler sees a person's leadership style as ingrained and thus more or less fixed, a problematic situation is most easily solved by exchanging the leader. For more information on Fiedler's model, see Chapter 3.24 on page 75f.

In 1969, American behavioral scientist Paul Hersey and leadership trainer and author Ken Blanchard published what was originally called the 'Life-Cycle Theory of Leadership' but was renamed the *Situational Leadership Model* in the mid-1970s. It postulates that leaders need to adapt their style to the maturity of their followers. The authors describe four levels of maturity:

M1: The person lacks the skills needed to perform a task and is therefore both unable and unwilling to do the task.

M2: The person is willing to work on the task but does not have the skills it requires and is thus unable to take responsibility for it.

M3: The person has the required skills and experience and is consequently able to perform the task but lacks confidence or willingness.

M4: The person has the required skills and experience and is confident and willing both to work on the task and to take responsibility for it.

Maturity influences followers' development, which in turn is seen as depending on their competence or capability and commitment or willingness. Maturity and development may be task-specific: team members may generally be both capable and willing but still show low maturity when asked to perform certain tasks or if put in a project group they do not like. Correspondingly, the leader's style should adjust not only to the group or individual but also to the task situation.

Depending on development levels, a leader may employ a range of styles:

- Followers with low competence (e.g. because they are low-skilled) but high commitment (e.g. because they have just entered the organization and want to prove themselves) require a *directing* style, meaning the leader defines the role of the person or group and provides specific instructions on how to perform them, including frequent progress check-ups, but does not provide much socio-emotional support.
- Followers with low competence and low commitment require a *coaching* style, providing both fairly detailed instructions and strong socio-emotional support by providing opinions and information, guidance, and positive reinforcement.
- Followers with high competence (e.g. researchers) but low or at least variable commitment (e.g. due to frequent organizational changes and insufficient management communication in the recent past) require a *supporting* style characterized by low directive behavior (because they are trusted to know their job well) but strong supporting behavior; this creates buy-in and motivation.
- Followers with high competence and high commitment require a *delegating* style in which they are, in essence, left in peace to do their jobs.

Clearly, these styles are reminiscent of similar styles described in other publications. For example, the directive style resembles both Lewin's authoritarian style and Blake and Mouton's authority-compliance style. The coaching and supporting styles are reminiscent of Blake and Mouton's team management and country-club management styles, respectively. And the delegating style shares many similarities with Lewin's laissez-faire style.

Although intuitively appealing, empirical evidence for the Situational Leadership Model is mixed; several large studies have failed to find support for key postulates. From the mid-1970s onwards, both authors independently continued to develop separate versions. For more information on this model, see Chapter 3.25 on page 79f.

Robert House's *Path-Goal Model*, published in 1971, postulates that a leader's behavior depends on the satisfaction, motivation, and performance of followers. The model derives its name from House's argument that it is the leader's responsibility to guide followers in selecting the best path to reach both organizational and personal goals. In a 1996 revision of the original theory, he also added a provision for changing leader behavior to complement subordinate's abilities and/or compensate for deficiencies. Leader effectiveness depends on followers'[1] motivation and satisfaction as well as their acceptance of the leader, which in turn depends on follower contingencies (skills and experience), environmental contingencies (task structure and team dynamics), and leader behavior (i.e. leadership style). House lists four such behaviors:

- directive,
- supportive,
- participative, and
- achievement-oriented.

Directive leadership is based on clear guidelines, performance standards, and controls as well as rewards and punishment where necessary. *Supportive* leaders are concerned for the needs, welfare,

---

[1] House originally used the term 'employees'.

and well-being of their followers and behave accordingly. *Partici-pative* leaders share information with their followers and involve them in decision-making. Finally, *achievement-oriented* leaders employ challenging goals to encourage followers to reach their maximum performance. In line with Greenleaf's Servant Leadership[1], leaders in this model do not seek power but rather serve as coaches and facilitators for their followers. In contrast to Fiedler's Contingency Model but in line with Hersey and Blanchard's Situational Leadership, the Path–Goal Model assumes that leaders can adopt any of the four leadership styles when the situation warrants it. These styles, however, are not seen as mutually exclusive.

The question of which leadership style is most appropriate under which circumstances is the basis for the *Vroom-Yetton-Jago Normative Decision Model*, a situational leadership model developed by Canadian-born Yale School of Management Professor Victor Vroom and Australian management scholar Phillip Yetton that was originally published in 1973 and later extended in collaboration with Arthur Jago in 1988.

The model suggests three leadership styles (autocratic, consultative, and collaborative), which are the basis for five decision-making processes. These are

- *Autocratic I* (A1) : the leader makes the decision without subordinate involvement using information that is readily available.
- *Autocratic II* (A2) : the leader obtains additional information from subordinates before making the decision but then makes the decision alone; the subordinates may or may not be informed.
- *Consultative l* (C1) : the leader discusses problems individually with subordinates and asks for input opinions, but there are no team meetings, and the leader makes the decision alone.

---

[1] See Chapter 2.7 on page 48f.

- *Consultative II* (C2) : the leader discusses problems with the team but makes the decision alone.
- *Group II* (G2) : the leader discusses problems with the team, focuses and directs discussions, and allows the group to make the decision.

Selection which of these processes is most appropriate depends on the answers to eight questions that deal with the decision quality requirement, the leader's information, the problem's structure, the probability of subordinate commitment, goal congruence between leader and subordinates, the likelihood of conflict between subordinates over the decision, and whether subordinate's have sufficient information to contribute to the decision or not. Depending on the answers to each of these, the most appropriate style may then be determined by using a decision tree[1]. For more information, see Chapter 3.26 on page 82f.

The Path-Goal Model and the Vroom-Yetton-Jago Normative Decision Model are examples of *transactional* leadership theory. Transactional leaders emphasize organization and processes, tasks, and control, and they exchange tangible rewards (such as bonuses or time off) for the work and loyalty of followers. Predominantly transactional leadership is frequently found in high-risk professions such as oil drilling. In contrast, *transformational* leaders focus on intrinsic needs of followers, provide a sense of mission, collaborate with followers to identify needed changes, and raise awareness about the desirability of certain outcomes. The concept of transformational leadership was introduced in 1978 by American historian and political scientist James McGregor Burns[2].

The twin concepts of transactional and transformational leadership correspond to some extent to the older dichotomy between task orientation and people orientation, with transformational leadership

---

[1] This decision tree was later replaced with a mathematics-based expert system.

[2] Burns actually referred to *transforming* leadership. The modern term *transformational* leadership was introduced by Bernard Bass in 1985.

frequently seen as superior. During the early 1990s, however, a view that gained prominence was that both are needed. This view came to be known as *Full Range of Leadership*, a term coined by Avolio and Bass in 1991. Among others, support was provided by a study of 726 leaders that found that transformational leadership alone did not lead to superior performance and that the most effective leader behavior included both transactional and transformational elements (O'Shea et al., 2009).

The Avolio and Bass Full Range of Leadership model includes nine elements (Antonakis, Avolio, and Sivasubramaniam, 2003):

- *Idealized influence (attributed)* refers to whether the leader is perceived as being confident, powerful, and focusing on higher ideals and ethics (i.e. perceived charisma).
- *Idealized influence (behavior)* denotes the actions of the leader that are objectively charismatic in nature and centered on values, beliefs, and a sense of mission.
- *Inspirational motivation* means the leader's ability to energize followers by viewing the future with optimism, stressing ambitious goals, and projecting a desirable, achievable vision.
- *Intellectual stimulation* refers to the leader's actions that challenge followers to think creatively and to find new ways to solve difficult problems.
- *Individualized consideration* denotes leader behaviors which contribute to follower satisfaction by advising, supporting, and paying attention to their individual needs, allowing them to develop and self-actualize.
- *Contingent rewards* means leader behaviors that are focused on clarifying role and task requirements and providing followers with material or psychological rewards based on the fulfillment of corresponding obligations.
- *Active management-by-exception* refers to the active controlling of task achievement by a leader intent on standards being met.

- *Passive management-by-exception* means a leader's behavior where intervention occurs only after mistakes have already happened or standards have not been met.
- *Laissez-faire* denotes the absence of leadership: a behavior in which the leader avoids making decisions, abdicates responsibility, and makes no use of authority.

The first five of these are the transformational and the next three the transactional components. The final one, laissez-faire leadership, is neither and acts as a counterpoint.

These theories are prescriptive in nature: they describe which practices leaders *should* employ. However, this may be more easily said than done. Just like everyone else, even excellent leaders are not always in equally good form; they are subject to external influences, such as good and bad news, and personal issues, such as health problems or particular memories of previous failures or difficult situations, and these may lead to mood swings, anxiety, and so forth. Some, however, are more resistant than others to such influences and issues.

The ability of a person or a system, such as an organization, to adapt to change is commonly described as *resilience*. In psychology, resilience is defined as the ability to properly adapt to stress and adversity—skills which are very important for leaders. In a 1993 psychometric study, Gail Wagnild and Heather Young found that the principal components of resilience were personal competence, which consists of aspects such as self-reliance, determination, resourcefulness, and perseverance, and acceptance of self and life, consisting of adaptability, mental balance, flexibility and a balanced perspective of life. They also found that resilience was positively linked to good physical health, life satisfaction, and morale but negatively linked to depression. In other words, good health and a positive disposition increase resilience, whereas depression reduces it. Leaders can and must develop and continuously monitor and strengthen their resilience to cope with the changing demands of their duties over the long term. Resilience is further discussed in Chapter 4.32[1].

2.6 Functional Leadership Theories

In contrast to trait and behavioral theories, *functional leadership theories* are less concerned with why something is done and more with how it gets done and what responsibilities the leader must take on to get there. At the center lies the assumption that effectiveness depends on a set of behaviors performed not just by the leader but by the entire group.

As early as 1953, American psychologist Edwin Fleishman reported that followers tended to view and rate their leader's behavior according to two aspects, consideration and initiating structure[2]. The former refers to showing concern and support, the latter to how the leader sets up tasks for instance with regard to task allocation, roles, performance standards, and evaluation. Two comparatively recent contributions to this field have become particularly influential, Adair's *Action Centered Leadership Model* and Kouzes and Posner's *Five Practices of Exemplary Leadership*.

John Adair, a former British military officer, academic, and management author, published his *Action-Centered Leadership Model* in 1973. It postulates that leaders have three main responsibilities:

- achieving tasks,
- managing the team, and
- managing individuals.

---

[1] See page 150f.

[2] In essence, of course, this echoes the people-orientation and task-orientation approaches found in many leadership theories and suggests that, if the group is seen as the origin of effectiveness, both are important in a leader (lending support to e.g. the Managerial Grid and the Full Range Leadership model).

Adair sees these responsibilities as overlapping, because the task needs a team to perform it, and the individual team members need to be at their personal best (i.e. fully developed), challenged, and motivated for the whole team to perform at its best. The associated "core functions" of leadership Adair initially listed were

- planning,
- initiating,
- controlling,
- supporting,
- informing, and
- evaluating.

These are, in essence, transactional. In a revised edition published in 1988, Adair changed them to defining the task, planning, briefing, controlling, evaluating, motivating, organizing, and setting an example. The older version, however, remains much better known.

Adair is also famous for his 'fifty-fifty' rule. This refers to the amount of influence each of two influencers wield in any given situation. For example, he postulated that 50% of a follower's motivation comes from within that person, while the other 50% is due to external influences such as leadership. Similarly, he saw 50% of team-building success as stemming from the team and 50% from the team's leader. And so on. Adair's contributions are discussed further in Chapter 4.1[1].

In 1987, James Kouzes and Barry Posner published *The Leadership Challenge*, in which they summarized the results of thousands of interviews and more than 75,000 written responses, listing the *Five Practices of Exemplary Leadership*, the five most common practices in which they found effective leaders engage:

---

[1] See page 117f.

- *Model the way* refers to the need for leaders to establish principles regarding how people at all levels should be treated and the way goals should be pursued, including breaking large, complex goals and changes into smaller interim goals. The leader sets the standard and then acts as a role model for the team.
- *Inspire a shared vision* refers to the need for leaders to envision the future, believe in their ability to make a difference, and make people see exciting possibilities.
- *Challenge the process* refers to the need for leaders to encourage outside-the-box thinking, move outside traditional boundaries, experiment and take risks, be innovative, and demand and foster change. Inevitable disappointments are seen as learning opportunities.
- *Enable others to act* refers to the need for leaders to actively involve others, make them feel capable and energetic, encourage collaboration, and build team spirit in an atmosphere of trust and dignity.
- *Encourage the heart* refers to the need for leaders to keep hope and determination alive, recognize individual contributions, share the rewards of team efforts, and celebrate accomplishments.

Kouzes and Posner are also well known for their *Leadership Practices Inventory*, a widely used leadership assessment tool.

2.7   Integrated Psychological Theory

Integrated Psychological Theory (IPT), which emerged in the early 2000s, examines what makes people listen to leaders. Two well-known concepts arising from it are Greenleaf's *Servant Leadership* and Scouller's *Three Levels of Leadership*.

American management and education scholar Robert Greenleaf is said to have been inspired by Herman Hesse's *Die Morgenland-fahrt*[1] to consider the serving aspects of leadership. He later distilled his thoughts on the subject into a theory that became known as *Servant Leadership*. Disillusioned by what he saw as the failure of the power-centered authoritarian leadership style that was prominent in U.S. institutions at the time, he took early retirement from AT&T, where had had worked for nearly forty years, to found the *Center for Applied Ethics* in 1964, which was renamed the *Greenleaf Center for Servant Leadership* in 1985. According to Greenleaf, 'servant' does not refer to servility but to a desire to help others. As his "best test" of servant leadership puts it (Greenleaf, 2002: 27):

Do those served grow as persons; do they, while being served, become healthier, wiser, freer, more autonomous, more likely themselves to become servants?

As such, servant leadership is really a philosophy of leadership, rather than a theory in the traditional sense. Other scholars have attempted to distill Greenleaf's ideas into conceptual frameworks. For example, leadership author Larry Spears (2010) identified ten characteristics of servant leaders:

- listening,
- empathy,
- healing,
- awareness,
- persuasion,
- conceptualization,
- foresight,
- stewardship,
- commitment to the growth of people, and
- building community.

---

[1] English title: *Journey to the East.*

According to Spears, effective leaders need both excellent listening skills and a high level of empathy. They also need to be able to heal relationships as well as their own spirit and that of others. They are both self-aware and socially aware, rely on the power of persuasion rather than positional authority, display good conceptual thinking and are able to look at the big picture, and show foresight and stewardship, meaning that they see the team or organization they run as something entrusted to them rather than owned by them. They are committed to the individual growth of people in their domain of influence, including growth that does not benefit the organization directly, and are able to instill a sense of community in those around them.

A second popular framework in this school of theory is provided by former CEO James Scouller. In his book *The Three Levels of Leadership*, published in 2011, he offers a review of older leadership theories and points to a number of shortcomings they exhibit, such as the original Trait School's failure to produce a list of universally agreed-upon leadership qualities, the Situational/Contingency School's assumption that leaders can change their styles at will, or the general neglect of most newer leadership theories to consider the leader's personality.

Scouller postulates that leadership happens on three levels:

- personal,
- private, and
- public.

Personal leadership (Scouller calls this the "inner level") refers both to the leader's skills and knowledge and to beliefs, emotions, and unconscious habits. So, in essence, personal leadership is about leading yourself. Scouller (2011: 15) puts it this way:

At its heart is the leader's self-awareness, his progress toward self-mastery and technical competence, and his sense of connection with those around him. It's the inner core, the source, of a leader's outer leadership effectiveness.

Scouller also asserts that leaders must develop what he calls leadership presence—which in essence is real, honest charisma[1]—because this is what compels others to follow a person.

The two "outer levels" in Scouller's model, private and public leadership, therefore depend on the leader's personal leadership. Specifically, they are concerned with the behaviors the leader must employ to address what Scouller calls the *Four Dimensions of Leadership*:

- a shared, motivating group purpose or vision,
- action, progress and results,
- collective unity (team spirit), and
- individual selection and motivation.

In this context, private leadership means leading individual team members, while public leadership is, for the purposes of this book, team leadership[2]. In other words, effective leaders have a sound moral compass and care about those around them, are able to heal rifts in relationships and inspire team spirit based on their ability to listen and read people, know what they can do and need themselves, outline the path to take rather than issue commands, know who owns the organization and what their duty is to those owners, have a vision of the future, and can think conceptually.

---

[1] See the discussion of charisma in Chapter 4.31 on page 150f.
[2] Scouller specifically refers to 'leadership of two or more people'.

2.8   Global Leadership Theory

Finally, the *Global Leadership School*, which originated in the early 2000s but integrated cross-cultural insights from decades of research in addition to important new research, is occasionally considered part of the Behavioral School because it is also concerned with leader effectiveness. However, it is chiefly concerned with examining the cultural transferability of leadership traits, behaviors, and competencies. As such, it is a cross-sectional research discipline that draws on psychology (especially leadership studies and personality research), culture studies (anthropology and sociology), and management. It examines which implicit leadership expectations are harbored by people in various cultures, which leader traits and behaviors are therefore valued in what way in each culture, and what contributes to cross-cultural and global leadership success. Understanding cultural differences and how they influence peoples' reactions to leader behaviors and management decisions contributes significantly to international leadership success.

In a wider sense, a variety of cross-cultural research can be counted part of Global Leadership research. Among the most well-known frameworks that emerged from this field are Edward T. Hall's (1959) concepts of polychronic vs. monochronic time, low vs. high context, and proxemics[1]; Florence Kluckhohn and Fred Strodtbeck's (1962) Values Orientation Theory; Geert Hofstede's (1980) Cultural Dimensions Theory; Fons Trompenaars and Charles Hampden-Turner's (1997) model of national culture differences; the World Values Survey, a multi-national, decade-long effort to explore and track people's values and beliefs in almost 100 countries; and Browaeys and Price's (2008) summative model of cultural dimensions. At the core of the Global Leadership School, however, lies its most important contribution to date: Robert House, Paul Hanges and

---

[1] Proxemics refers to the amount of space people need around them, which Hall divided into four zones: intimate, personal, social, and public.

Mansour Javidan's report of a long-term (1993-2003) study involving 170 researchers from 62 countries that collected data from 17,300 middle-managers. Published in 2004, it identified 22 leader attributes that are universally viewed positively and eight that are universally viewed negatively. It also identified six leadership styles that are found around the world, although only two of those styles were endorsed in all 62 countries as facilitators of leadership effectiveness.

Global leadership is covered in more detail in Chapter 5[1].

---

[1] See page 233f.

2.9   Summary Overview

Table 4 summarizes the development of modern leadership theory in broadly chronological order.

Table 4:   Evolution of Leadership Theory

Origin period	Leadership school	Contributors (examples)	Questions examined (examples)	Well-known tools and concepts
1840s	Great Man Theory	• Carlyle (1841) • Galton (1869)	• How can great leaders be identified?	• "Great leader" stories and anecdotes (e.g. biographies)
1930 to 1940s, since 1980s	Trait theories	• Cowley (1931) • Kenny and Zaccaro (1983)	• Which traits distinguish a leader from a non-leader? • What is the extent of differences between leaders and other people?	• 16 Personality Factors • Big Five personality traits • Alternative Five Model • NEO Personality Inventory • HEXACO model of personality structure • Emotional Intelligence
1940s to 1950s	Behavioral theories	• Lewin, Lippit, & White (1939) • McGregor (1960) • Blake and Mouton (1964)	• Which specific behaviors do leaders display? • Is leader behavior task or relationship oriented? • Which behavior is most effective?	• Lewin's Leadership Styles • Theory X and Theory Y • Blake-Mouton Managerial Grid
1950s	Power and influence theories	• French and Raven (1959)	• What is the importance of power in leader behavior? • What are the sources of leader power? • What sources of power are most relevant?	• French and Raven's Five Points of Power

Table 4:   Evolution of Leadership Theory (cont.)

Origin Period	Leadership School	• Contributors (examples)	• Questions examined (examples)	• Well-known tools and concepts
1960s	Situational/ Contingency Approach	• Fiedler (1958, 1967) • Hersey and Blanchard (1969) • House (1971) • Vroom and Yetton (1973) • Avolio and Bass (2002) • O'Shea et al. (2009)	• How will a specific situation affect leader behavior? • What is the most efficient leader behavior in a given situation? • What is the optimal combination of different leadership styles?	• Tannenbaum-Schmidt Leadership Continuum • Fiedler's Contingency Model • Hersey-Blanchard Situational Leadership Styles • House's Path-Goal Model • Vroom-Yetton-Jago Normative Decision Model • Full Range Model
1980s	Functional Leadership Theory	• Kouzes and Posner (1987) • Adair (1988)	• Which specific leader behaviors contribute to organizational or unit effectiveness?	• Five Practices of Exemplary Leadership • Adair's Action-Centered Leadership Model • Integrated Functional Leadership Model
2000s	Integrated Psychological Theory	• Scouller (2011)	• What makes people listen to leaders? • How can leaders gain presence?	• Scouller's Three Levels of Leadership • Servant Leadership
2000s	Global Leadership	• House, Hanges, and Javidan (2004)	• Which traits and behaviors are most effective in a specific culture and across cultures?	• Cultural Dimensions • Cultural Clusters • Cultural contingency of leader traits and behaviors • Six Universal Leadership Dimensions

Source: author.

2.10   Chapter Recap

TAKEAWAYS

What you should take away from this chapter:

1. The Great Man Theory assumes that history is shaped by great leaders and that leadership is best learned by studying them.

2. Trait-based leadership research attempts to identify traits which distinguish leaders from non-leaders. Initial attempts assumed that leaders are born, not made, and results were mixed, which led to strong criticism. Newer research relaxed this assumption and employed more advanced methods or organized previous results around established frameworks like the Big Five personality traits; it has identified a number of relationships between personality traits and the emergence and effectiveness of leaders.

3. Behavioral leadership research examines the kinds of behaviors successful leaders exhibit, the type of leadership styles they employ and have at their disposal, and the kind of behavioral modification successful leaders undergo. Among the most well-known frameworks are
   - Lewin's leadership styles,
   - McGregor's Theory X and Theory Y,
   - Blake and Mouton's Managerial Grid;
   - (mixed model) Emotional Intelligence, and
   - Goleman's Six Leadership Styles.

4. Power and influence research examines the nature, sources, and forms of the power and influence of leaders. Among the most well-known frameworks are
   - French and Raven's Five Points of Power, and
   - Cialdini's Six Principles of Influence.

5. The Situational and Contingency School is based on the notion of environmental 'fit': the need to match leaders with situational demands. Among the most well-known frameworks are
   - Tannenbaum and Schmidt's Leadership Continuum,
   - Fiedler's Contingency Theory,
   - Hersey and Blanchard's Situational Leadership model,
   - House's Path-Goal Theory, and the
   - Vroom-Yetton Normative Decision Model.

6. Functional leadership theories examine how things get done and what the leader's responsibilities are in that regard. Among the most well-known frameworks are
   - Fleishman's Consideration and Initiating Structure Theory,
   - Adair's Action Centered Leadership Model, and
   - Kouzes and Posner's Five Practices of Exemplary Leadership.

7. Integrated Psychological Theory attempts to integrate the strengths of earlier leadership theories while accounting for their shortcomings. Among the most well-known frameworks are
   - Greenleaf's Servant Leadership and
   - Scouller's Three Levels of Leadership model.

8. Global Leadership research examines the cultural transferability of leadership traits and competencies. Its major contributions to date are the various reports about findings of the GLOBE Project.

CHECK QUESTIONS

Try to answer the questions below. If you need help, check the sample answers in the annex.

1. What is the basic premise of the Great Man Theory?
2. What are Lewin's basic leadership styles?
3. What is the view of workers in McGregor's Theory X?
4. What are the two concerns on which the Managerial Grid is based, and what does it present as the optimal leadership style?
5. What are the sources of power in French and Raven's Five Points of Power?
6. Which forces should a leader consider, according to Tannenbaum and Schmidt's Leadership Continuum, when deciding which leadership style to employ?
7. According to Fiedler's Contingency Theory, what is the key determinant of leader effectiveness?
8. In Hersey and Blanchard's Situational Leadership model, to what do leaders need to adapt their style?
9. In House's Path-Goal Theory, on what does a leader's behavior depend?
10. Which are the three basic leadership styles in the Vroom-Yetton-Jago Normative Decision Model?
11. What is full range leadership?
12. According to Fleishman, on which two aspects do followers base their views and ratings of a leader's behavior?
13. Which are the three main responsibilities of leaders according to Adair's Action-Centered Leadership model?
14. What are Kouzes and Posner's Five Practices of Exemplary Leadership?

15. Which are the three levels in Scouller's leadership model, and to what do they refer?

16. According to Robert Greenleaf, for what does the word 'servant' in Servant Leadership stand?

17. What question lies at the center of the Global Leadership School of research?

3 TRAITS AND BEHAVIORS OF EFFECTIVE LEADERS

LEARNING OUTCOMES

After this chapter, you will:

- Understand the role personality plays in leader emergence and effectiveness, and
- Understand common leadership styles at your disposal and how to apply them.

3.1 Traits and Characteristics of Effective Leaders

Following the popularity of the Great Man Theory in the 19th century, the heyday of trait research occurred in the 1930s and 1940s. Somewhat inconclusive results led researchers to turn their attention to leader behaviors and styles in subsequent decades, but improved methodologies enabled a revival in trait research from the 1980s onwards.

Broadly speaking, leadership research can be separated into two large categories: leadership emergence and leadership effectiveness (Lord, De Vader, and Allinger, 1986). Leadership emergence examines whether someone is considered leader-like (Hogan, Curphy and Hogan, 1994), while leadership effectiveness considers a leader's performance in influencing and guiding the activities of his or her unit toward the achievement of its goals. Leadership research has attempted to identify the traits and behaviors that promote and hinder each of these aspects of leadership.

Traits can be defined as habitual patterns of disposition, thought, and emotion present in a person. They are relatively stable over time, differ from one person to another (e.g. some people are extravert whereas others are introvert), and influence behaviors. Over the years, leadership research has accumulated a large number of traits that have been linked to leader emergence and effectiveness. The vast number of traits claimed to be conducive to good leadership, the fact that these have tended to differ significantly from study to study, and the overall mixed empirical results have made these lists rather unhelpful for organizations in selecting future leaders. To address this problem, more recent research has categorized and grouped these traits further to make them easier to handle. The underlying assumption is that, based on the traits they exhibit, certain personality types are more likely to emerge as leaders and thus may also be more successful. A common typology of personality factors is the Big Five model, which is easily remembered with the acronym OCEAN:

- *O*penness,
- *C*onscientiousness,
- *E*xtraversion[1],
- *A*greeableness, and
- *N*euroticism.

Openness to experience refers to curiosity and an appreciation of adventure, unusual ideas, and new ways of doing things. An individual's openness can be located on a spectrum running between *inventive/curious* and *consistent/cautious*.

Conscientiousness captures a person's dependability and tendency to be organized. Very conscientious people exhibit strong self-discipline, achievement orientation, and a preference for planned rather than spontaneous behavior. The corresponding scale runs from *efficient/organized* to *easy-going/careless*.

Extraversion is frequently measured as *outgoing/energetic* vs. *solitary/reserved*. Extravert people are very sociable, assertive, and

---

[1] Often also spelled 'extroversion'.

talkative. They seek the company of others and display generally high energy levels.

Agreeableness indicates how cooperative and compassionate a person is. Low agreeableness is experienced by others as suspicious and antagonistic behavior. This construct is often measured as *friendly/compassionate* vs. *challenging/detached.*

Neuroticism expresses how easily a person experiences such negative emotions as anger, anxiety, and frustration. Neurotic people tend to display low self-esteem and are often seen as nervous and overly sensitive and excitable by others. The construct is often measured as *sensitive/nervous* vs. *secure/confident.*

A number of instruments based on the Big Five have been developed, such as the NEO PI-R[1], the NEO FFI[2], and particularly the OPQ32[3], which is frequently used in companies for leader selection and development, team building, and succession planning.

Other commonly found models of personalities and personality types include the Myers-Briggs Type Indicator, which is based on four type dichotomies[4], and Cattell's 16 Personality Factors[5].

Improved conceptual and methodological sophistication has enabled newer research to find broad support for the key postulates of the Trait School: personality does matter, and particular characteristics (such as those listed in Table 5 below) increase the likelihood that a person emerges and is accepted as a leader and that he or she is effective in a leadership position. For example, in a meta-analysis

---

[1] NEO PI-R stands for *Revised NEO Personality Inventory.* NEO originally stood for 'neuroticism', 'extraversion', and 'openness'. The revised version considers all of the Big Five personality factors. Additionally, it also reports on six subcategories (called facets) for each of them.

[2] The NEO FFI (*NEO Five-Factor Inventory*) is the short (60-item) version of the 240-item NEO PI-R.

[3] The OPQ32, or *Occupational Personality Questionnaire*, is a commercially available personality questionnaire based on the Big Five personality factors. It consists of 32 questions and is available in more than 30 languages.

[4] These type dichotomies are extraversion–intraversion, sensing–intuition, thinking–feeling, and judging–perception.

[5] The corresponding factors are warmth, reasoning, emotional stability, dominance, liveliness, rule-consciousness, social boldness, sensitivity, vigilance, abstractedness, privateness, apprehension, openness to change, self-reliance, perfectionism, and tension.

of 222 correlations from 73 samples organized according to the Big Five personality traits, Judge et al. (2002) found a clear link between the presence of certain traits and both leader emergence and leader effectiveness. Table 5 contains more details.

Table 5: **Predictive Power of the Big Five Personality Factors for Leader Emergence and Effectiveness**

Personality factors	Associated traits (examples)	Effect on leader emergence	Effect on leader effectiveness
Openness	Originality, creativity, non-conformity, adaptability.	Strongly positive	Positive
Conscientiousness	Initiative, persistence, tenacity, achievement motivation.	Strongly positive	Weakly positive
Extraversion	Dominance, sociability, self-monitoring, energetic disposition.	Strongly positive	Positive
Agreeableness	Cooperativeness, compassion, modesty, sensitivity, altruism, gentleness, need for affiliation.	Negative	Weakly positive
Neuroticism	Low self-esteem, hostility, anxiety, poor emotional adjustment.	Weakly negative	Weakly negative

Source: adapted from Judge et al. (2002)

Likewise, a study of middle managers in the Swiss subsidiary of a global HR firm by Seelhofer and Valeri (2017) also found support for the trait perspective, with the caveat that the specific traits depend on the organizational situation. In that particular high-pressure, sales-driven context, traits such as conscientiousness and detail orientation were better predictors of leadership success than, for instance, extraversion.

Zaccaro, Kemp, and Bader (2004) developed an empirically validated model of leader emergence, effectiveness, and advancement/promotion. The authors assume that, moderated by the leader's operating environment and leader processes, these outcomes are influenced both by what they call *distal attributes* such as cognitive abilities, personality, and motives/values and by *proximal attributes* such as social appraisal skills, problem-solving skills, and tacit knowledge or expertise.

3.2   Leadership Styles at Your Disposal

The evolution of leadership theory was introduced in the previous chapter. This section contains additional information and exercises related to leadership styles and their practical application.

As leadership research turned from traits to behaviors, new questions gained prominence, such as what leadership styles leaders theoretically have at their disposal, which ones are actually found in reality, whether there is a best style or whether 'best' depends on the particular situation, and if leaders can really just switch from one style to another if they want to.

As you will no doubt notice, the various typologies of leadership styles discussed below are not really competing or substitutive. They are largely complementary and provide different 'lenses' with which various levels of detail can be observed or analyzed in the same topic[1]. They reflect advances in leadership research.

3.21   Lewin's Leadership Styles

In 1939, a group of researchers led by psychologist Kurt Lewin attempted to classify different leadership approaches. In the process, they identified three major leadership styles:

- authoritarian (or autocratic),
- democratic (or participative), and
- laissez-faire.

---

[1] Although they may differ in some of their basic assumptions, such as whether leaders can adapt their style or not.

Lewin's leadership styles are described in Figure 3.

Figure 3: Lewin's Leadership Styles

Lewin's leadership styles		
Authoritarian (or *autocratic*)	**Democratic** (or *participative*)	**Laissez-faire** (or *delegative*)
The leader provides clear expectations of what should be done when and how. This is best applied when there is little time for group decisions or if the leader is most knowledgeable.	The leader encourages group members to participate but retains final say. This was generally found to be the most effective style in the study, because group members feel part of the process and are more motivated and creative.	The leader offers little or no guidance and leaves decision-making to group members. This can be effective if group members are highly qualified, but it often leads to poorly defined roles and a subsequent lack of motivation.

Source: based on Lewin, Lippit, and White (1939)

In the original study, leaders experienced the best results with a democratic style, despite the fact that reaching a solid decision may be difficult if decisiveness is lacking and there is a wide range of opinions. An authoritarian style was found to frequently cause high levels of discontent, although it may occasionally be warranted in cases involving inexperienced or unwilling teams or during times of crisis. Finally, a laissez-faire style may occasionally work well for teams of highly motivated and skilled experts without the need for central coordination. However, the study found that, generally, followers coordinated in this way did not invest the same energy and produced lower quality work than when they were more actively led. Therefore, the balance between a more democratic or a more laissez-faire mode depends on how long the team has worked together, how experienced its individual members are, and how specialized their tasks are, while an authoritarian mode should be avoided except in exceptional circumstances, such as during times of crisis.

This is still a well-known and widely used basic classification of leadership styles. Understanding your own preferred style and the potential uses of each of the other styles can help you be more effective as a leader. To determine your own preferred leadership style according to Lewin's classification, see *Exercise* 3 on page 99.

Note that Lewin's results were later put into cross-cultural perspective by research such as the GLOBE study. For example, an authoritarian style is generally received negatively in cultures with low power distance; in the Western world, democratic leadership is generally well-received and associated with good performance[1].

3.22   Tannenbaum and Schmidt's Leadership Continuum

In some ways a continuation and extension of Lewin's model, Tannenbaum and Schmidt's Leadership Continuum was introduced in 1958. Its details were explained in Chapter 2.5[2]. To reiterate the gist, the authors assume that leaders can move fluidly between seven styles on a continuum from boss-centered (or authoritarian) to subordinate-centered (or laissez-faire) leadership. These seven styles are:

- authoritarian,
- paternalistic,
- consultative I[3],
- consultative II,
- participative,
- democratic, and
- laissez-faire.

---

[1] In line with Lewin's original results, a study of middle managers in a global HR firm found that teams led by female leaders – who as a group exhibited significantly higher levels of participant leadership than their male counterparts – tended to outperform other teams (Seelhofer and Valeri, 2017).

[2] See page 34f.

[3] The difference between the Consultative I and II styles is how far along the path to a decision the leader already is: when using the former, he or she only presents ideas (which are then discussed) rather than a fully fledged (if tentative) decision to the team.

Even if this assumption may not hold[1], and the model's applicability is limited by the need to generalize and a lack of consideration of individuals, it provides a useful way to think about specific leadership challenges.

The authors also suggest that the choice of one of these seven leadership styles when facing a particular leadership challenge depends on what they call forces in the leader, the subordinates, and the situation, and each of the forces is determined by a number of aspects.

When considering the forces in the leader (i.e. yourself), you need to choose whether, based on your value system, you generally tend to trust or distrust people, how much confidence you have in your team overall (low, medium, high), whether you are more naturally directive or participative, and how personally secure you feel in uncertain situations. You also need to consider your team's need for independence, their readiness for responsibility, their tolerance for ambiguity, their interest in the task at hand, their identification with the organization, their skill level, and their expectation of participating in the decision-making process.

Finally, when considering the general situation, you need to determine whether the relevant organization[2] is centralized or decentralized overall, how effective the group (i.e. your team) currently is, whether the problem at hand is simple or complex, and how much time pressure you face.

In the original article, the authors provided only fairly abstract and generic advice on how to choose the most appropriate of these styles. Figure 4 provides a structured way to make that choice. To better understand how to apply this tool, perform Exercise 4 on page 102.

---

[1] Many leaders are unable to change their leadership style to fit a specific leadership situation, often due to an inability to assess it accurately.

[2] The relevant level is the one that determines the discretion with which your team can operate. In essence, it is the level that is the source of the organizational culture which determines your team's operational environment. For example, in a large corporation this may be the business unit or even the department, rather than the corporation as a whole.

Figure 4: Choosing a Style on the Leadership Continuum

A — FORCES IN THE LEADER

Value system		Confidence in team		
More distrusting	More trusting	Low	Moderate	High
1	2	1	2	3

Leadership inclinations		Feelings of security in an uncertain situation		
More naturally directive	More naturally participative	Low	Moderate	High
1	2	1	2	3

B — FORCES IN THE FOLLOWERS

Need for independence		Readiness for responsibility		Tolerance for ambiguity		Interest in the task		Identification with organization	
Low to medium	Medium to high	Low to medium	Medium to high	Low to medium	Medium to high	Low to medium	Medium to high	Low to medium	Medium to high
1	2	1	2	1	2	1	2	1	2

Skill level		Expectation of participating	
Medium to high	High	Low to medium	Medium to high
1	2	1	2

C — FORCES IN THE SITUATION

Type of organization		Group effectiveness		
Centralized	Decentralized	Low	Moderate	High
1	2	1	2	3

Nature of problem		Time pressure		
Simple	Complex	Low	Moderate	High
1	2	1	2	3

Total (A + B + C)

Score	Style	Description
15-16	Authoritarian	Leader makes decision and informs team.
17-18	Paternalistic	Leader makes decision and then convinces subordinates of its value.
19-20	Consultative I	Leader presents ideas and invites questions before making decision.
21-23	Consultative II	Leader presents tentative decision that is subject to change.
24-27	Participative	Leader presents problem to team and gets suggestions but retains final decision.
28-31	Democratic	Leader defines limits but delegates decision to team.
32-34	Laissez-faire	Leader allows subordinates to function within limits defined by higher instance.

Source: author; based on Tannenbaum and Schmidt (1958).

Illustration 3: Using the Leadership Continuum

Rhiz is a 29-year-old British civil engineer of Pakistani descent who has recently been promoted and given his first team. He's now working for the governing council of a large Northwest English metropolitan region that is currently undergoing major restructuring. His subordinates are also all engineers. Rhiz is rather introvert and tends not to trust people until he is sure he can. He also lacks experience and thus self-confidence, particularly in new or uncertain situations. His initial impression is that his team members are competent and quite interested in their work, but he does not yet know them that well. Based on his handover discussions with the previous team leader and his initial observations, his team members seem to be content to be told what to do and do not display an overt need for independence or participation despite being highly educated. However, he has noticed that, with one exception, they all seem to need constant updates and clarification. The government body for which the team works is quite bureaucratic, with slow, centralized decision making and moderate overall productivity at best. This is a constant source of frustration for the engineers, because their problems tend to be quite complex, and their solutions frequently depend on the input of others, which is often only slow and sporadic.

Rhiz is unsure what leadership and decision-making style he should try. On one hand, he is a very methodical person and feels the most natural approach for him would be to arrive at a decision by himself and then issue his orders. On the other hand, he remembers from business school that highly skilled teams often expect to take decisions as a group. He also remembers discussing the Tannenbaum-Schmidt Leadership Continuum in one class, and digs out his notes on it. Applying the corresponding principles, he decides to aim for an approach in which the leader presents a tentative decision that is then subject to change after consulting the team. Below is the decision matrix he used.

FORCES IN THE LEADER

Value system		Confidence in team			Leadership inclinations		Feelings of security in an uncertain situation		
More distrusting	More trusting	Low	Moderate	High	More naturally directive	More naturally participative	Low	Moderate	High
1	2	1	2	3	1	2	1	2	3
A 1			2		1		1		
5									

FORCES IN THE FOLLOWERS

Need for independence		Readiness for responsibility		Tolerance for ambiguity		Interest in the task		Identification with organization		Skill level		Expectation of participating	
Low to medium	Medium to high	Low to medium	Medium to high	Low to medium	Medium to high	Low to medium	Medium to high	Low to medium	Medium to high	Low to medium	Medium to high	Low to medium	Medium to high
1	2	1	2	1	2	1	2	1	2	1	2	1	2
B 1			2	1			2		2		2	1	
11													

FORCES IN THE SITUATION

Type of organization		Group effectiveness			Nature of problem		Time pressure		
Centralized	Decentralized	Low	Moderate	High	Simple	Complex	Low	Moderate	High
1	2	1	2	3	1	2	1	2	3
C 1			2			2	1		
6									

Total

A +B +C	15-16	17-18	19-20	21-23	24-27	28-31	32-34
	Authoritarian	Paternalistic	Consultative I	Consultative II	Participative	Democratic	Laissez-faire
	Leader makes decision and informs team.	Leader makes decision and then convinces subordinates of its value.	Leader presents ideas and invites questions before making decision.	Leader presents tentative decision that is subject to change.	Leader presents problem to team and gets suggestions but retains final decision.	Leader defines limits but delegates decision to team.	Leader allows subordinates to function within limits defined by higher instance.

3.23   Blake and Mouton's Managerial Grid

The Managerial Grid, developed by Blake and Mouton, is based on the assumption that people tend be both task-oriented and people-oriented but that one of the two usually predominates. In the original model, the labels used were *concern for production* (task orientation) and *concern for people* (people orientation). Depending on how evident each orientation is in a leader, five leadership styles[1] are distinguished:

- impoverished (later called indifferent) style,
- country-club management (later called accommodating) style,
- middle-of-the-road (later also called *status quo*) style,
- authority-compliance (previously called *produce-or-perish*) style, and
- team management (later called *sound*) style.

These styles and how each relates to the two concerns were introduced in Chapter 2.3[2]. According to Blake and Mouton, the optimal style to employ is the team management style, which incorporates high degrees of concern for both people and production.

The styles above are archetypes. In practice, a leader will normally exhibit a mixed orientation that displays some measure of both concerns. This is indicated by the zones in Figure 5. Nonetheless, the authors assume that a leader will tend to prefer a certain style.

In the *impoverished* style, the leader exerts minimal effort to complete the bare amount of work that is required to avoid being replaced. In the *country-club management* style, thoughtful attention to the needs of people regarding satisfying relationships leads to a friendly, comfortable work environment and tempo. The *middle-of-*

---

[1] Originally called management styles.
[2] See page 33f.

the-road style delivers adequate performance by balancing task efficiency with keeping morale at acceptable levels. In the *authority-compliance* style, efficiency results from arranging work conditions in a way that human elements interfere minimally. And when the t*eam management* style is employed, a purpose held in common by committed people, an atmosphere of trust and respect, and a leader who can get things done combine to result in superior performance.

Figure 5: The Managerial Grid

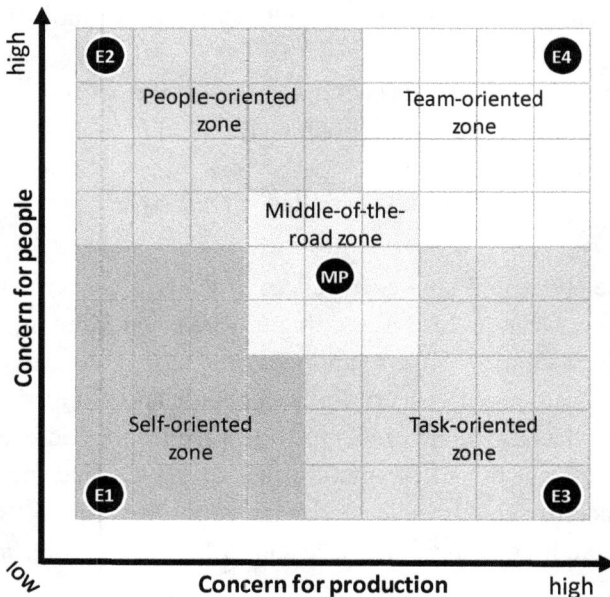

Positions in original Managerial Grid:
- E1: Impoverished style (1/1)
- E2: Country-club management style (1/9)
- MP: Middle-of-the-road style
- E3: Authority-compliance style (9/1)
- E4: Team management style (9/9)

Additional positions in updated Managerial Grid:
- E1, E2, E3, E4, or MP in order to maximize personal benefit: Opportunistic style
- Alternating between E2 and E3: Paternalistic style

Source: adapted from Blake and Mouton (1964) and McKee and Carlson (1999).

In 1999, the managerial grid model was updated by Rachel McKee and Bruce Carlson, who added two new styles (although 'behaviors' might be a more appropriate term):

- *Opportunistic (*or exploit and manipulate) style: the leader situationally selects the style that offers the greatest personal benefit to him or her.
- *Paternalistic (*or prescribe and guide) style: the leader alternates between country-club and authority-compliance, offering praise and support but discouraging challenges to his or her thinking.

In practice, these additions did not gain much traction, and most books on leadership refer to the original grid.

Identifying the style that you currently naturally prefer will increase your awareness of how you approach tasks and people and where your strengths and weaknesses may lie. Perform Exercise 5 on page 105 to determine your preferred style. This may also help you identify your personal development needs.

3.24   Fiedler's Contingency Theory

In his Contingency Theory of Leadership, American psychologist Fred Fiedler introduced the notion that team performance depends not just on the leadership style but also on what he called situational favorableness. Like the Managerial Grid, Fiedler's model uses the task orientation vs. people orientation dichotomy (although he uses the term 'human relations orientation' for the latter) to describe a leader's basic hardwiring.

Situation favorableness is determined by three factors:

- leader-member relations,
- task structure, and
- leader positional power.

Leader-member relations may be good or poor. Tasks may be structured or unstructured, and the leader's position power may be strong or weak.

Fiedler sees a need for task-oriented leaders particularly when relations are good and tasks are structured. If tasks are unstructured but the leader's position power is strong, a task-oriented leader is also seen as preferable, because effective teams need direction, and the leader's power ensures that people will do his or her bidding. However, when the leader and the team members work well together but the task is unstructured and the leader's position power is uncertain or weak, a people-oriented leader is preferred, because these teams require a lot of team-building, convincing, and pep-talking. This is often the case in ad-hoc project teams where team members do not report to the project head. The same is suggested for any situation in which leader-member relations are poor, with the exception of an extremely unfavorable situation where these bad relations are made worse by an unstructured task *and* weak positional power. In this exceptional situation, Fiedler's model suggests that a task-oriented leader will be more effective, because things just need to be done somehow, and among other things, this type of leader will be less distracted by emotions stemming from the poor situation.

In line with Lewin's notion of a preferred leadership style, Fiedler considers a leader's style to be ingrained and therefore more or less fixed. Consequently, if a situation changes significantly, the leader may have to be replaced because, in essence, this is easier than changing the entire team (which is also an option, however, and occasionally also happens, particularly in owner-run organizations). Where the situation shifts less rapidly over time, the leader may develop along with it, yet the model suggests that the more promising approach is still to modify the situation continuously to fit the leader, for instance through team-building activities (improving leader-member relations), formalizing processes (making tasks more structured), or by the organization granting more formal power to the leader, such as creating a formal reporting relationship between the leader and the members of an important project.

The table below summarizes Fiedler's recommendations for a leader type based on the various situational combinations.

Table 6:   Situation and Leader Type in the Fiedler Contingency Model

Influence factor for situational favourableness			Fiedler's recommendation
Leader/members	Task	Leader power	
Good relations	Structured	Strong	Task oriented leader
Good relations	Structured	Weak	Task oriented leader
Good relations	Unstructured	Strong	Task oriented leader
Good relations	Unstructured	Weak	People-oriented leader
Poor relations	Structured	Strong	People-oriented leader
Poor relations	Structured	Weak	People-oriented leader
Poor relations	Unstructured	Strong	People-oriented leader
Poor relations	Unstructured	Weak	Task oriented leader

Source: adapted from Fiedler (1967)

Stress , whether for the leader or for his or her followers stemming from superiors, the team, and the situation is seen as detrimental to leader effectiveness, and the ability to control the group situation is thus crucial for a leader. Additionally, Fiedler found that, perhaps counterintuitively, experience can impair performance under low-stress conditions. This is because it limits the leader's cognitive horizon and may lead him or her astray due to false familiarity[1]. However, it normally contributes to performance under high-stress conditions.

---

[1] False familiarity refers to a psychological reaction to new situations that seem to be similar to previously encountered ones. Often, a person will then jump to the conclusion that the same solution as last time will resolve the issue without further problem assessment or situation

One typical methodological problem in leadership style research is the reliance on self-reporting; the study results depend on people's self-view and how they report their own perceived attitudes and behaviors (for an example, see the exercises on page 99f.). Some people, even if they do not consciously misreport, have low self-awareness and can subconsciously deceive themselves when completing a questionnaire, perhaps to fit some anticipated 'ideal' answer or because they have somehow formed the impression that the researcher expects a particular answer.

Fiedler is also recognized in leadership research circles for the innovative way with which he attempted to circumvent this issue. Apart from his original research, his *least-preferred co-worker* (LPC) scale has also been used subsequently on a variety of other samples, such as soldiers (Posthuma, 1970) and students (Rowland and Gardner, 1973). Fiedler asked his test subjects to think of the one person with whom they found it hardest to work[1]. With that person in mind, they then had to indicate where they saw that person between a number of opposites, as in these examples:

Pleasant	1	2	3	4	5	6	7	8	Unpleasant
Supportive	1	2	3	4	5	6	7	8	Hostile
Harmonious	1	2	3	4	5	6	7	8	Quarrelsome
Kind	1	2	3	4	5	6	7	8	Unkind

Fiedler assumed that task-oriented leaders would be less harsh in their judgments about this person than people-oriented leaders, thus leading to a comparatively lower LPC score. Despite its name, therefore, the LPC scale is not really about the eponymous least-preferred co-worker. Instead, it captures the leader's emotional reaction to this person. See Exercise 6 on page 108.

---

analysis. Considering that situations are almost always different to previous situations in at least some ways, this can lead to incorrect decisions and/or incomplete solutions.

[1] Although the two often go together, this was expressly *not* the person least liked, just the one with whom one somehow could not cooperate at all.

3.25   Hersey and Blanchard's Situational Leadership

Hersey and Blanchard's *Situational Leadership Theory[1]* was published in 1969 and has since become highly influential, particularly in leadership training[2]. In contrast to Fiedler's Contingency Theory, this model assumes that leaders can adjust their leadership style as warranted by the situation. Thus, the model is only applicable in cases where the leader is able to do this.

Critical competencies of situational leaders are

- diagnosing the situation,
- adapting to the situation,
- communicating with followers and others, and
- advancing the task and people.

The authors postulate that the style a leader should employ depends on the follower's maturity[3], which in turn influences development. These maturity levels and the corresponding development levels influence the performance readiness of followers and therefore the style the leader should employ:

- A *directing style* is required if followers are unskilled but committed.
- A *coaching style* is required if followers are only marginally skilled and not committed.
- A *supporting style* is required if followers are quite skilled but not fully committed.
- A *delegating style* can be applied if followers are both highly skilled and highly committed.

---

[1] Hersey and Blanchard's theory was originally called the Life-Cycle Theory of Leadership.
[2] Also see Chapter 2.5 on page 31.
[3] In variations of the model, maturity and development are jointly referred to as "performance readiness".

Figure 6: Situational Leadership

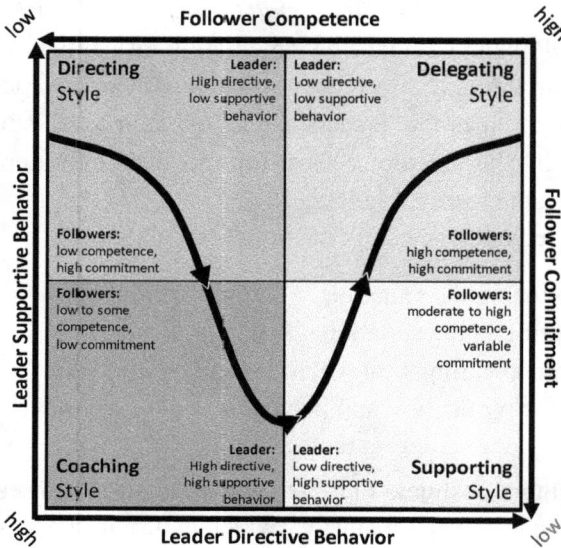

Source: adapted from Hersey and Blanchard (1969)

Importantly, the leader has to choose a style both for the team as a whole and for every individual team member. If the team is very homogeneous, the same style will conceivable apply to all—but that is often not the case.

Below is an example of a tool that can help you think systematically about your leadership approach to each team member as well as the team as a whole. Please note that tools like these can only help you think about your leadership situation and approach, but they do cannot tell you what to do. Leadership is complex, and you must rely on your experience, senses, and intuition to judge whether the approach you take actually works. Use Exercise 9 on page 115 to practice applying this tool.

Table 7: The Situational Leadership Team Portfolio

Leading the individual team members				Appropriate style for each team member
Team member	Competence 1: low; 3: medium; 5: high	Commitment 4: low; 6: variable; 8: high	Maturity Score (competence x commitment)	
...	...	...	...	...
...	...	...	...	...
...	...	...	...	...
...	...	...	...	...
...	...	...	...	...
...	...	...	...	...

Leading the team		Appropriate style for the overall team
Average maturity (sum of individual maturity scores divided by number of team members)	(Rounded average score)	(corresponding score in decision matrix* below)
	...	...

To determine the appropriate style, select the score below that is closest to the one above:

* Decision matrix		Commitment		
		Low (4)	Varying (6)	High (8)
Competence	Low (1)	(4) Directing Style (or terminate)	(6) Coaching Style	(8) Directing Style
	Medium (3)	(12) Coaching Style	(18) Supporting Style	(24) Supporting Style
	High (5)	(20) Coaching Style (or switch/enrich job)	(30) Delegating Style	(40) Delegating Style

Source: author, based on Hersey and Blanchard (1969).

3.26   The Vroom-Yetton-Jago Normative Decision Model

As previously explained[1], the Vroom-Yetton-Jago Normative Decision Model is a situational leadership model that is designed to suggest the most appropriate decision-making process in a given leadership situation, based on the answers to eight questions. According to Vroom and Yetton[2] (1973), the effectiveness of a decision depends on three outcomes:

1. the quality or rationality of the decision,
2. the acceptance or commitment on the part of the subordinates to execute the decision effectively, and
3. the amount of time required to make the decision.

The higher the quality of the decision needed, the more other people should be involved in the decision making. The same is true if acceptance by subordinates is crucial and if there is ample time.

The model suggests five decision-making processes, which are based on three basic leadership styles:

- autocratic,
- consultative, and
- collaborative.

The autocratic style corresponds to Lewin's autocratic, Goleman's commanding, and Hersey and Blanchard's directive styles, while the consultative style is in line with Lewin's participative-democratic substyle, and the collaborative style matches Lewin's fully democratic substyle and Goleman's affiliative style.

The decision-making processes that result from these three basic styles differ mainly in the amount of subordinate involvement. They are

---

[1] See Chapter 2.5 on page 29f.
[2] Vroom and Yetton themselves refer to Maier (1963).

- *Autocratic I* (A1): the leader makes the decision without subordinate involvement using available information.
- *Autocratic II* (A2): the leader obtains additional information from subordinates before making the decision but then makes the decision alone; the subordinates may or may not be informed.
- *Consultative l* (C1): the leader discusses problems individually with subordinates and asks for input, but there are no team meetings, and the leader makes the decision alone.
- *Consultative II* (C2): the leader discusses problems with the team but makes the decision alone.
- *Group II* (G2): the leader discusses problems with the team, focuses and directs discussions, and allows the group to make the decision.

The selection of the most appropriate of these processes depends on the answer to the following eight questions:

1. *Quality requirement*: Is there a critical quality requirement? Is one solution likely to be superior due to technical or rational reasons?
2. *Commitment requirement*: Is acceptance of the decision by subordinates critical to effective implementation?
3. *Leader information*: Do you have sufficient information to make a high-quality decision?
4. *Problem structure*: Is the problem structured?
5. *Commitment probability*: If you were to make the decision by yourself, is it reasonably certain that your subordinates would be committed to the decision?
6. *Goal congruence*: Do subordinates share the organizational goals to be attained in solving the problem?
7. *Subordinate conflict*: Is conflict among subordinates likely over preferred solutions?
8. *Subordinate information*: Do subordinates have sufficient information to contribute to a high-quality decision?

A yes-or-no answer to each question[1] leads along the decision tree in Figure 7 to the most appropriate decision-making process.

Figure 7: The Vroom-Yetton-Jago Normative Decision Model

Decision Question	Decision Tree	Processes
1. Quality requirement: Is there a quality requirement? Is one solution superior for technical or rational reasons?	Yes ... No	**A1** (Autocratic): leader makes decision without subordinate involvement using available information.
2. Commitment requirement: Is acceptance of the decision by subordinates critical?	Yes ... No ... Yes ... No	
3. Leader information Do you have sufficient information to make a high-quality decision?	Yes ... No ... Yes ... No	**A2** (Autocratic II): leader gets additional information from subordinates before making decision alone; subordinates may or may not be informed.
4. Problem structure Is the problem structured?	Yes ... No ... Yes ... No	**C1** (Consultative I): leader discusses issue individually with subordinates and asks for input before making decision alone without team meetings.
5. Commitment probability: If you were to make the decision alone, would your subordinates commit to it?	Yes ... No ... Yes ... No ... Yes ... No ... Yes ... No	**C2** (Consultative II): leader discusses problems with team but makes decision alone.
6. Goal congruence Do subordinates share the organizational goals to be attained in solving the problem?	Yes ... No ... Yes ... No ... Yes ... No ... Yes ... No	
7. Subordinate conflict Is conflict likely among subordinates over preferred solutions?	Yes ... No ... Yes ... No	**G2** (Group II): leader discusses problems with team, focuses and directs discussions, and allows group to make decision.
8. Subordinate information: Do subordinates have sufficient information to contribute to a high-quality decision?	Yes ... No ... Yes ... No	

Source: adapted from Vroom and Jago (1988)

---

[1] The formulation and sequence of questions changed slightly between model iterations. The questions listed here are from Vroom and Jago (1988).

To summarize the model's recommendations, a consultative style is recommended in cases where the problem is not clearly defined, the implementation depends on follower buy-in, there is sufficient time available, and/or the leader needs information from others to solve a particular problem. In contrast, an autocratic style is seen as more efficient when the leader is most knowledgeable about a subject or problem, the team is likely to accept the decision without any problems, there is time pressure, and/or if the leader feels confident enough to act alone.

3.27   Goleman's Six Emotional Leadership Styles

While neither the first nor by any means the only emotional intelligence model, Goleman's framework is arguably one of the most well known. First introduced in his 1995 bestseller *Emotional Intelligence*, it is based on the idea that emotional intelligence may matter just as much or more than traditional cognitive intelligence for the academic, professional, social, and interpersonal aspects of one's life. In *Working with Emotional Intelligence* (1998), he extended this argument to success in the workplace, and in *Primal Leadership* (Goleman, Boyatzis, and McKee, 2002) specifically to leadership.

In this model, emotional intelligence is defined as the ability to perceive, evaluate, and control emotions. A key postulate in Goleman's writings is that a leader's actions and behaviors influence the emotional state of his or her subordinates, just as the actions and behaviors of individual team members affect those around them. This is an important point, because psychological well-being is closely linked to performance (Wright and Cropanzano, 2000). According to this model, therefore, the leadership style employed may affect the followers' emotional well-being positively or negatively, depending on how the style fits them and their particular situations. Goleman claims that effective leaders will be able to switch seamlessly from one to the other and will typically use all of them in a given working week[1]. While this is a disputed point, and the model itself lacks empirical support, his framework is nonetheless an interesting and helpful tool to think about how to meet the emotional needs of subordinates and create resonance with them –in a particular situation. This holds true even for leaders who are not able to change styles situationally.

Goleman's model lists six leadership styles:

- visionary,
- coaching,
- affiliative,
- democratic,
- pace-setting, and
- commanding.

Each style is associated with a different leader mode, which can be summed up in a particular quote, and uses specific underlying emotional intelligence competencies, thereby creating resonance in a unique way. Leaders who employ a visionary style mobilize people toward a vision or "shared dream", which in turn creates resonance with followers. This approach can be summarized in the style quote "come with me" and is appropriate when change requires a new vision. The coaching style ("try this") is suitable to help competent, motivated followers improve performance, while the affiliative style ("people come first") can help to heal rifts, motivate during stress, and strengthen interpersonal connections. A democratic style ("what do you think?") facilitates consensus and buy-in and helps to gain valuable input from followers, while a pace-setting style ("do what I do, now") can be appropriate to achieve peak performance from competent and motivated teams.

---

[1] In his Harvard Business Review article *Leadership That Gets Results*, Goleman used the example of a golf pro who picks clubs from his bag based on the demands of a particular shot. Sometimes the selection will be pondered, but most often it is automatic. Goleman argues that it is the same with leadership styles, meaning a leader – sometimes after due consideration, often automatically selects the style best suited to a given leadership situation.

Table 8:   Goleman's Six Emotional Leadership Styles

Goleman's Six Emotional Leadership Styles		
Style	**Visionary** (earlier: authoritative)	**Coaching**	**Affiliative**
Leader mode	Mobilizes people toward a vision	Develops people for the future	Creates harmony and builds emotional bonds
Style quote	"Come with me."	"Try this."	"People come first."
Leader traits and behaviors	Inspires, believes in own vision, and explains how people's efforts contribute to the 'dream'	Listens, counsels, encourages, delegates; helps people identify own strengths and weaknesses	Promotes harmony, is nice and empathetic, boosts moral, and solves conflicts
Base EI competencies	Self-confidence, empathy, change catalyst	Empathy, self-awareness, developing others	Empathy, relationship-building, communication
How style builds resonance	Moving people towards the 'shared dream'	Connecting what a person wants with the organization's goals	Creating harmony by connecting people to each other
When appropriate	When change requires a new vision	To help competent, motivated followers improve performance	To heal rifts, motivate during stress, or strengthen connections
Basis	Transformational style (Bass, 1985)	Coaching style (Hersey and Blanchard, 1969)	Country-club management (Blake and Mouton, 1964)

Style	**Democratic**	**Pace-Setting**	**Commanding** (earlier: coercive)
Leader mode	Forges consensus through participation	Sets high standards for performance	Demands immediate compliance
Style line	"What do you think?"	"Do as I do, now"	"Do what I tell you."
Leader traits and behaviors	Superb listener, team worker, collaborator, influencer	High standards; impatient, low on empathy and collaboration; often micro-managing and numbers-driven	Commanding, threatening, tight control, monitoring closely, creating dissonance
Base EI competencies	Collaboration, team leadership, communication	Conscientious-ness, drive to achieve, initiative	Drive to achieve, initiative, self- control
How style builds resonance	Valuing input and getting commitment through participation	Meeting challenging and exciting goals	Soothing fears by giving clear directions in an emergency
When appropriate	To build consensus or buy-in; to get valuable input from followers	To get top results from competent and motivated teams	In a crisis and/or to kick-start urgent initiatives; with problem followers
Basis	Democratic style (Lewin, Lippit, and White, 1939)	Pace-setting style (Hersey and Blanchard, 1969)	Autocratic style (Lewin, Lippit, and White, 1939); directive style (Hersey and Blanchard, 1969)

Sources: adapted from Goleman (2000), Goleman, Boyatzis, and McKee (2002)

If these styles appear familiar, it is no coincidence. The visionary style incorporates aspects of Bass's transformational leadership. The coaching style corresponds to the Hersey and Blanchard style of the same name. The affiliative style is reminiscent of Blake and Mouton's country-club management style, while the democratic style matches Lewin's style of the same name. The commanding style resembles both Lewin's autocratic style and Hersey and Blanchard's directive style, and the pace-setting style is also in line with Hersey and Blanchard's supporting style. The additional aspect introduced by Goleman and his colleagues is the emotional effect associated with them.

3.28 GLOBE's Six Global Leadership Styles

As part of a major eleven-year effort by an international team of 170 researchers in 62 countries that aimed to test the cross-cultural application of leadership traits and behaviors, the *Global Leadership and Organizational Behavior Effectiveness* (GLOBE) study published in 2004 identified six leadership styles[1] that are found around the world:

- charismatic/value-based,
- team-oriented,
- participative,
- humane-oriented
- self-protective, and
- autonomous.

Charismatic/value-based leadership reflects the ability to inspire, motivate, and expect high performance from others on the basis of firmly held core values. *Team-oriented* leadership stresses effective team-building and implementation of a common goal among team members. Both of these styles were found to hold universal

---

[1] The study called these *culturally endorsed implicit leadership dimensions.*

appeal around the world. Interestingly, this was true for neither the *participative* style often favored in the Western world nor for what the authors termed *humane-oriented* leadership, which reflects supportive and considerate leadership and includes compassion and generosity. *Self-protective* leadership, which focuses on ensuring the safety and security of the leader, and *autonomous* leadership, which refers to independent and individualistic leadership, were both seen negatively in all cultures, albeit to varying degrees.

The topic of global leadership is discussed in Chapter 5[1].

---

[1] See page 239f.

3.3 Chapter Recap

What you should take away from this chapter:

1. The Big Five personality factors are openness, conscientiousness, extraversion, agreeableness, and neuroticism. The first three have a positive effect and the others a negative effect on leader emergence. Openness, conscientiousness, extraversion, and agreeableness also have a positive effect on leader effectiveness, whereas neuroticism's effect tends to be negative, although results are mixed.

2. Kurt Lewin and his collaborators identified three broad leadership styles: authoritarian (or autocratic), democratic (or participative), and laissez-faire (or delegative).

3. Tannenbaum and Schmidt assert that leadership styles exist on a continuum from fully autocratic to fully delegative. Their associated styles are authoritarian, paternalistic, consultative (I and II), participative, democratic, and laissez-faire.

4. Blake and Mouton's Managerial Grid is based on the assumption that a person's leadership style tends to be either person-oriented or task-oriented, though both orientations may be present in a leader's style to varying degrees. A leadership style which is neither person oriented nor task oriented is termed impoverished (later also indifferent). A solely person-oriented style is labelled country-club management, while the opposite is termed authority-compliance (later also produce-or-perish). Finally, a style that combines both aspects to a certain degree is called middle-of-the-road (later also named status quo), while one that incorporates them fully is called a team management (later also sound) style. The last one is seen as the ideal to which all leaders should aspire. In 1999, Rachel McKee and Bruce Carlson added two more styles: opportunistic (or exploit and manipulate), and paternalistic (or prescribe and guide).

5. Fiedler's Contingency Model assumes that team performance depends not just on the leader's leadership style, which is seen as either task-oriented or relationship-oriented, but also on situational favorableness, which is determined by three aspects: leader-member relations (good or poor), task structure (structured or unstructured), and leader positional power (strong or weak).

6. Hersey and Blanchard's Situational Leadership framework assumes that the ideal style a leader should employ in a given situation depends on the followers' development and maturity, which is equivalent to their competence and commitment. Unskilled but committed followers require a directing style, while a coaching style is required if followers are only marginally skilled and not committed. Skilled but not fully committed followers warrant a supporting style, while a delegating style can be applied if followers are both highly skilled and highly committed.

7. The Vroom-Yetton-Jago Normative Decision Model suggests a decision-making process based on the answers to eight questions to identify the most appropriate style for a given situation. These decision-making processes, based on three archetypal leadership styles, are autocratic (I and II), consultative (I and II), and group (II).

8. Based on the notion that the actions and behaviors of leaders influence the emotional states of their followers, Goleman's Emotional Intelligence model assumes that leaders are not merely able to switch between leadership styles as warranted but that they actually do so frequently and will use all of them in any given working week to create what the author calls resonance, a positive emotional response. His so-called Six Emotional Leadership Styles are visionary, coaching, affiliative, democratic, pace-setting, and commanding.

9. As part of a massive, long-term, cross-cultural research project (Project GLOBE), Robert House and his collaborators identified six leadership styles that were found around the world: charismatic/value-based, team-oriented, participative, humane-oriented, self-protective, and autonomous. The first two were universally seen positively, while the last two were seen negatively in all cultures.

CHECK QUESTIONS

Try to answer the questions below. If you need help, check the sample answers in the annex.

1. What are the two main strands of leadership research?
2. What is another name for trait research?
3. What are traits?
4. Which are the Big Five personality factors?
5. According to Kurt Lewin, what is a laissez-faire leadership style, and what is its effect?
6. What is the difference between the consultative I and consultative II styles in Tannenbaum and Schmidt's Leadership Continuum?
7. What are the two dimensions that determine a person's leadership style in the Blake-Mouton Managerial Grid?
8. According to Fiedler's Contingency Theory, when can it make sense to replace a leader?
9. What is the postulated effect of experience in Fiedler's Contingency Theory?
10. What is the logic behind Fiedler's Least-Preferred Co-worker (LPC) scale?
11. What is a fundamental difference between Fiedler's Contingency Theory and Hersey and Blanchard's Situational Leadership model?
12. What determines the appropriate leadership style in Hersey and Blanchard's Situational Leadership model?
13. What are the two fundamental leader behaviors in Hersey and Blanchard's Situational Leadership model?
14. What does the effectiveness of a decision depend on, according to the Vroom-Yetton-Jago Normative Decision Model?

15. In the Vroom-Yetton-Jago Normative Decision Model, which factors determine the level of subordinate involvement necessary in a decision?

16. What basic idea provides the basis for Goleman's Six Emotional Leadership Styles?

17. Which two of the six leadership styles found around the world by Project GLOBE held universal appeal?

3.4   Exercises

On the following pages, you will find various exercises related to the content of this chapter. If you need help, check the sample solutions in the annex.

Exercise 3   Your Preferred Leadership Style According to Lewin

Fill in the questionnaire below. For each question, select the answer which seems to apply to you the most.

#	Determinant	Your Answer				
		Almost always	Frequently	Occasionally	Rarely	Hardly ever
1	I always reserve the final decision-making authority in my team for myself.	5	4	3	2	1
2	I always try to include one or more employees in determining what to do and how to do it. However, I retain the final decision.	5	4	3	2	1
3	My employees and I always vote whenever a major decision has to be made.	5	4	3	2	1
4	I do not consider suggestions made by my employees, as I do not have the time,	5	4	3	2	1
5	I ask for employee ideas and input on upcoming plans and projects.	5	4	3	2	1
6	For a major decision to pass in my department, it must have the approval of each individual or the majority.	5	4	3	2	1
7	I tell my employees what has to be done and how to do it.	5	4	3	2	1
8	When things go wrong and I need to keep a project or process running on schedule, I call a meeting to get my worker's advice.	5	4	3	2	1
9	To send out information, I use email, memos, voice mail, or text; rarely is a meeting called. My workers are expected to act upon it.	5	4	3	2	1
10	When someone makes a mistake, I tell him or her not to ever do that again and make a note of it.	5	4	3	2	1
11	I want to create an environment where employees take ownership of the project. I allow them to participate in the decision-making process.	5	4	3	2	1
12	I allow my employees to determine what needs to be done and how to do it.	5	4	3	2	1
13	New hires are not allowed to make any decisions unless approved by me first.	5	4	3	2	1
14	I ask employees for their vision of where they see their jobs going and then use their vision where appropriate.	5	4	3	2	1

#	Determinant	Your Answer				
		Almost always	Frequently	Occasionally	Rarely	Hardly ever
15	My workers know more about their jobs than I do, so I allow them to make their own decisions.	5	4	3	2	1
16	When something goes wrong, I tell my employees that a procedure is not working correctly and I establish a new one.	5	4	3	2	1
17	I allow my employees to set priorities with my guidance.	5	4	3	2	1
18	I delegate tasks when implementing a new procedure or process.	5	4	3	2	1
19	I monitor my employees closely to ensure they are performing correctly.	5	4	3	2	1
20	When there are differences in role expectations, I work with them to resolve the differences.	5	4	3	2	1
21	Each individual is responsible for defining his or her job.	5	4	3	2	1
22	I like the power that my leadership position gives me over subordinates.	5	4	3	2	1
23	I like to use my leadership power to help subordinates grow.	5	4	3	2	1
24	I like to share my leadership power with my subordinates.	5	4	3	2	1
25	Employees must be directed or threatened with punishment in order to make them achieve organizational objectives.	5	4	3	2	1
26	Employees will exercise self-direction if they are committed to the objectives.	5	4	3	2	1
27	Employees have the right to determine their own organizational objectives.	5	4	3	2	1
28	Employees mainly seek security.	5	4	3	2	1
29	Employees know how to use creativity and ingenuity to solve organizational problems.	5	4	3	2	1
30	My employees can lead themselves just as well as I can.	5	4	3	2	1

Now fill in the numerical score of each item on the questionnaire in the list below, and then calculate the total for each column.

Item	Score	Item	Score	Item	Score
1		2		3	
4		5		6	
7		8		9	
10		11		12	
13		14		15	
16		17		18	
19		20		21	
22		23		24	
25		26		27	
28		29		30	
Total		Total		Total	

| Authoritarian style | Democratic style | Laissez-faire Style |

Source: Clark (1998).

Your preferred style is indicated by the highest of the three column scores. If it is 40 or more, this is a strong indicator of your preferred style. If a score is 20 or lower, then that would indicate that you really do not feel comfortable with that style. If the difference between the three scores is small, this might indicate that you are not fully aware of your normal operating mode, perhaps because you are new at leading and are still finding your way.

Exercise 4 Choosing a Style on the Leadership Continuum

Marc De Vries, 33, has been with the Belgian subsidiary of a large international retailer for the past six years. Although not considered a natural leader by his superiors, he has recently been promoted and has just taken over a team in the purchasing department. The promotion has boosted his self-confidence somewhat, although he remains rather insecure and nervous. Accordingly, he tends to have quite a hard time making decisions and prefers getting everyone's input before making up his mind, although he then frequently disregards his team members' advice. During his company-internal leadership, he repeatedly received the feedback that he needs to put more trust in other people.

Having spoken formally and informally to all team members several times now, he is fairly confident that they are generally up to the task but feels that some of them require additional training. The team lacks cohesiveness and performs acceptably but not very well. He has also noticed that most of his team members have a solid grasp of what they are supposed to do and do not appreciate being told how to do their jobs, even if they do not seem to particularly live for them. Nonetheless, he feels that some of them overestimate their own abilities and should not be given too much responsibility for the moment. After all, making sure that the right products are bought at the right time for the lowest price possible is no simple task, he feels.

Owing to the nature of the business, the team is always under some time pressure, even if this is not severe. Marc has also noticed that, with one exception, all team members tend to ask a lot of questions about any number of things that concern the company, but he does not have an answer to most of them because they are well above his paygrade. His team members are generally not shy when it comes to telling him what they feel he should do, and they clearly expect him to take their feedback into account when making decisions. At the same time, they seem to be rather indifferent to the company itself, mostly seeing their work there as a means to an end. In his discussions, the perceived high level of bureaucracy and the fact that almost all the important decisions are made at headquarters in the USA have emerged as important demotivators. Although the company has over 200,000 employees worldwide, it is quite ethnocentric, with the various international country organizations taking on the role of low-autonomy satellites.

Feeling unsure about how to deal with his team, Marc comes to you for advice about what style of leadership he should adopt.

Assignment

Based on this information, work through the leadership continuum decision model on the next page and determine the appropriate leadership style. Refer to Chapter 3.22 on page 69f. for an explanation.

FORCES IN THE LEADER

	Value system		Confidence in team			Leadership inclinations		Feelings of security in an uncertain situation		
	More distrusting	More trusting	Low	Moderate	High	More naturally directive	More naturally participative	Low	Moderate	High
A	1	2	1	2	3	1	2	1	2	3

FORCES IN THE FOLLOWERS

	Need for independence		Readiness for responsibility		Tolerance for ambiguity		Interest in the task		Identification with organization		Skill level		Expectation of participating	
	Low to medium	Medium to high	Low to medium	Medium to high	Low to medium	Medium to high	Low to medium	Medium to high	Low to medium	Medium to high	Low to medium	Medium to high	Low to medium	Medium to high
B	1	2	1	2	1	2	1	2	1	2	1	2	1	2

FORCES IN THE SITUATION

	Type of organization		Group effectiveness			Nature of problem		Time pressure		
	Centralized	Decentralized	Low	Moderate	High	Simple	Complex	Low	Moderate	High
C	1	2	1	2	3	1	2	1	2	3

A
+B
+C

Total

15-16	17-18	19-20	21-23	24-27	28-31	32-34
Authoritarian	Paternalistic	Consultative I	Consultative II	Participative	Democratic	Laissez-faire
Leader makes decision and informs team.	Leader makes decision and then convinces subordinates of its value.	Leader presents ideas and invites questions before making decision.	Leader presents tentative decision that is subject to change.	Leader presents problem to team and gets suggestions but retains final decision.	Leader defines limits but delegates decision to team.	Leader allows subordinates to function within limits defined by higher instance.

Exercise 5 Your Preferred Position in the Managerial Grid

Fill in the questionnaire below. For each question, select the answer which seems to apply to you the most.

#	Determinant	Your Answer				
		Almost always	Frequently	Occasionally	Rarely	Hardly ever
1	I encourage my team to participate in decisions and I try to implement their suggestions.	5	4	3	2	1
2	Nothing is more important than accomplishing a goal or task.	5	4	3	2	1
3	I monitor the schedule closely to ensure a task or project is completed in time.	5	4	3	2	1
4	I enjoy coaching people on new tasks and procedures.	5	4	3	2	1
5	The more challenging a task is, the more I enjoy it.	5	4	3	2	1
6	I encourage my employees to be creative about their job.	5	4	3	2	1
7	When seeing a complex task through to completion, I ensure that every detail is accounted for.	5	4	3	2	1
8	I find it easy to carry out several complicated tasks at the same time.	5	4	3	2	1
9	I enjoy reading articles, books, and journals about training, leadership, and psychology—and then putting what I have read into action.	5	4	3	2	1
10	When correcting mistakes, I do not worry about jeopardizing relationships.	5	4	3	2	1
11	I manage my time very efficiently.	5	4	3	2	1
12	I enjoy explaining the intricacies and details of a complex task or project to my employees.	5	4	3	2	1
13	Breaking large projects into small manageable tasks is second nature to me.	5	4	3	2	1

#	Determinant	Almost always	Frequently	Occasionally	Rarely	Hardly ever
		Your Answer				
14	Nothing is more important than building a great team.	5	4	3	2	1
15	I enjoy analyzing problems.	5	4	3	2	1
16	I honor other people's boundaries.	5	4	3	2	1
17	Counselling my employees to improve their performance or behavior is second nature to me.	5	4	3	2	1
18	I enjoy reading articles, books, and trade journals about my profession—and then implementing the new procedures I have learned.	5	4	3	2	1

Now fill in the numerical score of each item on the questionnaire in the list below, and then calculate the total for each column.

Item	Score
1	
4	
6	
9	
10	
12	
14	
16	
17	

Total	
Divide by 5	
X-Position	

Concern for production

Item	Score
2	
3	
5	
7	
8	
11	
13	
15	
18	

Total	
Divide by 5	
Y-Position	

Concern for people

Finally, visualize your result by entering it into the grid below:

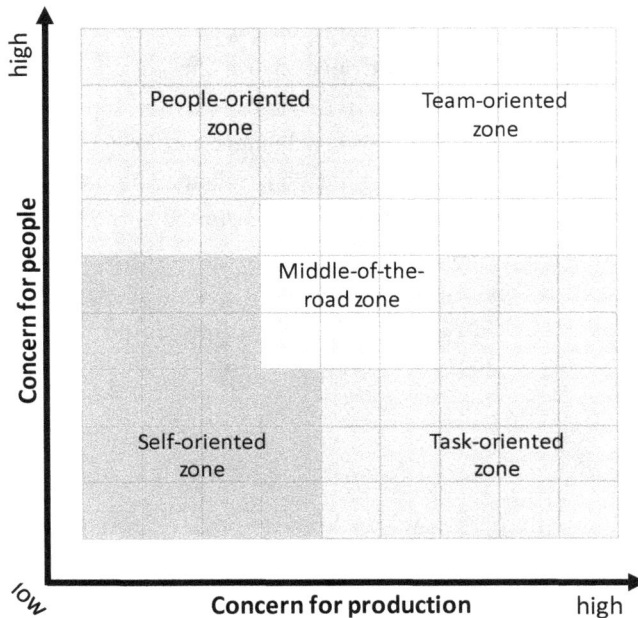

Reflect on the result:

- Is the result in line with your self-view? Why or why not?
- If you compare your position in the grid with the supposed ideal position (team management), what personal conclusions do you draw?
- What specific actions could potentially be helpful for you to further improve as a leader?

Also reflect on the methodology itself. What do you think of the basic idea? How do you rate the questionnaire? What could be improved?

Exercise 6 Determine your LPC Score

Fiedler's Contingency Theory of Leadership asserts that leaders basically display one of two styles, task oriented or relationship oriented. Which one is superior depends on the situation. As Fiedler considers the leadership style to be ingrained and therefore more or less fixed, meaning that in his view leaders cannot normally change their style at will, knowing which style a leader naturally prefers is important. In order to identify this but avoid the common self-report bias, he developed the Least Preferred Co-worker scale. It is based on the idea that task-oriented leaders will tend to be less harsh in their judgments of a person with whom they could not work well together.

Instructions

Think about a person with whom you can or could not work together at all. The point is that it should be a person with whom you had trouble getting a task or project done, not necessarily someone you dislike (although the two may go together, of course). Then fill in the questionnaire on the next page and describe that person by choosing the appropriate number for each of the 18 scales. Be as honest and precise as possible.

Note that some scales are reversed.

#	Attribute	Position that best describes LPC								Opposite
1	Open	8	7	6	5	4	3	2	1	Guarded
2	Unfriendly	1	2	3	4	5	6	7	8	Friendly
3	Pleasant	8	7	6	5	4	3	2	1	Unpleasant
4	Rejecting	1	2	3	4	5	6	7	8	Accepting
5	Warm	8	7	6	5	4	3	2	1	Cold
6	Tense	1	2	3	4	5	6	7	8	Relaxed
7	Interesting	8	7	6	5	4	3	2	1	Boring
8	Loyal	8	7	6	5	4	3	2	1	Backbiting
9	Nasty	1	2	3	4	5	6	7	8	Nice
10	Hostile	1	2	3	4	5	6	7	8	Supportive
11	Considerate	8	7	6	5	4	3	2	1	Inconsiderate
12	Insincere	1	2	3	4	5	6	7	8	Sincere
13	Unkind	1	2	3	4	5	6	7	8	Kind
14	Trustworthy	8	7	6	5	4	3	2	1	Untrustworthy
15	Gloomy	1	2	3	4	5	6	7	8	Friendly
16	Peacable	8	7	6	5	4	3	2	1	Quarrelsome
17	Emotionally distant	1	2	3	4	5	6	7	8	Emotionally open/close
18	Supportive	8	7	6	5	4	3	2	1	Hostile

Source: adapted from Fiedler, Chemers, and Mahar (1976).

Interpretation

Calculate the total sum of all the answers you selected in the questionnaire. Then compare your score with Fiedler's original interpretation below:

57 or less:	*low LPC*
	You are likely primarily task-oriented. According to Fiedler, these leaders are very effective at completing tasks, while relationship-building is a low priority.
58 to 63:	*middle LPC*
	You are able to switch between task-oriented and relationship-oriented styles. These leaders may be best suited to fluid situations that demand frequent switching between task-oriented and relationship-oriented leadership.
64 and above:	*high LPC*
	You are likely primarily relationship-oriented. According to Fiedler, these leaders are good at managing conflict and better able to make complex decisions.

Research found LPC to be a stable measure, with high test-retest stability (see e.g. Fiedler and Garcia, 1987).

Exercise 7   The Downturn—Situational Leadership

You are head of a team that sells cellular phone services for a major telecom company. You have been team leader for three years now and have been quite successful. Overall, the team has shown consistently good performance, although you have to do a lot of the work coordination yourself. Your team consists of five people.

Roger is 42 and has been in sales all his life. He is extravert, competitive, and very committed, but he tends to be a bit conservative, and his self-assurance can come across as arrogant. He also has a tendency to provoke others, sometimes hurting their feelings. He is not prone to complaining, but he occasionally mentions his frustration with the bureaucracy in your company and the fact that all fringe benefits of the past, such as company cars, are gone. He particularly thrives under pressure and always finds solutions to problems. His competence and performance are very high, and he is also quite good at exploring opportunities and developing contacts. He occasionally mentions not feeling challenged enough.

Manoj is 29 and quite timid for a salesperson. Although creative and unorthodox when solving problems, he often seems preoccupied and unable to communicate effectively. He is on a limited contract and seems to suffer from anxiety because of this. Additionally, he has repeatedly asked you for more responsibility and has not taken your refusal well. Although he is fairly competent when it comes to the company's products and services, his performance overall is considered low. He has recently been in discussions with other employers and is quite open about it.

Sonya is 51 and has recently transferred to sales from engineering. She is quite prickly and easily aggravated. She is brilliant with numbers—which none of the others are—but also has a tendency to focus on minor technicalities. She habitually laments that her contributions are not appreciated properly and that her office and other working conditions are inadequate. She can also occasionally be jealous of team members with higher sale performance and frequently mentions leaving for a better job elsewhere. This tends to upset and demotivate her co-workers. Her performance is considered average.

Bintang is 44, Indonesian by origin, highly competent, and well-liked in the team and organization. She is important for the team's harmony because she is very diplomatic and able to listen and resolve friction. She often discusses her work with you and occasionally mentions that all she misses are more opportunities for personal growth. As a single mother, she sometimes has to set priorities outside of work and greatly appreciates the necessary flexibility that you give her. Her biggest fear is losing her job.

Finally, Sarah is 33 and was the highest performer in the past three years, with stellar appraisals. Since she joined the company, she has become known particularly for seeing the big picture better than anyone else and for her ability to think strategically, but you know that she is also excellent at turning ideas into practical actions. She also used to have a real knack for finding errors and omissions, but she was also often reluctant to delegate. She never made a secret of the fact that her main motivation is money but was generally easygoing, quite open, and friendly. She has always seemed to you to be very motivated, and getting married six months ago seemed not to have changed that at first. However, in the past month or so, Sarah has started to come to work later and later, without explanation. She was never the most popular person on the team, and some of her co-workers have started to complain about this. She has also missed several team meetings and bilateral meetings with you, again without offering convincing explanations. You have noticed that she appears increasingly distracted and seems very tired all the time. Rumors have already started floating around the team and office. Some suggest she has marital problems, others say it is a psychological issue, and yet others suppose she has health problems.

You decide to get to the bottom of this.

Questions and Assignments

- Reflect on your options. What might be Sarah's issue? What could you do?
- Which of Hersey and Blanchard's leadership styles should be adopted in this case? Why?
- Assume you are calling Sarah in for a meeting and are preparing for it. What is your main meeting goal? Create an outline structure of how the meeting will ideally progress. What do you say and how do you act when, how, and why? What topics can you approach, and what not?

Optional Roleplay Exercise

In a leadership class of at least five people, assign one person to play Sarah and one to play the leader. Both set a meeting goal for themselves which they do not disclose before the debriefing after the exercise. 'Sarah' is told to react to the way the meeting progresses: peaceable if the tone is amicable and relaxed, but pushing back if necessary or shutting down if points that she does not want to discuss are raised. Then go through the meeting, following the agenda of the leader created as part of the last question above. The remaining students observe. Switch leaders as often as you want and time allows, each time using the agenda of the person playing the leader. The person playing Sarah should remain the same to make the roleplay as comparable as possible. Conduct a debriefing after each turn, discussing the goals of the leader and 'Sarah', the way the meeting was conducted, and the meeting's results.

Variation: the instructor tells each leader what style he or she should try to employ.

Exercise 8   Situational Leadership—Leading Teams

Assuming a leader is indeed able to adapt his leadership style to a specific situation, discuss and then recommend which style should be used in the following situations based on Hersey and Blanchard's model:

Situation 1	
Industry:	Semiconductor
Functional area:	Finance
Team members:	3 accountants (1 with a BSc in Finance; 2 with an MSc in Accounting, of which 1 also with a CPA).
Team dynamics:	Ups and downs; high fluctuation has recently stabilized.
Recommended leadership style:	

Situation 2	
Industry:	Telecom
Functional area:	Sales
Team members:	9 salespersons (2 with a BSc in Marketing, the rest with on-the-job training)
Team dynamics:	Very competitive; negative trend; high fluctuation.
Recommended leadership style:	

Situation 3	
Industry:	Commodity trading
Functional area:	Back office
Team members:	7 pool secretaries (all below the age of 25, with only basic training)
Team dynamics:	Highly committed; not very productive.
Recommended leadership style:	

Situation 4	
Industry:	Processed foods.
Functional area:	R&D
Team members:	6 food technologists (4 with an MSc, 2 with a PhD).
Team dynamics:	Positive; highly committed, energetic.
Recommended leadership style:	

Exercise 9   Situational Leadership—Leading *Your* Team

Reflect on your own leadership and your team. If you are not currently leading a team, refer to the situation described in Exercise 7 on page 111.

Hersey and Blanchard's Situational Leadership Theory suggests that the specific leadership style to be adopted vis-à-vis a specific team member or the team as a whole depends on follower development and maturity, which is equivalent to competence and commitment.

Instructions

Enter the names of your team members in the table on the next page. Then reflect on their competence and commitment and calculate the corresponding score. For example, if competence is medium but commitment is low, the corresponding score would be $3 \times 4 = 12$. Then look up the appropriate score in the decision matrix below.

Enter the names of your team members and your assessment of their competence and commitment. Calculate the overall score, then look up the appropriate style in the decision matrix and enter it in the column to the right. Finally, calculate the average for the whole team, find the closest score in the decision matrix, and enter the appropriate style in the corresponding box.

Please note that this is only a tool, not a law. Leadership is complex, and although deterministic approaches can help you think about the various issues, they do not tell you what to do. In other words, they can help you structure your thinking, but you must rely on your senses and intuition to judge whether the approach you take actually works.

Leading the individual team members				Appropriate style for the individual team members
Team member	Competence	Commitment	Maturity	
	1: low; 3: medium; 5: high	4: low; 6: variable; 8: high	Score (competence x commitment)	

Leading the team		Appropriate style for the overall team
Average maturity (sum of individual maturity scores diviced by number of team members)	(Rounded average score)	(corresponding score in decision matrix* below)

Determine the appropriate style:

* Decision matrix		Commitment		
		Low (4)	Varying (6)	High (8)
Competence	Low (1)	(4) Directing Style (or terminate)	(6) Coaching Style	(8) Directing Style
	Medium (3)	(12) Coaching Style	(18) Supporting Style	(24) Supporting Style
	High (5)	(20) Coaching Style (or switch/enrich job)	(30) Delegating Style	(40) Delegating Style

Exercise 10 Rolf and the Normative Decision Model

Rolf Schröder is a 44-year Bavarian upper-level manager working for a middle-sized producer of air treatment solutions in Berlin. He is facing a dilemma: He fears that the company is increasingly out of touch with its customers and that his unit is partly to blame. The company's main source of income is a line of stylish air purifiers; these account for almost 40% of overall revenues, but their sales have declined steadily over recent years. Rolf heads the company's marketing department, which consists of 21 people. Ever since he was promoted to the job four years ago, the unit department has been structured in seven teams: a small photography team (two people), a slightly larger creative design team (three people), a business intelligence unit (three people), a marketing services unit (four people), an online/digital team (four people), an event team (two people), and a marketing communications team (three people). This traditional structure has worked satisfactorily in the past, but Rolf feels that his people are too closely focused on their functions and not enough on the company's customers. Additionally, he has increasingly noticed a kind of silo thinking among his teams, with a subsequent lack of proper communication. Consequently, he is considering reorganizing his department to rectify this problem.

In a recent management seminar, he was introduced to what the instructors called "a new kind of organizational paradigm for the marketing department of the future": think, feel, do. The way he understood it, this model proposes to organize a marketing department as multiple, often temporary cross-functional teams that integrate the three main classes of new marketers: 'think' marketers use analytics to generate necessary market insights through data generation, mining, and modeling; 'do' marketers are focused on content and production; and 'feel' marketers are tasked with increasing consumer engagement. In its most radical form, the think-feel-do model would warrant creating short-term task forces for various marketing tasks that would include people with each kind of focus. Rolf feels that he could also use this basic idea to more permanently restructure his department, but he is unsure if his company is really ready for this quite radical departure from its traditional way of organizing. On the other hand, he *is* sure that the seminar he attended has left him well equipped to come up with a sensible solution for the new department structure, which cannot be said of his subordinates. However, his experience indicates that his direct reports expect to contribute to important decisions and will commit better to a solution if they are involved in the process.

Assignment

Use the figure on the next page to determine the most appropriate decision-making process for Rolf's dilemma.

For details on the Normative Decision Model, refer to Chapter 2.5 on page 38f. and Chapter 3.26 on page 82f.

Decision Question	Decision Tree	Processes

Decision Question

1. Quality requirement: Is there a quality requirement? Is one solution superior for technical or rational reasons?

2. Commitment requirement: Is acceptance of the decision by subordinates critical?

3. Leader information Do you have sufficient information to make a high-quality decision?

4. Problem structure Is the problem structured?

5. Commitment probability: If you were to make the decision alone, would your subordinates commit to it?

6. Goal congruence Do subordinates share the organizational goals to be attained in solving the problem?

7. Subordinate conflict Is conflict likely among subordinates over preferred solutions?

8. Subordinate information: Do subordinates have sufficient information to contribute to a high-quality decision?

Decision Tree

Yes / No

Yes / No / Yes / No — A1

Yes / No / Yes / No — A1

Yes / No / Yes / No — C2

Yes / No / Yes / No / Yes / No / Yes / No
A2 / C2 / A1 / G2

Yes / No / Yes / No / Yes / No / Yes / No
C2 / C2 / C2 / A2

Yes / No / Yes / No
G2 / C1 / A2

Yes / No / Yes / No
G2 / C2 / G2 / C2

Processes

A1 (Autocratic): leader makes decision without subordinate involvement using available information.

A2 (Autocratic II): leader gets additional information from subordinates before making decision alone; subordinates may or may not be informed.

C1 (Consultative I): leader discusses issue individually with subordinates and asks for input before making decision alone without team meetings.

C2 (Consultative II): leader discusses problems with team as a group but makes decision alone.

G2 (Group II): leader discusses problems with team, focuses and directs discussions, and allows group to make decision.

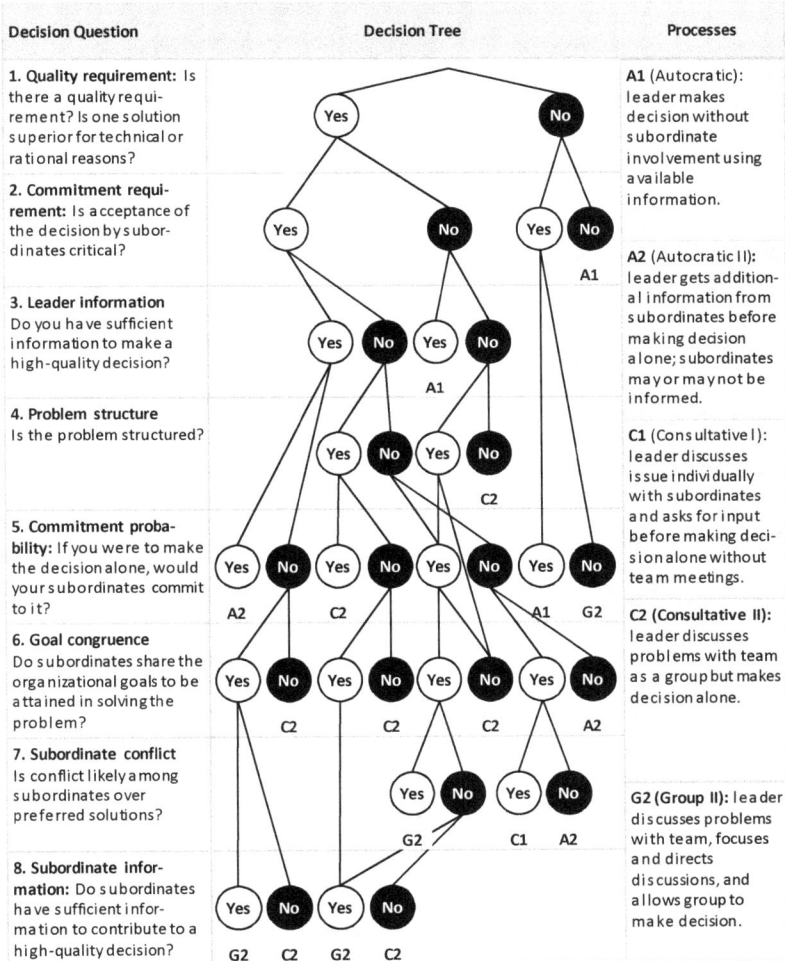

Source: adapted from Vroom and Jago (1988)

Exercise 11 Shehan's Behavior—Contrasting Leader Styles

This is a group exercise appropriate for leadership workshops with at least five (but preferably more) people. It requires a coach (or, if the group is self-organizing, a coordinator) and three roleplayers. The rest of the group are observers.

Situation (Roleplay)

You have been in your present job as head of an engineering team at a large construction company for 2 months. Shehan, a long-time member of your team, has recently started to make increasingly disparaging remarks about you and several of his co-workers, from what you hear mainly in private but also occasionally in public. This has really started to hurt the team harmony. Because he has been there a long time and because he claims to "know all the big bosses", the other co-workers either do not want to say anything or complain to you in an unhelpful way. So far, you have never personally witnessed his alleged behavior. You call Shehan in for a meeting.

Preparation

The coach selects one participant to play the role of Shehan and two additional participants to each play the leader. He or she then briefs the leaders on the approach to take. One is to use a very autocratic, confrontational style, while the other is to use a very democratic, harmony-oriented style. The coach also assigns Shehan one of two basic personalities:

- Introvert, meek, and submissive, or
- Extravert and confrontational.

In the next ten minutes, the two leaders reflect individually on how they want to proceed within the basic approach assigned to each and prepare for the meeting by compiling a brief meeting outline, including the meeting's goal(s) and rough structure. Meanwhile, Shehan decides on and thinks through a specific reason for the behavior he or she displays. Whether he or she will divulge this reason, and under which circumstances, is up to the roleplayer but should be in line with the basic personality assigned by the coach.

The rest of the group prepares for the debriefing discussion, for instance by writing down specific points they want to particularly observe. Following this, the meeting takes place twice, once with each leader. For training purposes, the coach will end the meeting after about 10-15 minutes—in reality, of course, it could take much longer. The debriefing takes place only after both leaders have had their turn, so that the two approaches can be contrasted during the discussion.

Variation 1: the instructor allows each leader to choose his or her own approach to the meeting.

Variation 2: if the group is large enough and there is sufficient time, *two* Shehans (displaying both basic personalities explained above) and *four* leaders may be selected. For maximum contrast, each of the four leaders could be asked to display one of four distinct approaches, perhaps by selecting from Goleman's Six Leadership Styles.

Note: If several iterations are concluded with differing personalities of Shehan, a debriefing should take place after each turn of two meetings.

Assignment

After each turn of two meetings, the rest of the group discusses:

- What was observed, that is, what actually happened?
- What worked, and what did not?
- What can be learned from the exercise?

4 PRIMARY LEADER RESPONSIBILITIES AND COMPETENCIES

LEARNING OUTCOMES

After this chapter, you should

- understand and appreciate your main responsibilities as a leader,
- understand what it takes to achieve tasks and missions,
- know how to increase or maintain your leadership presence and resilience, and
- know how to lead yourself, your team, and your team members.

4.1 The Integrated Functional Leadership Model

What are a leader's main responsibilities? This question is clearly relevant to how you set your priorities and focus your time and energy. As discussed previously[1], Adair's (1973) widely used Action-Centered Leadership model stresses, in line with Blake and Mouton's Managerial Grid model, that leaders should not be either task-oriented or person-oriented but rather both. Yes, leaders must devote part of their time to task-related activities, but they must also spend substantial time with their followers, both individually and with the team as a whole.

Adair also holds that leaders have three main responsibilities. The situation will dictate how much time is spent on each of the three responsibilities, but none should be neglected. Some authors distinguish between the terms 'leading' and 'managing', so, to slightly paraphrase Adair, a leader's main responsibilities are

---

[1] See Chapter 2.6 on page 45f.

achieving the task, leading and managing individuals, and leading and managing the team.

To *achieve the task,* you need to plan actions and initiatives, implement them together with your team, control the implementation, take corrective measures where necessary, and ensure an adequate flow of information, both vertically and horizontally. Occasionally, a distinction is also made between tasks and *missions,* the latter being understood as larger and more important[1].

Leading and managing the team involves creating opportunities for developing and maintaining relationships in your team[2] as well as providing decisions, information, and opportunities to interact as necessary. Scouller (2011) calls this *public leadership.*

Finally, *leading and managing individuals* includes motivating, assessing, training, developing, and where necessary disciplining team members in addition to assigning them tasks and providing decisions and information. Scouller (2011) calls this *private leadership.*

Scouller (2011) also mentions a third level of leadership, *personal leadership.* This is echoed by a number of authors (e.g. Goleman, 2000), who stress the leader's responsibility for self-discipline and self-management. Leading yourself is therefore an important element of effective leadership and should be explicitly included among the main responsibilities.

Consequently, your key responsibilities as a leader are

- getting the job done,
- leading and managing the team,
- leading and managing the team members, and
- leading and managing yourself.

---

[1] See Chapter 4.2 on page 129f. for more details.
[2] This is usually referred to as *team-building.*

The main functions of leadership that Adair originally mentioned are planning, initiating, controlling, supporting, informing, and evaluating. Two important leader activities, analyzing a situation and making a decision based on that analysis, are implicitly included but not specifically mentioned. Additionally, as the discussion of transactional leadership above[1] showed, the use of contingent rewards[2] has been found to increase follower commitment (Yammarino et al., 1997), satisfaction (Podsakoff, Todor, and Skov, 1982), and performance (Judge and Piccolo, 2004), and to enhance followers' perception of a leader's integrity (Parry and Proctor-Thomson, 2002). 'Rewards', in this context, is meant both positively and negatively and thus also includes punishment.

These three items (analyzing, deciding, and rewarding and punishing) should thus be added to the list. Consequently, the key functions of leadership are

- analyzing,
- deciding,
- planning,
- initiating,
- controlling,
- supporting,
- informing,
- evaluating, and
- rewarding and punishing.

One of the key criticisms of functional leadership theories concerns their primarily transactional nature. In a later edition of his model, Adair (1988) consequently partly addressed this by adding two transformational elements to his original core leader functions[3]:

---

[1] See Chapter 2.5 on page 42f.

[2] The leader clarifies the expectations, defines the rewards for meeting them, and issues those rewards upon success. This could include both monetary rewards (such as a bonus) and non-monetary rewards (such as time off or simply praise).

[3] See page 38.

motivating and *setting an example*. This raises the question which transformational leadership practices, beyond these two additions, are particularly useful when leading and managing.

As indicated in Chapter 2.5[1], transformational leadership has four basic components (Bass, 1985; Tracey and Hinkin, 1998): *idealized influence* refers to the leader serving as an ideal role model for his or her followers, leading to admiration, respect, and trust; *inspirational motivation* means the leader's ability to motivate and inspire followers through a shared vision; *individualized consideration* describes how the leader pays attention to team members and demonstrates genuine concern for their needs, feelings, and well-being; and *intellectual stimulation* denotes the leader's habit to challenge followers to be more creative and innovative. In Avolio and Bass's (1991) Full Range Leadership model, idealized influence is further split into two components: *idealized influence (attributed)* refers to the leader's influence based on his or her perception by followers, and *idealized influence (behavior)* means the leader's influence through charismatic actions.

An alternative but not fundamentally diverging view is provided by Kouzes and Posner (1987) in their book *The Five Practices of Exemplary Leadership.* On the basis of a large empirical study reported, the authors identify the top five practices in which effective leaders engage: *model the way, inspire a shared vision, challenge the process, enable others to act,* and *encourage the heart*[2]. As mentioned above[3], to do so consistently, leaders also need to be *resilient*: able to effectively deal with stress and adversity.

By including transformational practices, therefore, our emerging leadership model is in line with the concept of full range leadership, meaning leadership that is both transactional and transformational. Table 9 provides a comparison of key contributions to transforma-

---

[1] See page 44f.

[2] For an explanation of these practices, see page 39.

[3] See page 36.

tional leadership theory, identifies their core elements, and summarizes them. Grey cells indicate that the respective model does not contain that particular aspect.

Table 9: Analysis of Key Transformational Leadership Practices

Key contributions			Core elements	Summary practice
Adair (1973/88)	Kouzes and Posner (1987)	Avolio and Bass (1991)		
Motivating		Idealized influence (attributed)	Being viewed as confident and successful	Developing and sustaining presence
			Being viewed as powerful	
	Encourage the heart		Focusing on values and ethics	
			Fostering team spirit	Motivating and inspiring
	Inspire a shared vision	Inspirational motivation	Fostering a shared vision	
			Displaying calm optimism	
			Setting ambitious goals	
			Caring honestly	Showing real interest and consideration
			Showing interest	
			Communicating openly	
	Enable others to act	Individualized consideration	Advising	Enabling, challenging, and stimulating
			Supporting	
			Enabling growth and self-actualization	
	Challenge the process	Intellectual stimulation	Thinking creatively	
			Finding innovative solutions	
			Taking calculated risks	
			Fostering change	
Setting the example	Model the way	Idealized influence (behavior)	Setting an example	Setting a positive example
			Playing a positive role	
			Exploring and explaining solutions	Providing guidance and direction
			Establishing principles	
			Establishing rituals and traditions	

Source: author.

127

Additionally, *leadership presence* is an important asset of a leader because it compels others to follow that person. Furthermore, in order to be able to be able to lead effectively over a long period of time, leaders also need to develop their own *resilience*. Both concepts are explained in chapter 4.3.

The full list of key leadership practices in summarized form and augmented by presence and resilience is therefore

- providing guidance and direction,
- setting the positive example,
- developing and sustaining your presence and resilience,
- motivating and inspiring,
- showing real interest and consideration, and
- enabling, stimulating, and challenging.

By incorporating all these aspects, an integrated functional model of leadership emerges, as depicted in Figure 8.

Figure 8: Integrated Functional Leadership (IFL) Model

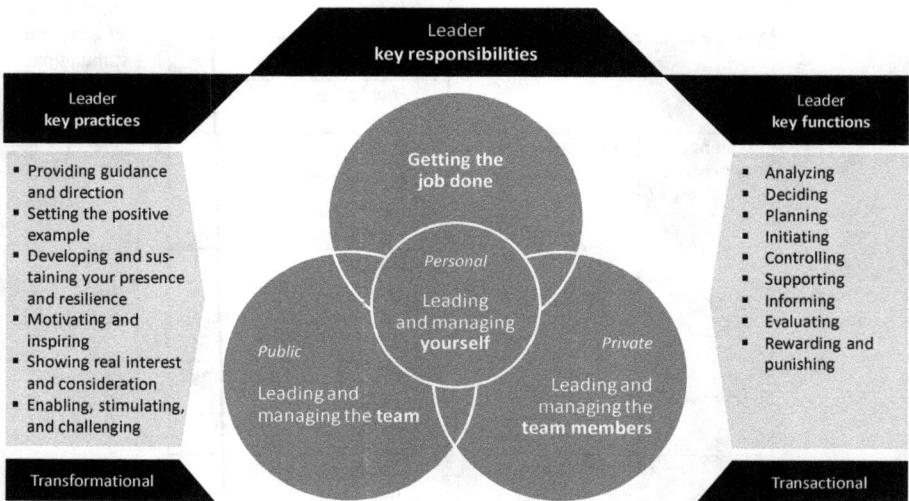

Source: author; partly based on Bass (1985), Adair (1988), Wagnild & Young (1993), and Scouller (2011).

In this model, the six key practices form the transformational base, and the nine key functions comprise the transactional base; from these two, a leader can operate effectively. Both of these apply to and affect all levels of leadership (personal, private, and public) and permeate everything you do as a leader. On the transformational side, all six key practices will influence and interact with each other. By providing clear guidance and direction and by setting a positive example, you will also motivate and inspire your team members. The same is true if you show real interest in and consideration for your team members. Developing your leadership presence will make it easier for you to achieve tasks and missions together with your followers, because they will more willingly do what you want, and increasing your resilience will make it easier for you to deal with setbacks and failures, which in turn will provide a positive example for your team members. On the transactional side, you will regularly need to analyze new or changed situations, decide on courses of action, plan how to proceed, initiate and control the implementation of your plans, support your team members in their tasks, inform them about important issues, evaluate their work and your own, and reward or punish good or bad performance and behavior.

The core of the model, however, are the four key responsibilities. The following sections explain them in more detail.

4.2   Getting the Job Done

The endless discussion about whether leadership and management are distinct things or not provides little practical help in achieving tasks and missions. If either leadership or management skills are lacking, success is unlikely. The key to getting the job done reliably is a confluence of transactional and transformational skills.

First, however, the terms *task* and mission must be clarified. Although the two terms are often used interchangeably, mission is more abstract than task. In most militaries, a mission is a generic term for an assignment, such as taking a town or providing disaster relief, which is provided together with the reason for it, its purpose, and the action to be taken. In business, the term is most commonly associated with an organization's mission statement, but it is also often found at lower levels. Tasks, on the other hand, are most frequently linked to project management, but they are also used in everyday interactions. Thus, a mission is a fairly general undertaking that in itself may consist of a number of tasks, which in turn may consist of smaller sub-tasks, and so on. For instance, a sales team's mission might be to establish a particular product as the market leader in a specific geographic area. Such a mission would involve a number of tasks, such as defining the specific customer requirements and identifying the triggers for the buying decision; adapting the product accordingly, if necessary; launching the product in the market; tracking the progress made; and taking additional or corrective measures as needed. Those tasks themselves could then be broken down into smaller subtasks. Defining the specific customer requirements might include conducting a survey and a series of interviews, followed by a written summary and analysis of the results. Adapting the product might entail changes to the product design, production process, or brand message. And so on.

Consequently, the two terms will be used as follows for the purpose of this book:

Task: *a specific piece of work to be completed.*

Mission: *an important general assignment that aims at securing a particular desired outcome.*

As highlighted in the Integrated Functional Leadership model[1], achieving tasks and missions—getting the job done—is a key responsibility of leadership. Success depends on a multitude of factors. Some of these are hard or even impossible for you to control, such as the outcome of organizational power games or pure luck. However, others, depend directly on you and your team. No man is an island, as the saying goes, and the active cooperation and contribution of your team is paramount. Specifically, three factors must be present in you and your team members alike: the right attitude, the right skills, and the right timing.

Figure 9: Success Factors for Achieving Tasks and Missions

- Leadership skills
  (self, team, individual)
- Management skills (planning, organizing, implementing)
- Job-related skills

Skills

- Conceptual skills
  - Analysis
  - Thinking in options
  - Concept development
  - Plan development

Task/ mission success factors

Attitude

- Sense of mission
- Spirit of cooperation
- Performance orientation
- Goal orientation
- Quality orientation
- Service orientation.

Timing

- Realistic and fair time planning
  - One-third/two-thirds rule
  - 80% in time instead of 100% too late

Source: author.

---

[1] See Figure 8 on page 130.

4.21 The Right Skills

An important job of you as the leader is to ensure that all the required functional and job-related skills are present in the team. Your personal skill set should include the leadership abilities required at the personal, private, and public levels as well as the management abilities needed to plan, organize, and implement the work. In the modern office environment, project management (which, in essence, is basically planning, organizing, and implementing) is a particularly important management skill to master.

A project is a temporary undertaking, usually with a clearly defined start and finish. As a leader, breaking down a large mission into subtasks will frequently result in various projects. In a traditional sense, project management consists of initiating, planning and designing, executing and constructing, monitoring and controlling, and completing or closing the project. Many project managers are self-taught. If you head a lot of projects or if you are responsible for very large or strategically important projects, however, it is a good idea for you to have some formal training. Various project management approaches are in common use, such as PRINCE2[1], CCPM[2], BRM[3], SCRUM[4], and HERMES[5], and plenty of courses are available to teach you how to use them.

---

[1] PRINCE stands for *projects in controlled environments* and is a structured project management approach that was originally developed in the United Kingdom as a government standard for IT projects. The first version was adopted in 1989. The number *2* in PRINCE2 refers to the second, more generic iteration of the method released in 1996.

[2] CCPM stands for *critical chain project management* and is a resource-focused project management approach that is more flexible than traditional critical path methodologies. It was first introduced by Eliyahu M. Goldratt in his 1997 book *Critical Chain*.

[3] BRM stands for *benefits realization management*, a change-oriented project management methodology that focuses on the alignment between organizational strategies and project results.

[4] SCRUM is an agile project management methodology that uses iterative and incremental practices and is increasingly used to manage complex projects, such as large software and product development efforts.

[5] HERMES is a simplified, flexible, and freely available project management approach developed and used by the Swiss government since 1975. In its latest iteration, it also incorporates support for agile development (e.g. with SCRUM). The acronym stands for *Handbuch der Elektronischen Rechenzentren des Bundes, eine Methode zur Entwicklung von Systemen* ('Manual of Federal Electronic Datacenters, a Method for Systems Development').

Also crucial are job-related skills, such measuring physical dimensions for a carpenter or understanding statistics for a quantitative researcher. Finally, conceptual skills are very important if the task involves any kind of planning or problem-solving. There are four basic conceptual skills:

- analysis,
- thinking in options,
- concept definition, and
- plan development.

Analysis is a key skill in the development of almost anything. When you analyze, you break a larger problem into its components, look at these from all perspectives using cogent reasoning and appropriate analytical tools, and employ sound logic to arrive at a justifiable conclusion. In other words, good decisions—a key component of effective leadership—are based on a thorough breakdown and evaluation of the current situation and often its possible future development paths, often referred to as scenarios. This is clearly an important ability for a leader. All the charisma and empathy in the world are worth nothing if you and your team then charge off in the completely wrong direction.

To some extent, sound analysis can be learned. Although logical thinking, for example, is easier for people with an analytical-rational rather than an intuitive-experiential cognitive style (something that depends significantly on genetics[1]), a multitude of analytical tools and frameworks are available to help you analyze various situations and problems in a proven, structured way regardless of your personality.

---

[1] A number of studies on twins (e.g. Grigorenko, LaBuda, and Carter, 1992; Finkel and McGue, 1993; McClearn et al., 1997; Bartels et al., 2002; Benyamin et al., 2005; Briley and Tucker-Drob, 2013) suggest that between sixty and eighty percent of the variation in most cognitive abilities of adults are due to genetic factors.

Some of the most commonly used analytical tools in business includes PESTEL[1] for the analysis of an organization's macro-environment; Michael Porter's Five Forces[2] framework for industry analysis; SWOT analysis for determining an organization's strategic fi) and Heinz Weihrich's extension, the TOWS matrix for developing strategic options based on SWOT 3; the Ansoff, McKinsey, and Boston Consulting Group matrices for strategic portfolio management; and ABC analysis[4] for object prioritization, such as customer or inventory categorization by importance. While some classroom learning can be helpful in understanding these tools, mastering them requires practice. In other words, the more you analyze, the better you become at it.

Thinking in options refers to the ability to see beyond the immediately obvious and identify multiple viable solutions to a problem. For example, if you buy a car, you probably first think about your basic needs (transporting kids, status, high mileage, and so on), then do some research on makes and models that would fulfill these, and then check around to see where you can get the best deal for your money before finally conducting the transaction. In essence, organizational problems can and should be handled in the same way: analyze the situation, identify various ways to solve the problem, compare these usually based on some pre-defined criteria, and then select the objectively best one. Thinking in options is a mindset as

---

[1] PESTEL is an acronym for *political, economic, social* (or socio-demographic), *technological, ecological,* and *legal.* dividing the macro-environment into these spheres and investigating them individually can be used to identify the key drivers of change in an organization's external environment.

[2] The five forces are the bargaining power of suppliers, the bargaining power of buyers, the threat of new entrants, the threat of substitution, and the competitive rivalry that exists in the industry.

[3] SWOT is an acronym for *strengths, weaknesses, opportunities,* and *threats.* The first two are internal and can be addressed and possibly changed over time; the other two are external and considered given, to be exploited or avoided. Based on the results of this analysis, strategic options can be developed that for example counter a threat by employing a particular strength or overcome a weakness by exploiting an opportunity. The acronym TOWS, which stands for the same aspects in reverse, signifies this second step.

[4] The three letters denote differing levels of significance, with A being the most and C the least important.

much as a skill. In fact, many people have a tendency to jump to conclusions. If they are presented with a problem, a solution often pops into their heads almost immediately, before reflecting on alternative solutions or really fully considering the ramifications and drawbacks. Frequently, someone will then stick doggedly to this initial gut reaction even when presented with objectively preferable alternatives. Thinking in options reduces the risk of implementing inferior, ill-considered solutions. Depending on the task, this may be done by you alone, but the combined brainpower of you and your team will generally arrive at superior, better considered solutions.

Options can be evaluated in various ways. If the problem is fairly simple or not many people are involved, comparing advantages and disadvantages will often be enough. For larger or more complex problems, a scoring matrix that includes the must-have and possibly nice-to-have factors may well suffice. Ideally, such a matrix contains an overview of what is common to all options; the key characteristics that make each option unique; each option's key advantages and disadvantages; how each option conforms to common 'killer criteria' (feasibility[1], acceptability[2], suitability[3], and completeness[4]); and how each scores according to defined, weighted criteria. This approach works quite well for most issues. For very complex problems, there are a number of multi-criteria decision-making (MCDM) approaches, usually computer-assisted, such as the analytical hierarchy process (AHP), a structured technique for organizing and analyzing complex decisions based on mathematics and psychology; the analytical network process (ANP), a more general form of the analytical hierarchy process in which problems are structured into networks instead of hierarchies; and the evidential reasoning (ER)

---

[1] An option is feasible if enough resources (people, finances) are available and if there is sufficient information and time to implement it.

[2] An option is acceptable if its consequences do not violate the organization's value system and conform with the expectations of key stakeholders (customers, employees, shareholders).

[3] An option is suitable if it addresses both the internal and external situations and is in line with the overall mission.

[4] An option is complete if it addresses all aspects of the problem it intends to solve.

approach, a method that uses both quantitative and qualitative criteria to deal with problems that exhibit various uncertainties.

Table 10 shows an example of how to structure such a matrix. Illustration 4 on page 137 provides an abbreviated example of how to apply it.

Table 10: Option Evaluation and Recommendation Matrix

Option		ONE		TWO		THREE	
Identifier							
Characterization							
Common aspects of all options		...					
Key aspects of each option		...		...		...	
Strengths/ advantages		...		...		...	
Weaknesses/ disadvantages		...		...		...	
Killer criteria (select 'yes' or 'no' for each criterion and option)							
Feasible regarding resources/constraints		Yes	No	Yes	No	Yes	No
Acceptable in its consequences		Yes	No	Yes	No	Yes	No
Suitable for external/ internal situation		Yes	No	Yes	No	Yes	No
Complete regarding critical success factors		Yes	No	Yes	No	Yes	No
Overall		Met	Not met	Met	Not met	Met	Not met

Additional decision criteria (set by the leader or the organization)							
Criteria	Weight (1-3)	Rating (1-5)	Score (Weight × Rating)	Rating (1-5)	Score (Weight × Rating)	Rating (1-5)	Score (Weight × Rating)
...	...	...	...	...	...	...	...
...	...	...	...	...	...	...	...
...	...	...	...	...	...	...	...
Overall score (sum)		...		...		...	
Recommendation to decision-maker(s)		...		...		...	

Source: author.

Illustration 4:   Evaluating Options

The following illustrates in abbreviated form how a purchasing unit in a medium-sized Swiss electronics company evaluated three vendor options. In order to avoid triggering any preconceptions and thus to remain as objective as possible, the actual vendor names were replaced with code names for the purpose of the analysis and subsequent board discussion.

Option	ONE	TWO	THREE
Identifier	**ALPHA**	**BRAVO**	**CHARLIE**

Characterization			
Common aspects of all options	All can fulfill our volume requirements. All offer similar rebates. All are Swiss or have representation in Switzerland and will agree to a choice of law clause naming Zurich.		
Key aspects of each option	Local market leader (SME)	International market-leader	Fast-growing regional player
Strengths/ advantages	▪ Familiar with local practices	▪ Established ▪ Reliable just-in-time delivery	▪ Reliable just-in-time delivery ▪ Aggressive pricing
Weaknesses/ disadvantages	▪ Just-in-time unreliable ▪ Lowest rebates	▪ Less familiar with local practices	▪ Risk of over-reach/pre-mature failure

Killer criteria						
Feasible regarding resources/constraints	Yes	No	Yes	No	Yes	No
Acceptable in its consequences	Yes	No	Yes	No	Yes	No
Suitable for external/ internal situation	Yes	No	Yes	No	Yes	No
Complete regarding critical success factors	Yes	No	Yes	No	Yes	No
Overall	Met	Not met	Met	Not met	Met	Not met

Additional decision criteria (set by the executive board)						
Criteria	Weight (1-3)	Rating (1-5)	Score (Weight x Rating)	Rating (1-5)	Score (Weight x Rating)	Rating (1-5)	Score (Weight x Rating)
Cost savings potential	3	2	6	3	9		
Existing trust	1	4	4	1	1	Killer criteria not met	
Cross-border risk	2	1	2	3	6		
Overall score (sum)		12		16			

Recommendation to executive board	Keep as backup	Switch to BRAVO	Do not consider

Concept definition is a partly creative and partly analytical activity. In essence, a concept is a rough idea of how to implement an option. The concept document may often be only a few sentences or paragraphs long, but various methodologies prescribe specific steps to arrive at this stage. For example, Kossiakoff et al. (2011) consider needs analysis, concept exploration, and concept definition to be integral steps in systems engineering concept definition. And Nelke (2012) considers formulating the vision and goals, identifying the stakeholders and their needs, formulating a value proposition, analyzing the consequences and risks, and prioritizing among alternatives as steps in the development of a business concept. The idea behind these and other methodologies is to transparently arrive at the finished concept in a structured, logical way while considering all relevant information. That is the analytical part. Fleshing out the concept is the creative part, and if you include your team in this as you should, it will often involve group creativity techniques, such as Osborn's brainstorming[1], Rohrbach's 635 method[2], and Bono's Six Thinking Hats, or even more advanced methodologies such as Altshuller's TRIZ[3] or Sickafus's USIT[4].

---

[1] Described by advertising executive Alex F. Osborn in his 1948 book *Your Creative Power*, this original group creativity method was developed because Osborn was frustrated with his employees' failure to develop creative ideas for advertising campaigns. The term was coined in 1939 by a team led by Osborn. The method is built around four basic ideas: go for quantity (generate as many ideas as possible), withhold criticism (first collect ideas, then discuss them), welcome wild ideas (think outside the box), and combine and improve ideas ("1+1=3").

[2] Also called *group brainwriting* or *6-3-5 brainwriting*, this method is similar to brainstorming but requires participants to write down their ideas rather than express them verbally. In its original form, as published by Bernd Rohrbach in the German sales magazine *Absatzwirtschaft* in 1969, it consists of six participants who, coordinated by a moderator, work in a circle to add three ideas each to a worksheet in a series of rounds lasting between five and ten minutes. At the end of each round, participants pass their worksheets on to the people on their right, allowing these to get inspiration from their predecessors. The process continues until each worksheet is completed, yielding a total of 108 ideas.

[3] TRIZ stands for *teoriya resheniya izobretatelskikh zadach*, meaning 'theory of the resolution of invention-related tasks'. It was originally developed from 1946 onwards by the Soviet inventor and science-fiction author Genrich Altshuller while working as a clerk in the Caspian Sea flotilla's inventions inspection department.

[4] USIT stands for *unified structured inventive thinking*. It is an extension of the TRIZ method introduced at Ford Motor Company and published in the 1997 book *Unified Structured Inventive Thinking – How to Invent*.

Even though the core concept in the sense outlined above may be quite short and to the point, it usually makes sense to include some framing information when pitching or explaining it to others. This is particularly important, of course, in cases where the concept document has to speak for itself, for example because it is only provided by email and not presented in person.

As a barebones structure for a generic concept brief, these seven elements work quite well:

1. necessary *background information* (e.g. task or mission received, including rationale and background; conditions, requirements, and restrictions, including legal; foundational documents, if any; and any other aspects that are relevant to the task or mission),

2. concept-related *goals* and *targets*[1] (specific, measurable, attainable, relevant, and time-based),

3. key *influence factors* (e.g. stakeholders and environmental change drivers),

4. overview of *options* that have been evaluated (including a justified recommendation),

5. actual *concept* (i.e. the basic idea of what you propose to do, based on the recommended/chosen option),

6. rough *timeline* (stating in broad strokes what needs to be done by when to implement the concept and fulfill the task or mission), and

7. *organizational and administrative aspects* (e.g. list of workgroup/team membership and structure, with contact information; rough estimate of additional resources and support needed).

---

[1] Although the two terms are not applied consistently in the literature and are often used synonymously, the position taken here is that targets are subordinate to goals—similarly to the relationship between mission and task—in the sense that a general goal must be derived from the mission or task given and may consist of one or several specific targets that flesh out how the goal is supposed to be achieved. For example, if the goal is to become the market leader with a certain product within three years, the associated targets might specify what sales growth and market share needs to be achieved in each year.

Plan development, finally, is the process of elaborating the concept and planning its implementation. Usually, part or all of the information contained in the concept brief will be repeated and described in more detail, along with additional information relevant to the plan's execution. If you and your team are writing a specific kind of plan, such as a business case or business plan, you may often be expected to follow a specific structure. Figure 10 contains three examples.

Figure 10: Examples of Business Plan Structures

Business Plan Content Recommendation		
U.S. Small Business Administration (SBA)	**Shell liveWIRE**	**Credit Suisse**
1. Executive Summary 2. Company Description 3. Market Analysis 4. Organization and Management 5. Service or Product Line 6. Marketing and Sales 7. Funding Request 8. Financial Projections 9. Appendix	1. Summary 2. The Business 3. Product or Service 4. The Market 5. Marketing Plan 6. Management and Organization 7. Break-Even Analysis 8. Financial Forecasts 9. Sensitivity or Risk Analysis 10. Financial Requirements 11. Appendices	1. Summary 2. Company and Strategy 3. Products and Services 4. Market and Customers 5. Competition 6. Marketing 7. Production, Delivery and Procurement 8. Research and Development 9. Location and Administration 10. Information and Communication Technology 11. Management, Instruments, Organization 12. Risk Analysis 13. Finance

Source: SBA (n.d.), Shell liveWIRE (2015), Credit Suisse (2016).

Clearly, the three institutions make similar but not identical content recommendations. In the end, however, that does not matter much. Whatever plan you write can be structured in any way you want as long as it is complete, logical, and easy to follow. For a generic plan, follow the concept structure outlined on page 139 and add details and subsections as required.

4.22   The Right Attitude

The right attitude is another key ingredient for getting the job done. In fact, having a positive, focused attitude is both a prerequisite for and partly a result of your efforts in leading yourself, the team, and the individual team members[1]. You are the role model for your team, and if your attitude is helpful and positive it will rub off on your team members.

Figure 11: The Leader Attitude Heptagon

Source: author.

---

[1] Also see Figure 8 on page 103.

The state of mind that you should cultivate in both yourself and your followers includes a clear sense of mission; a spirit of cooperation; reciprocal trust; and strong performance, goal, quality, and service orientation. These make up the leader attitude heptagon, as shown in Figure 11.

Maintaining the right attitude requires attention. Successful teams often acquire a kind of swagger that can eventually be detrimental to cooperation with other teams, while unsuccessful or unlucky teams may start to develop unwanted habits, such as taking overly long breaks or questioning at length every new task that comes their way. Fostering the right attitude in yourself and encouraging it in others will contribute to your team's success. Many people subconsciously emulate leaders they like or even admire[1], so your personal example can go a long way towards mentally aligning your team in a way that contributes to achieving your tasks and missions. Its efficiency and productivity and the satisfaction of external and internal customers will rise, while error rates will decline. Working on such a team will also be more enjoyable for its members, which in turn is important for their long-term health and well-being.

4.23   The Right Timing

Accomplishing a task or mission is essentially the same as completing a project, and time management is key to doing so successfully. A perfect solution too late may have no value, because the competition has already captured the market or an important board decision has already been taken without your input.

Your time planning should be both fair and realistic, and you should prioritize timely completion over perfection. A time plan is fair if it allocates the net available time[2], which will rarely be enough

---

[1] Also see Illustration 7 on page 135.

[2] Net time refers to the available time minus all periods during which you cannot or do not want to work on the assignment. For example, if a business plan is due early on May 2, it is now April 18 in the evening, and you and your team can work exclusively on that plan with

to do a perfect job, according to the one-third/two-thirds rule[1]: one third can be spent at your own level; two thirds should be reserved for subsequent levels. If, for example, a business division has been given the task to develop a new employee compensation system and implement it within six months, the division's staff unit should take no more than two months to develop and roll out the new system, because otherwise the line units will not have sufficient time for the implementation, which may include updating various documents (such as policies and hiring instructions) and holding many individual and group information and discussion sessions. All of these take time, which the staff unit should not take away from the line units.

Figure 12: The Time Planning Cascade

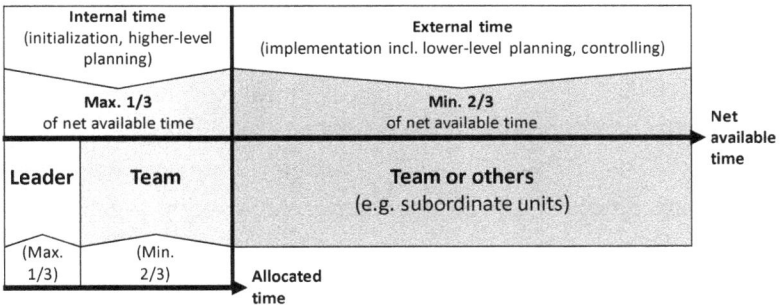

Source: author.

This applies at both functional and hierarchical levels: if you and your team work on something, you should not under any circumstances use more than one third, and ideally much less, of the net available time to prepare and issue your team's tasks, and if other levels of the organization are involved, you and your team together

---

the exception of a one-day team-building event on April 25, then the question is if you are willing to work evenings and weekends. If you stick to a work-day of e.g. eight hours and exclude both weekends that lie in that period, the net planning time will be eight days times eight hours of work, i.e. 64 hours. That time can be stretched if you are willing to be flexible and work on some or all evenings and/or one or both weekends.

[1] For very large tasks or missions, this ratio may be adjusted to one-fourth/three-fourths.

should not take more than one third to complete the project, task, or mission. And so on.

Remembering this rule is important, because people tend to lose sight of dependencies outside of their immediate sphere of responsibility whenever there is time pressure. Consequently, most leaders and support units have a tendency to take too much of the net available time for their own tasks, leaving too little for the subsequent levels.

A time plan is realistic if all tasks and subtasks have been allocated sufficient time to complete them to the quality required. Conversely, a time plan is unrealistic if there is insufficient time to complete tasks and subtasks at the minimally required level of detail and quality. With regard to this, a good (80%) solution in time is usually better than a perfect (100%) solution too late.

Managing your own time and that of your team are of equal importance. The former is vital to juggling your own tasks and duties—some of which will constitute bottlenecks for the overall task or mission—effectively with the time needed to coordinate, control, and support your team's work. Equally, managing your team's time plan is imperative because, in groups of people working together, not everyone has the full overview of all tasks at all times. That would likely consume too much valuable time, which would then not be available for actual work. This is particularly important if there is time pressure, which tends to be the norm. It falls to you, the leader, to ensure that the various tasks and subtasks are completed in time so as to stay on track overall and, since unforeseen things often happen, that the time plan is regularly checked and updated. This can be quite a demanding and occasionally distracting task, and it may be worth assigning someone to be the team's official timekeeper.

The key question is

When do we have to act in what way with what speed for how long and using which resources?

When refers to the latest possible moment in time that tasks and subtasks may be initiated in order to still accomplish the task or mission. Of course, it pays to start earlier whenever possible to avoid undue stress, but it is imperative to determine this 'point of no return' in order not to miss it. Naturally, accomplishing this requires you to have a solid understanding of the major work that needs to be performed, including its time requirements.

In what way refers to the specific tasks and subtasks that need to be completed. A key question is granularity: How detailed should you plan? If you do not have much time available and you spend almost all of it planning, this will be (very) counterproductive. On the other hand, if you do not spend any time identifying the key things that must be done, that will not enhance your chances of success either. As a general rule of thumb, the higher time pressure, the lower the granularity.

With what speed indicates that there may be less time available for some of these tasks and subtasks than should ideally be spent on them. There is also a resource planning implication: If a task is expected to take longer than the available time, adding more labor can help speed things up. Note, however, that this only works up to a certain threshold, after which the increasing effort required of the leader to coordinate the group members will slow the work down again. Generally, the more skilled the leader, the larger the optimally effective team can be (Liang, Rajan, and Ray, 2008). When accomplishing tasks or missions under time pressure, however, the various subgroups will often be self-organizing and, as a rule of thumb, should be no larger than three to four people.

For how long also has resource implications: If particular subtasks run on for a long time, more people may have to be added to that group so they can implement a work roster or shift plan. This is particularly important in preventing team members from exhausting themselves and eventually burning out if intense work must be performed over a long period of time. For example, paramedics, police officers, and firefighters all work in shifts because their service is needed around the clock. However, using more people may well also mean spending more money.

Using which resources, finally, refers to the need to match tasks and subtasks to available human, financial, and possibly other resources. How much money will we need for each subtask? Which should take priority? Who should do what? This last question should consider the particular strengths and weaknesses of each team member. Someone is fairly neurotic? He or she might make an excellent timekeeper. Others are quite creative? Put them in charge of brainstorming options. Some are very structured in their thinking? Let them develop the concept. One is a strong technical writer? Have him or her write the plan based on the concept. And so on. Note, however, that the particular task or mission is often larger than the available resources, and some or all team members will thus need to take on additional tasks, which will in turn require you to prioritize them.

Once all the parts of this time-related key question are answered, actual time planning can begin. In a nutshell, effective time management consists of

- identifying and allocating the overall net amount of time and person hours available,
- identifying and assessing the tasks and subtasks to be performed,
- identifying and prioritizing the internal and external milestones,
- crafting an internal and external time plan, and
- regularly monitoring and updating the time plan.

Identifying and allocating the overall net amount of time and person hours available should be the first step taken when completing any assignment under time pressure, because this creates a sense of urgency. Otherwise, too much valuable time might be spent on compiling the list of tasks and subtasks. If there is plenty of time available, however, it may make sense to reverse the order of these first two steps, depending on your preference.

Time pressure usually arises because either a deadline has been fixed or the task or mission should be completed as quickly as possible. The difference between net available time and person hours is that the net available time defines the timeline, while the net person-hours are just the total amount of hours your team can actually work on the task or mission. In other words, all milestones and the task or mission overall must be finished within the net available time, so you need to assign the net available person hours accordingly to the various tasks and subtasks. Obviously, your team members are much more than the sum of their work hours, and you certainly should not reduce them to this, but getting an initial idea of how many person hours are actually available helps you determine whether you can realistically complete the task in time or whether you need either additional labor or more time.

Optimally (i.e. without time pressure), you would first compile the list of major tasks and the most important subtasks, estimate how much time each will take and what the dependencies between them are, and then see in which sequence they must be completed and which tasks, if any, can be completed in parallel. In this way, you would arrive at the total time necessary for all tasks and thus also at the date and time by which the overall task or mission can be completed. This is the logic behind the popular critical path project-modeling technique, and it can also be used if finishing as quickly as possible rather than by a fixed deadline is the objective. Unfortunately, this is rarely the case. Normally, tasks or missions are issued along with a clear deadline. If that is the case, the method has to be adjusted by calculating the maximum planning time backwards from the defined end date and time, minus all periods during which you cannot (or do not want to) work on the assignment. This step therefore involves having at least a rough idea of the net available person hours. Illustration 5 on page 148 demonstrates how this is done.

Illustration 5: Calculating Net Times

On February 27, a quality team in the German subsidiary of a large multinational engineering company is tasked with creating a business process map along with the corresponding process descriptions for an upcoming quality audit. The documents are due for internal review by March 15. The team consists of five people, Chris (the team leader), Tom, Linda, Sonja, and Michael. They have been working together for quite a while now, and Chris trusts them completely. All have roughly similar backgrounds and experience. After getting the assignment, Chris decides to gather the team the next morning, rather than immediately, and instead spends the two hours which are left of the first day on getting up to speed on the task and organizing the upcoming work. She sits down and first calculates the net available time by going through the days in the assignment period. She plans to complete the entire task within regular work days, only using evenings and weekends as reserve time. Checking with each team member, she then compiles their individual availabilities. She needs these to calculate the net person hours at her disposal. Sonja is a single mother, so Chris does not want her to have to work evenings or weekends. When completed, the finished net time matrix looks like this:

Day	Date	Net available time			Net person-hours											
					Available regular hours						Available stretch hours					
		Regular	Stretch	Comments	Rob	Tom	Linda	Sonja	Michael	Total	Rob	Tom	Linda	Sonja	Michael	Total
Mo	27.02.20XX	2	0	Leader's time to get organized	2	0	0	0	0	2	0	0	0	0	0	0
Di	28.02.20XX	8	2	Evening: reserve/stretch time	8	8	8	8	8	40	2	2	2	0	2	8
Mi	01.03.20XX	8	2	Evening: reserve/stretch time	8	8	4	4	0	24	2	2	2	0	2	8
Do	02.03.20XX	6	2	Morning: 2-hour staff meeting	6	6	6	6	6	30	2	2	2	0	2	6
Fr	03.03.20XX	0	0	all day team workshop	0	0	0	0	0	0	0	0	0	0	0	0
Sa	04.03.20XX	0	4	Reserve; Linda abroad	0	0	0	0	0	0	4	4	0	0	4	12
So	05.03.20XX	0	0	Off-limits	0	0	0	0	0	0	0	0	0	0	0	0
Mo	06.03.20XX	8	2		8	8	8	0	8	32	2	2	2	0	2	8
Di	07.03.20XX	8	2		8	8	8	0	8	32	2	2	2	0	2	8
Mi	08.03.20XX	8	2		8	8	8	8	8	40	2	2	2	0	2	8
Do	09.03.20XX	4	0	Afternoon: Different project	4	4	4	4	4	20	4	4	4	0	4	16
Fr	10.03.20XX	8	0	Office party in the evening	7	7	7	7	7	35	0	0	0	0	0	0
Sa	11.03.20XX	0	8	Reserve	0	0	0	0	0	0	8	0	4	0	4	16
So	12.03.20XX	0	0	Off-limits	0	0	0	0	0	0	0	0	0	0	0	0
Mo	13.03.20XX	8	4		8	8	8	8	8	40	4	4	0	0	4	12
Di	14.03.20XX	0	8	Reserve	0	0	0	0	0	0						0
Mi	15.03.20XX	0	4	Reserve	0	0	0	0	0	0	4	4	0	0	0	8
	Total	68	40							295						110

Based on her quick calculations, Chris thus estimates that there are 68 net hours, about 8½ work days, available. In other words, the task has to be finished in 68 regular work hours from now, discounting all periods during which the team is unavailable (such as during a mandatory, all-day team workshop on Friday, March 3). If there are unforeseen problems, this can be stretched to 108 hours by working some or all evenings and weekends. On hand for the various subtasks are a total of 295 person hours from the five team members which can be stretched to a total of 405 person hours, if absolutely necessary. Working from this basis, she calculates the time requirements of the various tasks.

Identifying and assessing the tasks and subtasks to be performed is necessary to be able to develop a working timeline. The granularity depends on the time pressure involved: The more time you have, the more detailed you can be. At the very least, you should identify the first-level components of your work breakdown structure: those major tasks (if you work on a mission) or subtasks (if you work on a task) that form the main work packages you need to complete, because you will likely organize your milestones around them.

At the very least, you should identify the first-level components of your work breakdown structure—the main work packages you need to complete—because you will likely organize your milestones around them.

You also need to gain at least a rough idea of how long each will likely take so that you can realistically set internal deadlines and schedule meetings where necessary. Although logic will help, this is largely based on experienced. The more tasks and missions you complete, the easier it will become to gauge time requirements. There is no shame in asking someone with more experience if you are unsure.

Once you have compiled your work breakdown structure at the appropriate level, the next step is *identifying and prioritizing the internal and external milestones*. In its original meaning, a milestone literally is a stone set along the road that indicates the distance in miles to or from a particular place. Figuratively, a milestone is a significant juncture or intermediate result on the way to completing a whole, such as a task or mission. Usually, milestones coincide with the completion of major work packages. Often, it makes sense to get the team (or at least part of it) together for a meeting once a milestone has been met to synchronize them and get their views and inputs.

Once the net available time, the person hours at your disposal, and the work packages and milestones have been determined, a time and task allocation plan can be developed.

Illustration 6:   Time and Task Allocation

Lara and her team of four work in the corporate academy of a global steel producer. Out of the blue, they are tasked with the development of a four-day crisis management exercise for the company's senior management which will take place in less than two weeks. They will need to start from scratch because the team that had originally been charged with it has not done anything. On paper, there are roughly 10 days left, but by quickly calculating the net available time (see Illustration 5 on page 148), Lara realizes they really have only 32 hours. Luckily, all team members are present during that period, with about 95 person hours (h_p) available in total. As an immediate measure, Lara ensures the services of a division-level intern, Shanice, which raises that number to around 120 h_p. Next, the team leader sits down at her desk and thinks about what needs to be done. Eventually, she compiles the following list:

Tasks (level 1)		Person hours (est.)	Milestone
1	Concept	6 to 8 h_p	1
2	Venue/logistics	12 to 16 h_p	-
3	Base scenario	3 h_p (1 person) to 18 h_p (whole team)	2
4	Exercise plan and briefing	4 to 6 hp	-
5	Script (scenario roll-out and dilemmas)	8 to 12 h_p	3
6	Supporting documents and media	14 to 18 h_p	-
7	Umpires and coaches plan and briefing	6 to 8 h_p	-
8	Finished (physical) document packages	6 to 8 h_p	4
9	Presentations & templates (intro/debriefings)	4-6 h_p	-

With a relieved sigh, she realizes that she will have enough resources to complete the task in time. Next, she tries to fit these tasks onto her tight timeline—using the upper-bound time estimates to be on the safe side—and comes up with a rough time and task allocation plan. Note that, while this can still serve to coordinate the team, it is not a complete time plan; its purpose is only to check whether all the tasks can be done in time. The final time plan also has to consider non-project-related and external events.

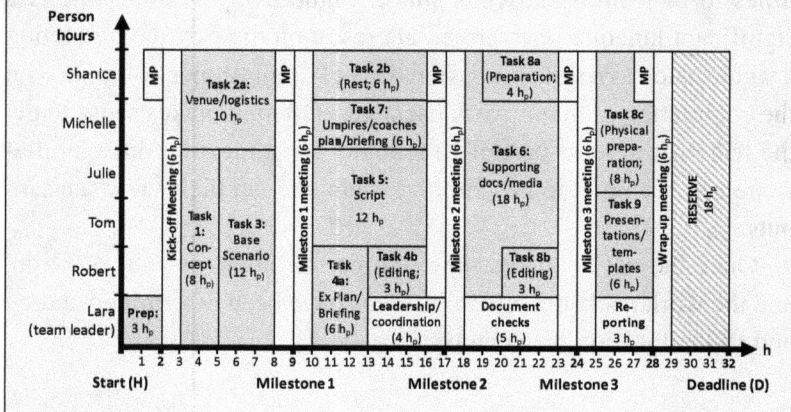

This helps you check whether the overall task or mission can realistically be completed within the given timeframe.

Such a plan plots *roughly* how the major work packages, milestones, and meetings are distributed among team members within the net available time. For an example, see Illustration 6 on page 150. Employ what works for you: if you have enough time and prefer the critical path method or some other technique, then by all means use that. If time is short, however, the above works well with some practice.

All the preliminary steps explained above were only precursors to *crafting an internal and external time plan*. This step depends on a solid understanding of the time pressure overall, the available labor, and the time requirements of the various major work packages.Based on a central timeline, a time plan should integrate both the internal and external views. The internal view includes at minimum all team milestones and ideally also all other team events. The external view encompasses major events related to important stakeholders and any relevant events and deadlines at the superior and subordinate levels.

There is a clear difference between the time and task allocation plan explained previously[1] and this final time plan. While the former is used to make sure we have enough labor to complete the overall task or mission in time, the latter is used both to coordinate the team member's efforts and to ensure that no important internal or external events or deadlines are missed. Consequently, if we have 32 net hours of time available within 10 days, the time and task allocation plan will only consider those 32 hours, while the actual time plan will consider all 10 days. If there is high time pressure, experienced leaders will often craft the time plan directly.

A time plan can take many shapes and forms. Below is a tried-and-tested sample structure that can be used as a starting point.

---

[1] See Illustration 6 on page 125.

Table 11: Sample Time Plan Structure

Time Plan	Day	DD.MM.YYYY												...	
	Time	8	9	10	11	12	13	14	15	16	17	18	...	...	...
Internal	Team leader														
	Team member 1														
	Team member 2														
	...														
	...														
External	Superior level														
	Subordinate level														
	Major stakeholders														
	...														
	...														

Source: author.

Remember that, even if there is a lot going on, it may be worth spending some extra minutes on a time plan that is self-explanatory. Not having to explain your time plan every five minutes will make this worthwhile.

An important aspect of realistic time planning is the inclusion of buffer[1] (or slack) times. These are small time windows inserted into the time plan that allow for ongoing tasks or unforeseen events to take up additional, and therefore. unplanned, time without jeopardizing the start of the next task. Of course, buffers should not be too long, particularly if there is high time pressure. If they are too short, however, they become ineffective. The trick is to strike the right balance. This depends on whether the task is routine or non-routine, the team's experience, and the length of the task to be buffered. The more non-routine and unpredictable a task and the less experienced a team, the more buffer time is warranted.

The table below suggests some standard buffer times. The actual buffer times warranted by a specific task may diverge considerably.

---

[1] In the critical path project management methodology, these slack or buffer times are also called *float*.

Table 12: Standard Buffer Times

Task duration	Task type *and/or* team experience	
	Routine *and/or* experienced	Non-routine *and/or* inexperienced
<60	5 min	10 min
60-90	10 min	20 min
90-180	15 min	30 min
>180	20 min	40 min

Source: author.

Coming up with a realistic, sensible time plan is often an iterative process. You, the leader, can start by constructing a very rough initial time plan in a few minutes of solitary work that allows you to initiate immediate measures and assign initial tasks. A more detailed and presentable time plan can then be created later on based on this initial draft, usually by someone you assign to this task.

The final step in ensuring the right timing is *regularly monitoring and updating the time plan*. This is not as trivial as it sounds: when there is high time pressure, teams often forget to update the time plan, even if it is clearly no longer in line with reality. This can and usually will lead to all sorts of problems, such as friction, misunderstandings, and missed deadlines, which in turn results in unnecessary stress for those involved. If there is too much of this, it can also jeopardize completion of the overall task or mission. So, once again, it is a good idea to assign an official timekeeper.

Ensuring the right timing is essential. Although the principles and techniques set out in this section may seem complicated and cumbersome at first, they should and quickly will become second nature. How detailed you plan and what tools you use, whether you use a pre-prepared form or just jot it down by hand on a napkin, is up to you based on your assessment of the particular situation. The more detailed your plan, the easier coordination of your team's various tasks will be, but the more precious time you will also consume yourself for this very act of diligent planning.

4.3 Leading and Managing Yourself

Ensuring the right skills, attitude, and timing is important for getting the job done. For long-term leadership success, however, leading yourself effectively is also very important. In this regard, you face five main challenges:

- developing and sustaining your leadership presence,
- developing and sustaining your resilience,
- setting a positive example,
- developing your emotional and social intelligence, and
- structuring your work and off-time.

The first three constitute key practices of interpersonal leadership; the other two are necessary prerequisites for these.

4.31 Developing and Sustaining Your Leadership Presence

As a leader, you need your team to get the job done. Even with identical education and experience, some leaders have a much easier time leading than others. These leaders possess a certain quality, frequently called *charisma*, that draws people to them. According to Bernard Bass (1985), charisma is based on two aspects of transformational leadership:

- Idealized influence[1]: the leader is seen as an authentic, credible role model with high integrity.
- Inspirational motivation: the leader has the ability to motivate followers by inspiring them with optimism, demanding goals, and a desirable, achievable vision.

---

[1] In Avolio and Bass's Full Range of Leadership model, idealized influence is divided into two elements: idealized influence (attributed) and idealized influence (behavior). Also see page 42.

James Scouller (2011) prefers the term *leadership presence* to charisma, because according to him a leader may appear charismatic yet really rely on a positional title and/or good acting skills. Presence, in his view, is deeper and more fundamental. Scouller himself puts it this way:

What is presence? At its root, it is wholeness – the rare but attainable inner alignment of self-identity, purpose and feelings that eventually leads to freedom from fear. It reveals itself as the magnetic, radiating effect you have on others when you're being the authentic you, giving them your full respect and attention, speaking honestly and letting your unique character traits flow. As leaders, we must be technically competent to gain others' respect, but it's our unique genuine presence that inspires people and prompts them to trust us – in short, to want us as their leader.

To develop and maintain your leadership presence, Scouller has three recommendations:

1. develop your technical know-how and skills,
2. cultivate a helpful[1] attitude towards other people, and
3. work on psychological self-mastery.

Having solid technical know-how and skills is important for the standing of a leader, particularly in expert teams. Cultivating a helpful attitude towards other people ensures the long-term maintenance of relationships in pursuit of a shared vision or shared goals. Finally, working on self-mastery—particularly high self-awareness and the ability to relinquish previously held limiting beliefs and attitudes—enables leaders to reduce self-esteem issues that make it difficult to connect with and appreciate colleagues and followers. In this context, *self-awareness* is an important construct. Understanding what makes you tick, how you appear to others, how you react to various

---

[1] Scouller himself calls this "the right attitude". It has been changed in this book to prevent confusion with the explanation of the *right attitude* given in Chapter 4.22.

stimuli such as complaining team members, and recognizing your own current state of mind and how it affects your interactions with others will help you to understand the reactions of the people you interact with much better, be they family, friends, or team members.

In addition to Scouller's psychological view, leadership presence also includes a physical aspect. As the word 'presence' implies, you need to be there for your people, both by *making* time for them and by *spending* time with them. If the going gets tough, you must be *seen* to be in the thick of it, leading your team from the front, being subjected to the same kinds of pressure and the same demands. As the discussion of situational leadership noted, though, not all team members may require the same leadership approach. The trick is to be both physically and mentally present, adjusting to the situation as warranted, being supportive rather than overbearing, leading each team member according to his or her needs (within the constraints of the situation), making timely decisions in which your team is included, and monitoring the implementation but not appearing dictatorial.

Successfully walking this fine line will enhance your standing and reputation as a leader and create trust, thus contributing to your leadership presence in addition to your psychological self-mastery and your technical and social skills.

4.32   Developing and Sustaining Your Resilience

As discussed in Chapter 2.5[1], *resilience* describes your ability to adapt to change, deal with stress, and recover from adversity. Gail Wagnild and Heather Young (1990: 166) define the concept thus:

'Resilience' connotes emotional stamina and has been used to describe persons who display courage and adaptability in the wake of life's misfortunes.

---

[1] See page 36. "

According to this view, *personal competence*, consisting of aspects such as self-reliance, determination, resourcefulness, and perseverance, and *acceptance of self and life*, consisting of adaptability, mental balance, flexibility and a balanced perspective of life, are the chief components of resilience, which the authors found to be positively linked to good physical health, life satisfaction, and morale, while reducing the likelihood of depression.

Particularly if you do not consider yourself to be a natural leader and you still feel insecure about your leadership abilities, your leadership-related duties may be a source of stress (or a *stressor*) for you. Avoiding excessive stress, however, is of major importance for your well-being in the long run.

In 2015, the Swiss Public Health Promotion Agency[1] estimated that more than a third of all Swiss employees suffered from frequent or very frequent stress. The percentage among leaders may well be even higher. The negative effects of stress include heart problems, reduced concentration and adaptability, low motivation, irritability, and frequent conflicts, and these may even lead to increased substance abuse and depression. This can negatively impact your effectiveness as a leader and, ultimately, also hurt your social relationships, including your family life. Obviously, this should be avoided.

A number of factors contribute to improved resilience (Cohen and Will, 1985; Beardslee, 1989, Caplan, 1990):

- your ability to correctly identify stressors,
- your ability to realistically assess your own capabilities,
- your self-confidence based on repeated successful problem solving, and
- your social support, such as a supportive relationship or a happy family life.

---

[1] *Gesundheitsförderung Schweiz* (gesundheitsfoerderung.ch).

In order to identify and thus avoid or mitigate stressors, you need to have a clear understanding of what stresses you. There are countless sources of stress, and what is considered stressful differs from person to person. Common occupational stressors (Snow, 1982; Hemingway and Smith, 1999; Elfering et al., 2005) include

- technical problems (e.g. malfunctioning IT),
- safety hazards (e.g. unsafe electrical wiring),
- cooperation problems (e.g. colleagues missing deadlines),
- a demotivating organizational climate (e.g. because of excessive gossip),
- social problems (e.g. abrasive colleagues),
- quantitative overload (e.g. too many meetings),
- qualitative overload (e.g. having to perform duties for which you feel unqualified),
- difficult decisions (e.g. firing an underperforming team member),
- clashes between work and private life (e.g. missing family functions because of work), and
- private issues that are brought into work (e.g. spouse caught having an affair).

Obviously, this is not a full list. And not all of them will stress you equally—or even at all. But in all likelihood, there are things that can stress you, and recognizing them is an important first step. Among the measures you can take to reduce stress and strengthen your resilience are

- adopting a positive outlook on life,
- initiating frequent, open dialog with both your own supervisor and your team members,
- ensuring a work environment in which you feel comfortable (or at least not chronically uncomfortable),
- clearly communicating your needs (including asking for help when necessary),

- clarifying expectations and roles (with regard to your team members and yourself as well as your supervisor),
- taking short, rejuvenating breaks,
- ensuring a healthy work-life balance (including making sufficient time for family and/or personal relationships), and
- making your physical and mental fitness a priority (including sufficient exercise and a healthy diet).

Although parts of this list may seem like esoteric mumbo-jumbo, there is ample evidence that daily positive emotions and a generally positive attitude reduce stress significantly (Tugade, Fredrickson, and Barret, 2004; Ong et al., 2006). Feeling comfortable with your surroundings can also produce positive emotions, so make sure you arrange and, if necessary, decorate the space in which you spend a lot of your time accordingly.

Communication is important for clarifying roles, expectations and needs, thereby reducing misunderstandings that can lead to anxiety, resentment, or emotional confrontations.

Asking for help when you need it does not make you a weak leader but is just common sense.

Finally, just as you need to recharge your cell phone once in a while, you also need to recharge mentally. Regularly taking a short break does wonders for your well-being, particularly if you are bogged down with constant meetings, as many leaders are. How long these breaks need to be and how often they should be taken differs from person to person. Some are sufficiently relaxed after just one or two short coffee-breaks even on a long day, others need to take five minutes every other hour or so. Whichever routine suits you, make an effort to get into the habit—for both your long-term leadership effectiveness and your personal well-being.

On a more general note, habitually ensuring a sensible work-life balance and a generally good level of fitness has been found to effectively prevent stress-related negative effects. Of course, this applies not just to you but also to those you lead. It is one of your leader duties to reduce their stress as much as you can, considering the circumstances and individual needs.

4.33   Setting the Positive Example

Whether you are aware of it or not, as a leader you are a role model for your people, either in a positive or in a negative way. Depending on the personalities of your subordinates, some will challenge you, some will emulate you, and others might try to distance themselves from you. However, none will be able to completely ignore you.

There is ample scientific evidence that the leader's example influences his or her team members: in the context of sales teams (Rich, 1997), public sector organizations (Schraeder, Tears, and Jordan, 2005), health professionals (Halcomb, 2005), and the promotion of organizational citizenship behavior (Yaffe and Kark, 2011), to name but a few. The leader's example is a signal to followers that an activity or behavior is worthwhile (Potters, Sefton, and Vesterlund, 2007). On most teams, some team members will inevitably start to consciously or subconsciously emulate their leader. This can occur in small ways, such as how people dress. For example, within a short time of Jeff Skilling, former CEO of failed Energy giant Enron[1], getting rid of his glasses following LASIK laser eye surgery, practically nobody in the company's management wore glasses. For a team-level example, see Illustration 7.

---

[1] This example is found in the 2005 documentary *Enron: The Smartest Guys in the Room*. It shows in exemplary fashion how, in a very hierarchical, single-minded, diversity-of-opinion-averse corporate culture, this need to emulate leaders can also have destructive effects. Hence, the emphasis on setting the *positive* example.

Illustration 7: Rob's Posse or the Black Hand

In a large British business consulting company, a floundering team of about 30 consultants and clerical staff were taken over by Rob, a white male approaching forty who had a reputation for turning underperforming projects and teams around. An outgoing, friendly person and a natural leader who obviously cared honestly for his subordinates, he was also well known for ignoring the implicit dress code of his organization. A self-described pragmatist, he resented having to wear a suit and tie to work every day as his predecessor had and almost all of his colleagues did. Instead, right from the start he wore formal dress only to formal business meetings, opting instead for black jeans and black dress shirts (or polo shirts on particularly hot days) to the office. Pretty soon, a pool was running within his new team about how long this behavior would be tolerated by his higher-ups. Issues that were gossiped about over coffee included his military background, with the black dress supposedly substituting for the uniform; the fact that he dressed in a way that was seen (particularly by some female colleagues) as either boring or (particularly by some male colleagues) as not sufficiently business-like; or his blatant refusal, as some others saw it, to conform to implicit expectations. He was well liked right off the bat, however, and the team's performance soon started to improve noticeably. After a few weeks, the gossip died down and people turned to other matters. At around the same time, some of the team started to dress in the same way; at first only a few, then more and more, until black became a common sight on the team. This led other teams to refer jokingly to Rob's team as the 'Black Hand', after the 19th century Spanish anarchist group. Within the team itself, the black dressers became known as 'Rob's Posse'. Rob, who was a keen observer and good listener, soon became aware of this but decided it was good for morale and let it go.

What can we learn from this example? Copying the leader's dress is a sign that Rob was well-liked and respected, yet this kind of behavior can also lead to unintended consequences and dynamics. If the convergence in dress—which signifies particularly strong bonds and loyalty among those team members and between them and the leader —is accepted by the others, this can be beneficial for both the work climate in the team and its performance. If, however, it is seen as the emergence of a self-styled 'elite' that is resented by others, this can lead to faction-building and in-fighting, which in turn will negatively impact both work climate and performance. The leader should thus carefully observe such dynamics and, if necessary, adapt his or her own behavior or, if warranted, discuss the issue with the team members in question or even the whole team.

Consequently, as a leader you can foster the kind of behavior you expect from your team members by not just telling them but also showing them. You want them to be on time? Make it a point to be on time yourself. You want them to think more positively? Make it a point to be optimistic yourself. You want them to show more team spirit and complain less about each other? Make it a point to stop complaining about your own boss in front of them.

4.34   Developing your Emotional and Social Intelligence

One of your most important assets as a leader, one that can be actively developed through training, is your emotional and social intelligence. It involves recognizing and processing emotional information as part of general problem-solving (Mayer and Geher, 1996). Based on self-awareness, self-management, social awareness, and relationship management skills, it enables leaders to manage their disruptive emotions in a way that enables them to focus and think clearly under pressure, stay flexible, and adapt to new realities ahead of time (Goleman, Boyatzis and McKee, 2002).

Although the term 'emotional intelligence' was made famous by American psychologist Daniel Goleman with his 1995 book of the same name, a similar construct, *social intelligence*, has been around since the early 20th century. The term was introduced in Edward Thorndike's writings on intelligence, published in 1920, and his subsequent research focused on what constitutes socially intelligent behavior.

An early attempt to combine the two concepts of emotional and social intelligence was Howard Gardner's 1983 book *Frames of Mind*, in which he asserted that *personal intelligence*[1] consisted of both intrapersonal and interpersonal intelligences.

---

[1] Gardner actually referred to *personal intelligences*, plural.

In 2006, American-Israeli psychologist Reuven Bar-On introduced his model of *emotional-social intelligence*[1] (ESI). He defined the construct as follows (Bar-On, 2006: 14):

Emotional-social intelligence is a cross-section of interrelated emotional and social competencies, skills and facilitators that determine how effectively we understand and express ourselves, understand others and relate with them, and cope with daily demands.

His model consists of ten key components and five facilitators of emotional-social intelligence. The ten key components are

- self-regard,
- interpersonal relationship,
- impulse control,
- problem-solving,
- emotional self-awareness,
- flexibility,
- reality testing,
- stress tolerance,
- assertiveness, and
- empathy.

The five facilitators are

- optimism,
- self-actualization,
- happiness,
- independence, and
- social responsibility.

---

[1] Inititally, Bar-On referred to the construct as *emotional and social intelligence*, but later shortened it (Bar-On, 2006).

Together, these key components and facilitators of emotional-social intelligence enable you to function effectively as a leader.

Self-regard refers to your ability to accurately perceive, understand, and accept yourself. It is hard to demonstrate real interest and consideration for your team if you do not like yourself. The same is true if you like yourself a little too much. Realistic self-regard needs time to develop and is hard to achieve. Frequent reality testing, as described further below, is therefore important.

Interpersonal relationship refers to your ability to generally relate well to others and establish mutually satisfying relationships. In part, this depends on your personality. If you are fairly extravert by nature, you probably have no problems meeting new people, yet to create stable, mutually satisfying relationships requires more than just an outgoing nature. Keeping promises, looking out for the other person, and being open and honest but diplomatic are also important.

Impulse control (or restraint) means your ability to effectively and constructively control your emotions. Obviously, this skill is closely linked to others, such as emotional self-awareness. If you do not recognize your own emotional state, you will likely 'infect' people with it. For example, if you are highly stressed and this shows very clearly during team meetings, you will automatically pass on some of that stress. If you are angry and short-tempered and lash out at subordinates, this will in turn make them angry. And so on. Recognizing your own emotions is the first step toward being able to cope with them. How you do this again depends a lot on your personality and experience. Some leaders avoid meetings, if at all possible, when in a bad mood. Others are able to tune out and bottle up their negative emotions to be dealt with later. If you have developed that ability, you might work through them after the work day by spending time with your family, going to the gym or for a run, or by any other positive means that help you. For example, a well-known Swiss Army officer deals with stress and negative emotions by splitting logs in his backyard—and then giving away the fruits of his labor as firewood to his friends. Note, however, that your work stress may spill over into your private life if you are unable to compartmentalize effectively like this. In that case, dealing with your negative emotions *before* you go home may be the right approach for you.

Emotional-social problem-solving means your capacity to solve problems of a personal and interpersonal nature effectively. Are you frustrated by some private or professional relationship? Find a way to deal with it, or your effectiveness as a leader will invariably suffer. Are team members going through a personal challenge such as a nasty divorce or a midlife crisis? They may need additional work to take their mind off these problems, or, conversely, they may need some time off to deal with them. Maybe they just need someone to talk to—or maybe they just want to be left alone. Sensing what someone, including you, needs emotionally and then satisfying that need is a very important leadership skill. Helping your team members to work through their issues—even by doing nothing, if that is the person's preference—forges strong bonds between leader and followers.

Emotional self-awareness is the ability to be aware of and understand your own emotions. Is there a team member or colleague with whom meetings invariably end in some kind of debate or even fight, although you like each other otherwise? Did you leave home in a huff after a fight with your spouse? Did your boss tick you off? Recognizing how you react to certain situations and how this reaction is influenced by your own emotional state will help you better manage these issues.

Flexibility refers to your ability to adapt and adjust your feelings and thinking to new situations. Most people do not really like change. Change increases uncertainty, and uncertainty can be threatening[1]. Since it is vital for organizations to adapt to changes in their environment, however, change may be inevitable. As a leader, it is

---

[1] Uncertainty avoidance is also culturally dependent; some cultures, such as Austria, have a much higher general propensity to avoid uncertainty than others, like Nepal or China. For details, see Chapter 5.

your responsibility both to be open to necessary change and to pro-actively identify areas in which you, your team, or your organization need to change.

Reality testing means objectively validating your feelings and thinking with external reality. An important tool at your disposal is encouraging open feedback from subordinates, colleagues, and su-periors.

Your *stress tolerance* is also influenced by your ability to effec-tively and constructively manage your emotions[1].

Assertiveness, in the context of emotional-social intelligence, re-fers to your ability to effectively and constructively express your emotions and views in a confident and self-assured manner without being aggressive.

Finally, *empathy*, one of the most important competencies, ena-bles you to be aware of—and, more importantly, understand—how others feel. In other words, this is the ability to see things through someone else's eyes. If you want to know why your team members resent certain practices, ask yourself how you would react to those practices if you were in their shoes. For example, in some compa-nies, staff are not allowed to sit at the same table as management during lunch. In cultures with low power distance, this may not go down well, and people may feel unappreciated. Empathy enables you to understand why people react the way they do. This ability is based on both intellectual and emotional faculties. Intellectually, you can anticipate, or at least recognize after the fact, why someone reacts in a certain way to a particular situation. This skill is based on your knowledge of the person as well as secondary knowledge (gained e.g. by reading, listening, or observing). Having actually lived through a comparable situation, however, will enable you to *feel* what the other person feels in that situation—an immeasurable advantage when trying to put yourself in someone's shoes. In other words, intelligence and experience are the cornerstones of empathy. If you want to know how your factory-floor workers feel, spend

---

[1] For more information on managing stress, see Chapter 4.32 on page 152f.

some time talking to them, for intellectual understanding, or doing the same kind of work, for emotional understanding. When leading soldiers as an officer, it helps to have been an ordinary infantryman at one point, too. When leading administrative staff, working alongside them for a while, even for just a few days, helps to really understand the issues they face.

Empathy is particularly vital in professions and functions where social skills are key, such as nursing, general practitioner medicine—and management. A number of studies have demonstrated that empathy can be actively trained (cf. e.g. Stepien and Baernstein, 2006; Klimecki et al., 2014), that training should usually include action components (i.e. learning-by-doing), and that positively empathic role models can foster higher levels of empathy in followers (Cotton, 1992). This is another example of the leader-emulation effect previously discussed[1].

These key components of emotional-social intelligence do not stand on their own. Just as plants need water, sunlight, nutrients, clean air, and healthy soil, these skills develop better in the right state of mind. In Bar-On's (2006) model, this 'soil' for emotional-social intelligence is provided in the form of key emotional enablers.

Optimism refers to your ability to be positive and see the brighter side of life. People are drawn to optimistic, confident leaders. This kind of positive leadership has been found, in turn, to increase employee optimism, engagement, and performance (Arakawa and Greenberg, 2007; Luthans et al., 2005; Seligman, 1998). The trick is not to let optimism turn into hubris, an exaggerated kind of optimism without a basis in fact.

Self-actualization occurs when you realize your goals and potential. An important factor in motivation theory, it allows leaders to retain their intrinsic motivation in the long term. To some extent, how congruent the goals of the organization, group, individual group member, and leader are depends on the various personalities involved at all levels. Self-serving leader goals that are transparently

---

[1] Also see Chapter 4.33 on page 156.

unrelated to the team's and organization's goals will be detrimental for overall leadership performance because they will tend to demotivate those followers who care about the common goals. On the other hand, completely neglecting yourself and simply being swept up in the current of everyday leadership chores and tasks will invariably cause you to lose your own motivation. The trick is to find a healthy balance.

Happiness is the state of feeling content with yourself, others, and life in general. In other words, it describes your emotional well-being. Think about a person you know who is sometimes ebullient and sometimes withdrawn or even sad: when is it easier to be around that person? A happy leader is an effective leader. Unfortunately, happiness does not always come easy. In fact, only about 40 percent of a person's happiness can be influenced intrinsically (through self-control, which can be practiced). Another 10 percent or so are due to current life circumstances (such as disposable income or health, which can, at least partly, be influenced), but a full 50 percent have been found to be genetically determined (Lyubomirsky, Sheldon, and Schkade, 2005). Making yourself happier in the short run by manipulating the 40-plus percent under your control is relatively simple: buy yourself a present, enjoy a delicious piece of cake, spend an afternoon outdoors, visit family, host a great team event, or do something else that makes you feel good. The real challenge is being *sustainably* happy. Newer research suggests that such happiness can be practiced. *Positive activity interventions*, or PAIs, involve simple, self-administered cognitive or behavioral strategies designed to mirror the thoughts and behaviors of naturally happy people and thus improve the happiness of the person performing them (Layous and Lyubomirsky, 2014). Among such PAIs are writing letters of gratitude to people who have done something nice for you, reflecting on the good things in your life, and performing acts of kindness to others. In her 2008 book *The How of Happiness*, American psychology professor Sonja Lyubomirsky discussed five factors that contribute to sustainable happiness:

- fostering positive emotions (through PAIs),
- optimal timing and variety (using these PAIs when they do the most good),
- social support (fulfilling the basic human need for affiliation),
- motivation, effort, and commitment (finding reasons to keep doing them), and
- habit (making doing them automatic).

Clearly, happiness and resilience[1] are closely linked: by being happy, you make yourself more resilient, and by being more resilient, you can be happier for longer periods of time. To recognize the importance of happiness and well-being as universal goals of humanity, the United Nations declared March 20 the International Day of Happiness.

Independence is present when you are self-reliant and free of emotional dependency on others. If you pathologically need (as opposed to enjoy) approval from your own boss, subordinates, or life partner, you are not emotionally independent. Self-confident, assertive, happy leaders tend to be healthily independent. If you realize that an unhealthy emotional dependence on someone else makes you unhappy and hampers your effectiveness as a leader, try to identify the roots of the problem. Some people are reminded of an overbearing parent when dealing with their boss, triggering subconscious behavioral responses that can be avoided once people become aware of them. Others are insecure, secretly or obviously, and need constant reassurance and validation in both their private and professional lives. Whatever the source of dependence may be, identifying and addressing it (perhaps by simply having a frank discussion with the person or group, or more drastically by changing jobs to get away from a domineering boss or breaking up with an emotionally controlling partner) and generally working on improving your self-

---

[1] Also see Chapter 4.32 on page 152f.

confidence will go a long way towards increasing your emotional independence.

Finally, *social group responsibility*[1] refers to a state of identifying with your social group and cooperating with others. This construct is closely related to loyalty. De Hoogh and Den Hartog (2008) define it more generally as having a moral–legal standard of conduct, internal obligation to the group, concern for others, concern about consequences, and self-judgment about actions.

To measure these key components and facilitators of emotional-social intelligence, Bar-On developed the *Emotional Quotient Inventory* (EQ-I), a self-report questionnaire that provides an estimate of someone's emotional-social intelligence based on questions about stress management and intrapersonal, interpersonal, and adaptive characteristics and skills. Initially published in 1997, it is one of the most widely used measures of emotional-social intelligence.

As evident from Table 13, the majority of emotional-social intelligence elements are actually more relevant for *self*-leadership than for individual and team leadership. Of course, being able to effectively lead and manage yourself also helps you lead your team because it makes you more authentic and leader-like. Importantly, the emotional and social competencies and facilitators in the ESI develop and increase more or less continuously from early childhood to about the age of forty, but their development can be accelerated considerably through training (Bar-On, 2006).

Overall, the emotional-social intelligence construct clearly overlaps considerably with that of resilience explained in the last section, particularly with regard to intrapersonal aspects, adaptability, and stress management. Therefore, developing your emotional-social intelligence will also improve your resilience.

---

[1] Bar-On refers to this factor simply as social responsibility. To prevent confusion with the widely used concept of corporate social responsibility, the 'group' has been added in this book.

Table 13: Emotional-Social Intelligence and Key Leader Responsibilities

Type		Element	Goal	Associated KLR*
Key Components	Interpersonal	Empathy	Be aware of and understand how others feel.	Leading and managing the team and the team members
		Interpersonal relationship	Establish mutually satisfying relationships and relate well to others.	
	Adaptability	Emotional-social problem-solving	Solve problems of a personal and interpersonal nature effectively.	
		Flexibility	Adapt and adjust your feelings and thinking to new situations.	Leading and managing yourself
		Reality testing	Objectively validate your feelings and thinking with external reality.	
	Intrapersonal	Emotional self-awareness	Be aware of and understand your own emotions.	
		Self-regard	Accurately perceive, understand, and accept yourself.	
		Assertiveness	Effectively and constructively express your emotions and views.	
	Stress management	Impulse control	Effectively and constructively control your emotions.	
		Stress tolerance	Effectively and constructively manage your emotions.	
Facilitators	General mood	Happiness	Feel content (with yourself, others, and life in general).	
		Optimism	Be positive and see the brighter side of life.	
	Intrapersonal	Self-actualization	Realize your goals and potential.	
		Independence	Be self-reliant and free of emotional dependency on others.	
	Interpersonal	Social responsibility	Identify with your social group and cooperate with others.	

KLR: Key Leader Responsibilities   Source: adapted from Bar-On (2006)

4.35   Room to Breathe: Structuring your Work and Off-Time

If you struggle to keep up with all your duties, it may be a good idea to structure your work and off-time, at least to some extent. This can significantly reduce uncertainty (a source of stress) and help you focus. Additionally, many leaders have a tendency to neglect their own needs because of work, which in the long run destabilizes their work-life balance and eventually also reduces their leadership performance. Consciously structuring your week can help you become aware of these issues. How you do this is up to you. Some people do this purely in their minds. Visualizing[1] it can be quite helpful, however, particularly if you need to coordinate with other people, such as family members.

In order to avoid the 'paralysis through analysis' trap, this week plan should not be too detailed. In other words, it is a tool that can help you achieve a certain balance rather than a project plan. It is sufficient to carve out broad blocks of time for particular activities. For example, a leader could assign a 'theme' to each day and then divide every day into rough chunks of about four hours, as shown in Table 14. For an actual example of such a week plan, see Illustration 8 on page 173.

Table 14: Sample Week's Structure

Week-day	Your Week						
	Monday	Tuesday	Wednes-day	Thursday	Friday	Saturday	Sunday
Day's Theme	...	...	...	...	...	...	...
Designated Activity Blocks							
Morning	...	...	...	... ...	...	...	...
Lunch-time	...		...			...	
After-noon	...		...			...	
Dinner/Evening	...	...		...	...	...	...

Source: author.

Such a plan is not immutable. Rather, it provides a rough structure that helps you focus and not do too many unrelated things at once, which is important, because this can drastically lower your efficiency and effectiveness. If the structure does not work anymore,

---

[1] Visualizing not in your mind but in the sense of giving it visible form, as in a sketch or diagram.

change it. Just make sure that you do not lose sight of the two main goals: improving efficiency and achieving balance between your work and your private life.

Illustration 8:   Paul's Week

Paul is a 43-year old mid-level manager in a large Austrian construction company. Friends and family alike describe him as a bit of a workaholic. For many years he has struggled with his work-life balance. This has led to a number of problems, such as weight issues, high blood pressure, and tensions with his wife. In a Living Healthier workshop that he very reluctantly attended after his boss signed him up, he learned, among various other things, about the importance of structuring one's work and off-time for stress relief. After discussing this first with both his wife and his best friend Christian, he rather unenthusiastically decided to give it a try.

Writing the first draft of his initial week plan helped him to realize that he did not, in fact, have anything resembling balance between his work and private life. This encouraged him to finally make an effort. His second draft looked like this:

Paul's Week							
Week-day	Monday	Tuesday	Wednes-day	Thurs-day	Friday	Saturday	Sunday
Day's Theme	Admin	Firm-level	Team-level	Customers/ Projects		'Me'-time	Family
Designated Activity Blocks							
Morning	Internal work and/or meetings	Board or strategic project work and/or meet-ings	Team and bilateral meetings	Customer meet-ings and/or pro-ject work		Language lessons	Family
Lunch-time	Fitness		Fitness	Business lunches		Family	
After-noon	Internal work and/or meetings		Team and bilateral meetings	Customer meet-ings and/or pro-ject work		Sports or kid's sports	
Dinner/ Evening	Personal admin	Family or business functions		Squash	Spouse	Personal or family time	

Six months late,r he swears by this method and explains that he cannot understand why he did not start earlier. Visualizing his week's structure helped him to realize how little time he had actually spent on himself and his family. It also helped him to focus better, which in turn saved him time and increased his efficiency by grouping similar work so that he could allocate more work for private activities.

A solid work-life balance increases your resilience, prevents burnout syndrome, and increases both your general well-being and thus your effectiveness as a leader.

Finally, most leaders find it helpful (albeit not necessarily enjoyable) to keep a to-do list. It helps you keep track of your own tasks and the priorities you originally assigned them as well as those of your team members. At its most basic, such a list should clearly and unambiguously identify a task (e.g. by assigning it a number) and explain its essence, who is responsible for it, when it is due, and possibly what progress has been made so far. For the sake of efficiency, it often makes sense to keep only one to-do list for both your personal tasks and those assigned to other people, although that will depend on your preferences. Table 15 shows a sample structure.

Table 15: Sample To-Do List

Item	Task	Created	Assigned	Due	%	Status	Comments
..	..	..	..	..		..	..
123	Q4 financial reporting	Sept. 10, 2015	Rob Meister	Jan. 18, 2016	80%	Overdue	Final approval by CEO necessary
124	Update marketing plan	Feb. 17, 2016	Lori Loughlin	May 5, 2016	30%	On track	Coordinate with production
125	Update strategic reporting	Jan. 7, 2016	Myself	Feb. 29, 2016	30%	On track	Coordinate with Corporate Center
..	..	..	..	..		..	..

Source: author.

4.4 Leading and Managing Individuals

The way that you manage to lead yourself will show in the way that you lead others. If you have good leadership presence and bring a positive spirit to the job, people will follow you much more readily. Apart from the team as a whole, you also need to find an individualized approach to each team member. As their leader, you fulfill four basic roles:

- teacher/coach,
- facilitator/enabler,
- conflict manager, and
- challenger/enforcer.

As a *teacher/coach*, it is your job not just to demand results but also to show your team members how to achieve these, and to work with them and support them if they struggle. Just as in sports, this requires a solid understanding of whatever it is the team is supposed to do. Naturally, it is easier to coach a softball or football team if you have played softball or football yourself. Making sure that your technical skills are up to standard, mentioned in the discussion of leadership presence[1], will allow you to fulfill this role more easily.

As a *facilitator/enabler*, you create the appropriate work conditions, procure the necessary information, and open the right doors for your team to do its best work. You also give your team members necessary and individually appropriate leeway and responsibility. This does not just increase their motivation; it also improves the team's overall efficiency and will eventually reduce the demands on your time. Having the right attitude[2], particularly with regard to service orientation, will make it easier to fulfill this particular role.

---

[1] See Chapter 4.31 on page 150f.
[2] See Figure 11, The Leader Attitude Heptagon on page 137.

As a *conflict manager*, you handle three types of conflict that can occur in your team:

- relationship conflict (based on disagreements that may have nothing to do with work),
- task conflict (stemming from disagreements about what work needs to be done), and
- process conflict (arising from disagreements about how to do the work and who should do what).

Conflict can cause tension and antagonism and may thus interfere with people's satisfaction and eventually the team's performance. In fact, effective conflict management has consistently been shown to be beneficial for group performance (cf. e.g. Way, Jimmieson and Bordia, 2016; De Dreu and Weingart, 2003). On the other hand, a number of studies have reported that low levels of conflict may actually be constructive because this forces people to confront issues, open their minds to differing perspectives, and be creative (De Dreu and Weingart, 2003). As a leader, therefore, you do not need to crush every little spark of discord, but you must be able to resolve those conflicts that threaten the team's harmony. For example, while some competition among team members, or between team members and you, which can also happen, may be healthy and beneficial, too much of it can lead to personal animosities that need to be handled so they do not start to distract people from their work and thus impact the team's performance negatively.

Managing conflict in your team or between you and a team member is a tricky business; you need to remain (or at least appear to remain) unfazed when a team member seeks a confrontation with you and stay impartial when team members fight with each other, but you also need to follow your basic sense of right and wrong and take a clear stand against unacceptable behavior such as bullying.

There are various tools that can help you better understand your conflict behavior, such as the Thomas–Kilmann Conflict Mode Instrument[1] or Clark's DISC assessment[2].

Finally, as a *challenger/enforcer* you make sure that everybody does their best work and contributes appropriately to the team while adhering to defined standards. This requires a light touch: not everybody who is in a bit of a slump is an incorrigible slacker, and coming down hard on someone at the first sign of a dip in the quality or quantity of their work can be very counterproductive. Often, a temporary decrease in performance may be due to family trouble or some kind of health or psychological issue, such as a mid-life crisis. If you tread softly and offer support instead of increasing the pressure during this difficult time, the team member may often emerge more motivated than before. The important thing is to discuss and clearly define and limit this period. Of course, if somebody demonstrates neither the required performance nor the right attitude and does not contribute to the team in any other relevant way, it may eventually be time to say goodbye. Such decisions should be a last resort, however, and should not be taken lightly.

In this role as challenger and enforcer, you may also play devil's advocate, poking holes in explanations, playing what-if games, and encouraging your team members to defend their work. Obviously, this should not be done simply to put someone in his or her place. Rather, it should be a joint attempt to check if work is up to commonly understood and communicated standards and if offered solutions are feasible, acceptable, suitable, and complete. However, some people are very touchy about their work, so it pays to be completely open and honest about your motivation for this approach and what you aim to achieve by it. You question certain aspects of the work, not the person. It is very important to make sure this difference is understood. Note that there is a cross-cultural aspect to this

---

[1] The TK-CMI lists five conflict behaviors based on assertiveness and cooperativeness.

[2] DISC assessment is based on William M. Marston's DISC theory which asserts that people express their emotions using four types of behavior: dominance, inducement, submission, or compliance.

and that separating the issue from the person may be harder for some than for others, depending on their cultural background[1].

As a leader, you will switch fluently between these roles, depending on the situation and your interactions with the team as a whole and with the individual team members.

Figure 13: The Four Basic Leader Interaction Roles

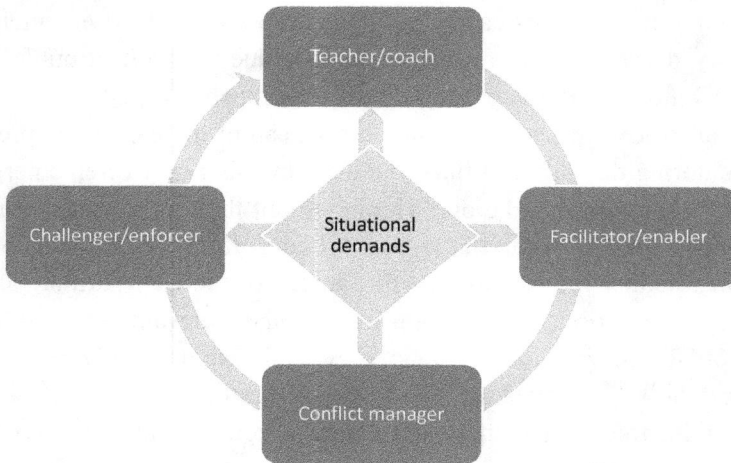

Source: author.

Regardless of which role takes precedence at any one moment, you always face four main challenges when it comes to the individuals on your team: how to motivate or even inspire them, how to show them where to go and what to do, how to get the best out of them, and how to show you care. If you meet these challenges for every single team member, the logic goes, the team as a whole is covered, too. Information and communication are important for this. Therefore, you need to systematically provide interaction opportunities. Your people need to know when they will have access to you for help and decisions. This formalized list of regular meetings with

---

[1] For more details, see Chapter 5.26 on page 265f.

your subordinates is called your *leadership rhythm*. Therefore, leading individuals involves four key leader practices[1] and a facilitator practice:

- motivating and inspiring them,
- providing guidance and direction to them,
- enabling, stimulating, and challenging them,
- showing real interest and consideration, and
- setting an appropriate leadership rhythm.

Clearly, these practices are all linked. By providing guidance and direction, you also inspire, and through enabling, stimulating, and challenging you also contribute to motivation, as you do by inspiring and showing real, authentic interest and consideration for your people or by giving them sufficient face-to-face interaction possibilities with you. Leadership is a holistic challenge.

4.41   Motivating and Inspiring

Motivated people work better and harder. To achieve optimal team performance, therefore, it is necessary for you to understand what makes each team member tick. General frameworks of motivation can guide you, but only knowing your followers as well as possible will help you truly understand how to motivate them. Important components of motivating your team members are

- a *vision* that is shared between you and your follower(s),
- *goal congruence* between your goals as the leader, the team's goals, and the individual team members' goals,
- *rewards* contingent on reaching these goals, and
- *perceived fairness* of these rewards relative to others.

---

[1] Also see Figure 8 on page 124.

In the management literature, motivation is frequently a result of job satisfaction. One of the earliest and most famous theories of job satisfaction is Edwin A. Locke's *Range of Affect Theory*, published in 1976. It postulates that work satisfaction is determined by the perceived discrepancy between what a person *wants* from a job and what he or she currently *has*. This relationship is moderated by personal values. In other words, someone who values money highly will be more dissatisfied by perceived differences between their own salary and that of co-workers of equal standing than someone who cares less about money.

Job satisfaction is to some extent intrinsic. Studies on identical twins raised apart have found similar job satisfaction levels despite differing jobs[1]. Judge, Locke, and Durham (1997) thus proposed the *Core Self-Evaluations Model*. It does not replace affect theory but rather complements and extends its range by suggesting that this intrinsic job satisfaction (in other words, someone's baseline satisfaction) depends on a person's self-view with regard to four core aspects:

- *self-esteem*,. the value placed on one's self,
- general *self-efficacy*, the strength of the belief in one's own competence,
- *locus of control*, whether one believes in control over one's own life (internal locus) or in control of outside forces (external locus), and
- *neuroticism*, one's personality-driven tendency to experience negative feelings such as anxiety, moodiness, envy, frustration, or jealousy.

Higher self-esteem and self-efficacy and an internal locus of control increase job satisfaction, while higher levels of neuroticism and an external locus of control decrease it.

---

[1] The stream of research based on this idea has become known as the *dispositional approach*.

On a side note, cultural differences may be relevant to the locus of control: people from collectivistic societies such as China, Indonesia, and Brazil are more likely to have an external locus of control than people from an individualistic society such as New Zealand, the USA, and Switzerland (Hamid, 1994).

People with a naturally higher level of job satisfaction may still be dissatisfied by perceived differences in an aspect of the job that they value, but they will tend to be more satisfied across their work life overall. As a leader, therefore, the trick is to know whether each of your team members is naturally more or less satisfied. Once you have established this baseline, it is much easier for you to separate legitimate grievances from simple venting.

Personality also plays a role in this. Extravert people will usually tell you what bugs them, but you will have to be more sensitive vis-à-vis quieter followers; they may have serious issues with something even if they are not telling you. The frequently voiced leadership advice "if they aren't telling, it's not worth knowing" is patently wrong. In fact, serious dissonance in teams often starts with introvert team members not talking about something they perceive as a major offense. Instead, they often swallow their pride and say nothing, but the issue can stay with them for a long time, negatively influencing and possibly jeopardizing their relationships with you and the other team members. As the leader, you need to be aware of what is going on in your team, and you should have a solid understanding of the satisfaction level of each team member at any given time.

In order to fully understand statements and reactions, however, you also need to understand what your followers' main motivators are. Humans are motivated by a variety of things. A good summary is provided by Maslow's hierarchy of needs. Although originally not an empirically validated model, his framework has been widely used and taught since its first publication in his 1943 paper *A Theory of Human Motivation*.

Maslow introduced the idea that humans have five basic needs that must be satisfied in sequence:

- physiological (e.g. food and drink),
- safety (e.g. from harm),
- love (e.g. by a spouse or family members),
- esteem (e.g. as accorded by peers), and
- self-actualization (e.g. through meaningful work).

Satisfying a higher need (such as esteem) without satisfying a more basic need (such as safety) does not lead to sustainable motivation. This makes intuitive sense. Your colleagues' admiration is not worth that much in a work setting in which someone can die from an accident at any time, as in the early Chicago meat plants. Only when acceptable safety levels have been established are higher-level needs such as esteem really relevant for motivation.

Maslow's theory has been criticized over the years, with studies finding mixed results when trying to empirically validate its basic premise. Some professions, such as firefighting or police work, are inherently dangerous. Nonetheless, those are also the professions in which camaraderie and peer appreciation play a vital role, despite the unsafe work. Maslow's hierarchy of needs must therefore be understood as a relative framework. A fire station that is contaminated with asbestos will demotivate even the most resilient firefighters, regardless of the admiration they receive from others, while going into a building on fire is just part of the job.

A more detailed perspective is provided by American psychologist Frederick Herzberg's *Two-Factor Theory*[1], introduced in 1959. This theory links job satisfaction and motivation by asserting that certain factors in a job setting cause satisfaction, while other factors cause dissatisfaction. Only when a person is satisfied can he or she also be motivated. In other words, eliminating dissatisfiers

---

[1] Also called the *Motivator-Hygiene Theory* and *Dual-Factor Theory*.

such as bad team spirit or unsafe working conditions will not automatically lead to motivated employees. Rather, two sets of factors, termed hygiene factors and motivational factors, are responsible for ensuring motivation. Consider a situation in which a team is both dissatisfied and demotivated. Paying attention to extrinsic hygiene factors such as pay, status, security, working conditions, fringe benefits, policies and admin practices, and interpersonal relationships and team spirit will lead to satisfied but still unmotivated team members. Only intrinsic factors are able to inspire long-term motivation. Such motivators, according to Herzberg, are such things as meaningful work, challenging tasks, a sense of achievement, recognition for a job well done, the increased responsibility that comes with it, and opportunities for personal growth. Only by paying attention to all of these factors can long-term motivation be achieved.

Figure 14: Herzberg's Two-Factor Theory of Motivation

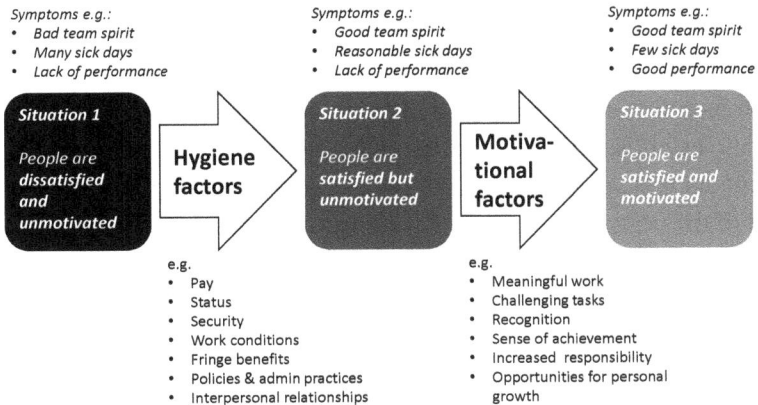

Source: based on Herzberg (1968).

Motivation and inspiration are not quite the same. Inspirational leadership specifically involves the awakening and amplifying of follower motivation (Banerji and Krishnan, 2000). Stories of inspirational leaders abound. It seems to be a natural tendency of many people to want to look up to leaders who inspire them. As one of the main aspects of transformational leadership, inspiration refers to a leader's ability to act as a model, communicate a vision, and use symbols to focus efforts (Hartog, Muijen, and Koopman, 1997). Inspirational leaders go beyond simple performance-versus-reward transactions and have a deep impact on their followers and their organizations, including facilitating change (Waldman, Balthazard, and Peterson, 2011). Note that the terms 'inspirational' and 'charismatic' (or charisma-like) are often used interchangeably in this context[1].

Key factors that contribute to inspiring followers are (Bass and Stogdill, 1990)

- pride,
- respect,
- confidence, and
- trust.

Pride is often the result of visible success and a sense of belonging. Hence, if a particular team member or the team as a whole has been mentioned favorably in a meeting with higher-ups, pass it on. Aim to establish routines and traditions that make your team and its members feel special within the organization (but, importantly, as a part of the organization, even if the best part). And be a positive role model to your team that makes them compare any other leader in the organization to you, taking pride in the fact that, at least in their eyes, their leader is the best.

Respect is what your followers feel towards you if they see you as a positive role model. Not everyone can garner respect in the same way, and not every situation warrants the same approach. In the military, your physical prowess may be a crucial aspect, while this normally has little or no impact in business. Your personal values and

---

[1] See e.g. Bass and Stogdill's (1990) best-selling *Handbook of Leadership*.

ethics are also important. Competence, fairness, authenticity, dependability, and a certain predictability (in a positive sense) are key aspects frequently mentioned when asking people about what factors cause them to respect a leader. Additionally, respect is reciprocal; if you do not respect your team members, they will soon notice and in turn lose respect for you.

Confidence is the notion that things will turn out positively. This feeling is fed by positive past experiences, trust in the leader, co-workers, and one's self, and positive reinforcement. Confident teams perform better, and teams are confident if their individual members feel confident. Hence, to instill confidence in your team members, you have to earn their respect and be a positive role model. Additionally, you should arrange frequent, open dialog within the team so everyone knows about each other's success and failures, strengths, and weaknesses, celebrate successes and share best practice examples, and occasionally 'massage the soul' of team members who need it at that point.

Trust exists if one person is willing to rely on another. To foster trust, positive past experiences, such as of a leader keeping his or her word, are once again important. Trust does not exist right from the start in a relationship; it must be built.

To motivate and inspire, you should make sure that both hygiene and motivational factors are properly considered. Additionally, you should aim to instill a sense of pride in your team members, earn their respect, fill them with confidence in their own and the team's overall ability, and foster trust between the team's members and between the team and you.

4.42   Providing Individual Guidance and Direction

If individual team members are motivated, the team is motivated. However, all motivation, inspiration, and stimulation will do no good if it remains unclear what needs to be done. Providing guidance and direction for your followers involves a number of things.

It includes Adair's (1973, 1988) advice to "set the example", Kouzes and Posner's (1987) recommendation to "model the way"', and various elements of Avolio and Bass's (1991) idealized influence (for a reminder of these aspects, see section 4.1 on page 123). But it is even more than that. Based on the shared vision and goals necessary for sustained motivation, you need to explore and explain solutions and establish principles, rituals, and traditions.

Depending on the maturity of particular followers, the emphasis when discussing possible solutions may lie more on exploring or explaining. Even though it may initially be slower and more demanding for you as a leader, it pays to let team members arrive at solutions themselves while, if necessary, coaching them on the way. This will increase both their self-confidence and their problem-solving ability, eventually increasing performance and decreasing the need for supervision.

Additionally, establishing accepted principles, rituals, and traditions can also all contribute to a reduction in your leadership load, freeing up capacity for other tasks[1].

Even if your followers are highly experienced, skilled, and self-managing, every team member will at times require guidance from you. Mostly, this will be about job-related issues, but occasionally private matters may also pop up. How you package your guidance can go a long way towards making that team member feel more secure and appreciated—and thus more effective.

4.43   Enabling, Stimulating, and Challenging

To do their jobs properly, the authority and responsibility of your team members must be aligned and commensurate with their assigned tasks. Together, they form the enabling triangle (also known as TAR[2]).

---

[1] This point is further explored in Chapter 4.54 on page 204 and Chapter 6.1 on page 320.

[2] TAR refers to task, authority, and responsibility.

Figure 15: The Enabling Triangle (TAR)

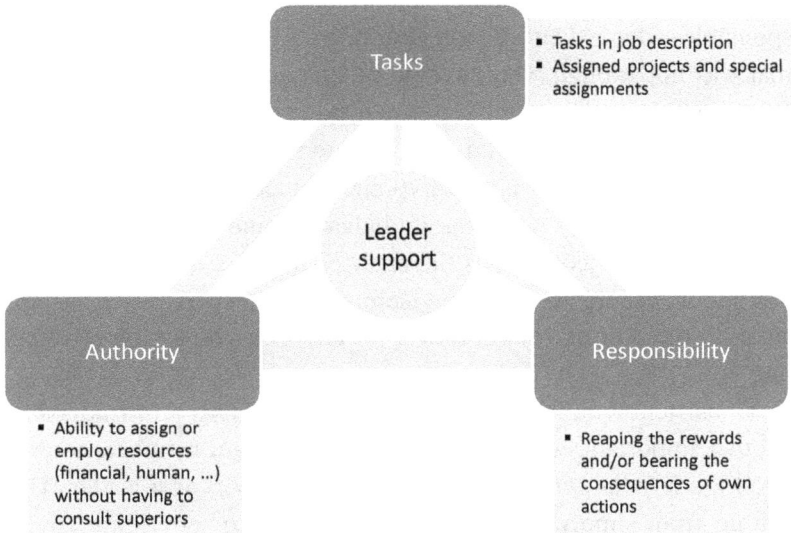

Tasks
- Tasks in job description
- Assigned projects and special assignments

Leader support

Authority
- Ability to assign or employ resources (financial, human, ...) without having to consult superiors

Responsibility
- Reaping the rewards and/or bearing the consequences of own actions

Source: author.

Authority here does not refer to power in the Weberian sense[1] but indicates what team members are allowed to do without consulting superiors.

Responsibility means having to bear the consequences of failure but also receiving recognition and perhaps rewards for success.

And *tasks* can be both those that are standard for a particular job (and, ideally, specified in the job description) and additionally assigned projects and duties.

In reality, these three elements are frequently misaligned. Imagine that you are selected to head a new project of strategic importance for your organization, such as developing a new product or service. Despite its significance, the project is not assigned any full-

---

[1] In his 1922 essay *Die drei reinen Typen der legitimen Herrschaft* ("The Three Types of Legitimate Rule"), German sociologist Max Weber identified three types of authority used to legitimize a ruler's right to rule: rational-legal (or bureaucratic), traditional, and charismatic.

time members. Rather, all project team members are seconded part-time from their line units. You have no direct reward or punishment powers, so success or failure—for which you will be held fully responsible—depend entirely on your powers of persuasion. And as if that was not enough, you have no budget authority whatsoever, so for even the smallest purchases you need to get the project sponsor's signature, a very busy (and thus hard to reach) woman. Does that sound familiar? In this not-so-hypothetical example, the three TAR elements are clearly not properly balanced, and just as clearly this reduces or even jeopardizes the chances of success. Consequently, you should ensure that the three factors are aligned as closely as possible, to the best of your abilities, for any task you assign to someone.

Consistent with Robert Greenleaf's notion of servant leadership, another important element of enabling your team members to do a good job is your general, often unbidden, support as a leader. This can go from simply spreading the good word or providing advice and expertise to passing on contacts you have inside or outside the organization to opening doors to superiors, and so on. It also includes developing your team members and helping them grow professionally and personally, aiming to increase their skills (e.g. through training), responsibilities (through progressively more difficult assignments), and self-confidence (through successes and positive feedback).

In addition to this enabler function, successful leaders also manage to stimulate their team members intellectually and emotionally with their ideas, enthusiasm, and positive example, as well as by calling them out if they try to take inappropriate shortcuts and by continuously challenging them to find even better ways of solving problems.

4.44   Showing Real Interest and Consideration

As a rule, most people appreciate it if their boss shows she or he cares. This has been a well-known maxim ever since the Hawthorne experiments[1] and is an aspect that is frequently emphasized in leadership training. As a result, even bosses who do not really care for their followers[2] are aware of it and at least pay lip service to its implications, often quite successfully fooling those with less-developed social senses by asking superficial questions in pre-arranged settings. However, on any team there will normally be a few people who see right through this kind of behavior and in the long-term will not tolerate it. Even if they do not openly challenge such a boss (who will often be quite immune to criticism and possibly also vindictive), they will make their opinions known to their colleagues. This will inevitably lead to tensions within the team or between team and leader. Therefore, an effective leader should honestly be interested in the people he or she leads, caring for their thoughts and physical and emotional well-being. Very task-oriented leaders are thus not well suited to leadership of teams that require a lot of emotional support. If you really have no interest in the people you lead, you will find it hard to achieve long-term leadership success; you might be best suited to leading mature teams with high degrees of autonomy and clearly defined, stable tasks, rather than less mature teams that still need to be formed or where the task nature constantly changes.

---

[1] The Hawthorne experiments were commissioned by the management of the Hawthorne Works, a Western Electric plant outside Chicago, with the aim of determining whether differing levels of lighting influenced worker productivity. Taking place between 1924 and 1932, the experiments did indeed find increasing levels of productivity when changes were made. In a 1958 analysis of these experiments, however, these effects were attributed not to the actual lighting change but to the fact that workers knew they were under observation, giving rise to the well-known term *Hawthorne effect*. The effect is considered to be real despite the fact that a 2011 examination of the original data by economists Stephen Levitt and John List found it to be wholly attributable to the fact that lighting changes were always introduced on Sundays, which meant the first day of measurement that captured the supposed effect of the lighting change actually reflected the day of rest the workers had had.

[2] In any organization, a certain number of leaders will have personalities that in psychology are considered part of the so-called 'dark triad': narcissism, Machiavellianism, and psychopathy. Among other things, these are characterized by excessively high self-regard and an uncaring attitude towards other people.

Such teams require a higher degree of interaction among team members, which, as the leader, you might have to facilitate. A certain interest in others, however, should be a basic hiring and promotion requirement for any leader.

4.45 Setting an Appropriate Leadership Rhythm

As previously discussed, making time for your people is very important, both for morale and the smooth running of things. In fact, the existence or absence of opportunities for clear face-to-face interaction has a significant psychological impact on most followers. Making time for them is not just functionally relevant to exchanging information, discussing problems, and making decisions; it is also a sign of your appreciation of them which they will value. Failing to stick to the rhythm can also demotivate them.

An important tool for this is your leadership rhythm. Basically, this is just a systematic plan of when you meet with whom. These meetings should be regular, hence the term 'rhythm'. Some units include them in a general team agenda. The difference is that the leadership rhythm is focused exclusively on events related to your leader duties. It is a tool for you as the leader. From the perspective of the team and the individual team members, only the events in which they participate are interesting. Keeping the leadership rhythm and the team agenda separate is recommended.

Mostly, the leadership rhythm will address your direct reports, but you may also want to include a wider range of people if, for instance, you are responsible for major projects. Meeting length will depend on the complexity of the issues to be discussed, but as a general rule of thumb a meeting of this kind should not normally exceed 90 minutes[1]. Often, if you are well prepared, an hour might be enough.

Table 16 shows an example of a leadership rhythm for a team of five people.

---

[1] For more information about managing meetings, see Chapter 4.55 on page 208.

Table 16: Sample Team Leadership Rhythm

Meeting	Participants	Rhythm	Weekday	Time slot	Target week			
					1	2	3	4
Team								
Team meeting	All direct reports (unit heads)	Fortnight	Wednes-day	0900-1030	X		X	
Team coffee+tea	Whole team (vol-untary)	Weekly	Tuesday	1000-1015	X	X	X	X
Team workshop	Whole team (man-datory)	Annually, October	Friday	0800-1800		X		
Team dinner	Whole team (vol-untary)	Annually, April	Tuesday	1800-2100				X
Individuals								
Bilateral meeting 1	Direct report 1	Fortnight	Wednes-days	0900-1030		X		X
Bilateral meeting 2	Direct report 2	Fortnight	Wednes-days	1045-1215		X		X
Bilateral meeting 3	Direct report 3	Fortnight	Wednes-days	1430-1600		X		X
Bilateral meeting 4	Direct report 4	Fortnight	Wednes-days	1045-1215	X		X	
Bilateral meeting 5	Direct report 5	Fortnight	Wednes-days	1430-1600	X		X	

Source: author.

The leadership rhythm should reflect the leader's weekly struc-ture, as mentioned previously[1]. It pays to group bilateral meetings with your direct reports so you can focus on those issues during a clearly defined time slot. This will be particularly helpful if you tend to work in a monochronic[2] fashion. For example, Wednesday is the dedicated leadership day in the team leadership rhythm depicted in Table 16. This frees up all other days for other work except for one Friday a year for the team workshop and whatever evening events your team holds.

The concept of the leadership rhythm is scalable. As unit size grows, more time will likely need to be devoted to leadership-related duties. The same is true for follower commitment and competence;

---

[1] Also see Chapter 4.35 on page 145.
[2] Also see Chapter 5.21 on page 247.

the lower either is, the more direct interaction is required. Table 17 shows a sample leadership rhythm for a department of around 50 people, divided into five teams plus a small staff unit.

Table 17: Sample Department Leadership Rhythm

Meeting	Participants	Rhythm	Weekday	Time slot	Target week			
					1	2	3	4
Team								
Leader team meeting	All direct reports (team leaders)	Fortnight	Wednesdays	0900-1030	X		X	
Full staff meeting	All department staff (mandatory)	Monthly	Monday	1330-1500			X	
Department coffee+tea	All department staff (voluntary)	Weekly	Tuesday	1000-1015	X	X	X	X
Department workshop	All department staff (mandatory)	Annually, October	Friday	0800-1800		X		
Department dinner	All department staff (voluntary)	Annually, April	Tuesday	1800-2100				X
Focus Days 1	All staff (no vacation)	February	Tue-Thu	0800-1800			X	
Focus Days 2	All staff (no vacation)	August	Tue-Thu	0800-1800			X	
Deputy Lunch	All deputy team leaders	Twice a year	Monday	1200-1400	X			
Individuals								
Bilateral meeting 1	Team leader 1	Fortnight	Wednesdays	0900-1030		X		X
Bilateral meeting 2	Team leader 2	Fortnight	Wednesdays	1045-1215		X		X
Bilateral meeting 3	Team leader 3	Fortnight	Wednesdays	1430-1600		X		X
Bilateral meeting 4	Team leader 4	Fortnight	Wednesdays	1045-1215	X		X	
Bilateral meeting 5	Team leader 5	Fortnight	Wednesdays	1430-1600	X		X	
Bilateral Meeting 6	Department Chief of Staff	Weekly	Monday	0900-1030	X	X	X	X
External								
Strategic projects progress meeting	Project heads	Monthly	Monday	1500-1700		X		

Source: author.

In this example, the department head structures his or her week as follows: Mondays are for internal and administrative issues. Tuesdays are for duties at the next higher level, such as division leader meetings or executive board meetings, depending on the organization's size. Wednesdays are for leadership duties related to the department's main responsibilities, such as producing a product or offering a service, which is why the leader team meeting and the bilateral meetings with the team leaders are scheduled on that day. Finally, Thursday and Friday are reserved for external duties, such as meeting customers or working on projects.

Focus days are intended for getting projects that are lagging, if not in implementation then at least in documentation, back on track and/or working on something as a team, such as coming up with ideas for a new product, service, or problem solution. To do this, people need to be around, which means that they should not take any vacation time then. It is thus a good idea to check school break dates and other relevant dates, such as bank holidays, and work around them when scheduling these activities. The example above features two blocks of three focus days each, spaced apart in a roughly half-year interval.

Additionally, a deputy team leader lunch twice a year gives the department head—who mainly interacts with his direct reports or the department as a whole—a chance to pick the deputies' brains and explore their ideas and concerns.

There is also a weekly team coffee and tea slot on Tuesdays, an annual team workshop devoted to spending time together on solving fun problems away from the office in the fall, and an annual team dinner that combines learning something new with quality downtime in the spring. All these activities are intended to strengthen the team's spirit and increase the effectiveness and efficiency of team work because, among other benefits, they help the team members to get to know each other better.

4.5   Leading and Managing Teams

Members of high-performing teams support each other, work well together, share common goals, and take pride in their team and their membership in it. As the saying goes, the whole is more than the sum of its parts. As the leader, you play an important role in facilitating this by building the team and providing guidance and direction. You also need to know what is going on and set and enforce standards. Additionally, running productive meetings is an often underappreciated yet highly important skill that influences both the productivity of your team and its spirit. How often have you sat in a meeting and wished you were somewhere else? Unproductive, inefficient meetings are not just a nuisance; they are a waste of time and money. Management thinker Peter Drucker identified running productive meetings as one of the key skills of effective executives (Drucker, 2004).

In a nutshell, effectively leading and managing a team therefore involves

- building and developing the team,
- providing guidance and direction (to the team as a whole),
- staying on top of things,
- setting and enforcing standards, and
- running productive meetings.

Providing guidance and direction is a key leadership practice.[1] The other four are necessary and important facilitator practices. Without team coherence (people appreciating one another and looking out for each other), there can be no long-term fruitful collaboration, and without collaboration, there is no sustainable performance. If you do not stay on top of things, the wrong things may be done despite all the team spirit and collaboration. And if you do not set

---

[1]Also see Figure 8 on page 124.

and enforce standards, you will spend all your time checking and rechecking results.

Figure 16 summarizes these deliberations and provides an overview of what each practice entails. These aspects are then discussed in more detail further below.

Figure 16: Five Key Elements of Team Management

- Select and hire
- Form and shape
- Foster team coherence and collaboration
- Create highlights

Build and develop the team

- Set the standards
- Explain the standards
- Live the standards
- Check compliance

Set and enforce standards

Run productive meetings

Provide guidance and direction

- Goals
- Topics
- Responsibilities
- Times

- Explain
- Establish principles, rituals, and traditions

- Collect and assess information
- Adapt, improvise, overcome

Stay on top of things

Source: author.

4.51   Building and Developing the Team

Team coherence and collaboration are important prerequisites for performance. Obviously, fostering these is easier if you are able to pick your own team members. In most cases, however, a new leader will take over an existing team; forming and shaping the team by hiring new team members can be a lengthy process. In other words, as a leader, you must normally learn to work with what you have got, whether you like it or not.

Unfortunately, even mature teams in which the members like and support each other may not perform optimally. Having fun is good for team cohesion and therefore for performance, but there is such a thing as having too much fun. If the main point of every work day becomes playing pranks on each other and goofing off, then of course performance will suffer. Successful teamwork depends on fruitful collaboration among the team members, which in turn is based on the following conditions (Friend and Cook, 1992):

- the existence of mutual goals,
- parity among participants,
- shared responsibility for participation and outcomes, and
- sharing of resources among team members.

Even if *mutual goals* exist, they may not be obvious to your followers. As repeatedly mentioned, one of your key jobs as a leader is to provide guidance and direction for your team. This includes pointing out the existence and substance of mutual goals and the benefits of jointly pursuing them.

All teams have an internal pecking order, but the differences in perceived status and social standing should not be such that they jeopardize the team's working together. Yet, although shown to be conducive to good team work, this *parity* among team members — the absence of hierarchical or social distinctions that hinder communication and may lead to resentment—is not alone a sufficient condition for excellent performance. Teams also need to be well balanced with regard to the personalities represented on them and the roles the individual team members take on.

One of the best-known team role typologies is Belbin's *Nine Team Roles*. Based on a study of team roles in management teams conducted between 1969 and 1981, it was first published in 1981[1] and has been continuously updated since then (Belbin, 2012). While

---

[1] In fact, Belbin identified only eight team roles in his initial 1981 publication, but in a 1993 update, he revised some of them and added a ninth, 'the specialist'.

empirical support has been limited, it is widely used among managers and management trainers around the world.

Table 18: Belbin's Nine Team Roles

Main concern	Role	Team role contributions	Allowable weaknesses
Intellectual problem-solving	Plant	▪ Creative, imaginative, unorthodox ▪ Solves difficult problems	▪ Ignores incidentals ▪ Too preoccupied to communicate effectively
	Specialist	▪ Single-minded, self-starting, dedicated ▪ Provides knowledge and skills in rare supply	▪ Contributes only on a narrow front. Dwells on technicalities
	Monitor/ Evaluator	▪ Sober, strategic, discerning ▪ Sees all options ▪ Judges accurately	▪ Lacks drive and ability to inspire others
Action	Implementer[1]	▪ Disciplined, reliable, conservative, efficient ▪ Turns ideas into practical actions	▪ Somewhat inflexible ▪ Slow to respond to new possibilities
	Shaper	▪ Challenging, dynamic, thrives under pressure ▪ Has the drive and courage to overcome obstacles	▪ Prone to provocation ▪ Tends to offend people's feelings
	Completer/ Finisher	▪ Painstaking, conscientious, anxious ▪ Searches out errors and omissions ▪ Delivers on time	▪ Inclined to worry unduly ▪ Reluctant to delegate
Relation-ships	Teamworker	▪ Co-operative, mild, perceptive, diplomatic ▪ Listens, builds, averts friction	▪ Indecisive in crunch situations
	Coordinator[2]	▪ Mature, confident, a good chairperson ▪ Clarifies goals, promotes decision-making, delegates well	▪ Can often be seen as manipulative ▪ Offloads personal work
	Resource Investigator	▪ Extravert, enthusiastic, communicative ▪ Explores opportunities ▪ Develops contacts	▪ Over-optimistic ▪ Loses interest once initial enthusiasm has passed

Source: adapted from Belbin (2012)

Belbin asserts that teams are balanced when all nine of the roles in his model are represented at the 'natural' level[3]. Since many or

---

[1] Called 'company worker' in earlier versions.

[2] Called 'chairman' in earlier versions.

[3] According to Belbin, this means a score of 70 or above when using his *Belbin Team Role Inventory*.

even most teams have fewer than nine people on them, team members may thus fulfill multiple roles. In fact, Belbin's framework assumes that a person has a natural (or strongest) role but may also be suited for one or several additional roles.

Belbin's framework is by no means the only typology of team roles. Some authors have suggested models with as many as fifteen different roles (Davis et al., 1992). Others, however, argue that the relevant distinctions are actually much less complicated than in Belbin's model. For example, Fisher, Hunter, and Macrosson (1998) assert that the main thing is to ensure a good mix of relationship-oriented and task-oriented team members.

Regardless of which team role typology you subscribe to, it is obviously much easier to ensure a good balance if you are able to pick your own team. Unfortunately, this is rarely the case. Team-building is thus an important aspect of leadership. Fruitful collaboration cannot be ordered, but it *can* be assisted. Depending on what stage of development a team has reached, the leader's role in this may vary. In fact, all teams go through a series of phases. According to American educational psychologist Bruce Tuckman, who first introduced this model in 1965, it is both necessary and inevitable for a team go through these stages for it to ultimately deliver results.

New or significantly changed teams first undergo a *forming* phase in which the individual team members get to know one another and familiarize themselves with the challenges ahead and the corresponding goals, which may be either introduced by a directive leader or facilitated by a participative leader. Team members behave constructively but quite independently, with no strong bonds between team members yet. In this phase, the leader can support team-building by creating formal opportunities to get to know each other's personalities, strengths, and weaknesses. Possibilities range from simple introduction rounds in early team meetings to elaborate events with professional coaches and a variety of team-building and problem-solving exercises.

In the *storming* phase, personality clashes and personal opinions about each other emerge and are voiced, leading to disagreements that must be resolved before the team can move on. The leader has to ensure these do not become destructive, as the team may otherwise become so mired in conflict that it is unable to emerge from this stage. The leader's role at this stage is therefore as a moderator and creator of opportunities for reconciliation and as a provider of clear direction, which reduces conflict arising from uncertainty.

In the *norming* phase, resolved disagreements and clarified roles lead to a strong sense of unity and team spirit. All team members begin to share in the responsibility for achieving tasks and attaining goals and are able to tolerate each other's quirks and whims. The leader's role at this stage is as a facilitator of creativity and outside-the-box thinking, because the need and focus on harmony can lead to the suppression of unpopular or controversial opinions.

In the *performing* phase, the team's members have finally reached a competent, motivated, and autonomous work state in which decisions are frequently made by the whole team. In addition to participating actively in the team's work, the leader's role in this stage is as an enabler, ensuring the right circumstances for the team's success. This can include providing infrastructure, managing the workload so high-performers do not burn out, or protecting the team from political power games. Once the team has reached this final stage, naturally more directive than participative leaders can be quite detrimental to the team's motivation and performance, particularly if they also have a tendency to micromanage.

Following an analysis of research conducted since the publication of his initial article, in 1977 Tuckman added a fifth stage: *adjourning*. This occurs when the task assigned to the team is completed or reassigned and the team thus becomes obsolete, regardless of where in the team development process it finds itself. The team can then either be dissolved or merged with another team. The leader's role at this stage is both as a moderator of the closing process and the team member's personal feelings and as the supervisor and pace-setter of the administrative shut-down processes.

Note that the process of team building and development is never quite finished. Both external and internal factors may lead a team to revert to earlier stages. Most teams go through many such cycles, and the demands on the leader's ability to recognize this and adjust his or her style accordingly are therefore quite high.

Table 19 summarizes this.

Table 19: The Leader's Role in Team Development

Stage	Key aspects	Leader's role	Dangers to performance	
			...from the team	...from the leader
Forming	Team members get to know each other, the challenges ahead, and the associated goals.	▪ Direction-setter ▪ Facilitator of team members' getting to know one another	▪ Individualistic behavior ▪ Insufficient engagement	▪ Inadequate direction ▪ Obstruction of relationship building
Storming	Personality clashes, prejudices, and unclear roles lead to disagreements.	▪ Moderator ▪ Provider of opportunities for reconciliation	▪ Disruptions due to personality clashes and prejudices	▪ Participation in team strife ▪ Ignoring conflicts (and hoping they go away)
Norming	Resolved disagreements and clarified roles enable emerging team spirit and a sense of shared responsibility for achievements	▪ Facilitator of creativity ▪ Participant	▪ Lack of buy-in ▪ Rejection of emerging norms	▪ Losing sight of the big picture ▪ Failure to consider viable alternatives
Performing	Competent, motivated team members accomplish tasks efficiently and effectively	▪ Enabler ▪ Participant	▪ Fragmentation ▪ Rejection of necessary leader interventions	▪ Over-immersion ('forgetting' leadership role)
Adjourning	The task is completed and the team dissolves.	▪ Moderator of adjournment ▪ Supervisor of shut-down processes	▪ Inability to move on	▪ Glorification of 'good old days' makes it harder for team members to move on

Source: author; partly based on Tuckman (1977).

Illustration 9: Planned Highlights

At the beginning of 2017, the Department of International Business at the Zurich University of Applied Science consisted of around 50 people from 14 countries speaking more than 20 languages in addition to the lingua franca, English. In light of this diversity, the department's varied tasks (teaching, consulting, and research plus providing international services to the business school), and the fact that its offices were spread across different buildings, the department head considered that providing information and fostering mutual understanding and appreciation were key for team coherence and collaboration. Information needs were intended to be satisfied through a consistent leadership rhythm that included regular face-to-face time with all of the department's seven team leaders, a monthly all-hands meeting, and an annual one-to-one with all department members. However, team coherence was thought to be best enhanced through more informal events. The limited funds available for team events had traditionally been spent on a team Christmas event. Following discussions with the department's members, who were mostly of the opinion that the run-up to Christmas was busy enough, and considering there was already a large event for the business school as a whole, the department head decided to replace the department Christmas event with a series of smaller ones that better reflected the team's diverse origins and organization. These were augmented by an annual full-day outdoor team workshop and several smaller but regular get-together opportunities. Over time, the following list of activities emerged:

Highlight	Description	Frequency	Attendance
Outdoor team-building workshop	A day spent literally out in the woods conducting a series of team puzzles and other physically harmless but mentally challenging team-building exercises	Annually (October)	Mandatory
Intercultural evening	After-work get-together, with dinner arranged around a theme linked to one of the department's seven units, which organized them in turn. Examples included Chinese New Year, an American Thanksgiving, a Scandinavian Midsummer event, Oriental Night, and the very popular St. Patrick's Day event	About once every quarter	Voluntary
Brown-bag lunches	Learning opportunities at noon where everybody brings their own lunch and somebody introduces a topic of interest	Infrequent	Voluntary
Rooftop Friday	After-work drinks on the roof-top terrace of the main office building	Monthly (last Friday)	Voluntary
Coffee chat	Informal get-together for a coffee and chat, alternating between office buildings	Weekly (Tuesdays)	Voluntary

The motivation of individual team members and the coherence of the team as a whole can also be increased by actively creating the occasional highlight. The type and frequency will depend on the particular team and the available budgets, of course, and the importance of such events may be higher in earlier stages of team development, but highlights are always useful for generating team stories and promoting positive feelings, if nothing else. Whether this involves giving the team members a chance to unwind and let their hair down over pizza and beer, getting together for a team barbecue, or organizing a cultural event, what is important is that the activity is really seen as a highlight by the whole team, not just the leader. To gauge this in advance, you have to know your people. Even if something does not work out as planned, the fact that you made an effort will be appreciated. What is important is that you, the leader, actively think about what kind of highlights will work best with your team as well as which are compatible with company rules and then ensure that they happen with appropriate regularity. Illustration 9 provides an example.

4.52   Providing Team Guidance and Direction

When explaining the bigger picture, providing background information, or fostering a shared vision, it will often be much more efficient to get the whole team together rather than explaining everything several times. As with individuals, providing guidance and direction for the team as a whole involves setting a personal example, fostering a shared vision and shared goals, exploring and explaining solutions, establishing principles, and establishing rituals and traditions[1]. The last point is particularly important for the team as a whole; rituals and traditions, as long as they are not demeaning or exclusionary[2], can bring a team closer together and foster a sense of

---

[1] For a more detailed explanation of these points, see page 157f.

[2] An example of a negative ritual that has become an unfortunate tradition is the hazing ritual for new entrants found in many boarding schools and some armed forces.

belonging. Such rituals and traditions may be simple, such as a regular team coffee meeting or an annual team workshop, or more elaborate, such as recurring award ceremonies, joint skiing weekends, or an annual city trip the team takes together on a private basis; what is important is that they are understood and accepted by the team and that the team members do not just go through the motions out of fear or a desire to please the boss. Ideally, therefore, the team will establish its own rituals and traditions over time. However, most new teams need some help from the team leader along the way; as the leader, you have an important role in kick-starting these rituals and traditions. Providing guidance and direction is an ongoing job.

4.53   Staying on Top of Things: Situational Awareness

Although you will never know everything, making decisions depends on understanding a situation as well as possible. With specialized, big problems, that seems self-evident. But what about all the small, day-to-day decisions you make as a team leader?

It pays for a leader to stay on top of things. This means big-picture issues such as the direction in which your organization is headed, tactical issues such as what kinds of tasks might be next coming your team's way, or team-internal operational stuff such as who is underperforming, who has problems at home, or who does not get along with whom.

To increase your chances of staying on top of things, there are five key things you should do:

- foster a culture of transparency,
- keep your ear to the ground,
- earn a reputation for integrity,
- ask pointed questions, and
- keep track.

Fostering a culture of transparency is the first step in ensuring that information will reach both you and the others on the team that need it. Eventually, it will also make people come to you to actively share information rather than you having to seek them out. Usually, such a culture of transparency does not come about on its own. In fact, in a survey among mid-level managers, international management speaker and consultant Carol Kinsey Goman (2002) found a widespread unwillingness on the part of both leaders and followers to share information because of a belief in knowledge as power, insecurity about the actual value of the information possessed, a lack of trust, fear of negative consequences, and the bad example of superiors also withholding information.

Fostering a culture of transparency requires that all these issues are addressed. Clearly, your behavior as the leader will play a large role in this. First, you must explicitly declare your expectations, because while some people will no doubt exhibit the desired behavior naturally, it is unrealistic to expect that this applies to all your followers. And you also need to set an example personally. Speak the truth, even if it is uncomfortable. Share relevant[1] information regularly (unless it is *really* confidential) and avoid handing it out piecemeal. Prove to your people that you can be trusted and that you trust them; encourage them to tell you the unvarnished truth without fear of backlash. Eventually, this will contribute to an open culture that will help you stay on top of things.

Keeping your ear to the ground means being able to glean important insights by closely observing the world around you as well as being plugged into the usual official and unofficial channels of information. Sources of information can be found in all sorts of places, from publications to management retreats and from meetings over bilateral discussions to informal coffee get-togethers and after-

---

[1] To determine whether a piece of information is relevant, ask yourself if the person or persons to whom you consider entrusting it will be able to do their job better if they possess it, now or in the future. However, avoid becoming the office gossip; bosses who frequently share personal details about team members or other co-workers tend to lose the respect and trust of their followers.

work drinks. In fact, although often regarded as distasteful and unreliable, office gossip may also yield insights that help you interpret official information. The difficult thing is to separate fact from fiction reliably, but gossip usually contains at least an element of truth. Combining formal and informal statements that people consider established fact with insights gleaned from gossip and your own observations can enable you to compose a kind of mental picture from many overlapping—and frequently also contradictory—data points. Perhaps you have seen one of those pictures of a face that is actually composed of many smaller faces: not all of those ideally fit the overall image, yet together they form a clearly recognizable larger face. In a nutshell, creating this larger face out of many small faces is the essence of intelligence work. And like an intelligence analyst, a leader must acquire all sorts of information that help her or him to connect the relevant dots. Doing this requires constant acquisition and interpretation of pertinent information from all sorts of official and unofficial sources, such as books and magazines, newspapers, industry and company publications, superiors, peers, followers, and other co-workers.

Earning a reputation for integrity is clearly related to the previous point. Your personal integrity must be unquestionable if you want people to share information openly with you. Being honest in your dealings with others is a key ingredient. Another point of principal importance is keeping your word, particularly if you have nothing to gain or even something to lose from it. This includes confidentiality. Frequently, someone will only share something with you on condition of anonymity, expressly or implied. Think before agreeing to it; confidentiality limits the way you can use the information in your leadership duties. Juggling too many bits of confidential information also increases the chance of tripping up and inadvertently spilling the beans. If you agree to confidentiality in order to receive the information, you must protect it at all costs. Nothing ruins your reputation for integrity quicker than breaking your word, particularly if this has a detrimental effect on the original source or, even worse, if you clearly do it to protect yourself.

Asking pointed questions is the counterpart to keeping your ear to the ground. It is uncommon for people to tell you exactly what you need to know in the exact order and level of detail you want, and asking good questions is thus an important leadership tool. While this may seem trivial, it does take some preparation. Pointed questions are worded and asked in such a way that they are hard to avoid or answer in an ambiguous manner. For this, you need to be clear in your own mind about the purpose of the conversation. For instance, are you looking for facts or an opinion? You should also be aware of your discussion partner's frame of reference (e.g. his or her education, background, and job context) and adjust your language accordingly. This may mean adjusting the actual language, if you speak several and believe the discussion will be more fruitful in a particular tongue. It also means adjusting the language register: speaking in a way that helps your conversation partner relate to you and using terms and expressions with which he or she feels comfortable. Your questions should be focused, unambiguous, easily understood, and worded in a neutral way. Avoid asking leading questions that are designed to elicit a particular response. Try to anticipate sore spots, points or areas about which the conversation partner feels uncomfortable or insecure, and prepare probing questions or illustrative examples. Additionally, it may be a good idea to include some questions to which you already know the answer. It will help you gauge how honestly you are being answered. Note, though, that people who give you incomplete or incorrect answers may not be actively trying to mislead you. Just like you, they may base their assessment on incomplete information and, depending on their personalities, may not feel secure enough to admit they do not know the answer to the questions you ask. Therefore, the more you know and understand your discussion partner, the better you will be able to put his or her answers into perspective.

Finally, *keeping track* is crucial to really staying on top of things long term. It is a rare person who can mentally store all relevant information and access it whenever necessary, although you may know someone like that. For the rest of us, keeping track essentially means taking notes and periodically reviewing, interpreting, and updating them. Some leaders do this by keeping a journal (online or offline); others compile folders full of documents. The important thing is that you have a system and you either take notes yourself or closely supervise the process. Unfortunately, as discussed previously, a common leader attitude, particularly in business, is that the leader's job is merely to think about the big picture, while the small stuff is best left to 'underlings'. If you want to organize your team that way, that is up to you, but it is not the best way to stay on top of things. The team's chances of success are certainly not enhanced if your secretary, should you have one, is fully informed about the situation while you think grand thoughts and work on your charisma in blissful ignorance.

That is not to say that there can be no sensible division of labor between leaders and support staff in this regard, but the leader is responsible for ensuring documentation and retaining full situational awareness at all times. Depending on your skill set, if keeping track is more effectively done with the help of an assistant, then so be it. Just remember that, normally, information will stay in your head much better if you actually write it down yourself. But as the leader, you are your own judge of the level of detail at which you want to keep notes and track progress or tasks assigned and decisions made, as well as the means of transcribing and storing this and other information. For example, many leaders still keep an old-school journal. Others take notes on their tablets or laptops. What is important is that you organize these notes in a way that allows you to access them easily and to find relevant items whenever they are needed.

Among the things you should keep track of are

- decisions,
- tasks assigned to or by you,
- important deadlines, and
- other information relevant to your team's mission.

Decisions are often tracked in meeting minutes, while tasks and deadlines may be kept in to-do lists[1]. You should also keep track of information that you consider relevant to your team's mission, as well as other items you deem worthy of keeping. Ideally, this is done as soon as you become aware of it.

Figure 17 summarizes these deliberations.

Figure 17: Five Key Activities for Staying on Top of Things

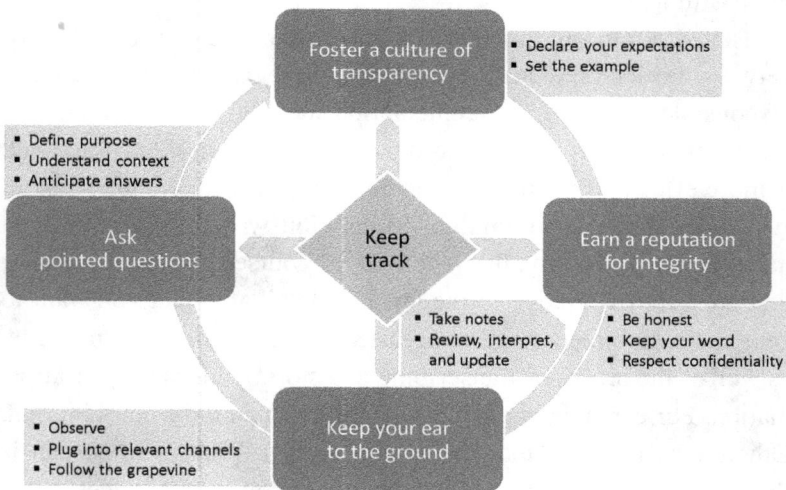

- Declare your expectations
- Set the example

Foster a culture of transparency

- Define purpose
- Understand context
- Anticipate answers

Ask pointed questions

Keep track

Earn a reputation for integrity

- Take notes
- Review, interpret, and update

- Be honest
- Keep your word
- Respect confidentiality

- Observe
- Plug into relevant channels
- Follow the grapevine

Keep your ear to the ground

Source: author.

---

[1] See Table 15 on page 147.

4.54   Setting and Enforcing Standards

Setting clear and realistic standards can help you increase team performance while simultaneously lowering your leadership workload. Standards should be unambiguously stated and measurable so that there is no leeway in either their interpretation or the assessment of the corresponding performance. In addition to content and desired outcome, other commonly defined elements include time, quality, quantity, and maximum cost expectations for specific tasks. Once set, these standards must then be enforced stringently if they are to be completely effective. Trust and your personal example play an important role in this. If someone has consistently performed well and delivered high quality in the past, you will probably also trust that person to do a good job on their current task and will give him or her considerable leeway. New entrants or team members that have repeatedly failed to meet your expectations may need to be monitored much more closely. And if you as the leader do not stick to deadlines, your team may start to wonder why they have to.

In the end, you are the judge of what you consider important to standardize on your team and how you do it. You may not be completely free in this, depending on whether or not your organization adheres to a specific management system[1]. Even if there are no such requirements, it is a good idea to think about which procedures and tasks should be standardized. Leaders are busy people, and, as mentioned above, a main function of clear and transparent standards is to lower your transactional leadership workload by reducing the time you have to spend controlling the work done by your team. Of course, some people want—or, in fact, need—to keep a much closer eye on things than others. That is a question of personality and trust. For example, more neurotic leaders have a tendency to micromanage (Seelhofer and Valeri, 2017). And if trust is lacking, a supervisor

---

[1] Examples of well-known management systems include those of the International Organization for Standardization (ISO), such as ISO 9001 (quality management), ISO 14001 (environmental management), and ISO 50001 (energy management).

will watch a particular team member more closely. Setting and enforcing standards does not fundamentally change that, but it does systematically increase the efficiency and quality of a team's work by reducing uncertainty and friction.

Among other things, uncertainty and the resulting friction may arise from unclear instructions, a lack of knowledge about the type or quality of work expected, and erratic or moody behavior on the part of the decision-maker. It can be mitigated by clearly and transparently stating

- the specific task to be performed,
- the expected outcomes (type, quantity, and quality),
- the associated milestones and deadlines, and
- all other information necessary to meet expectations.

It pays to ask some check questions after assigning the task, just to make sure these points are all understood, and understood in the same way by everyone. Additionally, it is a good idea to issue these standards in writing, with your signature. This adds gravity and increases the positive psychological pressure to conform to them[1]. At the same time, the reduced uncertainty both increases motivation and reduces the need for supervision, while the implied trust you place in the person or persons charged with the task further raises motivation. In this way, the overall efficiency and quality of the task's performance—and, in the end, overall work—is increased.

Many tasks recur, however, and you can also reduce your leadership load by issuing *general performance expectations* (GPEs)[2]. These state the above points in generalized terms for generic tasks, such as for project applications or specific reports. They may also refer to or require use of specific formats or templates. This way, once your followers have understood your expectations and are able

---

[1] Where necessary, the task assignee may also add her or his signature to the document, which further increases the pressure to perform but at the same time may reduce motivation because it may be seen as indicating a lack of trust.

[2] Often also referred to as *general performance standards*.

to perform accordingly, the need for constant supervision and explanation is much reduced. Figure 18 shows an example.

Figure 18: Sample General Performance Expectation (GPE)

GPE	4	Marketing & Sales		
Overview				
Task	Market penetration report		**Issued**	Feb. 2, 20XX
Task owner	piro (deputy: meis)		**Assigned by**	kong
Task description	Regularly compose and distribute report about state of implementation of market penetration plan			
Budget	Max. 20 hours total, no cash-out			
Timing (due/milestones)	H (published/sent out): March 31, June 30, Sept. 30, Dec. 20. Milestones: 1. First draft to head of Marketing & Sales: H – 1 week 2. Annotation with answers to board questions: H + 2 weeks			
Expected outcome				
Type	Report (email)		**Quantity**	1-3 pages
Recipients	Executive board members		**CC**	Department heads
Description	Activity and progress report, starting with an executive summary (max. ½ page) and then detailing: ▪ Progress made since last report ▪ Problems encountered and countermeasures taken ▪ Finances (budget spent and left) ▪ Additional resources and support required.			
Assessment criteria	1: Content and language quality 2: Professional layout 3: Timely delivery			
Quality	Content: ▪ Integration of all relevant information collected by market research ▪ Clear separation of facts and interpretation ▪ Clear marking of assumptions ▪ Logical narrative without redundancies or unnecessary meandering. Style: ▪ HTML-formatted ▪ Edited, flawless language and orthography ▪ In line with CD/CI			
Additional information and remarks				
▪ Board members served on due date; distribution to CC recipients with a one-day delay.				

Source: author.

Striking the right balance between what to standardize and what not will depend on a number of things, such as the general nature of your team's work; your own personality as the leader; your followers' individual personalities, maturity, and need for independence; and the trust that exists between you and your team. You do not want to stifle creativity and motivation, but neither do you want to have to check every single piece of work yourself to make sure each conforms to your expectations. As previously discussed, some team members will need more coaching and/or supervision than others. However, standardization should not be targeted at individual but, as the word implies, at everyone that is involved in a given task, both now and in the future.

Finally, once you have defined and communicated the standards you consider important, it may also be necessary to train your team. While this temporarily increases your own workload, it allows you to judge first-hand whether the tasks are well understood and realistic. It also enables your team members to ask questions that help them understand your reasoning, which in turn increases buy-in.

4.55   Running Productive Meetings

Meetings mirror the kind of management prevalent in an organization: generally well-run meetings indicate good management, while leaders who cannot efficiently and effectively run a meeting are not good leaders (Elsayed-Elkhouly and Lazarus, 1997).

The continuing internationalization of business has meant that electronic means of information sharing and decision-making have become more prominent. It is clearly cheaper and faster to convene a meeting via videoconferencing than face-to-face if the participants are spread across several countries. Nonetheless, running productive meetings is still a key skill for a leader. For example, a 2002 meta-study of 22 published and 5 unpublished studies that compared business (i.e. face-to-face) meetings with electronic means of coordination found that meetings were superior in their decision-making effectiveness and speed as well as participant satisfaction (Baltes et al., 2002). Although technology has advanced further since then, and collaborative tools can significantly improve workflow, decisions and orders are still best communicated in face-to-face meetings, because they allow the leader to explain his or her reasoning, answer questions, check that objectives and plans are correctly understood, and issue tasks with everyone hearing what everyone else is doing, all in one sitting. It also allows them to read non-verbal signs and subliminal messages. None of the other means of collaborative decision making, either through asynchronous communication means such as email or synchronous methods such as the phone or even video conferencing, can do all of the above, as is evident in Table 20.

Table 20: Communication Means in Groupwork

Type	Communication Means	Explain rationale	Answer questions	Ask check questions	Issue tasks	Provide record	Read mood/ non-verbal signals	Immediacy
Synchronous	Face-to-face (meeting)	Yes	Yes	Yes	Yes	Manually	Yes	High
	Group video chats (e.g. Skype)	Yes	Yes	Yes	Yes	Manually	Limited	Medium
	Web conferencing	Yes	Yes	Yes	Yes	Automatic	Limited	Medium
	Telephone conferencing	Yes	Yes	Yes	Yes	Manually	No	Medium
Semi-synchronous	Group text chats (e.g. WhatsApp, Skype)	Yes	Yes	Yes	Yes	Automatic	No	Low
Asynchronous	Social media messaging threads	Yes	Yes	Yes	Yes	Automatic	No	Low
	SMS (text)	Limited	Yes	Yes	Limited	Limited	No	Medium
	Email	Yes	Yes	Yes	Yes	Automatic	No	Low

Source: author.

Running successful, productive meetings that do not seem to be part of a surrogate social life for the initiator but serve a clear purpose depends on the following five aspects:

- Meeting rationale (purpose, goals),
- Meeting preparation (structure, content, duration, venue),
- Meeting invitation (participants, agenda, other documents),
- Meeting management (active), and
- Meeting follow-up (minutes),

Meeting rationale: ask yourself critically why the meeting is necessary. Is a face-to-face meeting really the best way to achieve your objectives? What is the purpose of the meeting? Could the same purpose be served differently, perhaps by using email or web conferencing? What are the meeting's goals? Do you want to update everyone, get progress reports, or make decisions? How should the participants prepare for it? What is the desired outcome?

Meeting preparation: define the meeting's structure and content, set a clear time limit, and define where it will take place. At this point, you should also decide who will take notes and compile the minutes and what form these should take. Content and structure are normally indicated in the meeting's agenda, which will ideally be sent out along with the meeting's invitation. If the meeting involves a mixture of information sharing and decisions to be made, do the former first so that everyone has the full picture, then deal with the decisions to be made. The meeting itself should be as short as possible but as long as necessary[1]. As a rule of thumb, meetings should not exceed two hours, if at all possible, and most good meetings will take less than 90 minutes.

You also need to decide where to meet. Although seemingly trivial, a detail that new leaders often forget is to make sure a room is available. Do you have access to a big enough office or do you need

---

[1] Of course, this depends on the specific topic and possibly the meeting frequency. Board meetings, for example, may take place only once a month but then take half a day or longer.

a conference room? How is that obtained, and who will do it? These questions need to be answered before the invitation is sent out. Finally, any handouts and documents that will be discussed at the meeting need to be prepared as well. While these may be sent out after the invitation, they should be provided early enough before the meeting that participants have time to prepare.

Meeting invitation: once these first two points have been settled, the meeting invitation and agenda can be sent out. The invitation should explain the meeting's rationale and goals and include the full agenda, which in turn should include all the relevant basic information for participants. Figure 19 shows an example of an agenda for a meeting of team leaders in a department.

Figure 19: Sample Team Meeting Agenda

Agenda Leader Team Meeting	Department of International Business		
Date	26.01.20XX	**Participants**	vepa, konti, sepp, froh, supi
Time	09.00 – 10.30	**Excused** (reason)	roml (on vacation), faul (sick)
Pages	1	**Guests** (item)	saun (3.2)
Inviter (phone)	seda (6642)	**Enclosures**	Financial report Q4

Item	Content	Who	From...to	(min)
1.	**Welcome/introduction**			
1.1	Overview/goals/duration	seda	09.00 – 09.05	(5')
2.	**Infos** (hot news, focus of activities, key problems)			
2.1	Department-level	seda	09.05 – 09.20	(15')
2.2	Team-level	all	09.20 – 09.40	(20')
3.	**Discussion**			
3.1	Contents of next strategy workshop	all	09.40 – 09.55	(15')
3.2	Product line updates: short list selection	all	09.55 – 10.15	(20')
4.	**Summary & conclusions, outlook**			
4.1	Summary of key points and decisions	seda	10.15 – 10.20	(5')
4.2	Miscellany/varia	seda	10.20 – 10.30	(10')
4.3	Next meeting	seda	10.30	

Source: author.

Who you should invite depends on the meeting's goals. Insecure leaders sometimes try to stick to a small circle of trusted colleagues or, conversely, invite anyone that might be upset about not being invited. Neither approach, however, is good for organizational efficiency. As a rule of thumb, only people who have something to contribute or will profit from the information shared or decisions made should be invited. Figure 20 displays an example agenda for an all-hands meeting in a department.

Figure 20: Sample Department Meeting Agenda

Agenda Full Staff Meeting | Department of International Business

Date	27.01.20XX	Participants	All department employees
Time	11.00 – 12.30	Excused (reason)	roml (on vacation), faul (sick)
Pages	1	Guests (item)	Trula (2.1)
Inviter (phone)	seda (6642)	Enclosures	New HR Compensation Policy (2.1)

Item	Content	Who	From...to	(min)
1.	**Welcome/introduction**			
1.1	Overview/goals/duration	seda	11.00 – 11.05	(5')
2.	**Infos** (hot news, focus of activities, key problems)			
2.1	Corporate-level	seda	11.05 – 11.10	(5')
2.1	Division-level	seda	11.10 – 11.20	(10')
2.1	Department level	seda	11.20 – 11.35	(15')
3.	**Team reports**			
3.1	Staff unit	Team leader	11.35 – 11.40	(5')
3.2	Product team 1	Team leader	11.40 – 11.45	(5')
3.3	Product team 2	Team leader	11.45 – 11.50	(5')
3.4	Product team 3	Team leader	11.50 – 11.55	(5')
3.5	Product team 4	Team leader	11.55 – 12.00	(5')
4.	**Input**			
4.1	Team 3: New product line initiative	Team leader	12.00 – 12.15	(5')
5.	**Outlook**			
5.1	Miscellany/varia	Seda	12.15 – 12.25	(10')
5.2	Planned absences	Seda	12.25 – 12.30	(5')
5.3	Next meeting	seda	12.30	

Source: author.

The invitation is still often sent by email, although groupware tools[1] can make the process more efficient. You should also state how the participants are expected to prepare for the meeting. Although it could be sent in any form, the agenda is often included as an email or calendar attachment so that the participants can print a standardized, formatted version to bring to the meeting.

---

[1] Examples include project management systems (in which the meeting is just part of the project workflow) and more generic workflow systems (which allow collaborative management of documents and tasks).

Meeting management: no two meetings are exactly alike. Nonetheless, the following basic structure generally works quite well:

1. Open the meeting by welcoming everyone and thanking them for attending.
2. Remind everyone of the meeting's purpose and goals.
3. Go through a quick introduction round, if not all participants know each other yet. Name tags may also be a good idea in such a case.
4. If necessary or applicable, review and formally accept the last meeting's minutes and review the team's to-do list.
5. Review the agenda. If there is time and you think it is appropriate, ask if there are any additional items that should be discussed at the end of the meeting.
6. Go through the agenda items one by one. Provide a short summary of the main points discussed and any decision taken at the end of each item. This will make it easier for the participants to remember them, and it will also make it easier for you or the person taking notes to compile the meeting minutes later on.
7. Deal briefly with additional items requested by participants (see point 4). This part of the meeting is usually listed in the agenda as 'varia' or 'miscellany' and should normally take no more than fifteen minutes. If it turns out that an item will require a full-blown discussion, defer it to a separate meeting.
8. Go around the table, specifically addressing each participant and dealing with any further questions they may have.
9. Summarize the meeting's key outcomes (making sure all participants understand them in the same way), state any new additions to the to-do list, and define the next steps.
10. If necessary, determine the date, time, and location for the next meeting.
11. Close the meeting.

Meetings have a tendency to get out of hand if not actively managed. Depending on the individual participants' personalities, some will try to dominate the proceedings, while others will avoid potential conflict at any cost. As the inviter, you will normally lead the participants through the agenda items, moderate the discussion, and summarize the findings, consensus, or decisions at the end. You will have to strike a sensible balance between staying on course, which may necessitate cutting some endless, circular discussions short, and allowing everyone who has something to contribute to speak. If you fulfill your role too aggressively, people might feel they lost face and be upset or demotivated, but if you are too passive, the meeting will invariably veer off course and take much longer than announced. This is a matter of experience, as is setting realistic time slots for the various agenda items. If you are a new leader, err on the side of caution and assign generous time slots. It is also a good idea to factor in a time reserve of ten to fifteen minutes at the end. There are usually no complaints if a meeting ends earlier than planned, whereas meetings that run on too long are rarely seen in a positive light.

As the meeting manager, always arrive a little early and expect the participants to be on time, too. Stick to the agenda; after all, you put a lot of thought into it. Do not tolerate side conversations, but be friendly when you ask people to focus on the topic at hand. Lead and moderate the meeting actively, but do not try to impose your personal opinion, and make sure everyone is heard. In other words, your opinion matters and should be voiced just as those of the other participants, but it should be clearly separated from your role as meeting manager. In general, it is a good idea when asking for opinions from participants to let the youngest or most junior members go first and then work upwards by seniority. In this way, these participants are less influenced by what they believe their more senior or older colleagues want to hear, and you will get more honest input. The downside is that this can appear quite formalistic and hierarchical to the participants, particularly on teams with a very egalitarian culture, such as expert teams. It also brings the added danger of each realizing their place in your mental pecking order, with corresponding potentially negative effects for motivation. This can be dealt with by assigning seating by age and/or seniority. Then, if you ask for opinions, you can just go around the table, which may seem more natural. Of course, participants may figure out the reason for the seating arrangements, particularly if this is not commonly done in your organization, which will then leave you in the same position as before. You must judge whether this approach makes sense in a given situation and whether you should explicitly mention what you are doing or not.

Finally, depending on how experienced your team is in working together, it may be a good idea to briefly review the meeting performance at the end. Was the agenda distributed early enough to allow everyone to prepare properly? Did they actually do so? Was there enough time for discussion of the various items on the agenda? How efficient and effective was the meeting? Taking a bit of time to answer these and similar questions may help to improve meeting performance.

Meeting follow-up: the minutes (i.e. the summary of key findings and decisions) should be distributed to the participants within a reasonable amount of time after the meeting[1]. Following their distribution, there is usually a defined period for correction of any errors, omissions, or ambiguities before they are considered final. In the case of more formal meetings, such as board or committee meetings, these may also have to be formally accepted by the participants, either by (usually written) consent or following their formal discussion during a subsequent meeting[2].

Not every meeting requires minutes. For example, if an all-hands meeting takes place regularly and its purpose is simply to update

---

[1] While the definition of what is 'reasonable' depends on factors such as the meeting's duration and circumstances or the workload of the person or persons compiling the minutes, there should be a clearly communicated standard. One widely used benchmark is four days.

[2] This is normally done at the beginning of the meeting, right after the introduction.

everyone, you may decide to dispense with the minutes. If you discuss anything that is important or unique enough to warrant a written record, however, minutes are a must. They should be as brief as possible but as long as necessary. A basic decision to be made in advance is what purpose they need to serve and what level of detail is required. Do they need to be a verbatim transcript of everything that was said, as in some legal proceedings, for example, should they summarize all relevant information about the meeting and its content in a way that people can understand everything without the need to consult further documents, or is a summary of decisions sufficient? Depending on your requirements, preparation for the minutes before and during the meeting will vary. If you need a verbatim transcript, you will normally need either the services of a specialist (such as a stenographer) or an audio or video recording of the meeting, coupled with specialist speech-to-text software and additional editing work.

If you only need a record of decisions made, you will most likely be able to write the minutes right during the meeting, without additional help. If so, you can then project your notes directly onto a screen in the meeting room, if a digital projector is available. This allows the meeting's participants to read along with what you write and voice any objections or suggestions right there and then. In this way, the minutes are ready and accepted by the end of the meeting.

The most common form of minutes, however, is in between these two extremes, containing a summary of key information and findings and including a description of each discussion item. This type of minutes takes longer to compile than a mere decision protocol, but it is much faster than a verbatim transcript and can be produced even more efficiently by preparing it as far as possible before the meeting. Specifically, information such as date, time, venue, and participants and a brief introduction to each discussion item can be entered beforehand, with additional empty space allocated to later describing key outcomes and decisions taken. These can then be filled in during the meeting itself, which will facilitate speedy completion and distribution of the minutes after the meeting. The easiest form to do this is in table format. Figure 21 shows an example. It is based on the agenda for the leader team meeting introduced in Figure 19[1].

Figure 21: Sample Pre-Prepared Meeting Minutes

Minutes Leader Team Meeting | Department of International Business

Meeting Date	26.01.20XX	Participants	vepa, konti, sepp, froh, supi
Time	09.00 – 10.30	Excused (reason)	roml (on vacation), faul (sick)
Pages	3	Guests (item)	saun (3.2)
Inviter (phone)	seda (6642)	Linked documents	Financial report Q4
Compiled by	seda	Date of acceptance	31.01.20XX

Item	Content	Content	Decisions and key findings
1.	Welcome/introduction		
1.1	Overview/ goals/duration	...	...
2.	Infos (hot news, focus of activities, key problems)		
2.1	Department-level	...	...
2.2	Team-level	...	...
3.	Discussion		
3.1	Contents of next strategy workshop	...	...
3.2	Product line updates: short list selection	...	...
4.	Summary & conclusions, outlook		
4.1	Summary of key points and decisions	...	...
4.2	Miscellany/ varia		...
4.3	Next meeting	...	...

Source: author.

As with the decision protocol, if you project this during the meeting, participants can voice their objections and suggestions directly. This will significantly reduce the number of corrections to the minutes after the meeting.

While not a foolproof guarantee for success, following these tips and principles will help you hold effective and efficient meetings.

---

[1] See page 188.

4.6   Chapter Recap

What you should take away from this chapter:

1. The Integrated Functional Leadership model consists of four key leadership responsibilities (achieving tasks and missions; leading yourself; leading the team; and leading the individual team members), six key practices (providing guidance and direction; setting the positive example; developing and sustaining presence and resilience; motivating and inspiring; showing real interest and consideration; and enabling, stimulating, and challenging), and nine key functions (analyzing; deciding; planning; initiating; controlling; supporting; informing; evaluating; and rewarding).

2. A mission is an important general assignment that aims at securing a specific desired outcome, while a task is a specific piece of work to be completed.

3. Getting the job done (i.e. achieving tasks and missions) depends on three elements: the right skills (leadership, management, job-related, conceptual), the right attitude, and the right timing.

4. The four basic conceptual skills are analysis, thinking in options, concept definition, and plan development.

5. Fostering the right attitude to complete tasks and missions depends on seven aspects: a sense of mission, a spirit of cooperation, goal orientation, service orientation, quality orientation, performance orientation, and reciprocal trust.

6. The one-third/two-thirds rule holds that a superior (unit) should use no more (and preferably less) than one third of the overall net available time for a task or mission before passing orders or assignments and properly divided associated tasks down the line.

7. The key question in time planning is: When do we have to act in what way with what speed for how long and using which resources?

8. In essence, time planning consists of five steps: identifying and allocating the overall net amount of time and person hours available, identifying and assessing the (sub-)tasks to be performed, identifying and prioritizing the relevant internal and external milestones, crafting an internal and external time plan, and constantly monitoring and regularly updating the time plan.

9. The internal time plan minimally includes all team milestones, while the external time plan accounts for major events related to important stakeholders and events and deadlines at the superior and subordinate level.

10. Leading yourself involves five main challenges: developing and sustaining your leadership presence, developing and sustaining your resilience, setting the positive example, developing your emotional and social intelligence, and structuring your work and off-time.

11. The four basic leader interaction roles—the roles you will variously fulfill, depending on situational needs—are teacher/coach, facilitator/enabler, conflict manager, and challenger/enforcer.

12. The five main challenges when leading individual team members are motivating and inspiring; providing individual guidance and direction; enabling, stimulating, and challenging; showing real interest and consideration; and setting an appropriate leadership rhythm.

13. The five key elements of team leadership are building and developing the team, providing team guidance and direction, staying on top of things, setting and enforcing standards, and running productive meetings.

14. Successful team work depends on four factors: the existence of mutual goals, parity among participants, shared responsibility for participation and outcomes, and sharing of resources among team members.

CHECK QUESTIONS

Try to answer the questions below. If you need help, check the sample answers in the annex.

1. What are your main responsibilities as a leader?
2. What are the nine transactional leader functions?
3. What are the six transformational leadership key practices?
4. What is the key rationale for thinking in options?
5. What is a concept?
6. Why should identifying and allocating the overall net amount of time and person hours available be the first step in time planning when under time pressure?
7. What are buffer times, and why are they important?
8. How can you develop your leadership presence?
9. Which four elements contribute to improving your resilience?
10. What are four key components for motivating team members?
11. What is the core premise of Herzberg's theory of motivation?
12. When completing a task, which other two factors must be in balance with the demands of this task?
13. Belbin's nine team roles are grouped into three classes of three roles each, based on three differing basic concerns (or orientations). What are these concerns?
14. What are the five stages in Tuckman's team development model?

4.7　Exercises

On the following pages, you will find various exercises related to the content of this chapter. If you need help, check the sample solutions in the annex.

Exercise 12 Core Leadership Functions and Responsibilities

Reflecting on your own leadership and that of others, identify and discuss at least one specific example of an important leader activity for each core function of leadership and for each of the core leader responsibilities, and fill in the table below.

Core functions of leadership	Core leader responsibilities			
	Accomplish the task	Manage your-self	Manage the team	Manage indi-viduals
Analyzing				
Deciding				
Planning				
Initiating				
Controlling				
Supporting				
Informing				
Evaluating				
Rewarding				

Exercise 13 Exemplary Leadership Practices

Reflect on which particular leader traits and behaviors are required for each of the core leader practices identified in Chapter 4 and fill in the table below. Provide an example of a leader you believe demonstrates or has demonstrated those traits in exemplary fashion.

Key leader practices	Supporting leader traits & behaviors	Leader examples
Provide guidance and direction		
Set a positive example		
Develop and sustain presence and resilience		
Motivate and inspire the team and followers		
Show real interest and consideration		
Enable, stimulate, and challenge.		

Exercise 14 Personal Leadership and Leadership Presence

Reflect on your own real, planned, or envisioned leadership abilities and fill in the table below.

Personal leadership area	Self-view ("where am I now?")	Development activities to get ready for an existing, planned, or envisioned leadership position ("where do I need to be?")
Developing technical know-how and skills		
Cultivating the right attitude towards other people		
Working on psychological self-mastery		

Exercise 15 Testing Your Personality

A prerequisite for solid leadership is realistic self-assessment. Personality tests have been developed to identify a person's personality type. These are based on established empirical insights and use standardized rating scales. To understand how such tests work and, provided you are new to personality testing, to potentially gain additional insights or food for thought about your own personality type, complete the following free online personality tests:

- *16 Personalities* (using the same system and background as the Myers-Briggs Type Indicator): www.16personalities.com
- *The TypeFinder* (also based on the Myers-Briggs Type Indicator): www.truity.com/test/type-finder-research-edition
- *The Big Five Personality Test* (based on the Big Five personality factors): www.truity.com/test/big-five-personality-test

For best results, it is paramount that you answer as truthfully as possible. Results are for you alone and will not be discussed in groups. Once you are finished, answer the questions below:

1. According to the tests, what personality type are you?
2. Were the results consistent across tests? If not, do you have any idea why not?
3. Are the results in line with your self-view? Were there aspects with which you disagree? Why?

Exercise 16   Measuring Your Resilience

Resilience describes a person's ability to adapt to change, deal with stress, and recover from adversity. It is an important leader attribute whose absence can severely affect long-term leadership performance and leader well-being. Among key factors that contribute to improved resilience are a person's self-confidence and social support and the ability to correctly identify stressors and realistically assess his or her capabilities.

Instructions

Below is a list of statements. Please read each statement carefully and rate how frequently you feel or act in the manner described. Try to answer each question as honestly as you can; you answer only for yourself. There are no right or wrong answers or trick questions. Once completed, summarize your scores for your total resilience quotient (REQ). In essence, the higher your REQ score, the higher your resilience level. The maximum score is 120.

For your orientation, the average score in repeat applications of the instrument to undergraduate and graduate students was around 85, with men generally showing slightly higher resilience than women. Broken down into quartiles, scores might be interpreted as follows:

- High resilience: 91 to 120
- Moderate resilience: 61 to 90
- Limited resilience: 31 to 60
- Low resilience: 0 to 30

Please note that this interpretation is not scientifically validated.

The questionnaire below can be used to gauge your own current resilience levels as well as those of your followers. Its efficacy depends on honest reflection and complete openness when selecting the appropriate answer to each question.

#	Determinant	Your Answer				
		Almost always	Frequently	Occasionally	Rarely	Hardly ever
1	I generally have a positive view of life and consider myself an optimist	4	3	2	1	0
2	I often feel stressed	0	1	2	3	4
3	I frequently discuss their roles and what they entail with my subordinates	4	3	2	1	0
4	Sometimes I cannot force myself do things even if I know I should do them	0	1	2	3	4
5	I tend to take things one day at a time	4	3	2	1	0
6	I do not have anyone who supports me mentally and emotionally	0	1	2	3	4
7	I take regular rejuvenating breaks, even if they are just short ones	4	3	2	1	0
8	I rarely discuss their and my own expectations with my superiors	0	1	2	3	4
9	I generally have a good understanding of what causes me stress	4	3	2	1	0
10	Sometimes I do not have enough energy to do what I know I have to do	0	1	2	3	4
11	I feel proud that I have accomplished important things in my life	4	3	2	1	0
12	I tend to worry about possible problems in the future	0	1	2	3	4
13	Once I have set my mind to a task, I always see it through	4	3	2	1	0
14	I feel that I cannot handle many issues at the same time without getting overwhelmed	0	1	2	3	4

#	Determinant	Almost always	Frequently	Occasionally	Rarely	Hardly ever
15	When things do not go as planned, I always find a way to get them back on track	4	3	2	1	0
16	I consider myself lacking in self-discipline	0	1	2	3	4
17	I normally have no problems accepting changed circumstances and adapt quickly	4	3	2	1	0
18	I do not get around to regularly working out	0	1	2	3	4
19	I feel that I have a clear and realistic understanding of my strengths and weaknesses	4	3	2	1	0
20	I rarely ask for help even if I know I would need it	0	1	2	3	4
21	I frequently discuss their and my own expectations with my subordinates	4	3	2	1	0
22	I tend to take a long time to bounce back if something really gets to me	0	1	2	3	4
23	My belief in myself gets me through hard times	4	3	2	1	0
24	My self-view of strengths and weaknesses is not always in line with outside feedback	0	1	2	3	4
25	I have someone or several people that I can always rely on, no matter what	4	3	2	1	0
26	I frequently worry that I might not be up to a task	0	1	2	3	4
27	In an emergency, I am someone others can rely on	4	3	2	1	0
28	I tend to dwell on things even if I cannot change them	0	1	2	3	4
29	I enjoy challenging my mind and actively seek opportunities to do so	4	3	2	1	0
30	I do not have a healthy work-life balance	0	1	2	3	4

Source: author; partly based on Seelhofer and Valeri (2017).

Exercise 17 Measuring Your Empathy

Empathy is a highly important leader attribute that can significantly increase leadership performance. However, extremely high levels of empathy may actually decrease your performance, because others' negative emotions can drag you down. Measuring your empathy levels and reflecting on them is thus an important part of leading yourself. The question is how empathy can be reliably measured.

Chartered psychologist Simon Baron-Cohen and his colleague Sally Wheelwright of the University of Cambridge in the United Kingdom developed a 60-item questionnaire designed to measure empathy in adults, the Empathy Quotient (EQ). It has been widely used to measure empathy in a variety of settings (Baron-Cohen and Wheelwright, 2004), and the full version is available online[1].

Based on a review of widely accepted empathy scales, Canadian researchers Nathan Spreng, Margaret McKinnon, Raymond Mar, and Brian Levine developed the Toronto Empathy Questionnaire (TEQ), a short 16-item measurement tool that was shown to correlate closely with Baron-Cohen's and Wheelwright's much longer version (Spreng et al., 2009). It has been used in different cultural contexts and has been shown to be a short but reliable instrument with high internal consistency and construct validity.

As previously discussed[2], empathy can be increased through reflection and experience, but it can also be actively trained. Additionally, positively empathic role models can inspire higher levels of empathy in followers. In other words, if you display sufficient levels of empathy, this will rub off on your followers, which can be particularly important if they also have leadership duties that contribute to overall performance.

---

[1] E.g. at https://psychology-tools.com/empathy-quotient
[2] See section 0.

Instructions

Below is a list of statements. Please read each statement carefully and rate how frequently you feel or act in the manner described. Try to answer each question as honestly as you can; you answer only for yourself. There are no right or wrong answers or trick questions. Once completed, summarize your scores for your total TEQ score. In essence, the higher your TEQ score, the higher your empathy levels. The maximum score is 64.

For your orientation, the average score in several studies[1] of healthy young adults using the TEQ instrument was around 45 (Spreng et al., 2009; Totan, Doğan, and Sapmaz, 2012), with women generally showing slightly higher empathy than men (47 vs. 44).

Broken down into quartiles, scores might be interpreted as follows:

- High empathy: 49 to 64
- Moderate empathy: 33 to 48
- Limited empathy: 17 to 32
- Low empathy: 0 to 16

Please note that this interpretation is not scientifically validated.

The questionnaire below can be used to gauge your own current empathy levels as well as those of your followers. Its efficacy depends on honest reflection and complete openness when selecting the appropriate answer to each question.

---

[1] See Spreng et al. (2009).

#	Determinant	Almost always	Frequently	Occasionally	Rarely	Hardly ever
				Your Answer		
1	When someone else is feeling excited, I tend to get excited, too.	4	3	2	1	0
2	Other people's misfortunes do not disturb me much.	0	1	2	3	4
3	It upsets me to see someone being treated disrespectfully	4	3	2	1	0
4	I remain unaffected when someone close to me is happy	0	1	2	3	4
5	I enjoy making other people feel better	4	3	2	1	0
6	I have tender, concerned feelings for people less fortunate than me	4	3	2	1	0
7	When friends talk about their problems, I try to steer the conversation towards something else	0	1	2	3	4
8	I can tell when others are sad even when they do not say anything	4	3	2	1	0
9	I find that I am in tune with other people's moods	4	3	2	1	0
10	I do not feel sympathy for people who cause their own serious illnesses	0	1	2	3	4
11	I become irritated when someone cries	0	1	2	3	4
12	I am not really interested in how other people feel	0	1	2	3	4
13	I get a strong urge to help when I see someone who is upset	4	3	2	1	0
14	When I see someone being treated unfairly, I do not feel very much pity for them	0	1	2	3	4
15	I find it silly for people to cry out of happiness	0	1	2	3	4
16	When I see someone being taken advantage of, I feel kind of protective towards him/her.	4	3	2	1	0

Source: adapted from Spreng et al. (2009).

Exercise 18 Checking Your Team's Balance

Reflect on your own leadership and your team. If you do not currently lead a team, refer to the situation described in Exercise 7 on page 111 and use the description of those team members to complete the exercise.

British researcher and management theorist Raymond Meredith Belbin developed his famous typology of team roles (see Table 18 on page 197) during the 1970s. It remains one of the most widely used frameworks to assess the composition of management teams. Complete use of the typology depends on a 360-degree assessment of the various team members. Assuming that you as the leader know your team members very well, you can conduct a rough assessment of your team's balance by simple reflection.

Instructions

Enter the names of your team members in the table below. Then go through the table on page 197 and think honestly about each of them. What are their natural roles? What other roles are they able to assume if necessary? What are their strengths and weaknesses?

If you believe that a particular role corresponds to a team member's natural role, enter 'N'. If that team member can assume any of the other roles if necessary, enter 'A' into the respective field. Once you have completed this process, check if all team roles are represented[1]. Enter 'Y' (for 'yes') in the corresponding field if the role is represented as a natural role, 'P' (for 'partially') if it is represented as a secondary role, and 'N' (for 'no') if it is not represented.

---

[1] Note that Belbin assumed a team to be balanced only if all nine roles were represented as the natural role of team members. Since most teams are smaller than nine (often as small as three or four) and people tend to have only one or two natural roles, you may relax this assumption; and aim for balance in the representation of all nine team roles, either as people's natural role or as a secondary role they may assume if necessary.

Team Members	Belbin's Team Roles (N=natural role of team member; A=role may be assumed if necessary)								
	Plant	Specialist	Monitor/ Evaluator	Implementer	Shaper	Completer/ Finisher	Teamworker	Coordinator	Resource Investigator
1									
2									
3									
4									
5									
6									
7									
8									
9									
10									
11									
12									
Represented? (Yes/Partially/No)									
Take-aways/ comments	1								

Exercise 19 Checking Your People's Motivation

Reflect on your own leadership and your team. If you do not currently lead a team, refer to the situation described in Exercise 7 on page 111 and use the description of those team members to complete the exercise.

Fredrick Herzberg's Two-Factor Theory asserts that motivation depends on two sets of factors: hygiene factors such as pay, status, and working conditions, and motivational factors such as meaningful work, recognition, and a sense of achievement. If you have people on your team who are obviously demotivated, it pays to get to the bottom of this, because a team is more than the sum of its parts, and motivated team members contribute to superior performance.

Instructions

Enter the names of your team members in the form below. Then determine for each member if you believe that person is currently satisfied and motivated. If so, then go to the next person. If not, then answer the remaining questions on the right and add any comments (e.g. rumors you have heard, bits and pieces of information you have gathered in the coffee room, things the person said to you in the past, and so on) you believe are relevant to the current situation.

This exercise can contribute to your preparation before discussing these issues with the affected team members.

| Person seems to be overall 2: mostly satisfied 1: somewhat dissatisfied 0: highly dissatisfied | Person seems to be dissatisfied with... A: pay; B: status; C: security; D: working conditions; E: fringe benefits; F: bureaucratic procedures; G: team relations O: other (please specify) | Person seems to be overall 2: mostly motivated; 1: somewhat unmotivated; 0: highly unmotivated | Person seems to be demotivated by lack of... A: meaningful work, B: challenging tasks; C: recognition; D: sense of achievement; E: increased responsibility; F: opportunities for personal growth O: other (please specify) |

Team Members	Satisfaction	Dissatisfiers	Motivation	Demotivators	Comments
1					
2					
3					
4					
5					
6					
7					
8					
9					
10					
11					
12					
Team overall					
Take-aways/ comments					

5 LEADING ACROSS BORDERS AND CULTURES

LEARNING OUTCOMES

After this chapter, you should be able to

- differentiate between the various types of culture that influence a person's personality, attitudes, and behaviors,
- identify areas of leadership in which culture may play a role,
- explain major frameworks of culture,
- explain which leadership traits are viewed positively and negatively around the world, and
- use the GLOBE results to reflect on your own cross-cultural leadership behavior.

5.1 The Concept of Culture

As Chapter 2 indicated, modern leadership theory evolved predominantly in a culturally fairly homogeneous setting, first in the United States and then later across the Western world. Although there are culturally contingent local leadership traditions in many parts of the world, systematic empirical research on these differences leading to frameworks that are helpful to international leaders and managers is rare and fairly new.

Understanding culture is an important determinant of success in international projects and assignments. A number of studies have found that over half of international efforts fail (Lientz and Rea, 2003; Kealy et al., 2006). Moreover, if working internationally is challenging, then leading across cultures has to be doubly so. Leadership is complex, and cross-cultural differences accentuate this complexity. When leading across cultures, problems often arise from the following four factors:

- communication blunders (both verbal and non-verbal),
- stereotypes and prejudices,
- offense against tradition and religion, and
- offense against deeply held (usually implicit) values and taboos.

Successful international managers are respectful of others, possess the ability to listen and observe, are patient and mentally flexible, show initiative, and can tolerate ambiguity (Daniels, Radebaugh, and Sullivan, 2009). Two key factors to becoming cross-culturally proficient are emotional-social intelligence and international experience. Together, they will help you recognize both potential problems in advance and when offense has been caused after the fact. Nobody can know everything, and realizing that someone reacts differently than expected is an important first step to recognizing and resolving a cultural blunder. Tradition, religion, core values, and taboos can all be studied, and culture-specific verbal and non-verbal communication can be trained. Recognizing your own stereotypes and prejudices is harder, but once you are able to see them and how they relate to your work, you will have taken an important step towards preventing unintentional cross-cultural problems. You will also need good leadership and management skills, cross-cultural communication skills, and a solid working knowledge of the particular culture or cultures in question.

So, what is culture? Like with many such terms, it can signify a variety of things. Merriam-Webster's dictionary lists six distinct meanings, relating, among other things, to the arts, agriculture, and education. What are relevant to leadership, however, are only the social aspects of culture, which the dictionary lists as follows:

- the integrated pattern of human knowledge, belief, and behavior that depends upon the capacity for learning and transmitting knowledge to succeeding generations;
- the customary beliefs, social forms, and material traits of a racial, religious, or social group;
- the characteristic features of everyday existence (such as diversions or a way of life) shared by people in a place or time;
- the set of values, conventions, or social practices associated with a particular field, activity, or societal characteristic; and
- the set of shared attitudes, values, goals, and practices that characterizes an institution or organization.

Definitions used in the management and leadership literature reflect this. Below are examples of how important contributors to the literature have defined culture.

Table 21: Definitions of Culture in the Management Literature

Authors	Definitions
Edgar Schein (1980)	"Culture is a set of basic assumptions—shared solutions to universal problems of external adaptation (how to survive) and internal integration (how to stay together)—which have evolved over time and are handed down from one generation to the next."
Fons Trompenaars (1998)	"Culture is the way a group of people solve problems and approach dilemmas. Culture is like gravity—you don't notice it until you jump."
Geert Hofstede (2001)	"Culture is the collective programming of the mind that distinguishes the members of one category of people from another."
Charles Hill (2002)	"Culture is a system of values and norms that are shared among a group of people and when taken together constitute a design for living."
House et al. (2004)	"Culture is the ability of an individual to influence, motivate, and enable others to contribute toward the effectiveness and success of the organizations of which they are members."

A number of authors have likened culture to an onion[1] or an iceberg[2] to make the concept more accessible. Just as with an iceberg, only the 'tip' of culture is visible in things like language, art, and food, while the vast majority of what defines culture—things like gender roles, leadership expectations, taboos, attitudes to power and hierarchy, ideas about friendship, and so on—is 'below the waterline' and thus invisible. And just like an onion, culture has a number of layers. Its core comprises deeply held assumptions, attitudes, and values. These lead to a next layer of norms the society gives itself and rituals that reflect these, which in turn lead to 'heroes' that epitomize and symbols that reflect them. Without peeling the onion, only the outermost layers are visible.

Commonly, two types of culture are of particular interest in management and leadership, societal and organizational culture. There are additional kinds of cultures that may influence a person to varying degrees, however, namely membership-group culture, reference-group culture, and generational culture.

Properly delineating *societal cultures* is difficult. Apart from questions such as how to define groups and at what level of analysis to distinguish between them, it is also intensely political. For example, the United States is a well-known melting pot of diverse cultures and traditions that continue to be a constant issue in domestic politics, yet there are also unique cultural traits that are universally identified abroad simply as 'American'. In India, the world's second-most populous country, 122 major languages are spoken, and six major religions[3] are practiced by more than one million people each, according to its 2001 national census. And even Switzerland, a small country of merely 8.3 million people, is commonly divided into

---

[1] See e.g. Hofstede (1980) or Schein (1980).

[2] The iceberg view of culture was originally proposed by Edward T. Hall in 1976.

[3] Hinduism, Buddhism, Islam, Christianity, Sikhism, and Jainism.

seven culturally distinct greater regions[1] and has four national languages[2]. German, the common language in the majority language area of the country, is not even widely spoken in daily life, however; instead, the area's inhabitants speak a large number of local and regional dialects which are linguistically attributed to three differing language traditions[3]. Some of them are mutually intelligible only with substantial difficulty[4]. There are also clearly noticeable cultural differences between administrative divisions, from the cantons at the federal level all the way down to individual communities. So, which is the proper level of analysis when thinking about leadership-relevant cultural differences in Switzerland?

To approach this issue, older research frequently used national culture as an easier-to-handle substitute for societal culture. However, the diversity within many countries renders this a problematic approach. Recognizing that a common language is an important factor in the genesis of distinct cultures, more recent research has tended to delineate cultures by language areas, which makes the analysis more granular, if still somewhat approximate. See Illustration 10 for an example of how geography can influence language.

In parallel to societal and national culture, *organizational culture* has been a focus of management research since the 1960s. The main premise of this line of research is that, just as geography influences the genesis of distinct societal cultures, organizational boundaries and divisions lead to distinct corporate cultures and subcultures. Geert Hofstede, the *éminence grise* of culture researchers, defines organizational culture as "the way in which members of an organization relate to each other, their work and the outside world in comparison to other organizations".

---

[1] Northwestern, Central, and Eastern Switzerland; the Espace Mittelland (literally translated 'middle land area'); the Ticino (the Italian-speaking South of Switzerland); and the Lake Geneva and Zurich regions.

[2] German, French, Italian, and Romansh.

[3] Low, high, and highest Allemanic.

[4] For example, the word for 'boy' in standard German is 'Junge'. In the Eastern Swiss dialects, it is 'Bueb' and in the Bernese dialect 'Giel' (which is actually pronounced 'giu').

Illustration 10:   Dutch in the Middle

The interconnectedness of geography and language is particularly evident in the case of English, Dutch, and German. Historically, all three are related West Germanic languages. While the grammar of modern Dutch is more similar to German, there are many Dutch words that are identical or very close to either their English or German counterparts (or both).

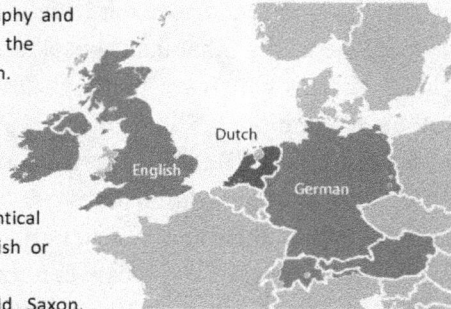

German developed out of Old Saxon, which was closely related to Old Dutch. After a shift in consonants in High German, Old High German emerged about 700 AD, and this in turn became Middle High German around the 11th century owing to increased use of German at court. Early New High German followed after further displacement of Latin as the courtly language in the Germanic territories of the Holy Roman and Austrian empires, finally leading to Modern High German after complete standardization of the written language in 1901.

Dutch grew out of the Frankish language spoken after the 3rd century BC, which evolved naturally into Old Dutch (also called Old Low Franconian) spoken between the 5th and 12th centuries and then Middle Dutch, spoken between the 12th and 15th centuries. Modern Dutch eventually followed after a lengthy process of standardization.

Old English originated from the Anglo-Frisian Germanic dialects brought to Britain by Saxon, Angle, and Frisian invaders in the mid-5th to 7th centuries BC. Heavily influenced by the Nordic language spoken by the Danes and Norse that raided and eventually settled parts of the island between the 8th and 11th centuries and the Norman conquest after 1066, the language evolved into Middle English and eventually into modern English.

Below are some examples that attest to the similarities in the three languages, with words that clearly share a common root:

English	Dutch	German
alarm	alarm	Alarm
beer	bier	Bier
better	beter	besser
book	boek	Buch
brown	bruin	braun
church	kerk	Kirche
day	dag	Tag
evening	avond	Abend

English	Dutch	German
good	goed	gut
green	groen	grün
mother	moeder	Mutter
needle	naald	Nadel
sleep	slaap	Schlaf
stone	steen	Stein
us	ons	uns
warm	warm	warm

All three languages also include a number of words of French origin, owing to the Norman conquest of England, intermittent French rule in the Low Countries, and the role of French as the *lingua franca* of commerce, diplomacy, and international relations in Renaissance Europe.

Barney (1986) refers to "a complex set of values, beliefs, assumptions, and symbols that define the way in which a firm conducts its business".

These descriptions are clearly reminiscent of the general definitions of culture introduced at the beginning of this chapter. As such, therefore, organizations may be viewed as possessing a particular kind of subculture, although they differ in the way they emerge and evolve. In line with this, national culture has been shown to be reflected in organizational cultures. For example, Trompenaars and Hampden-Turner (1997) identified four archetypes of corporate cultures[1] that were strongly influenced by societal cultural aspects.

Additionally, there are *generational cultures*. For example, Millennials[2] are supposed to bring attitudes and beliefs to work that are distinct from those of Baby Boomers[3] or members of Generation X[4].

Finally, a person may also be influenced by subcultures, both those of groups to which the person belongs (*membership groups*) and those to which he or she aspires (*reference groups*). Good examples include interest-based clubs and associations, such as political parties, sports clubs, online gaming clans, or celebrity fan clubs. All of these have distinct sets of expected behavior and often thought which are reflected in rituals and artefacts[5] and may or may not embed themselves in the attitudes and behaviors of a person[6].

Figure 22 depicts these overlapping types of culture. All of them influence how a person acts and feels. Illustration 11 provides an example.

---

[1] The four were the fulfillment-oriented *incubator* culture, the project-oriented *guided missile* culture, the role-oriented *Eiffel Tower* culture, and the power-oriented *family* culture.

[2] Millennials (or Generation Y) are generally defined as those born between 1980 and 2000.

[3] Baby Boomers are those born between about 1945 and 1964.

[4] Members of Generation X are those born between about 1965 and 1979.

[5] Artefacts are tangible objects that signify group membership, such as logos, memorabilia, and clothing.

[6] Arguably, a person may choose, say, a political party because that party already reflects his or her beliefs. However, it seems logical that group membership over time leads to either reinforcement, expansion, or modification of those beliefs.

Figure 22: Cultural Influences on a Leader

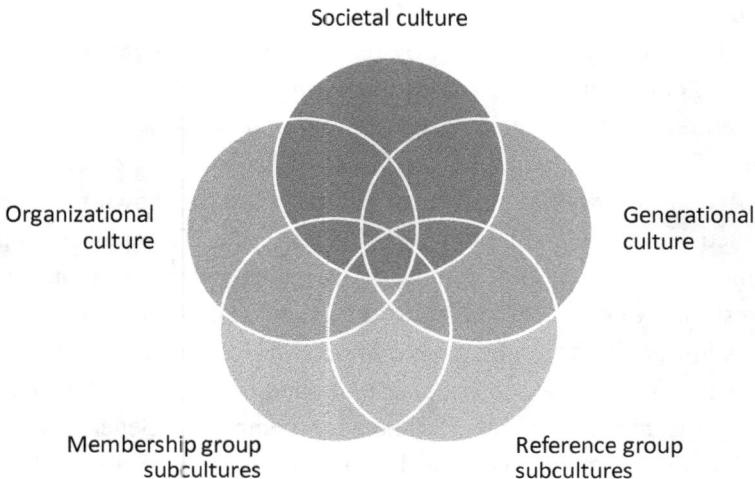

Societal culture

Organizational culture

Generational culture

Membership group subcultures

Reference group subcultures

The dominant view in psychology today is that personality is formed early but will, to some extent, continue to evolve throughout a person's lifespan (Roberts, Wood, and Caspi, 2010). Societal culture will thus influence a person's personality from childhood through adolescence into adulthood. This is the most formative part of a person's life and a time without substantial reflection on those usually subconscious influencing factors. Conversely, the influence of a particular group subculture will depend on the duration of exposure and the person's basic personality make-up, such as whether he or she adapts easily or feels a need to 'go along to get along'. The same is likely true for individual and group behaviors. In most cases, leaders and followers will come from the same organization, which reduces the disruptive effect of organizational culture[1].

---

[1] In cases where not all project members come from the same organization, the influence of differing organizational cultures can be quite evident. This is illustrated by the difficulties in integrating organizational cultures after a merger or acquisition or when working together on multinational missions that include members of different armed forces. As a small example, in the Swiss Army's German-speaking units the word *Rapport* means a meeting, while in the

Illustration 11:   Michael's Cultural Influences

Michael is a 44-year old Eastern Swiss associate professor at an internationally well-known university and an Army officer. He grew up in in the mountainous Toggenburg region and now lives in St.Gallen, Switzerland's 8th largest city and the region's center. Before his academic career, he worked in business consulting for almost a decade. Because he started his academic career rather late, he has not yet received a full professorship but clearly aspires to one. After nearly a quarter-century in the Swiss Army's part-time militia system, he has risen to the rank of colonel. He is a former battalion commander and a member of the general staff, an elite group of highly trained staff officers with extensive command experience. He has also been a keen soccer player since his early teens and currently plays for Bühler AG's senior team (FC BUZ) in the Swiss Corporate and Hobby Sport league. Although he has neither the time nor, increasingly, the energy to keep up with the younger players on the first team, he nonetheless compares his own abilities to theirs and is not always happy with himself because of that.

In summary, Michael's cultural influences are

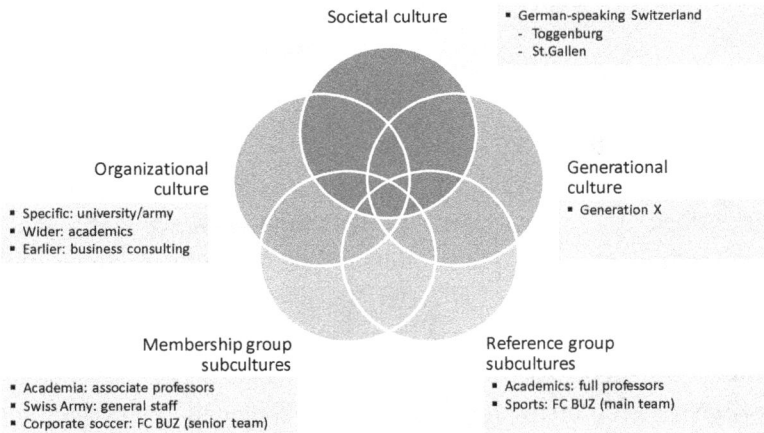

Societal culture
- German-speaking Switzerland
  - Toggenburg
  - St.Gallen

Organizational culture
- Specific: university/army
- Wider: academics
- Earlier: business consulting

Generational culture
- Generation X

Membership group subcultures
- Academia: associate professors
- Swiss Army: general staff
- Corporate soccer: FC BUZ (senior team)

Reference group subcultures
- Academics: full professors
- Sports: FC BUZ (main team)

Generational culture will normally be either highly visible, which makes it quite easy to spot, or completely absent. And group subcultural aspects tend to be compartmentalized (meaning someone will not exhibit sports club behavior at work, for example).

---

neighboring Austrian Army—which uses the same language—the exact same word denotes the result of writing someone up for an infraction or offense, something completely different.

Therefore, cross-cultural differences will arguably be the main source of potential misunderstandings and will thus be the focus of the following sections.

5.2 Influential Frameworks of Culture

Over the past decades, a number of studies have attempted to shed light on cross-cultural aspects of management and have given rise to several well-known models. Although none of these focus specifically on leadership, their findings are helpful to international leaders when forming expectations about culturally different groups of people. The most influential of these are discussed below. Explicitly leadership-oriented cross-cultural research will be discussed later in Chapter 5.3[1].

5.21 Hall

Arguably the first framework for cross-cultural management was introduced by American anthropologist Edward T. Hall in 1959. It described differing ways of looking at time. *Monochronic* managers prefer to do one task after another and assign their attention serially, because, for them, time is linear. This is reflected, for example, in the fact that these managers will typically shut the door during a meeting and not take calls. *Polychronic* managers, on the other hand, will tend to do many things at the same time and assign their attention in parallel. Time, to them, is non-linear. Often, such a manager may leave the door open and take calls throughout a meeting. As long as both leaders and followers are used to the same style, this is not generally a problem. However, mixing polychronic leaders with monochronic teams or vice versa can thoroughly frustrate both

---

[1] See page 274f.

leader and team, particularly if they are not actively aware of this difference.

Hall later also introduced the ideas of proxemics and high- and low-context cultures. *Proxemics* refers to the fact that, depending on their cultural background, individuals need differing amounts of space around them to feel comfortable. Hall divided this space into four distance zones (intimate, personal, social, and public) but suggested that differing cultures may have differing space patterns: what is intimate in one culture may be social in another, and so on. What is relevant for most leader-follower interactions is the social distance. When members of cultures used to more social distance, such as Northern Europeans, interact with those used to less, such as Southern Europeans, this can lead to (often unrecognized) friction.

Context refers to how much information is transmitted in a message. Low-context cultures tend to spell out everything that is required to understand a social situation, while in high-context cultures more implicit knowledge is required on the part of the recipient. This is manifested, for example, in how detailed contracts tend to be.

5.22   Kluckhohn and Strodtbeck

A few years later, in 1962, American social anthropologists Florence Kluckhohn and Fred Strodtbeck published *Variations in Value Orientations*, which was linked to the Harvard Values Project. The authors postulated that peoples' attitudes, in essence the building blocks of culture, are based on a relatively small number of stable values. Their *Values Orientation Theory* suggests that all cultures must answer a limited number of universal problems but that different cultures have different preferences regarding the solution to those problems, which they choose from a set of universally known, value-based answers. These questions are

- What aspect of time should be our primary focus?
- What is our relationship with our natural environment?

- How should we relate with others?
- What is the prime motivation for our behavior?
- What is the nature of human nature?
- How do we think about and use space?

The first question refers to our *use of time*. Should we focus on the past, present, or future? Should our decisions therefore be guided mostly by tradition, by our immediate needs, or by our predicted long-term future needs?

The next question deals with our *relationship with nature*. Should we try to dominate, direct, and change it, are we its powerless slaves who can only submit, or should we try to live in harmony with it?

The third question touches on our *relationships with people*. What do we prefer, lineal (hierarchical) or collateral (egalitarian) relationships? Or does that depend on the individual? Incidentally, do we prefer basically individualistic or collectivistic social structures?

The fourth question involves our preferred *mode of activity*. Is it enough to just be, to do everything in its own time and be spontaneous, without pursuing higher ambitions? Or is the main point continuous personal development[1]? Or should our main focus be on achieving tangible goals?

The fifth question deals with *human nature*. Are we basically good or bad? Or does it depend on circumstances?

The sixth and final question concerns our view and *use of space*. To whom does the space around us belong? Just us or everyone? Is it therefore public and can be used by anyone? Or is it private and cannot be used by anyone else without permission?

How members of a culture habitually answer these questions defines their culture.

Table 22 summarizes these deliberations.

---

[1] Kluckhohn and Strodtbeck calls this *being-in-becoming*.

Although not as well-known as other models of culture, Kluck-hohn and Strodtbeck's theory has strongly influenced subsequent culture research and is reflected in a number of other frameworks, such as those of Hofstede, Trompenaars, Browaeys and Price, and GLOBE.

Table 22: Kluckhohn and Strodtbeck's Values Orientation Theory

Cultural dimension	Questions (paraphrased)	Value orientations
Use of time	What aspect of time should be our primary focus?	Past, present, or future.
Relationship with nature	What is our relationship with our natural environment?	Mastery, submission, or harmony.
Relationships with people	How should we relate with others?	Lineally (hierarchically), collaterally (as equals), or individualistically.
Mode of activity	What is the prime motivation for our behavior?	Being (expressing yourself), being-in-becoming (growing as a person), or achieving.
Human na-ture	What is the nature of human nature?	Good, mixed (changeable), or bad.
Use of space	How do we think about and use space?	Private, mixed, or public.

Source: adapted from Kluckhohn and Strodtbeck (1961).

5.23   Hofstede

Dutch-born Geert Hofstede was professor of organizational anthropology and international management at the University of Maastricht and director of the university's Center for Intercultural Cooperation. In the early 1970s, he and his team conducted a study that would become seminal of work-related attitudes for IBM which produced more than 116,000 responses from sales and service personnel in over 70 countries. The questionnaires they used were translated into 25 different languages. The respondents were well matched, performed comparable jobs for the same employer, and had similar educational backgrounds in each country. The research team's main argument was that, because of this, any differences found had to be attributable to national culture. The survey was repeated four years later, with comparable results. Based on the analysis of the combined results, Hofstede published *Culture's Consequences* in 1980, a groundbreaking study of how values are influenced by culture. His framework has been widely used and integrated into other kinds of research, such as on the role of cultural distance in market entry (e.g. Kogut and Singh, 1988).

In his *Value/Belief Theory*, Hofstede originally saw culture as consisting of four seemingly dichotomous constructs he called *cultural dimensions*:

- individualism vs. collectivism,
- low vs. high power distance,
- masculinity vs. femininity, and
- low vs. high uncertainty avoidance.

Later, Hofstede added two more dimensions:

- long-term vs. short-term orientation[1], and
- indulgence vs. restraint.

These dimensions are not, however, actually dichotomous. Instead, they represent scales on which countries are positioned. For example, the USA was found to be highly individualistic and Guatemala highly collectivistic, while Argentina was between the two.

Individualism refers to how closely knit the society in a culture is. In very individualistic societies, individuals will care mainly for themselves and their immediate family, while in less individualistic, more collectivistic or communitarian cultures, individuals will tend to rely on particular membership groups, such as extended families, to care for them and protect them in exchange for loyalty.

Power distance indicates the extent to which social inequalities and an unequal distribution of power are accepted in a culture.

---

[1] Hofstede originally referred to this dimension as the 'Confucian dynamism'.

Illustration 12:   Cultural Comparison Using Hofstede's Scores

Peter Moskin is a 34-year old British manager working for a large oil and gas firm. He has recently been informed that his application to head up the company's rep office in Mexico City has been accepted, effective six weeks from now. Following his arrival there, he will be responsible for 32 employees (28 Mexican and four British). To prepare for this assignment, he examines a graph of the cultural differences using Hofstede's culture scores[1]:

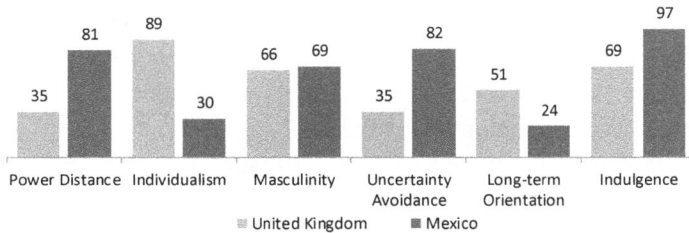

Visually, it immediately seems that there are fairly large differences in the power distance, individualism, and uncertainty avoidance of the two countries, while there are less pronounced variances in long-term orientation and indulgence and hardly any discrepancy in masculinity. Using information available at Hofstede's official website[1], Peter then compiles the following insights:

Cultural dimension	Cultural preference		Some key differences to consider about how to manage in Mexico
	UK	Mexico	
Power distance	Egalitarian	Hierar-chical	• Proper use of formal titles is important • First names only when comfort level is clear • Ideal boss is less participative and more 'be-nevolent dictator'
	Quite different		
Individual-ism	Highly indi-vidualistic	Collec-tivistic	• Loyalty is very important • Leadership style should be group-oriented • Work groups are like a kind of family • Independent thinking may be less common
	Quite different		
Masculinity	Masculine	Masculine	• Communication, meetings, and conflict res-olution, the value placed on assertiveness and decisiveness, performance, and compe-tition will likely be similar
	Quite similar		
Uncer-tainty avoidance	Low	High	• Thinking outside the box is uncommon • There is an emotional need for rules • 'Winging it' may not be accepted • More frequent communication necessary
	Quite different		
Long-term orientation	Unclear	Normative	• Traditions are very important • Quick wins are crucial
	Somewhat different		
Indulgence	Indulgent	Indulgent	• Optimism and a positive attitude are valued • Leisure time and generosity are important
	Quite similar		

[1] Source: geert-hofstede.com, retrieved 2017/06/15.

Masculinity refers to whether a society tends to prefer achievement, heroism, assertiveness, and status (which would indicate high masculinity) or whether the dominant concerns are for the quality of life, cooperation, modesty, and caring for the weak (which Hofstede attributed to femininity).

Uncertainty avoidance specifies the degree to which members of a culture try to avoid ambiguity and uncertainty.

Long-term oriented cultures tend to emphasize frugality and parsimony and particularly honor education to prepare for the future, while cultures that score low on this dimension tend to be resistant to change and to emphasize tradition

Finally, *indulgence* indicates how people deal with their urges and impulses. High indulgence would indicate that members of that culture tend to give in to these, while low indulgence would indicate restraint.

As explained, a culture will score somewhere between the two endpoints of each of these constructs. Significant differences in cultures manifest themselves as large gaps between the scores of two cultures in the same dimension.

By analyzing these differences and what they mean, leaders can form approximate expectations about where potential leadership problems may lie in an international assignment or how a group of employees abroad might react to certain management initiatives, such as performance-based pay schemes. An example is provided in Illustration 12.

It is worth pointing out that the GLOBE project[1]—which in contrast to earlier models like Hofstede's differentiated between cultural values and practices—reassessed some of Hofstede's dimensions and found that they were not consistently linked to the GLOBE values scores as would have been expected, although Hofstede's scores were generally correlated with one of the two.

---

[1] See Chapter 5 on page 246.

5.24   The World Values Survey

The *World Values Survey* (WVS) is a major research project that began in 1981 and is continued by a global network of social scientists who have conducted representative surveys in almost 100 countries since its inception. In each country, between 1,000 and 3,500 people are polled. By 2017, the project's database contained interviews with over 400,000 respondents from around the world, covering a full range of countries from very poor to very rich.

The WVS aims to identify changes in the beliefs, values, and motivations of people throughout the world and to help scientists and policy-makers understand them. It uses a rigorous research design with a common questionnaire[1] to explore people's values and beliefs, how they change over time, and what social and political impact they have. A major insight is that people's beliefs tend to play a key role in gender equality, economic development, and the emergence and development of democratic institutions and effective government.

In regular, roughly five-year intervals (called 'waves'), the WVS examines a number of aspects:

- support for democracy,
- tolerance of foreigners and ethnic minorities,
- support for gender equality,
- the role of religion (and changing levels of religiosity),
- the impact of globalization,
- attitudes towards the environment, work, family, politics, national identity, culture, and diversity, and
- insecurity and subjective well-being.

By 2017, six waves of data collection had been completed, with the seventh in progress.

---

[1] The questionnaire used in the fifth wave, for example, contained 250 questions.

The various waves have led to the interesting insight that culture groups as defined in the WVS shift over time. These shifts are clearly evident in the map's various iterations.

One outcome of the analysis of WVS data is the *Inglehart–Welzel Cultural Map.* The version based on the 2010-2014 WVS wave is depicted in Figure 23.

Figure 23: World Values Survey Cultural Clusters

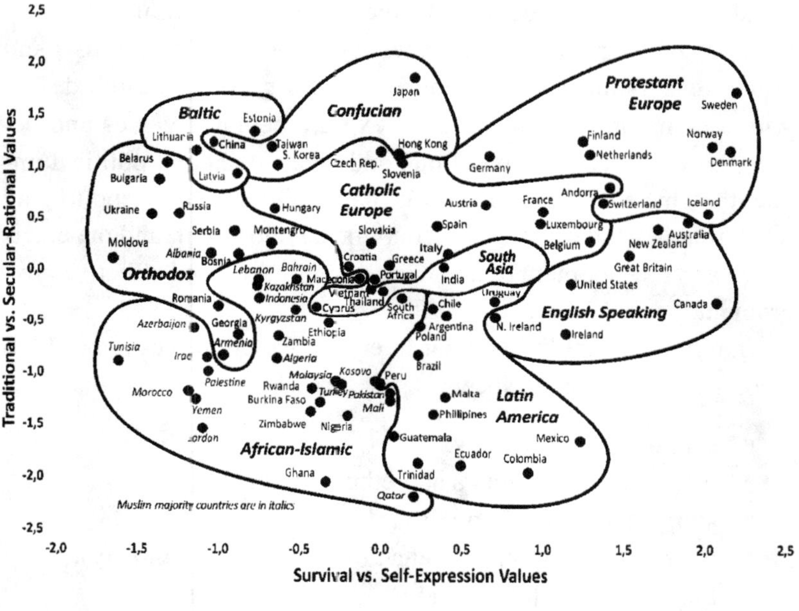

Source: www.worldvaluessurvey.org, retrieved 2017/06/24.

The Inglehart–Welzel Cultural Map is based on the concept that, in essence, there are two major dimensions of cultural variation:

- traditional vs. secular-rational values, and
- survival vs. self-expression values.

As in other models, a particular culture will be placed somewhere in between these the two extremes.

Traditional value cultures emphasize the role of religion, authority, and conservative family values. In contrast, *secular-rational* value cultures are more accepting of practices such as divorce and abortion.

Additionally, *survival* value cultures are very security-conscious, both in the physical and financial sense, while *self-expression* value cultures show a higher tolerance for immigrants, care about equal rights, and expect to participate in economic and political decision-making.

The WVS results have frequently been cited in the international press, particularly the results about happiness, and the data has been applied in various ways. For example, Inglehart and Baker (2000) used aggregate data from the first three waves to test the hypothesis that economic development is linked to systematic changes in basic values. They found that, while economic progress causes shifts away from absolute towards increasingly rational, tolerant, and participatory values and norms, the broad cultural heritage of a society—the lingering effect left by a long-lasting religion or ideology, such as Catholicism, Confucianism, and Communism—is persistently reflected in these values despite modernization.

5.25   Schwartz

Shalom H. Schwartz, an American-Israeli social psychologist and professor of psychology, published his *Theory of Basic Values* in 1992. Values, in this context, are broad motivational goals rather than attitudes towards specific actions or behaviors. According to Schwartz, basic human values can be identified by examining the most fundamental needs of humans, which he considers to be individual biological needs, the need to smoothly coordinate and cooperate with others, and the need of groups to survive and thrive. He sees these values as universal. In his original study, over 60,000 respondents in 20 countries[1] were examined using both self-report and observational instruments. Extensive empirical testing on samples from more than 80 countries in the quarter century since the study's introduction has provided further support.

Building, among others, on Hofstede's research (which he had followed closely for a number of years), Schwartz identified ten basic human values:

- self-direction,
- stimulation,
- hedonism,
- achievement,
- power,
- security,
- conformity,
- tradition,
- benevolence, and
- universalism.

Each of these ten values has a central underlying motivational goal. Interestingly, while the importance of these values differs widely between individuals, the priority ranking at the societal level (i.e. when individual ratings were averaged across all respondents from that group) was more or less the same in all countries. Benevolence, universalism, and self-direction values were consistently found to be most important, while stimulation and power values were least important. An obvious implication for leaders is that these values and their relative importance must be considered when setting policies and introducing management actions.

Schwartz further grouped these values into four categories that form a circular continuum:

---

[1] Australia, Brazil, China, Estonia, Finland, Germany, Greece, Hong Kong, Israel, Italy, Japan, the Netherlands, New Zealand, Poland, Portugal, Spain, Taiwan, the United States, Venezuela, and Zimbabwe.

- self-transcendence,
- self-enhancement,
- openness to change, and
- conservation.

Table 23 lists these groups with their values and the associated central motivational goals.

Table 23: Schwartz's Basic Values and Underlying Motivational Goals

Group	Value	Central motivational goals
Self-trans-cendence	Universalism	Understanding, appreciation, tolerance, and protection of the welfare of all people and for nature.
	Benevolence	Preserving and enhancing the welfare of those with whom one is in frequent personal contact (the 'in-group').
Self-en-hancement	Hedonism	Pleasure or sensuous gratification for oneself.
	Power	Social status and prestige, control or dominance over people and resources.
	Achievement	Personal success through demonstrating competence according to social standards.
Openness to change	Self-direction	Independent thought and action--choosing, creating, exploring.
	Stimulation	Excitement, novelty, and challenge in life.
Conserva-tion	Security	Safety, harmony, and stability of society, of relationships, and of self.
	Conformity	Restraint of actions, inclinations, and impulses likely to upset or harm others and violate social expectations or norms.
	Tradition	Respect, commitment, and acceptance of the customs and ideas that one's culture or religion provides.

Source: based on Schwartz (1992).

According to Schwartz, societies everywhere experienced the same kinds of conflicts: openness to change values contrasted with conservation values, and self-enhancement frequently clashed with self-transcendence. How societies overall resolve these conflicts— in other words, in which direction they tend to lean—is one source of cross-cultural differences.

Following up on this line of research, Schwartz developed his *Theory of Cultural Value Orientations*, a model of culture he considers distinct from others insofar as its components are seen as interdependent rather than orthogonal; they are statistically independent. At the theory's core lies the assumption that cultural value orientations emerge and evolve when societies deal with basic issues and problems of regulating human activity. Specifically, three critical questions that all societies face were considered:

1. What is the nature of the relation between the person and the group, and what are the boundaries between them?
2. How can the society guarantee that people behave in a responsible manner that preserves the social fabric?
3. How does the society regulate how people manage their relations to the natural and social world?

The cultural response to each of these issues is captured in one of three *cultural value dimensions* which provide bipolar alternative answers:

1. autonomy vs. embeddedness,
2. egalitarianism vs. hierarchy, and
3. harmony vs. mastery.

These three dimensions incorporate seven *cultural value orientations*—seven rather than six because, in the first dimension, *autonomy* actually consists of two types of autonomy, intellectual and affective. These seven archetypes of cultural value orientations identified by Schwartz are

- intellectual autonomy,
- affective autonomy,
- embeddedness,
- egalitarianism,
- hierarchy,
- harmony, and
- mastery.

According to Schwartz, the shared and opposing assumptions that underlie cultural values lead to a coherent circular structure that reflects cultural orientations' compatibility, by being adjacent in the circle, and incompatibility, by being distant in the circle. Figure 24 depicts this circular structure and provides examples of countries that score particularly highly in each value orientation.

Figure 24: Schwartz's Cultural Value Orientations

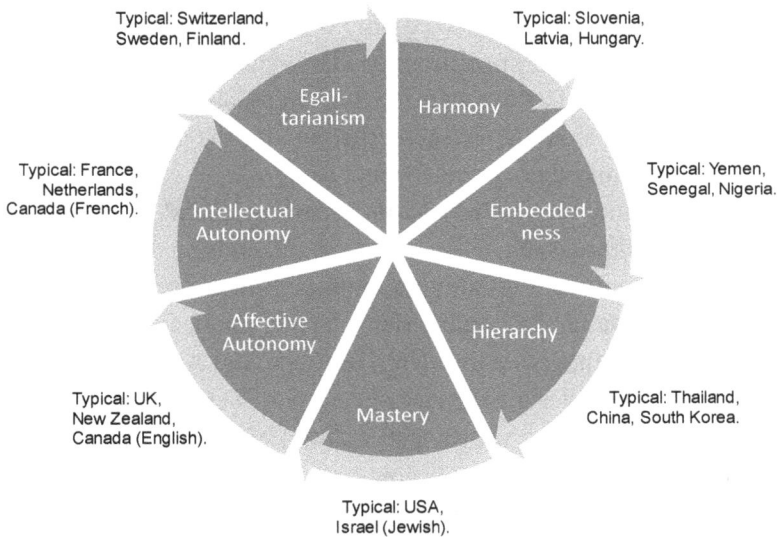

Source: based on Schwartz (2006).

Intellectual autonomy means that individuals are encouraged to pursue their own ideas and intellectual directions independently of group consensus. *Affective autonomy* refers to a situation in which individuals are encouraged to pursue positive experiences for themselves emotionally rather than intellectually. *Embeddedness* denotes a state in which a culture emphasizes maintaining a given status quo and limiting actions that might disrupt group solidarity or the traditional order.

In the second dimension, *mastery* connotes encouraging active self-assertion to direct or change the natural and social environment with the aim of reaching both group and personal goals. In other words, a prevailing attitude in these cultures is that people are the masters of their own fate as well as nature. In contrast, *harmony* cultures emphasize fitting into the world as it is, trying to appreciate and understand rather than to direct, change, or exploit.

Finally, in the third and final dimension, *hierarchy* means encouraging individuals to accept the hierarchical distribution of roles and their consequences and to comply with the rules and obligations attached to their own specific roles. The opposite, *egalitarianism*, correspondingly refers to a state in which individuals are encouraged to cooperate, to look out for each other and for the group, and to act for the benefit of others because they want to.

For example, embeddedness and hierarchy tend to appear together in a culture, such as in Ghana, Nepal, and Iran. Likewise, affective autonomy and mastery are both high in cultures such as Japan and Australia, and egalitarianism and intellectual autonomy characterize cultures like Sweden, Denmark, and Austria.

Table 24 provides a summary overview of Schwartz's theory.

Schwartz (2008) also provided cultural clusters, groups of culturally comparable societies. In contrast to most other models of culture, he developed these cultural patterns empirically rather than theoretically. Based on an analysis of his extensive data, he identified eight culturally distinct world regions:

- Western European,
- Eastern European (Orthodox),
- East Central and Baltic European,
- English-speaking,
- Latin American,
- South and Southeast Asian,
- Confucian-influenced, and
- Muslim Middle-Eastern and Sub-Saharan African.

Table 24: Schwartz's Model of Cultural Value Orientations

Underlying societal issue	Cultural value dimension	Cultural value orientation	Explanation	Important values (examples)
What is the nature of the relation between the person and the group, and what are the boundaries between them?	Autonomy vs. embeddedness	Intellectual autonomy	Encourages individuals to pursue their own ideas and intellectual directions independently.	Broadmindedness, curiosity, creativity.
		Affective autonomy	Encourages individuals to pursue affectively positive experiences for themselves.	Pleasure, exciting and varied life.
		Embeddedness	Emphasizes maintaining the status quo and limiting actions that might disrupt in-group solidarity or the traditional order.	Social order, respect for tradition, security, obedience, wisdom.
How can the society guarantee that people behave in a responsible manner that preserves the social fabric?	Mastery vs. harmony	Mastery	Encourages active self-assertion in order to master, direct, and change the natural and social environment to attain group or personal goals.	Ambition, success, daring, competence.
		Harmony	Emphasizes fitting into the world as it is, trying to understand and appreciate rather than to change, direct, or to exploit.	World at peace, unity with nature, protecting the environment
How does the society regulate how people manage their relations to the natural and social world?	Hierarchy vs. egalitarianism	Hierarchy	Encourages individuals to take the hierarchical distribution of roles for granted and to comply with the obligations and rules attached to their roles.	Social power, authority, humility, wealth.
		Egalitarianism	Encourages individuals to commit to cooperation, to feel concern for everyone's welfare, and to act for the benefit of others as a matter of choice.	Equality, social justice, responsibility, help, honesty.

Source: based on Schwartz (2006).

Table 25 provides an overview of Schwartz's cultural patterns and the cultures that belong to each.

Table 25: Schwartz's Cultural Patterns

Cultural Pattern	Countries
Western European	Switzerland, Germany[1], Italy, Finland, Spain, Sweden, Belgium, Denmark, Austria, Canada (French part)*, Netherlands, Portugal, Greece, France.
Eastern European (Orthodox)	Bulgaria, Croatia, Cyprus (Greek part)*, Macedonia, Romania, Peru*, Russia, Serbia[2], Ukraine, Turkey*·
East Central and Baltic Europe	Slovenia, Czech Republic, Latvia, Hungary, Estonia, Bosnia and Herzegovina, Georgia, Poland,
English-speaking	New Zealand, UK, Canada (English part), Ireland, Australia, USA, Israel (Jewish population)*
Latin American	Argentina, Brazil, Chile, Costa Rica, Mexico, Venezuela.
South and Southeast Asia	India, Indonesia, Malaysia, Nepal, Philippines, Singapore
Confucian-influenced	Hong Kong, South Korea, Thailand, Taiwan, Japan*
Muslim Middle-Eastern and Sub-Saharan African	Bolivia*, Cameroon, Ethiopia, Iran, Israel (Arab population), Jordan, Namibia, South Africa, Uganda, Yemen, Zimbabwe,

Cultures whose cultural pattern does not correspond to their geographic location.

Source: adapted from Schwartz (2006, 2008).

Schwartz asserts that common languages, religions, or histories likely play a role in the cultural closeness within these regions, as does the diffusion of values, practices, and institutions across national borders over time. Interestingly, however, the influence of geographic proximity may be less important than shared heritage. For example, French Canada is culturally more similar to Western Europe, and particularly France, than to Canada's English-speaking part. Likewise, the Jewish population of Israel has more in common with the English-speaking countries than with other Middle-Eastern cultures. Among other factors, this may be linked to the fact that

---

[1] Schwartz originally distinguished between the former East and West of Germany, although both were located within the Western European cluster.

[2] In Schwartz's original article, he still referred to 'Yugoslavia'.

about half of it is of Ashkenazi[1] heritage and that Palestine was a British mandate for 30 years before the founding of modern Israel.

When these clusters are seen as cultural patterns rather than strict geographic world regions, there are a few outliers whose cultures do not fit their location. In addition to the two examples mentioned above, these are Bolivia, which is closer to Muslim Middle-Eastern and Sub-Saharan African culture than the other Latin American cultures, Turkey, the Greek part of Cyprus, and Peru, which are all closer to orthodox Eastern European culture than the cultures of their geographic neighbors. Japan also does not really fit the cultural pattern of its neighbors, since its culture, although Confucian-influenced, is considerably lower in embeddedness and hierarchy and higher in intellectual autonomy and harmony.

Although innovative, Schwartz's original research was based mostly[2] on samples of teachers and students. To account for this, he also examined distinct subsamples based on age, gender, and occupation (Schwartz, 2006), with results that were consistent with the original analysis. Later research using a variety of samples also found clear support for his model, which can thus be considered well-established.

---

[1] Ashkenazi Jews (or Ashkenazim) are Jews whose ancestors settled along the Rhine in what is today Western Germany and Northern France in the early Middle Ages and later migrated into Eastern Europe. They are one of two major groups of historically European Jews, the other being the Sephardim, who emerged as a distinct group on the Iberian Peninsula around the year 1000. According to most estimates, today Ashkenazim account for over 90% of American Jews and about three quarters of all Jews worldwide.

[2] Specifically, Schwartz analyzed 88 samples of school teachers from 64 cultures, 132 samples of college students in 77 cultures, and 16 representative national or regional samples from 13 cultures, coming to a total of 55,022 respondents from 72 countries and 81 cultural groups (Schwartz, 2008).

5.26   Trompenaars and Hampden-Turner

Another well-known framework was introduced by Dutch management consultant Fons Trompenaars in 1993 and updated in 1997, together with British management philosopher Charles Hampden-Turner. In *Riding the Waves of Culture*, they introduced a construct of culture that integrated previous research and added several aspects. Their model lists five dimensions that are based on human interaction and two that are value-based:

- universalism vs. particularism,
- individualism vs. collectivism,
- neutral vs. emotional,   *Interaction-based*
- specific vs. diffuse,
- achievement vs. ascription,
- sequential vs. synchronic
  (attitudes to time), and   *Value-based*
- internal vs. external control
  (attitudes to the environment).

Individualism vs. collectivism and *sequential vs. synchronic* are closely related to Hofstede's dimensions of individualism and long-term orientation (which, in turn, are based on Kluckhohn and Strodtbeck's corresponding constructs).

Specific vs. diffuse corresponds partly to Hall's high vs. low context construct but is actually based on Kurt Lewin's (1939) Field Theory, which asserts that an individual's psychology is the result of the sum of environmental factors and that this psychology in turn influences that environment. Lewin coined the term *life space* to refer to the sum of all factors that influence a person's behavior at a given moment. Using this basic idea, Trompenaars and Hampden-Turner (1993) used the image of a peach, with soft flesh but a hard inner center, to illustrate how all individuals have an innermost, private core and a public space around it. The size of these spaces—

that is, what is considered private and what public—varies from culture to culture. One consequence of this is a variation in how strongly people differentiate between, for example, social roles: is your boss your boss only at work or also on the weekends when you meet him or her in the supermarket? To illustrate this, the authors explain that in German culture the private space tends to be quite large, while in Anglo-American culture it tends to be much smaller. Therefore, most Germans would consider such items as their refrigerator or car private, while for most Americans these would be seen as part of the public sphere. Additionally, Germans tend to not further segment these spaces, while Americans do. For an American, you may be a 'work friend' or a 'gym friend', while according to the authors friendship is friendship for most Germans, who will thus protect their private space much longer. Once you are a friend, however, you will often be so for life. American friendships tend to be much more fluid. More generally, specific cultures (which Lewin called *U-types*) tend to interact in their public spaces, while in diffuse relationships (*G-types*) the public *and* private spaces are shared. Specific cultures tend to thus clearly separate their work and private life, while the two are connected in diffuse cultures. Criticizing an idea in a specific culture is usually not taken very personally, while in diffuse cultures the idea will often be seen as representing the person, and criticism of the idea thus as criticism of the person. Without recognizing this fundamental difference, conflict between people from specific and diffuse cultures will often be almost inevitable.

Universalism vs. particularism refers to how members of a culture regard the rule of law: is it 'rules are rules' regardless of circumstances or does the social situation influence how rules are applied?

Neutral vs. emotional indicates how a culture deals with emotions, particularly in public.

Achievement vs. ascription refers to how a culture assigns status: what is more important, to achieve a doctorate and successfully complete a major project or to be the daughter or son of the company's founder?

Internal vs. external control is a construct that, at a general level, is very similar to Kluckhohn and Strodtbeck's (1961) question of humanity's mastery of the environment and, at a personal level, to Rotter's (1966) notion of a locus of control. It indicates how someone feels about the forces of nature and, by extension, life: do we, and should we, control them, or do they control us? More generally, does life just happen to us or are we the masters of our own destiny?

Like other frameworks, these dimensions allow a group of people's attitudes and values to be characterized and compared. Despite methodological questions that are occasionally raised, Trompenaars' framework has become very influential. In 1999, *Business* magazine named Trompenaars one of the top five management consultants in the world.

5.27 Lewis

Richard D. Lewis, a British linguist, communication consultant, and writer, first published his phenomenally successful bestseller *When Cultures Collide* in 1996. In it, he introduced a rough classification system for the world's cultures:

- *linear-active*: task-oriented, highly organized, cool, factual, decisive planners,
- *multi-active*: relationship-oriented, loquacious interrelators (i.e. connection facilitators), and
- *reactive*: respect-oriented, compromising, accommodating listeners.

Although highly influential, Lewis' model differs from others inasmuch as it is based mostly on his personal experiences rather than extensive empirical research. It is nonetheless a helpful framework to think about both groups and individuals, although at a rather abstract level.

According to Lewis, the root cause of cross-cultural problems is not nationality per se but rather cultural category: people from geographically disparate cultures may get along fine overall if they are of the same type, as in the case of multi-active Italians and Argentinians, or there may be constant misunderstandings and cultural tension between geographically much closer cultures, such as multi-active French and linear-active Germans. Distinct cultures may emerge based on a multitude of factors such as shared heritage (e.g. Hungarian minorities in Slovakia and Serbia) or regional geographic location (e.g. Southern culture in the United States). Overall, however, Lewis sees all of the world's cultures, to a greater or lesser degree, in one of the three categories above. Specifically, he positions them on one of three scales (linear-active–multi-active, linear-active–reactive, multi-active–reactive) that together form a triangle, as depicted in Figure 25.

Figure 25: Lewis' Model of Culture

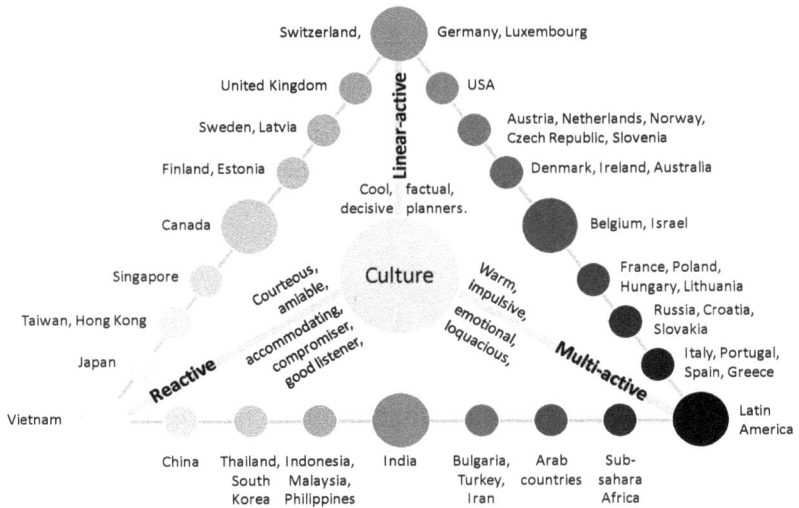

Source: based on Lewis (2006)

273

For each of the three cultural categories, Lewis mentions traits and behaviors which he considers typical, as listed in Table 26.

Table 26: Archetypal Traits and Behaviors in Lewis' Model of Culture

Trait/behavior	Linear-active	Multi-active	Reactive
Focus	Rather introvert	Extravert	Introvert
Patience	Is patient	Is impatient	Is patient
Loquaciousness	Is often quiet	Is often talkative	Is often silent
Privacy/ inquisitiveness	Minds own business, values privacy	Inquisitive, sociable	Respectful, good listener
Communication	Sticks to facts, tends to be brief, rarely interrupts	Juggles facts, can talk endlessly, interrupts frequently	Considers statements as promises, summarizes well, never interrupts
Relationship behavior	Job-oriented, unemotional, separates private from professional	People-oriented, emotional, interweaves private and professional	People-oriented, quietly caring, connects private and professional
Planning behavior	Plans ahead methodically, sticks to plans	Plans grand outline only, changes plans frequently	Looks at general principles, makes only small changes to plans
Project behavior	Compartmentalizes projects	Lets one project influence another	Sees whole picture
Process and hierarchy behavior	Follows correct procedures, respects authority	Pulls strings, circumvents authority (seeks out key person)	Networks, respects authority
Work style	Does one thing at a time, works fixed hours	Does several things at once, works any hours	Reacts, works flexible hours
Punctuality	Is punctual	Is not punctual	Is punctual
Time management	Dominated by timetables	Unpredictable timetable	Reacts to partner's timetable
Discussion behavior	Confronts with logic	Confronts emotionally	Avoids confrontation
Body language	Limited	Unrestricted	Subtle
Face attitude	Dislikes losing face	Has ready excuses	Must not lose face

Source: adapted from Lewis (2006: 33-34).

5.28   Browaeys and Price

A more recent, summative model of culture is provided by Browaeys and Price (2008). It divides culture into eight dimensions which together are assumed to capture a person's corresponding values and attitudes. All of them are taken from previous research, specifically Hall (1959), Kluckhohn and Strodtbeck (1961), and Hofstede (1980, 2001). These dimensions are

- time focus,
- time orientation,
- action,
- competition.
- power,
- space,
- structure, and
- communication.

Time focus refers to how a person prefers to work, serially (monochronic) or in parallel (polychronic).

Time orientation concerns a culture's attitude vis-à-vis the past, present, and future. What is the influence of traditions and of immediate or potential future situational needs?

Action refers to whether people prefer to *be* or to *do*. It also relates to how we gain status, through achievements or by ascription (because we are a relative of the boss, for example).

Competition means a culture's preferred mode of working together, whether competitive or collaborative.

Power deals with the acceptance of unequal power distributions and preferred organizational structures, whether hierarchical or egalitarian.

Space deals with peoples' attitude to the space around them. How much personal space around us do we need to feel comfortable? Is our care part of our private or public sphere? What about our house? What about the bedroom or kitchen? What about the food cupboard[1]?

---

[1] Specifically, can your friends walk in and out of your house like family members? If not, is it at least fine if they just turn up unannounced or do you expect them to announce their visit beforehand? The more you consider your house off-limits, the more is is part of private

Structure concerns people's preferred social organizational form, individualistic or collectivistic, and the relation between individual and group.

And, finally, *communication* can be very explicit, without relying on a lot of extraneous information (low-context) or indirect, in a way that hides the real message in what is said or written and requires knowledge of the context to understand it (high-context).

All of these dimensions correspond to constructs from earlier research, as shown in Table 27.

Table 27: Browaeys and Price's Cultural Dimensions

Cultural dimension		Origins/influence
Content	Orientations	
Time focus	Monochronic or polychronic	Hall: monochronic vs. polychromic.
Space	Public or private	Kluckhohn and Strodtbeck: space.
Structure	Individualism or collectivism	Kluckhohn and Strodtbeck: relating to others.
Action	Doing or being	Kluckhohn and Strodtbeck: structure.
Time orientation	Past, present, or future	Kluckhohn and Strodtbeck: time; WVS: tradition vs. secular-rational values.
Power	Hierarchy or equality	Hofstede: power distance.
Communication	High or low context	Hall: high vs. low context.
Competition	Competitive or cooperative	Hofstede: masculine vs. feminine; WVS: survival vs. self-expression values.

Source: Browaeys and Price (2008).

Like other models of culture, the Browaeys and Price framework can be used to compile a cultural profile of a person. The results can then be presented in a spidergram, which makes them more visually accessible. Illustration 13 contains an example.

Illustration 13: Lena's Culture Profile

Lena is a 28-year old Swiss national who has grown up in the German-speaking part of Switzerland and has been working for Migros, one of Switzerland's largest retailers, for the past six years. She is currently pursuing a part-time Master's degree in business management, and she has just been promoted to assistant manager of one of Migros' local supermarkets. Her team of sales clerks is culturally quite diverse, with the following nationalities represented: Bosnian, Brazilian, German, Italian, Macedonian, Portuguese, and Swiss. Although all of them reside in Switzerland, and about half of them have grown up there, some cultural differences are quite obvious to Lena, and she occasionally struggles with them. In her cross-cultural leadership and management class, Lena was recently introduced to the Browaeys and Price model of culture[1], and she feels it might be helpful when reflecting on her own cultural make-up. To determine where she stands vis-à-vis each dimension, she uses this table:

Value	Dimension							
	Time focus	Commu-nication	Struc-ture	Space	Power	Compe-tition	Action	Time ori-entation
1	Mono-chronic	Low context	Individ-ualistic	Private	Equality	Cooper-ative	Being	Past
2								
3								Present
4								
5	Poly-chronic	High context	Collec-tivistic	Public	Hierar-chy	Com-petitive	Doing	Future

She then plots her position in each of these dimensions, eventually arriving at the spidergram below.

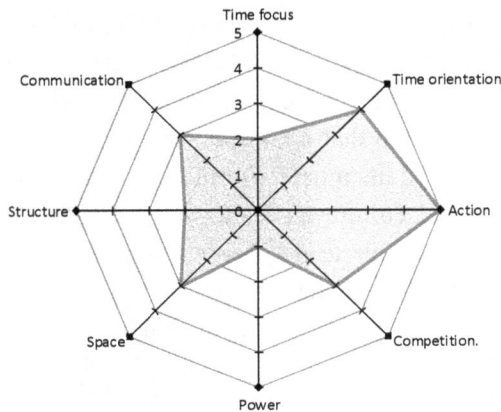

[1] Source: dimensions taken from Browaeys and Price (2008).

Note, however, that in order to do so you need either to know that person well or to have access to someone who does. Also remember that, as with other cultural frameworks, data on particular cultures derived through research cannot be applied at the individual level, only the group level.

5.3   Global Leadership

Global leadership is the study and practice of leading across borders and cultures. It is an interdisciplinary, cross-sectional academic discipline that draws on psychology, culture studies, and business and management studies. In a looser sense, general cross-cultural management research may also be counted as part of this field of study. However, specifically leadership-oriented cross-cultural research is still quite rare. The most important such study to date is the *Global Leadership and Organizational Behavior Effectiveness* (GLOBE) project, a long-term (1993-2003) effort involving over 200 researchers from 62 countries that collected data from 17,300 middle-managers in 951 organizations in the food-processing, telecommunications, and financial services industries.

Based on a mixed-methods approach that included quantitative and qualitative elements[1], the GLOBE research effort was conducted in three phases. Phase 1 involved developing measures of culture and leadership that could be used across societies. Phase 2 empirically assessed the impact of fundamental attributes of societal and organizational culture on leadership, and Phase 3 studied the effectiveness of certain leader behaviors at senior organizational levels. A projected fourth phase aims to confirm and extend previous findings and increase insights into causality.

---

[1] Specifically, a quantitative survey about societal, organizational, and leadership-specific aspects, additional in-depth interviews plus a media analysis were conducted in each of the societies studied.

Rooted in Implicit Leadership Theory (ILT), Value/Belief Theory, and Structural Contingency Theory, the GLOBE study aimed to test the cross-cultural generalizability of leadership insights and moved the leadership discussion away from individual motivations and towards cultural ones as the major determinants of international leadership emergence and effectiveness.

The project's design was based on thirteen propositions (House, Hanges, and Javidan, 2004):

1. Societal cultural values affect what leaders do.
2. Leaders affect organization form, culture, and practices.
3. Societal cultural values and practices affect organizational culture and practices.
4. Organizational culture and practices affect what leaders do.
5. Societal culture influences how people share implicit leadership theories.
6. Organizational form, culture, and practices influence how people share implicit leadership theories.
7. Strategic organizational contingencies affect organizational form, culture, and practices and leader behaviors.
8. Strategic organizational contingencies affect leader attributes and behavior.
9. Cultural forces moderate the relationship between strategic organizational contingencies and organizational form, culture, and practices.
10. Leader acceptance depends on the interaction between culturally endorsed implicit leadership theories and leader attributes and behaviors.
11. The interaction between leader attributes and behaviors and organizational contingencies moderates leader effectiveness.
12. Leader acceptance influences leader effectiveness.
13. Leader effectiveness influences leader acceptance.

A core question in culture research is the conceptualization of culture. Hall, Kluckhohn and Strodtbeck, Hofstede, Trompenaars, Schwartz, Lewis, and others all saw culture somewhat differently. It makes a substantial difference whether culture is conceptualized in two dimensions, as in the Inglehart-Welzel Map, or in seven very different dimensions, as in Trompenaars' model.

Based on the propositions above and on prior research but adding several previously neglected aspects, GLOBE viewed culture reflected in nine dimensions:

- *Uncertainty avoidance*: the extent to which a society, organization, or group relies on social norms, rules, and procedures to alleviate the unpredictability of future events.
- *Power distance*: the degree to which members of a collective expect power to be distributed equally.
- *Collectivism I (institutional)*: the degree to which organizational and societal institutional practices encourage and reward the collective distribution of resources and collective action.
- *Collectivism II (in-group)*: the degree to which individuals express pride, loyalty, and cohesiveness in their organizations and families.
- *Gender egalitarianism*: the degree to which a collective minimizes gender inequality.
- *Assertiveness*: the degree to which individuals are assertive, confrontational, and aggressive in their relationships.
- *Future orientation*: the extent to which individuals engage in future-oriented behaviors such as delaying gratification, planning, and investing in the future.
- *Performance orientation*: the degree to which a collective encourages and rewards group members for performance improvement and excellence.
- *Humane orientation*: the degree to which a collective encourages and rewards individuals for being fair, altruistic, generous, caring, and kind to others.

Again building on previous research[1], the GLOBE team then proposed so-called *cultural clusters*[2], i.e. groups of cultures that are similar to each other but distinct in comparison to other cultures outside the cluster. A total of ten such clusters were defined:

- Confucian Asia,
- Southern Asia,
- Latin America,
- Anglo (English-speaking countries),
- Eastern Europe,
- Germanic Europe,
- Latin Europe,
- Nordic Europe,
- Middle East, and
- Sub-Saharan Africa.

It is clearly apparent that they correspond closely to Schwartz's cultural patterns[3]. They are also more or less in line with the division of the world into 'civilizations' that Samuel Huntington postulated[4] in his *Clash of Civilizations* hypothesis (Huntington, 1993, 1995). While Schwartz's cultural patterns are empirically established divisions, the other two are based on theory. In contrast to Huntington's political point of view, GLOBE's aim was to examine leadership, and to do so they looked at societies (distinct cultural groups) rather than politically defined nations, like most previous research. Nonetheless, all three frameworks are quite similar.

Due to this similarity and owing to the empirical validation of Schwartz's model, the GLOBE clusters can also be considered well-established. Table 28 compares them. Countries are listed by GLOBE cluster in Table 29.

---

[1] See e.g. Inglehart (1997).

[2] The clusters were defined before the actual research began and were not a result of it. The study results, however, largely confirmed the existence of these clusters.

[3] Also see Table 25 on page 237.

[4] It is noteworthy that Huntington wrote from a political perspective, not a cultural one.

Table 28: The World's Cultures—GLOBE, Schwartz, and Huntington

GLOBE	Schwartz	Huntington
Confucian Asia	Confucian-influenced	Sinic
		Japanese
Southern Asia	South and Southeast Asian	Buddhist
		Hindu
Latin America	Latin American	Latin American
Anglo	English-speaking	Western
Nordic Europe	Western European	
Germanic Europe		
Latin Europe		
Eastern Europe	Eastern European (orthodox)	Orthodox
	East Central and Baltic European	
Middle East	Muslim Middle-Eastern and Sub-Saharan African	Islamic
Sub-Saharan Africa		African

Source: based on Huntington (1993, 1935); House, Hanges and Javidan (2004); and Schwartz (2008).

Significantly, and unlike previous research efforts, GLOBE distinguishes clearly between societal *values* and *practices*, between what *should be* and what actually *is*. To put it differently, values constitute the kind of social norms members of that culture generally would like to see in place, while practices reflect how they really tend to behave. While the distinction makes the results more granular and precise, it also makes them harder to work with. As an international leader trying to prepare for a cross-cultural assignment, the question is on which of the two you should rely. This is significant, because they may well not always correspond.

As a leader, it is important to be aware of the distinction between values and practices. People may hold a particular value dear and react quite negatively when it is violated, although their outward behavior may diverge owing to positive or negative incentives, such as group pressure or monetary rewards. In fact, in all cultures some practices contradict the corresponding values[1].

Table 29: The GLOBE Cultural Clusters

Cluster	Cultures		
Confucian Asia	• China • Hong Kong	• Japan • Singapore	• South Korea • Taiwan
Southern Asia	• India • Indonesia	• Iran • Malaysia	• Philippines • Thailand
Latin America	• Argentina • Bolivia • Brazil • Colombia	• Costa Rica • Ecuador • El Salvador	• Guatemala • Mexico • Venezuela
Anglo	• Australia • Canada (English) • England	• Ireland • New Zealand	• South Africa (White) • United States
Eastern Europe	• Albania • Georgia • Greece	• Hungary • Poland • Romania	• Russia • Slovenia
Germanic Europe	• Austria • Germany (East)	• Germany (West) • Netherlands	• Switzerland (German)
Latin Europe	• France • Israel	• Italy • Portugal	• Spain • Switzerland (French)
Nordic Europe	• Denmark	• Finland	• Sweden
Middle East	• Egypt • Kuwait	• Morocco • Qatar	• Turkey
Sub-Saharan Africa	• Namibia • Nigeria	• South Africa (Black) • Zambia	• Zimbabwe

Source: based on House, Hanges and Javidan (2004).

For each of the nine GLOBE dimensions of culture, Table 30 lists the three countries with the highest and the three with the lowest score for practices (P) and values (V).

---

[1] In an analysis of the GLOBE data, Hadwick (2011) found that practices and values for seven of the nine dimensions are negatively correlated, indicating a general tendency for individuals to act differently from how they believe society should operate.

Table 30: Examples of GLOBE Cultural Values and Practices

Cultural Dimensions (World P/V)**	Cultural practices*		Cultural values*	
	Highest 3	Lowest 3	Highest 3	Lowest 3
Uncertainty Avoidance *(4.17/4.61)*	• Switzerland (5.37) • Sweden (5.32) • Singapore (5.31)	• Guatemala (3.30) • Hungary (3.12) • Russia (2.88)	• Thailand (5.61) • Nigeria (5.60) • Albania (5.37)	• Germany (3.32) • Netherlands (3.24) • Switzerland (3.16)
Power Distance *(5.14/2.77)*	• Morocco (5.80) • Nigeria (5.80) • El Salvador (5.68)	• South Africa (Black) (4.11) • Denmark (3.89) • Czech Rep. (3.59)	• Czech Rep. (4.35) • South Africa (Black) (3.65) • N. Zealand (3.53)	• Spain (2.26) • Finland (2.19) • Colombia (2.04)
Collectivism I (institutional) *(4.24/4.71)*	• Sweden (5.22) • S. Korea (5.20) • Japan (5.19)	• Germany (East) (3.56) • Hungary (3.53) • Greece (3.25)	• El Salvador (5.65) • Brazil (5.62) • Iran (5.54)	• Russia (3.89) • Czech Rep. (3.85) • Georgia (3.83)
Collectivism II (in-group) *(5.10/5.64)*	• Philippines (6.36) • Georgia (6.19) • Iran (6.03)	• Sweden (3.66) • Denmark (3.53) • Czech Rep. (3.18)	• El Salvador (6.52) • Colombia (6.25) • N. Zealand (6.21)	• South Africa (Black) (4.99) • Switzerland (4.94) • Czech Rep. (4.06)
Gender egalitarianism *(3.38/4.50)*	• Hungary (4.08) • Russia (4.07) • Poland (4.02)	• Egypt (2.81) • Kuwait (2.58) • S. Korea (2.50)	• England (5.17) • Sweden (5.15) • Ireland (5.14)	• Kuwait (3.45) • Qatar (3.38) • Egypt (3.18)
Assertiveness *(4.12/3.83)*	• Albania (4.89) • Nigeria (4.79) • Hungary (4.79)	• Switzerland (French) (3.47) • N. Zealand (3.42) • Sweden (3.38)	• Japan (5.56) • China (5.44) • Philippines (5.14)	• Russia (2.83) • Austria (2.81) • Turkey (2.66)
Future orientation *(3.84/5.44)*	• Singapore (5.07) • Switzerland (4.73) • South Africa (Black) (4.64)	• Poland (3.11) • Argentina (3.08) • Russia (2.88)	• Thailand (6.20) • Namibia (6.12) • Zimbabwe (6.07)	• China (4.73) • Denmark (4.33) • Czech Rep. (2.95)
Performance orientation *(4.10/5.88)*	• Switzerland (4.94) • Singapore (4.90) • Albania (4.81)	• Russia (3.39) • Venezuela (3.32) • Greece (3.20)	• El Salvador (6.58) • Zimbabwe (6.45) • Colombia (6.42)	• Japan (5.17) • South Africa (Black) (4.92) • Czech Rep. (2.35)
Humane orientation *(4.09/5.39)*	Zambia (5.23) Philippines (5.12) Ireland (4.96)	Greece (3.34) Spain (3.32) Germany (W) (3.18)	Nigeria (6.09) Finland (5.81) Singapore (5.79)	Costa Rica (4.99) N. Zealand (4.49) Czech Rep. (3.39)

*in descending order of magnitude (GLOBE scale 1-7).
** as represented by the 62 countries in the GLOBE study sample.
Where not otherwise specified, Switzerland refers to the German-speaking part, while Germany refers to the former West Germany.

Source: author;
derived from GLOBE raw data.

A strong discrepancy between practices and values for a cultural dimension is an indicator of a potential cross-cultural trouble spot for leaders. Values are ingrained, and people are often not consciously aware of them, while practices are more visible. Violating a societal value will often generate a fairly emotional response and can be considered a serious *faux pas*. Since practices are the observable manifestations of the culture, however, foreigners tend to orient themselves by these—and may thus unwittingly violate divergent cultural values. By observing and imitating only the local practices without considering the much more elusive values, the foreign manager may miss out on a chance to improve team morale and effectiveness by taking into account the team member's often subconscious wishes. On the other hand, the cultural practices themselves may lead to expectations ("we have always done it this way, so who are you to change it?"). This is a clear cross-cultural dilemma that GLOBE can help to resolve.

So, if practices and values are very different, which should guide you? There is no general rule on this. A real-life situation is always much more complex than numbers in a book. On the other hand, models can be a good starting point from which to identify potential trouble spots as the basis for discussions with trusted cultural insiders. It can therefore be instructive to examine the differences between societal practices and values.

Table 31 lists the three countries with the largest and the three with the smallest difference for each of the GLOBE cultural dimensions. The actual numerical divergence (from 1 to 7) is provided in brackets. The overall mean for the 'world', here meaning the entire sample of 62 countries, is also provided. A positive number indicates that the practice is larger than the value, a negative number denotes the opposite.

Table 31: Intra-Culture Differences Between Values and Practices

Cultural Dimension	Intra-cultural differences between cultural values and practices*	
	Top 3 (largest)	Bottom 3 (smallest)
Uncertainty avoidance (World: -0.44)	• Switzerland (German) (2.21) • Russia (2.19) • Germany (West) (1.90)	• France (0.17) • United States (0.15) • Malaysia (0.10)
Power distance (World: 2.37)	• Colombia (3.52) • Argentina (3.31) • Ecuador (3.30)	• Bolivia (1.10) • Czech Republic (-0.77) • South Africa (Black) (0.46)
Collectivism I (institutional) (World: -0.48)	• Greece (-2.15) • El Salvador (-1.94) • Brazil (-1.79)	• England (-0.04) • Ireland (0.04) • USA (0.03)
Collectivism II (in-group) (World: -0.54)	• New Zealand (-2.54) • Sweden (-2.38) • Denmark (-1.97)	• Thailand (-0.06) • Brazil (0.02) • Indonesia (0.01)
Gender egalitarianism (World: -1.12)	• Switzerland (-1.96) • Ireland (-1.93) • Germany (East) (-1.84)	• Georgia (-0.18) • Russia (-0.11) • Czech Republic (0.01)
Assertiveness (World: 0.30)	• Japan (-1.97) • Turkey (1.87) • Austria (1.81)	• Ireland (-0.07) • Bolivia (0.05) • Namibia (0.00)
Future orientation (World: -1.60)	• Thailand (-2.78) • Argentina (-2.70) • Guatemala (-2.67)	• Singapore (-0.44) • Denmark (0.11) • Switzerland (German) (-0.06)
Performance orientation (World: -1.78)	• Venezuela (-3.03) • El Salvador (-2.86) • Portugal (-2.80)	• Singapore (-0.82) • South Korea (-0.71) • South Africa (Black) (-0.25)
Humane orientation (World: -1.30)	• Spain (-2.37) • Singapore (-2.30) • Germany (West) (-2.28)	• Philippines (-0.24) • Thailand (-0.21) • New Zealand (-0.16)

*in descending order of magnitude (GLOBE scale 1-7); negative numbers indicate values> practices. **as represented by the 62 countries in the GLOBE study sample.

Source: author; derived from GLOBE raw data.

The clear distinction between values and practices also enabled the GLOBE study to show that those of Hofstede's cultural dimensions which had a counterpart in GLOBE generally correlated positively with either practices or values, but not both. For example, Hofstede's uncertainty dimension is related to GLOBE's corresponding cultural value but not practices. The same is true for Hofstede's individualism construct, which is related to GLOBE's institutional collectivism values. Conversely, results for Hofstede's power distance dimension are significantly positively correlated with the GLOBE power distance practices but not the corresponding values. The same goes for Hofstede's masculinity construct, which is in line with GLOBE assertiveness practices. And so on. Relying solely on Hofstede, which is still the most widely used framework of culture, may thus be insufficient.

To illustrate this, Switzerland has medium uncertainty avoidance, according to Hofstede. GLOBE, on the other hand, indicates a cultural paradox for the German-speaking part of Switzerland[1] which shows the third lowest values score but the highest practices score for uncertainty avoidance[2] out of all cultures studied. This indicates that avoiding the unknown is not *seen* as something of major importance in German-speaking Switzerland, yet people actually *do* go to great lengths to reduce uncertainty and have very clear and strong expectations regarding, for example, the amount of information they require about what is going on in their organization. Thus, although the societal *value* is in line with Hofstede's results, relying solely on this information when leading a group from that culture may lead to unexpected reactions, because the actual practices are quite different.

Table 32 contains an overview of the differences between practices and values for all nine of GLOBE's cultural dimensions for the Germanic Europe cultural cluster.

---

[1] GLOBE distinguishes between the French and the German-speaking part and shows a clear difference between the two.

[2] The actual score of 3.2 is considered medium, which is in line with Hofstede's result for the same dimension and culture.

Table 32: In-Culture Practice/Value Differences: Germanic Europe

Culture	GLOBE cultural dimension with corresponding difference* between cultural practices and values for each country								
	Uncertainty Avoidance	Power Distance	Institutional Collectivism	In-Group Collectivism	Gender Egalitarianism	Assertiveness	Future Orientation	Performance Orientation	Humane Orientation
Austria	1.50	2.51	-0.43	-0.41	-1.74	1.81	-0.66	-1.66	-2.04
Germany (East)	1.22	2.85	-1.12	-0.70	-1.84	1.51	-1.28	-2.00	-2.04
Germany (West)	1.90	2.71	-1.03	-1.16	-1.80	1.46	-0.58	-1.77	-2.28
Netherlands	1.45	1.66	-0.09	-1.47	-1.48	1.30	-0.45	-1.17	-1.34
Switzerland (German)	2.21	2.46	-0.63	-0.97	-1.96	1.30	-0.06	-0.89	-1.94

Legend: ☐ Small difference ☐ Medium difference ☐ Large difference

*Differences of more than 1/6 of the 7-point scale are considered medium, those of more than 1/3 as high.

Source: author; derived from GLOBE raw data.

The cultural leadership dilemma created by the discrepancy between cultural values and practices is clearly evident. In the case of Austria, for example, there are large intra-cultural differences for power distance and medium differences for uncertainty avoidance, gender egalitarianism, assertiveness, performance orientation, and humane orientation. In the case of the Netherlands, there are no large differences, but medium differences exist for uncertainty avoidance, power distance, in-group collectivism, gender egalitarianism, assertiveness, performance orientation, and humane orientation.

Table 33 provides the same kind of overview for the Anglo cultural cluster.

Table 33: In-Culture Practice/Value Differences: Anglo

Culture	GLOBE cultural dimension with corresponding difference* between cultural practices and values for each country								
	Uncertainty Avoidance	Power Distance	Institutional Collectivism	In-Group Collectivism	Gender Egalitarianism	Assertiveness	Future Orientation	Performance Orientation	Humane Orientation
Australia	0.41	1.96	-0.11	-1.58	-1.62	0.47	-1.06	-1.53	-1.30
Canada (English)	0.82	2.12	0.21	-1.71	-1.41	-0.09	-0.91	-1.66	-1.15
England	0.54	2.35	-0.04	-1.46	-1.50	0.44	-0.78	-1.81	-1.71
Ireland	0.28	2.45	0.04	-0.59	-1.93	-0.07	-1.24	-1.62	-0.51
New Zealand	0.66	1.36	0.61	-2.54	-1.01	-0.12	-2.07	-1.18	-0.16
South Africa (White)	-0.58	2.53	0.24	-1.42	-1.32	0.91	-1.54	-2.12	-2.17
USA	0.15	2.03	0.03	-1.51	-1.72	0.23	-1.16	-1.65	-1.36

Legend: ☐ Small difference   ☐ Medium difference   ☐ Large difference

*Differences of more than 1/6 of the 7-point scale are considered medium, those of more than 1/3 as high.   Source: author; derived from GLOBE raw data.

As in the case of Germanic Europe, there are considerable discrepancies between practices and values. In the case of England, for example, there is a large difference for power distance and medium differences for in-group collectivism, gender egalitarianism, performance orientation, and humane orientation. It is noteworthy that, for the entire cluster, the scores for gender egalitarianism, future orientation, performance orientation, and humane orientation are consistently negative, meaning that actual practices are lower than values.

Finally, Table 34 presents the practice/value differences for the Confucian Asia cluster.

Table 34: In-Culture Practice/Value Differences: Confucian

Culture	GLOBE cultural dimension with corresponding difference* between cultural practices and values for each country								
	Uncertainty Avoidance	Power Distance	Institutional Collectivism	In-Group Collectivism	Gender Egalitarianism	Assertiveness	Future Orientation	Performance Orientation	Humane Orientation
China	-0.34	1.94	0.21	0.71	-0.62	-1.68	-0.98	-1.22	-0.96
Hong Kong	-0.31	1.72	-0.30	0.21	-0.89	-0.14	-1.47	-0.85	-1.42
Japan	-0.26	2.25	1.20	-0.63	-1.14	-1.97	-0.96	-0.96	-1.11
Singapore	1.09	1.95	0.35	0.14	-0.81	-0.23	-0.44	-0.82	-2.30
South Korea	-1.12	3.06	1.30	0.13	-1.73	0.64	-1.72	-0.71	-1.79
Taiwan	-0.97	2.09	-0.56	0.14	-0.88	0.64	-1.24	-1.18	-1.15

Legend: ☐ Small difference   ☐ Medium difference   ☐ Large difference

*Differences of more than 1/6 of the 7-point scale are considered medium, those of more than 1/3 as high.

Source: author; derived from GLOBE raw data.

It is immediately evident that, overall, the cultures in this cluster exhibit smaller practice/value differences than the other two clusters examined. Although the practice scores for power distance are again all higher than the values score, only South Korea shows a large difference in this dimension. As a whole, the majority of dimensions for the bulk of cultures show only relatively small differences. An interesting comparison can be made between Singapore and Japan regarding humane orientation; despite comparable levels of economic development, Singapore's difference between practice and values for this dimension is more than twice as large as that for Japan. In fact, Japan shows higher practice and lower value scores, which accounts for the smaller difference. Conceivably, this may be a function of Singapore's colonial past and its correspondingly closer ties to the Anglo cluster.

The GLOBE project also studied specifically leadership-oriented aspects. Just as with societal culture, the researchers distinguished between practices and values. A key question in this regard was the universality of findings: whether certain leadership traits and behaviors would support or reduce leadership effectiveness in all or just a few societies.

A large number of leadership attributes were initially identified through a review of the extant literature. These were then reduced in an iterative process[1] and a pilot study conducted. Based on the results of the pilot study, the researchers then used factor analysis to derive 21 universal leadership scales (termed 'first-order factors') from the large list of attributes. Each of these well-established[2] scales is an aggregate of several of the original items, and together they can be used to describe leadership in all cultures.

Table 35 lists these 21 first-order factors.

---

[1] Initially, over 700 items were considered. These were then assessed regarding their cross-cultural generalizability with several techniques—Q-sorting, item analysis, and translation–back-translation—and items difficult to translate or problematic in some cultures were deleted. This reduced the initial number of items to 379.

[2] The psychometric properties of the GLOBE scales were found to meet or exceed conventional standards when subjecting them to a series of empirical tests using both quantitative (e.g., exploratory factor analysis, multilevel confirmatory factor analysis, reliability analysis) and qualitative (e.g. Q-sorts, item-evaluation reports) methodologies (Den Hartog et al., 1999).

Table 35: GLOBE Universal Leadership Scales (First-Order Factors)

Leadership scale (first-order factor)	Associated leader attributes
Administratively competent	Orderly, administratively skilled, organized, good administrator.
Autocratic	Autocratic, dictatorial, bossy, elitist.
Autonomous	Individualistic, independent, autonomous, unique.
Charismatic I: visionary	Foresight, prepared, anticipatory, plans ahead.
Charismatic II: inspirational	Enthusiastic, positive, morale booster, motive arouser.
Charismatic III: self-sacrificial	Risk taker, self-sacrificial, convincing.
Conflict Inducer	Normative, secretive, intra-group competitor.
Decisive	Willful, decisive, logical, intuitive.
Diplomatic	Diplomatic, worldly, win-win problem-solver, effective bargainer.
Face saver	Indirect, avoids negatives, evasive.
Humane orientation	Generous, compassionate.
Integrity	Honest, sincere, just, trustworthy.
Malevolent	Hostile, dishonest, vindictive, irritable.
Modesty	Modest, self-effacing, patient.
Non-participative	Non-delegator, micro-manager, non-egalitarian, individually oriented.
Performance-oriented	Improvement-oriented, excellence-oriented, performance-oriented.
Procedural	Ritualistic, formal, habitual, procedural.
Self-centered	Self-centered, non-participative, loner, asocial.
Status-consciousness	Status-conscious, class-conscious.
Team I: collaborative team orientation	Group-oriented, collaborative, loyal, consultative.
Team II: team integrator	Communicative, team builder, informed, integrator.

Source: Hanges and Dickson (2004).

Additional, second-order factor analysis revealed the existence of six underlying, universal factors:

- charismatic/value-based,
- team oriented,
- self-protective,
- participative,
- humane oriented, and
- autonomous.

Each of these can be described in terms of the leadership scales previously discussed. In practical terms, these six second-order factors correspond to leadership styles in other models whose existence around the world has been empirically validated.

Table 36 provides an overview.

Table 36: GLOBE Leadership Styles and Associated Leadership Scales

Global culturally endorsed implicit leadership (CLT) dimensions (GLOBE leadership styles found around the world)		
Charismatic/value-based reflects the ability to inspire, motivate, and expect high performance from others on the basis of firm core values.	**Team oriented** stresses effective team-building and implementation of a common goal among team members.	**Self-protective** focuses on ensuring the safety and security of a leader.
Associated leadership scales (first-order factors): ■ Charismatic/visionary ■ Charismatic/inspirational ■ Charismatic/self-sacrificing ■ Integrity ■ Decisive ■ Performance oriented	*Associated leadership scales (first-order factors):* ■ Team collaborative ■ Team integrative ■ Diplomatic ■ Not malevolent ■ Administratively competent	*Associated leadership scales (first-order factors):* ■ Self-centered ■ Status conscious ■ Conflict inducer ■ Face saver ■ Procedural
Participative reflects the degree to which managers involve others in making and implementing decisions.	**Humane oriented** reflects supportive and considerate leadership and includes compassion and generosity.	**Autonomous** refers to independent and individualistic leadership without much consultation or interaction.
Associated leadership scales (first-order factors): ■ Charismatic/Visionary ■ Non-autocratic ■ Participative	*Associated leadership scales (first-order factors):* ■ Modesty ■ Humane-oriented	*Associated leadership scales (first-order factors):* ■ Autonomous

Source: based on House, Hanges, and Javidan (2004).

Charismatic/value-based leadership is reminiscent of Bass's transformational leadership and Goleman's visionary style. The team-oriented style is comparable to Blake and Mouton's country-club management. The self-protective style is similar to Blake and

Mouton's impoverished style. The participative style corresponds to both Lewin's and Goleman's democratic style. The humane-oriented style combines Goleman's coaching and affiliative styles and partly also Hersey and Blanchard's coaching and supporting styles. And the autonomous style contains elements of Lewins' laissez-faire, Tannenbaum and Schmidt's paternalistic and laissez-faire, and Blake and Mouton's authority-compliance styles.

Although all six styles were found around the world, only two of them held appeal in all cultures examined: charismatic/value-based and team-oriented. Figure 26 demonstrates this.

Figure 26: World View of GLOBE Leadership Styles

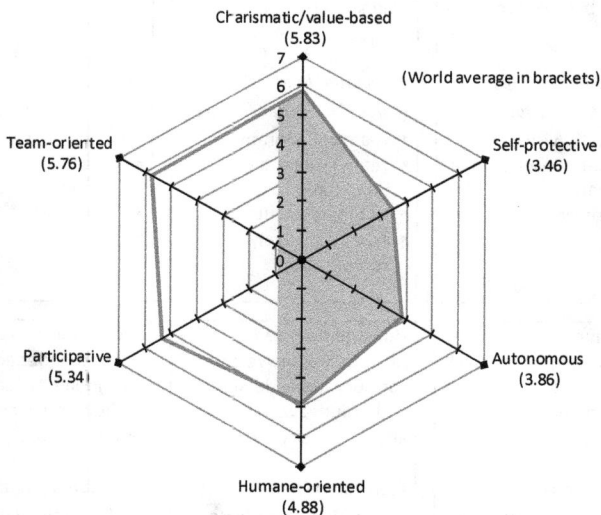

'World' as represented by the 62 countries in the study.   Source: author; compiled from GLOBE raw data.

This finding clearly challenged established leadership paradigms, such as the long-held view in the West that a participative leadership approach is normally preferable to other styles.

Figure 27 details how each of GLOBE's universal styles is viewed in each of the GLOBE cultural clusters.

Figure 27: Cultural Cluster View of GLOBE Leadership Styles

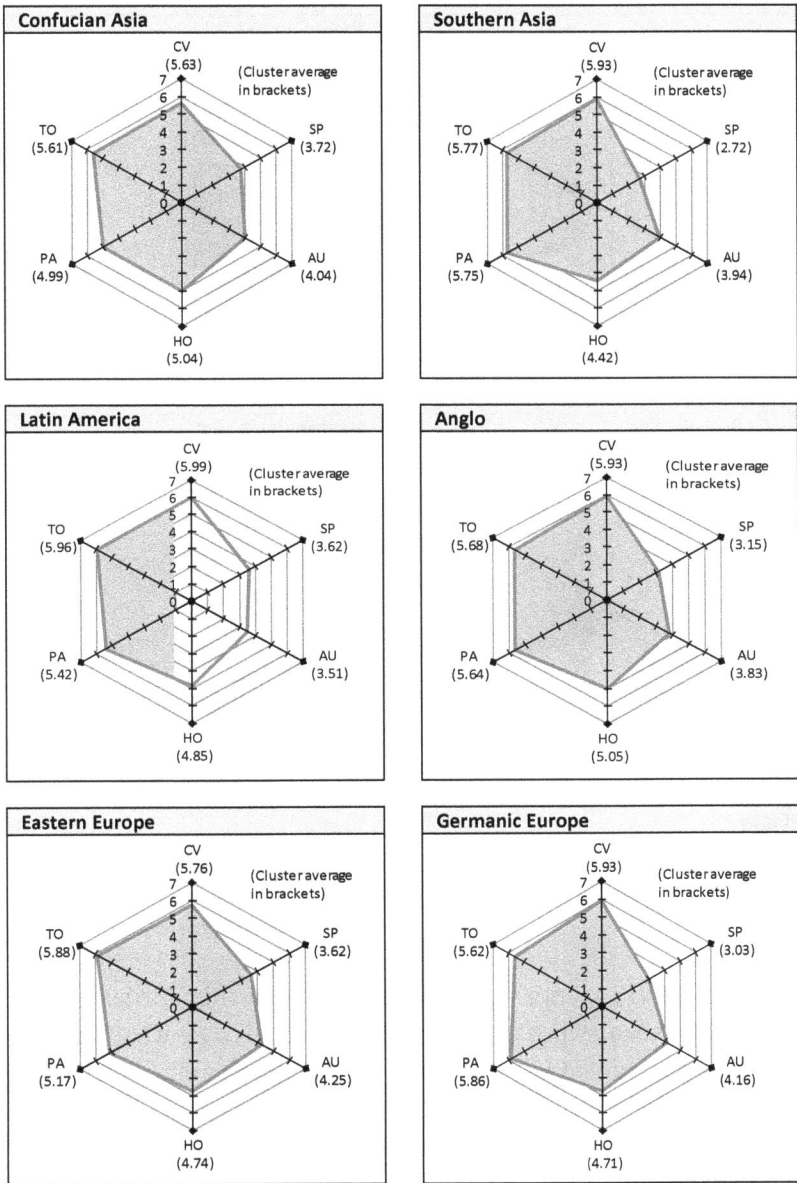

Confucian Asia

CV (5.63)
SP (3.72)
AU (4.04)
HO (5.04)
PA (4.99)
TO (5.61)
(Cluster average in brackets)

Southern Asia

CV (5.93)
SP (2.72)
AU (3.94)
HO (4.42)
PA (5.75)
TO (5.77)
(Cluster average in brackets)

Latin America

CV (5.99)
SP (3.62)
AU (3.51)
HO (4.85)
PA (5.42)
TO (5.96)
(Cluster average in brackets)

Anglo

CV (5.93)
SP (3.15)
AU (3.83)
HO (5.05)
PA (5.64)
TO (5.68)
(Cluster average in brackets)

Eastern Europe

CV (5.76)
SP (3.62)
AU (4.25)
HO (4.74)
PA (5.17)
TO (5.88)
(Cluster average in brackets)

Germanic Europe

CV (5.93)
SP (3.03)
AU (4.16)
HO (4.71)
PA (5.86)
TO (5.62)
(Cluster average in brackets)

295

Figure 27:   Cultural Cluster View of GLOBE Leadership Styles (cont.)

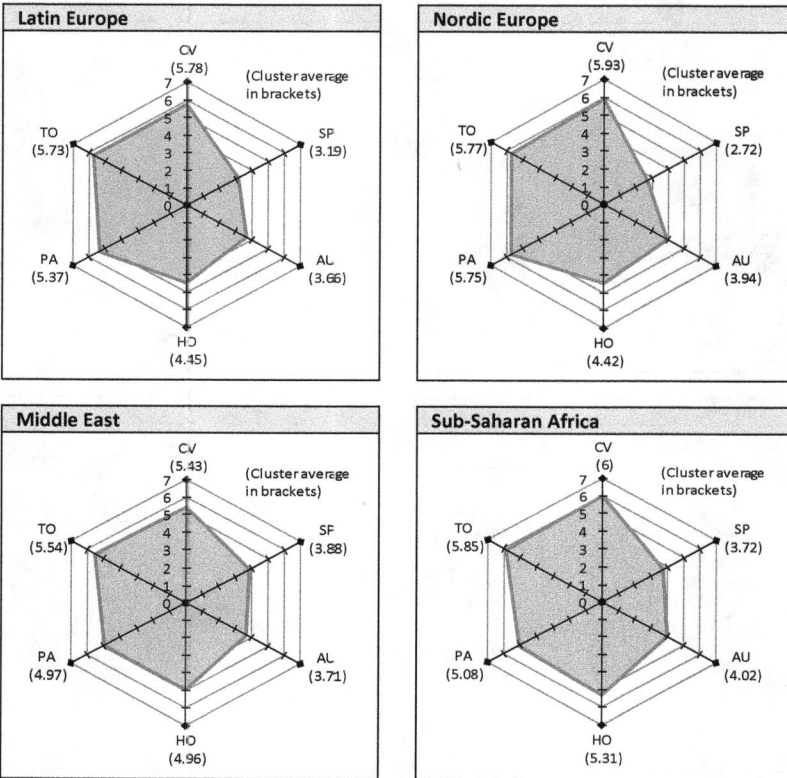

Legend:

CV	Charismatic/value-based	TO	Team-oriented	PA	Participative
HO	Humane-oriented	AU	Autonomous	SP	Self-protective

Source: author; compiled from GLOBE raw data.

The GLOBE team also found that 22 leadership attributes were universally seen as positive and eight as negative by what the middle-managers polled in the study considered outstanding leadership, while the rest were culturally contingent: seen positively in some cultures and negatively in others. These attributes are listed in Table 37.

Table 37: Universal and Culturally Contingent Leader Attributes

Universally desirable	Culturally contingent (examples)		Universally undesirable
■ Administratively skilled	■ Ambitious	■ Intuitive	■ Asocial
■ Communicative	■ Anticipatory	■ Logical	■ Dictatorial
■ Confidence builder	■ Autonomous	■ Micro-manager	■ Egocentric
■ Coordinator	■ Cautious	■ Orderly	■ Irritable
■ Decisive	■ Class conscious	■ Procedural	■ Loner
■ Dependable	■ Compassionate	■ Provocateur	■ Non-cooperative
■ Dynamic	■ Cunning	■ Risk taker	■ Non-explicit
■ Effective bar-gainer	■ Domineering	■ Ruler	■ Ruthless
■ Encouraging	■ Elitist	■ Self-effacing	
■ Excellence-oriented	■ Enthusiastic	■ Self-sacrificial	
■ Foresightful	■ Evasive	■ Sensitive	
■ Honest	■ Formal	■ Sincere	
■ Informed	■ Habitual	■ Status-conscious	
■ Intelligent	■ Independent	■ Subdued	
■ Just	■ Indirect	■ Unique	
■ Motivational	■ Individualistic	■ Willful	
■ Motive arouser	■ Intra-group competitor	■ Worldly	
■ Plans ahead	■ Intra-group conflict avoider		
■ Positive			
■ Team builder			
■ Trustworthy			
■ Win-win problem solver			

Source: based on House, Hanges, and Javidan (2004).

This clearly indicates that ideas of outstanding leadership differ between cultures. Societal culture will influence implicit leadership expectations, and these in turn will affect preferred leadership styles. Table 38 puts this into perspective by summarizing the societal practices (P) and values (V) for a select number of cultures, the consensus on what constitutes outstanding leadership in each culture, and the preferred leadership style.

As the proponents of the emotional intelligence school have emphasized, cognitive intelligence alone is not sufficient for effective leadership across borders.

Table 38: Culturally Contingent Outstanding Leader Attributes

Cluster	Culture	Societal culture	Attributes expected of outstanding leaders (summary)	Preferred style
Confucian Asia	Hong Kong	UA: medium; PD: medium; IC: medium; GC: high; GE: medium; AS: medium; FO: medium P, high V; PO: medium P, high V; HO: medium P, high V.	Administratively competent; decisive; focuses on results and performance; frugal, industrious, and pragmatic; maintains harmony, order, and discipline.	Autocratic, with little subordinate consultation or discretion.
Southern Asia	India	UA: medium; PD: high P, low V; IC: medium; GC: high; GE: low P, medium V; AS: medium; FO: medium P, high V; PO: medium P, high V; HO: medium P, high V.	Charismatic and action-oriented, administratively competent and introspective; has high integrity and a collective outlook.	Charismatic/value-based, with autocratic tendencies.
Latin America	Mexico	UA: medium P, high V; PD: high P, low V; IC: medium; GC: high; GE: medium; AS: medium; FO: medium P, high V; PO: medium P, high V; HO: medium P, high V.	Highly directive, assertive, and autocratic but charismatic; uses a system of rewards and punishments; patriarchal; supportive of followers; maintains pleasant personal relationships with subordinates through showing respect and empathy.	Team-oriented, with autocratic tendencies.
Anglo	England	UA: medium P, high V; PD: high P, low V; IC: medium; GC: high; GE: medium; AS: medium; FO: medium P, high V; PO: medium P, high V; HO: medium P, high V.	Decisive, visionary and inspirational; highly capable and performance-oriented; diplomatic; has high integrity; is approachable.	Charismatic/value-based.
	USA	UA: medium; PD: medium P, low V; IC: medium; GC: medium P, high V; GE: medium P, high V; AS: medium; FO: medium P, high V; PO: medium P, high V; HO: medium P, high V.	Excellence-oriented and able to stand out through individual achievements; authentic and trustworthy; inspirational and focused; decisive and action-oriented; change-seeking; caring and participative; promotes team spirit.	Charismatic/value-based.
Eastern Europe	Russia	UA: low P, high V; PD: high P, low V; IC: medium; GC: high; GE: medium; AS: medium P, low V; FO: low P, high V; PO: medium P, high V; HO: medium P, high V.	Visionary, decisive, and administratively competent; performance-oriented and inspirational; can focus team on performance, can get things done.	Charismatic/value-based.

Table 38:   *Culturally Contingent Outstanding Leader Attributes (cont.)*

Cluster	Culture	Societal culture	Attributes expected of outstanding leaders (summary)	Preferred style
Germanic Europe	Germany (West)	UA: high P, medium V; PD: high P, low V; IC: medium; GC: medium P, high V; GE: medium; AS: medium; FO: medium; PO: medium P, high V; HO: medium P, high V.	Highly performance-oriented and unemotional but participative ("tough on the issue, tough on the person, participative in nature"); direct in communication, does not shy away from confrontation.	Participative, with autonomous tendencies in decision-making.
	Switzerland (German)	UA: high P, medium V; PD: medium P, low V; IC: medium; GC: medium; GE: low P, medium V; AS: medium; FO: medium; PO: medium P, high V; HO: medium P, high V.	Consensus-oriented, egalitarian, and highly participative; humble and modest in manners; authentic and capable; efficiency-oriented and pragmatic; serves as a positive role model.	Participative, with emphasis on subordinate consultation in decision-making.
Latin Europe	France	UA: medium; PD: high P, low V; IC: medium; GC: medium P, high V; GE: medium; AS: medium; FO: medium P, high V; PO: medium P, high V; HO: medium P, high V.	Visionary and dynamic, collaborative and team oriented; is able to adapt to the structure of the workplace and integrate in the respective work milieu's complex network of personal relations.	Participative, with emphasis on social roles.
Nordic Europe	Finland	UA: high P, medium V; PD: medium P, low V; IC: medium; GC: medium P, high V; GE: medium; AS: medium; FO: medium P, high V; PO: medium P, high V; HO: medium P, high V.	Visionary and decisive but egalitarian and participative; combines teamwork and individuality; manages by objectives.	Charismatic/value-based.
Middle East	Turkey	UA: medium; PD: high P, low V; IC: medium P, high V; GC: high; GE: low P, medium V; AS: medium P, low V; FO: medium P, high V; PO: medium P, high V; HO: medium P, high V.	Visionary, decisive, and administratively competent; diplomatic and a team integrator; has high integrity.	Team-oriented.

Legend:

CV: Charismatic/value-based; TO: team-oriented;
PA: Participative; HO: humane-oriented;
AU: autonomous; SP: self-protective.

Scale:

Low: 1.00–2.98 (33rd percentile);
medium: 2.98–4.96 (66th percentile);
high: 4.96–7.00

Source: compiled from GLOBE raw data and Chhokar, Brodbeck, and House (2008).

Successful global leaders show high degrees of emotional-social intelligence and have a good understanding of the key responsibilities of leadership. They start out as good leaders in their own cultural context, are endowed with mental openness and flexibility, and possess relevant international experience. And they continually develop and hone their skills.

The five most important factors for developing your global leadership potential are

- developing your emotional-social intelligence,
- cross-cultural training,
- increasing exposure to cross-cultural/global leadership through international projects and assignments, and
- continuous leadership development.

In conclusion, the GLOBE study and the global leadership research it led to have contributed significantly to our understanding of how both culture and leadership work, both across and within cultures. It should not be forgotten, however, that the data of the original GLOBE study reflects the 1990s and early 2000s. Although distinctive underlying cultural traditions have been found to be quite persistent (see e.g. Inglehart and Baker, 2000), cultures may change over time, as demonstrated by the World Values Survey[1]. Even if cultures are fundamentally comparatively stable, attitudes (which, according to Kluckhohn and Strodtbeck, are based on a comparatively small number of basic values) certainly do change. Whether regarding women in the workplace, gay marriage, or marijuana, public opinion has changed significantly on a number of issues in many cultures over the past two decades. It is therefore quite likely some change has also occurred in leadership-related attitudes. GLOBE is an impressive feat, yet it is nonetheless a relatively minor aid in your quest for cross-cultural leadership success. There really is no way around immersing yourself in the new culture if you are

---

[1] See Chapter 5.24 on page 228.

on international assignment. Learn the language and talk to the locals as often as you can. And if you lead a multi-cultural team, you will have to deal with and get to know all the individuals on it. The GLOBE framework and other models can be a good starting point, but no more.

5.4   A Final Word about Applying Culture Research

As repeatedly mentioned, all the models of culture introduced over the course of this chapter have their uses but are not intended to be applied to individuals. In particular, those that are based on large sets of empirical data allow important insights into specific cultures and enable you, within limits, to form expectations about behaviors and attitudes of groups from these cultures. However, because these insights are based on the averaged answers of many people, it is almost guaranteed that no Chinese or American or German or any other foreign individual you meet corresponds exactly to those model expectations. Does that mean they are useless when dealing with individuals? No, it does not.

They are a useful starting point for reflection when you are trying to make sense of the (to you) strange behavior of someone from another culture. They also enable you to help that person become aware of his or her own cultural background and possible differences to yours, and they allow you to discuss such possible differences in a structured way.

Although in reality the number of direct reports you lead will normally not exceed eight to ten, even if you are responsible for large projects or whole departments, you should also be able to quite accurately gauge many typical reactions of the group to, for example, management practices such as performance-based pay schemes. It is therefore worth spending the time needed to get to know these frameworks well.

5.5 Chapter Recap

TAKEAWAYS

What you should take away from this chapter:

1. Cross-cultural problems are often caused by one of the following four factors:
   - communication blunders (both verbal and non-verbal),
   - stereotypes and prejudices,
   - offense against tradition and religion, and
   - offense against deeply held (usually implicit) values and taboos.

2. In management and leadership, two types of culture are of particular interest:
   - societal culture, and
   - organizational culture.

3. A person is influenced by five types of culture:
   - societal culture,
   - organizational culture,
   - generational culture,
   - membership group subcultures, and
   - reference group subcultures.

4. American anthropologist Edward T. Hall is best remembered for three cultural concepts:
   - monochronic vs. polychronic cultures,
   - high vs. low context cultures, and
   - proxemics.

5. American social anthropologists Florence Kluckhohn and Fred Strodtbeck's Values Orientation Theory suggests that all cultures must answer a limited number of universal problems (use of time, relationship with nature, relationships with people, mode of activity, human nature, use of space), but that different cultures have different preferences regarding the universally known, finite value-based solutions to these.

6. The six dimensions in Hofstede's framework (four originals and two added later) are
   - individualism vs. collectivism,
   - low vs. high power distance,
   - masculinity vs. femininity,
   - low vs. high uncertainty avoidance,
   - long-term vs. short-term orientation, and
   - indulgence vs. restraint.

7. In regular, roughly five-year intervals (called 'waves'), the WVS examines seven aspects:
   - support for democracy,
   - tolerance of foreigners and ethnic minorities,
   - support for gender equality,
   - the role of religion (and changing levels of religiosity),
   - the impact of globalization,
   - attitudes towards the environment, work, family, politics, national identity, culture, and diversity, and
   - insecurity and subjective well-being.

8. Schwartz's seven archetypes of cultural value orientations are
   - intellectual autonomy,
   - affective autonomy,
   - embeddedness,
   - egalitarianism,
   - hierarchy,
   - harmony, and
   - mastery.

9. Schwartz's three dimensions of culture are
   - autonomy vs. embeddedness,
   - egalitarianism vs. hierarchy, and
   - harmony vs. mastery.

10. Schwartz's ten basic human values are
    – self-direction,
    – stimulation,
    – hedonism,
    – achievement,
    – power,
    – security,
    – conformity,
    – tradition,
    – benevolence, and
    – universalism.

11. Trompenaars' and Hampden-Turner's framework of culture consists of seven dimensions, of which the first five are interaction-based and the other two value-based:
    – universalism vs. particularism,
    – individualism vs. collectivism,
    – neutral vs. emotional,
    – specific vs. diffuse,
    – achievement vs. ascription,
    – sequential vs. synchronic (attitudes to time), and
    – internal vs. external control (attitudes to the environment).

12. Lewis classifies the world's cultures into three rough types:
    – linear-active: task-oriented, highly organized, cool, factual, decisive planners,
    – multi-active: relationship-oriented, loquacious interrelators (i.e. connection facilitators), and
    – reactive: respect-oriented, compromising, accommodating listeners.

13. The Browaeys and Price model of culture consists of eight dimensions:
    - time focus,
    - space,
    - structure,
    - action,
    - time orientation,
    - power,
    - communication, and
    - competition.

14. The GLOBE cultural clusters are
    - Confucian Asia,
    - Southern Asia,
    - Latin America,
    - Anglo (English-speaking countries),
    - Eastern Europe,
    - Germanic Europe,
    - Latin Europe,
    - Nordic Europe,
    - Middle East, and
    - Sub-Saharan Africa.

15. The GLOBE model of culture encompasses nine dimensions:
    - uncertainty avoidance,
    - power distance,
    - collectivism i: institutional,
    - collectivism ii: in-group,
    - gender egalitarianism,
    - assertiveness,
    - future orientation,
    - performance orientation, and
    - humane orientation.

16. The 21 GLOBE universal leadership scales are
    – administratively competent,
    – autocratic,
    – autonomous,
    – charismatic i: visionary,
    – charismatic ii: inspirational,
    – charismatic iii: self-sacrificial,
    – conflict inducer,
    – decisive,
    – diplomatic,
    – face saver
    – humane orientation,
    – integrity,
    – malevolent,
    – modesty,
    – non-participative,
    – performance-oriented,
    – procedural,
    – self-centered,
    – status-consciousness,
    – team i: collaborative team orientation, and
    – team ii: team integrator.

17. The six GLOBE leadership styles are:
    – charismatic/value-based
    – team oriented
    – self-protective
    – participative
    – humane oriented, and
    – autonomous.

18. The five most important factors for developing your global leader-
    ship potential are
    – developing your emotional-social intelligence,
    – cross-cultural training,
    – increasing exposure to cross-cultural/global leadership
      through international projects and assignments, and
    – continuous leadership development.

CHECK QUESTIONS

Try to answer the questions below. If you need help, check the sample answers in the annex.

1. From a cultural perspective, what needs to be kept in mind regarding the development of modern leadership theory?
2. Which four factors often cause problems when leading across cultures?
3. What are two key factors for becoming cross-culturally proficient?
4. Why is nationality a problematic proxy for culture?
5. Which five types of culture influence a person?
6. What is the topic of Edward T. Hall's proxemics concept?
7. Which are the five fundamental questions in Kluckhohn and Strodtbeck's Values Orientation Theory?
8. How can Hofstede's framework be used to identify significant differences between cultures with which someone is not familiar?
9. Which are the two major value dimensions on which the Inglehart-Welzel Map is based?
10. Which are the three fundamental questions underlying Schwartz's Theory of Cultural Values Orientation?
11. What is Trompenaars' and Hampden-Turner's cultural dimension internal vs. external control about?
12. According to Lewis, what is the cause of cross-cultural problems?
13. What is the focus of the cultural dimension time orientation in Browaeys and Price's model of culture?
14. What is global leadership in the business management sense?
15. What is the difference between GLOBE and Hofstede's or Trompenaars' models of culture regarding value orientation?
16. In the GLOBE framework, what is uncertainty avoidance?

17. What is the difference between cultural practices and values, according to GLOBE?

18. For an international leader, what is the significance of large gaps between cultural values and practices for a relevant culture?

19. Which are the eight universally (i.e. globally) undesirable leadership attributes identified by GLOBE?

20. Although cultural models can only be applied at the group level, strictly speaking, what are their potential uses at the individual level?

5.6   Exercises

On the following pages, you will find various exercises related to the content of this chapter. If you need help, check the sample solutions in the annex.

Exercise 20 Your Cultural Profile

This exercise uses the Browaeys and Price model of culture to describe a person's cultural make-up. Since you are probably the person that knows you best, use the example of yourself to practice. Determine your own cultural profile by selecting the answers that best represent you from the rubric on the next pages. Select one answer for each cultural dimension. Then plot the corresponding positions in the spidergram figure below and connect them.

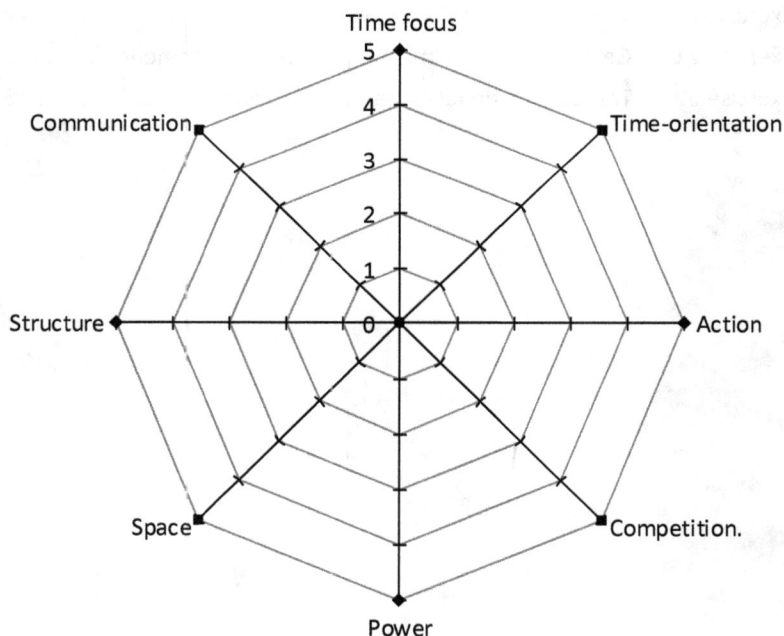

For an explanation of the Browaeys and Price model, see chapter 5.28 on page 274. For an example, see Illustration 13 on page 277.

Cultural Aspects	Score				
	1	2	3	4	5
Time focus	monochronic ⟵⟶ polychronic				
	I prefer to concentrate on one thing, finish it, then do the next one. Working on several things simultaneously makes me uncomfortable.	I prefer to work on one thing after another, but I feel comfortable if I have several things on my plate at the same time.	I do not care if I do one thing after another or many at the same time and feel comfortable with both.	I prefer to do several things at the same time; having to work on one thing after another frustrates me.	I tend to do many things at the same time and feel comfortable with it.
Structure	individualistic ⟵⟶ collectivistic				
	My priority is to take care of myself and my immediate family.	My priority is to take care of myself, my family and friends.	Myself, my family, and my social group are equally important.	My social group and society at large should come first, but I should not forget myself, either.	It is more important to look out for society than for myself.
Space	private ⟵⟶ public				
	When talking to someone, if they step closer than a large step, I get uncomfortable; my home is off-limits to new people I meet.	When talking to someone, if they step closer than one regular step, I get uncomfortable; also, I rarely invite someone new to my house.	When talking to someone, it's fine if they step a bit closer than one regular step; I occasionally invite someone new to my house.	I am comfortable if someone talks to me fairly close up; also, I frequently invite someone new to my house.	I am comfortable if someone talks to me very close; also, people constantly come and go at my home.
Action	being ⟵⟶ doing				
	I enjoy life, want to express myself, and live in the moment.	I generally enjoy life, sometimes want to express myself, and often live in the moment.	I primarily want to grow as a person.	I mostly enjoy doing things and achieving personal goals; recognition and promotion are sometimes important to me.	I enjoy doing things and achieving personal goals; recognition and promotion are important to me.

	past ⟷ future				
Time orientation	Traditions are very important; we can learn much from the past.	Traditions are fairly important; we can learn some things from the past.	I generally live in the present.	I frequently think about the future.	I am mostly concerned with the future.
	equality ⟷ hierarchy				
Power	I frequently question hierarchy and go outside of channels; I expect my boss to consult me before making any decisions that affect me.	I frequently question hierarchy and go outside of channels; I expect my boss to consult me before making major decisions that affect me.	I generally accept but occasionally question hierarchy and on rare occasions go outside of channels; I appreciate if my boss consults me before making major decisions that affect me.	I mostly accept hierarchy and hardly ever go outside of channels; I do not expect my boss to consult me before making decisions.	I accept hierarchy without questions and never go outside of channels; I do not expect my boss to consult me before making decisions.
	low context ⟷ high context				
Communication	I tend to be very explicit when talking or writing and try to include everything the recipient might need to know.	I tend to be fairly explicit when talking or writing and try to include the key points the recipient needs to know.	I include what the recipient need to know when talking or writing, but I don't waste time by repeating stuff that is probably already known	I am normally fairly brief when talking or writing and expect the recipient to understand the rest based on the context without spelling it out in detail.	I am normally very brief when talking or writing and expect the recipient to understand the rest based on the context.
	cooperative ⟷ competitive				
Competition	In business, relationships and consensus are the most important aspects.	In business, relationships and consensus are more important as profit and competition.	In business, relationships and consensus are as important as profit and competition.	Competition and achieving profits are quite important in business.	Profit and competition are the main purpose of business.

Source: author.

Exercise 21 Getting Ready for the International Assignment

You are head of a department at an international fashion company. Richard, a 32-year old Brit from Hastings in South England and one of your team leaders, has just been selected to head your company's small subsidiary in Sri Lanka. He asked you for some advice about the cross-cultural issues he might expect based on research about the two cultures. You believe he has enough emotional-social intelligence that he will be able to make the leap from cultural average to individual. Before your meeting, you want to compare the cultural profile of the two countries by applying Hofstede's Value/Belief Theory of culture.

Fill in the table below by using online sources to determine the cultural preferences for Sri Lanka and draw conclusions for Richard. For an example, see Illustration 12 on page 257.

Cultural dimension	Cultural preference		Some key differences to consider regarding how to manage in Sri Lanka
	UK	Sri Lanka	
Power distance	Egalitarian		
	Difference:		
Individualism	Highly indi-vidualistic		
	Difference:		
Masculinity	Masculine		
	Difference:		
Uncertainty avoidance	Low		
	Difference:		
Long-term orientation	Unclear		
	Difference:		
Indulgence	Indulgent		
	Difference:		

Exercise 22 The Dysfunctional Cross-Cultural Team

You are the head of the central staff unit at a major international semi-conductor corporation's holding company. Your unit consists of five teams: Legal (3 people), HR (4 people), IT (8 people), Marketing & Communications (14 people), and Business Development (4 people). You have been in your present job for a little more than a year now. Things are generally going well, but two teams, Legal and Business Development, do currently not perform according to your expectations. Both teams' leaders have recently left, and in both cases, you have temporarily taken the helm.

Legal consists of more or less autonomous experts that can be called upon by line units as warranted. Nonetheless, its members seem to be in constant competition regarding both professional matters (e.g. who gets the biggest cases) and their private life (e.g. who drives the nicest car, goes on the most expensive vacation, and so on). Claudette, the French team leader, has a hard time enforcing corporate policy and decisions and struggles to maintain the respect of her team, partly owing to her frequent emotional outbursts. The attitude of most team members is quite cynical. Additionally, one of its senior lawyers, Tom, constantly complains and urges the others to question most decisions taken by both the team's leader, Claudette, and you as her supervisor. There is no real need for joint team work, since most corporate cases only involve one lawyer at a time, but you feel that the tension evident in the team is bad for morale, if not for performance, then certainly for the long-term well-being of its team members. Additionally, this team has become quite insular and detached from the rest of your unit. In your opinion, their meetings are essentially showrooms for Claudette's status-seeking behavior and mainly used for top-down communication. There is no real involvement in the larger purpose of the organization as a whole, and most of them see their meetings as a waste of time. Motivation overall is low.

Business Development is a similar story, although that team needs to work together closely, with many interlinkages and dependencies in their work. Nonetheless, for the past few months it has also suffered from internal strife. The team consists of four people. The leader, Shun, is from Singapore and of Chinese ethnicity. He is 38, cool under pressure, and not prone to emotional outbursts. He also keeps his opinion to himself and does not solicit his team's opinion much before making decisions. Laura is German and very direct. It is clearly very important to her to make others see her point of view and, if at all possible, convince them of it. She is 31, blonde and small, and she frequently complains about not being taken seriously by others. Although showing promise, she is still inexperienced and quite often makes mistakes. Bheka is a 27-year old black South African and the prankster on the team. Some of his pranks are really funny, in your view, but it is clear that most of his team does not appreciate them at all. This goes particularly for Laura and Shun, who both occasionally give him a hard time because of it. He is quite emotional and very receptive to praise and any kind of interest in him. You consider his performance adequate, but you are concerned that he has become emotionally detached from the team. The fourth team member, John, is a Caucasian American and, at 49, the subordinate in your unit with the longest tenure in the company and the highest performance. He is usually quite optimistic and positive about any tasks that come his way, loves challenges, and gets frustrated if others do not keep up with him. He is the most outspoken of the four about what he considers to be a bad team. He feels that the team has no unity and that its members do not stick together or support each other. However, he and Laura frequently meet for an after-work drink, in which they are occasionally joined by Bheka. Shun considers this to be inappropriate behavior and has counselled them to stop it, to which both have replied that it is none of his business and that he is only their boss during the work day. Following this exchange, Shun has complained to you and strongly requested that John—the ringleader in his view—be fired; in your company, all personnel decisions need to be approved by the next-higher supervisor. You have refused. This and similar incidents have left Shun somewhat bitter and, in John's view, even more aloof than normally.

John and Tom from Legal are good friends. On the other hand, John and Claudette, the head of the Legal team, have a personal feud. Asked about this, Claudette once told you that she intensely dislikes it if people who are not at her hierarchical level pester her with questions and requests—something John often does. On the other hand, John is very clear about the fact that, based on his experience and skill, he considers himself at least the equal of Claudette, despite the difference in hierarchy. He has also repeatedly said in public that it is completely inefficient and a waste of everybody's time to always go through channels.

Questions and Assignments

- Characterize the legal team. What dynamics are at work? What would you recommend?
- Explain which of GLOBE's leadership styles Shun exhibits. Is this appropriate, given the team?
- Describe the problems on the business development team. Which aspects are likely cultural, which individual in origin?
- With regard to individual relationships, which GLOBE leadership style would you recommend Shun tries to adopt with each of his team members? Why?

6 COMMON LEADERSHIP PRINCIPLES AND MISTAKES

LEARNING OUTCOMES

After this chapter, you should be able to

- understand common leadership principles and how to apply them, and
- understand common leadership mistakes and how to avoid them.

When first starting out, most leaders make very similar kinds of mistakes. As a leader, you are under constant observation. Everything you do will be observed and judged. That may be unfair, but it is the way things are. Otto von Bismarck is supposed to have said: "fools say that they learn by experience – I prefer to profit by others' experience". While learning from your own experience certainly does not make you a fool, there is nothing wrong with trying to jumpstart your leadership abilities by learning from the mistakes of others. This is what leadership principles are for. Leadership principles and leadership mistakes are flip sides of the same coin; one refers to desirable leadership behaviors and the other to undesirable ones.

Leadership mistakes are very common. In fact, it is safe to say that all leaders make mistakes. However, what actually constitutes a mistake is not that clear-cut. As was demonstrated in Chapter 5[1], implicit expectations people have of leaders are inherently culture-bound, and what is considered a mistake in one culture may not be in another. It is important to keep the cultural context in mind, therefore, when discussing the dos and don'ts of leadership. Based on the

---

[1] See page 216f.

insights gained through the GLOBE study among other things, the deliberations in this chapter are deemed to be universally applicable, although their relevance may vary between cultures[1].

6.1   Ten Fundamental Leadership Principles

A leadership principle[2] is a general behavioral guideline that can help leaders increase their effectiveness and prevent common leadership mistakes. Below are ten leadership principles for the modern leader:

1. understand and respect your leader responsibilities,
2. avoid globally disliked leadership behaviors,
3. conform to implicit leadership expectations in your cultural context,
4. declare your expectations clearly,
5. be technically and administratively proficient,
6. be sure of what you say and why you say it,
7. go the extra mile,
8. take care of your people,
9. be present and authentic, and
10. maintain your integrity at all times.

The selection of these principles is based on established research[3], the author's almost three decades of leadership experience in a variety of cultural contexts, and occasionally some common sense. They incorporate the elements of transformational leadership

---

[1] The concept of face, for example, exists in all cultures but is much more dominant and complex in Asian than Western cultures.

[2] Note that leadership *principles* are distinct from leadership *directives*, which are a way to communicate a leader's intent in a formalized, usually written, way to reduce the need for one-to-one interaction in larger organizations. This is detailed in volume 2 of this book series, *Organizational Leadership*.

[3] Particularly Avolio and Bass (1991, 2002), Cohen (1998), the GLOBE study (i.e. House, Hanges and Javidan, 2004; and Chhokar, Brodbeck, and House, 2008), Scouller (2011), and Seelhofer and Valeri (2017).

and leadership presence previously explained and are in line with your key responsibilities as a leader.

Principle 1: Understand and respect your leader responsibilities

Your key responsibilities as a leader, together with key leadership functions and practices, were outlined in Chapter 4[1] and summarized in Figure 8[2]. To reiterate, they are

- getting the job done,
- leading and managing the team,
- leading and managing the team members, and
- leading and managing yourself.

You should have a clear and solid understanding of what each entails and what skills and competencies they require of you. If you are still unsure, go back to Chapter 4 and study it again. You should also occasionally take some time to reflect on where you stand with regard to each, what you do well, and where you could and want to improve.

Principle 2: Avoid globally disliked leadership behaviors

Some people do not like it when you show too much interest in them, others are unhappy if you do not inquire regularly how they are and what they do. Leaders have to find their own particular way with each and every one of their subordinates. This is influenced both by your and their personality and by culture, which in turn shapes personality.

---

[1] See page 98f.
[2] See page 103.

Nonetheless, according to the GLOBE study (House, Hanges, and Javidan, 2004), eight behaviors are considered unacceptable for leaders around the world:

- being *dictatorial* (i.e. autocratic) in the way you lead your team (e.g. by never consulting them or by demanding absolute obedience without questions),
- being *egocentric* (e.g. by claiming team successes as your own or by presenting personal successes rather than team successes to others),
- being *ruthless* in the pursuit of goals, both organizational and (particularly) personal,
- being frequently *irritable* in your interactions with others,
- being *asocial* (i.e. inconsiderate of or hostile to others),
- being a *loner* that shuns human interaction and communicates poorly,
- being *non-explicit* (i.e. not giving clear instructions or a straight answer), and
- being *non-cooperative* vertically and/or horizontally (i.e. with your subordinates, superiors, and/or colleagues).

As a leader, be mindful of these and avoid both acting in these fashions and being seen in these ways. Reflect periodically and honestly whether you have recently engaged in any of these behaviors, and if so, whether this was an excusable exception—it rarely is—or a pattern. If you notice the latter, ask yourself where this comes from and under which circumstances it emerges, then try to avoid either that circumstance, which is easier, or change your behavior, which is much harder. Ask for feedback from trusted colleagues and subordinates if you are unsure.

Principle 3: Conform to implicit leadership expectations in your cultural leader context

Apart from globally disliked leader behaviors, the GLOBE study (House, Hanges, and Javidan, 2004) also demonstrated that the perception of the majority of leader behaviors is culturally contingent, with many behaviors being seen positively in one culture but negatively in another. Understanding the cultural leadership context or contexts in which you operate is thus crucial. What is considered an exceptional leader? Which behaviors are expected of such leaders? There are many sources for such knowledge: trusted friends or colleagues with substantial leadership experience in the culture or cultures relevant to you, cross-culturally comparative research such as the GLOBE study, talks with your subordinates from those areas, cross-cultural trainings, familiarization visits, and so on. For an overview of leader behaviors expected of outstanding leaders in select cultures, see Table 38 on page 298.

Principle 4: Declare your expectations clearly

If a task is not completed according to your expectations, there are three possibilities: the team member charged with it was unable to do it or unwilling to do it, or you did not explain it correctly. Leaders with low self-awareness will often automatically attribute blame to the team member in such a situation. In cases where there is a sender–receiver problem, meaning inadequately voiced expectations on your part, rather than an actual screw-up on your follower's part, this can jeopardize both that team member's motivation and your reputation as a leader.

As previously explained[1], communication is a very important leader skill. Neither your team members nor your colleagues or superiors are mind readers. Communication is also strongly culturally

---

[1] See Chapter 5 on page 216f.

contingent. *That* you clearly declare your expectations is paramount, therefore; *how* you do it depends on the context. When issuing orders, always ask yourself if you really explained not only what you wanted in sufficient clarity and detail but also in a way that is acceptable to the team member or members in question. Did you clearly spell out the expected outcome? Did you check, for instance by asking a few pointed questions at the end, that your intent was correctly understood? Did you make sure that all those involved could save face?

If you notice a pattern of work that is not carried out according to your wishes, try putting your expectations in writing (e.g. in the form of a written task order). In fact, it is a good idea to always put important tasks in writing (either specifically or, for recurring tasks, in the form of a GPE[1]). It may also be a good idea to sign this document because people tend to pay more attention to a signed order. For non-routine tasks, always discuss the performance and outcome you expect from the team members involved with them before they start their work.

Principle 5: Be technically and administratively proficient

As mentioned before, a leader's reputation is an important asset, and what you know and are able to do is a big part of this. However, the military principle that a leader should be at least as well (or preferably even better) trained than the people he or she leads cannot always be applied in the business world. Perhaps you head a team of experts, and it would clearly be unreasonable to expect you to know everything about what they do. Even in that case, however, it behooves you well to understand at least the basics of what they are doing. For example, a business information project manager will normally not be as well versed in computer programming as his team members, but his reputation will be enhanced—and his life as a leader made

---

[1] General Performance Expectation; see Figure 18 on page 184.

considerably easier—if he knows how to write passable code himself and can gauge the quality of the code his people write.

Additionally, a leader must also be skilled administratively. Not only is this a universally expected attribute of an outstanding leader in all 62 countries examined in the GLOBE study[1]; if you create extra work for your team or make them look bad due to your administrative incompetence, your standing will suffer greatly, no matter how nice you are and how close your rapport with your team is otherwise. It is thus in your very own interest to make sure you are on top of your administrative duties. If you have a strongly management-oriented leadership role and feel less than confident in your administrative abilities, getting some formal business administration training as part of your leadership development may be a good idea. To prepare for higher management roles, a formal degree with a strong administrative focus (such as an MBA[2] or Executive MBA) may be worth considering. See Chapter 7 for more information on leadership development, too.

Principle 6: Be sure of what you say to whom and why you say it

In order to not appear weak, inexperienced or insecure, leaders sometimes feel pressured to state something with finality, even if they are less than sure. Although understandable from an emotional point of view, if it later on turns out you were wrong, your reputation and your followers' motivation will be hurt much more than if you had simply admitted you were uncertain. Of course, constantly proclaiming that you do not know or are not sure will also lead to the kind of reputation you do not want. This is a trade-off between the

---

[1] Only three of the 62 (or 5%) scores for this attribute were in the upper medium range (for France, Qatar, and New Zealand), while the rest were all in the high range. The lowest score was 4.53 (out of 7) in the case of France, the highest 6.42 in the case of Iran, and the mean score across all countries 5.78.

[2] *Master of Business Administration,* generally a graduate/postgraduate business degree for non-business graduates, such as engineers, medical doctors, or psychologists. An Executive MBA is usually a part-time MBA degree for more experienced students who already have substantial management and some leadership experience.

human need for information[1] and your desire to appear competent and not be held accountable for faulty statements. Additionally, some cultures (particularly the Chinese)[2] will tend to perceive even informal statements as promises, in which case you need to be doubly careful.

Consequently, always be careful when communicating something. Ask yourself in advance not just *how* you want to say it but also *why* you say it and to *whom* it should be addressed. Is your statement sufficiently based on established fact? Is now the right time for this statement? Could the information be improved if you waited a bit? Conversely, does the situation allow you to wait? Will your team accept the delay? Do the people you address need to know or want to know? If the latter, should they know? These are the kinds of questions you need to answer for yourself before making any kind of official statement.

Even unofficial statements, however, need to be well considered. Occasionally, it may feel tempting to engage in a bit of office gossip, particularly if you have a close relationship with your team. Unfortunately, this can also negatively impact your reputation, especially your reputation for integrity. For example, becoming known as someone who speaks negatively about others behind their backs, even someone outside the team, like a superior, will generally have a detrimental effect on the trust between you and your team. As their leader, your people will generally hold you to a higher standard than themselves or their colleagues, or even other leaders with whom they do not work directly. Unfair? Maybe. But that is life for a leader.

---

[1] This human need for information is strongly influenced by culture and the organization's current situation. Specifically, the stronger uncertainty avoidance is and the less the organization operates in normal mode, the higher the information needs are. In other words, people in an organization in crisis in Switzerland (which has one of the world's highest uncertainty avoidance practices) will have much higher information needs than people in an organization in normal operating mode in Hungary (which has one of the world's lowest uncertainty avoidance practices). In neither case, however, is information unimportant or irrelevant.

[2] Also see Lewis (2006).

Principle 7: Go the extra mile

Whether you like it or not, you are the role model for your team members. If you are slacking, so will they. If you show uncommon commitment, so will they. Once again, this is a matter of reputation: if you become known as a quitter or as someone who unloads unpleasant tasks on others or leaves them high and dry as soon as the first obstacle or alternative opportunity appears, your people will either stop following you, if they have that option, or show only lackluster commitment. Why should they invest their time and emotions if they feel you do not? Conversely, if you have a reputation for always getting there no matter what, and preferably while maintaining good working relationships on your team, people will follow you even when the obstacles seem almost insurmountable. In the interest of overall team performance, therefore, it is a good idea to be the benchmark for the kind of commitment you expect from others.

Principle 8: Take care of your people

In 1998, American business professor and former fighter pilot and U.S. Air Force major general William A. Cohen polled 200 business leaders with military experience and asked them what they considered the most important leadership lessons. Literally all of them mentioned taking care of their people as one of the essential leadership duties. Or, as Virgin Group founder and chairman Sir Richard Branson put it in a 2015 blog post: "Take care of your people and they'll take care of your business".

Why is that? A 2015 Gallup report found that more than two-thirds of American workers are disengaged, meaning they are emotionally detached from their work because they feel their contribution, and by extension they themselves, do not matter in the grand scheme of things. It seems quite feasible that the numbers are similar in other developed countries. In line with Herzberg's Theory of Motivation[1], by showing them over and over again that they matter and that you care about them, the level of engagement of your team members will increase noticeably. How you do this will depend on a number of factors, such as your personal style, the team's character, the individual team members' expectations, and the means at your disposal. What is important is that you do it and that you do it consistently.

Taking care of your people does not imply putting them before the mission. Sometimes the mission will come first and sometimes the people. But the important point is not just that your team members feel well taken care of; what is equally essential is for them to see and believe that you are not putting yourself ahead of them. To provide a brief analogy, just as the cowboys of old saw to their horses first before eating, you make sure the mission is in hand and your people have what they need before satisfying your own needs[2].

In summary, taking care of your people will help them be motivated and will contribute to reciprocal trust and loyalty—both necessary conditions for superior performance.

Principle 9: Lead from the front

There is a saying which exists in many similar shapes and forms and epitomizes the need to lead from the front: "It is easier to pull a piece of rope than to push it."

Of course, likening your team to a piece of rope is a tricky proposition, but if you think about it, the metaphor holds up well; your team can either be completely slack and inert or fully taut and at work, depending on your leadership and the team's maturity[3].

---

[1] See Chapter 4.41 on page 151f.

[2] Sometimes this may literally be about eating. In the Swiss Army infantry, for example, it is a standing principle that people eat in inverse order of rank when having meals in the field: first the common soldiers, then the non-commissioned officers, and finally the officers.

[3] Also see Chapter 3.25 on page 75.

The Israel Defense Forces are famous for their 'follow me!' ethos, which is firmly embedded in the organization's culture and seen as an important aspect in the IDF's effectiveness. The alternative, to lead from the back, was practiced by the Soviet Army of World War II, based on the argument that the state had spent too much time and money training an officer to throw him away—which of course implied that the same was not true for the common soldier. It was also the Soviet Army that developed a unique remedy for its soldiery's reluctance or even refusal to move forward, often into withering machine gun fire: to position political officers (so-called *commissars* or *politruks*) with pistols behind the advancing soldiers who would shoot them in the back when they stopped or tried to turn around. Obviously, this is neither literally nor figuratively an option for a modern leader and was, in fact, one of the main reasons for the widespread demoralization of Soviet troops at the time.

In contrast, the highest losses in the U.S. Army of World War II were among platoon leaders and company commanders[1], precisely because they were taught and expected to lead from the front. In a business context, being out in front makes a leader more vulnerable to office politics and increases the chance that she or he is blamed for failures.

So why, then, should anybody do this? Being right there at the frontline, seeing directly what is happening and sharing the danger with them is seen as the best way to get soldiers to do something inherently dangerous and quite possibly lethal. The same goes, figuratively, for business. Remember that a key responsibility of leadership is getting the job done. If your people do not see you share their efforts and hardships, this will be very difficult. Clearly, there is a big difference between "follow me!" and "forward, folks, and let me know when we've won!"

---

[1] In most armies, a platoon leader will lead somewhere around 30-40 soldiers and non-commissioned officers, while a company commander will lead between about 150 and 250 soldiers, non-commissioned officers, and junior officers.

Although there is a distinct difference between the military and business insofar as the latter will not normally pose a danger to life and limb, occupational burn-out, which is the result of prolonged job-related stress, has become all too common in corporate life, and an important stressor is the sense of inequity arising from the impression that the boss does not carry his or her fair share of the burden and, by extension, care about her or his people. By making it evident that you do, in fact, shoulder your fair share or more, that you understand exactly what is happening at the literal or figurative frontline, and that you do not ask something of your people that you are unwilling to do yourself, this particular stressor is much reduced, your people are encouraged, and their motivation is increased. At the same time, it will help you to fully appreciate and understand the situation in a way that would not be possible otherwise.

Even in a job where it is impractical to be out and about with your people all the time, having some first-hand frontline experience is paramount. If you head a team of salespeople, you should make at least the occasional sale yourself[1]. If you are a manager in a bank, you will ideally see a customer once in a while. And if you work in a manufacturing company, it is good to show your face on the factory floor regularly. Of course, there are plenty of contrary examples. In many hospitals, the chief administrator is not a medical doctor and may thus not fully appreciate the pressures at the Hippocratic front. Likewise, in plenty of universities, there is a clear separation between faculty and administration, with administrators often having only a rudimentary grasp of teaching and research at best. And in both corporations and armed forces, there are plenty of senior leaders who have risen through the ranks mainly due to successfully avoiding blame for any kind of failure, often chiefly by not having done much of anything. Depending on your personal outlook, this may be considered personal success, but it is not good leadership.

---

[1] As shown in Seelhofer and Valeri (2017), however, directly competing with subordinates for sales may well be counterproductive.

From both ethical and practical points of view, there is no alternative to leading from the front for long-term team leadership success. Saying "the project is behind; I need some people to work over the weekend to catch up" is clearly not the same as saying "the project is behind; I will be working this weekend to catch up, and I need some people to help me". If you get out in front, your people will follow you.

Principle 10: Maintain your integrity at all times

Integrity, defined as adherence to moral principles, should be a goal by itself without any particular need for additional reasons. Nonetheless, maintaining absolute integrity is also in your best interest from a practical angle. Why is that?

People need role models. A leader's behavior, both good and bad, will influence that of followers. Whether the leader plays favorites within the team, takes home the odd package of office paper once in a while, or profits from cronyism or bribery, inevitably someone will notice and feel "hey, if he/she can do it…" This can really hurt the team's harmony and, eventually, performance. It can reduce the team's trust in you and make them take you less seriously, even if you are an excellent leader otherwise. And it can potentially expose you to the threat of blackmail, which clearly is not a tenable position for a leader.

A leader's reputation is his or her capital. If you have a reputation for maintaining unconditional integrity even at the price of your own needs and profit, people will follow you more willingly.

6.2   Ten Classic Leadership Mistakes

Every leader makes mistakes. The only thing to do is learn from them, take corrective measures, move on, and try not to make the same mistake again. Below is a list of very common leadership mistakes you should try to avoid:

1. setting higher standards for your subordinates than for yourself,
2. persistently delegating tasks that you are unwilling to do yourself,
3. causing subordinates to lose face,
4. inconsistent communication,
5. refusing to admit mistakes,
6. creating ethical dilemmas for your subordinates,
7. imposing collective punishment,
8. breaking promises,
9. disloyalty downwards or upwards, and
10. stealing credit.

As you can see, these mistakes are inextricably interwoven with the leadership principles laid out before. By following the principles, all of these mistakes can be avoided; by avoiding these mistakes, you take a big step towards adhering to the principles. And doing both together will make you a more successful leader.

Mistake 1: Setting higher standards for your subordinates than for yourself

As explained in Chapter 4.54[1], setting clear and realistic standards can help you increase team performance while simultaneously lowering your leadership workload. Unfortunately, some leaders have a tendency to demand more of their team than they are willing to do

---

[1] See page 181f.

themselves. Maybe you have also caught yourself doing this at one time or another. It is human nature to optimize. However, it does not take long before your people notice, and that will be very bad for both their motivation and your reputation.

If you declare expectations, you must take pains to also stick to them diligently. Your people may not like it, but at least they see that you keep yourself to the same standards you demand of them. If not, they will either also stop paying attention to them or, if they fear your punishment, merely pay lip service to them. For example, for fifty years the founder and CEO of a medium-sized Swiss railway components producer demanded that all his employees were in the office by 7.30 a.m. While the vast majority of them grumbled constantly about this, they all saw that he was always already there when they came in, so at least he stuck to his own unpopular rule. In fact, he made it a point to be in the office by 6.30 a.m. at the latest, even when approaching ninety years of age. After he finally stepped down, his successor upheld the rule, but it quickly became evident that he had no intention of abiding by it himself, and it did not take long for the rest of the staff to stop paying attention, too. The rule became an empty shell.

You are the role model for your team. Keeping yourself to the same (or preferably an even higher) standard than your subordinates is part of this and will positively influence not just your reputation for integrity and reliability but also your team members' motivation.

Mistake 2: Persistently delegating tasks you are unwilling to do yourself

A second temptation that many leaders give in to is to unload tedious or literally or figuratively dangerous tasks on subordinates. There is, in principle, nothing wrong with delegating. In fact, the ability to delegate smartly is an important leadership skill. The question is how to most effectively utilize the overall resources of a team. An infantry company commander is not best utilized by personally storming a machine gun nest, and a claims team leader in an insurance company may not be most effectively employed by personally making payments while the rest of the team waits. In most cases, it will be better to delegate those jobs and so keep the overview and move the overall mission forward. On the other hand, there may be times when the leader *is* the best woman or man for the job. The classic leadership mistake described here does not refer to such cases. Instead, it is about tasks that are clearly, inherently yours to do and for which there is no reason to pass them on other than you not feeling like doing them and having the power to delegate. Eventually, this will become obvious to your team and reduce your standing in their eyes. For example, a university hired a former top manager to head one of its departments. Although he had a PhD, the university required him to complete a one-year didactics course. Claiming to be too busy, he delegated his written assignments (which he was required to pass to complete the course) to his assistant. Obviously, this is unacceptable behavior, akin to cheating in an exam, and it quickly made the rounds and lowered his already difficult standing in the eyes of his department even further.

An often-heard excuse for this kind of behavior is that a manager's time is too valuable to be spent on tedious tasks such as filling in expense claims or writing progress reports for projects. That may, in fact, be true when there is something of more value to the organization that could be done instead. Frequently, however, this is not the case, and the sole reason for delegating is the leader's unwillingness to deal with the task. For example, a team leader in a London-based advertising agency who was on the road frequently was in the habit of reserving the last half-day of the work month to catch up with her administrative duties, particularly her expenses. Initially, she did them herself, basically because there was no other way; in her company, mid-level executives no longer had personal secretaries. Then, during a high-pressure, major project for a multinational oil corporation, she convinced one of the department pool secretaries to take on her administrative duties, "in order to also make a contribution to the project", as she explained. After four months, the project was finished, but the executive had decided that her time was too valuable to do her expenses herself again. Instead, she began to take that half-day off "to recharge her batteries", as she put it. This quickly made the rounds in the department and started to really hurt her standing among her own team, who heard it from the pool secretaries during coffee breaks and lunch.

Even worse from a motivational viewpoint is the delegation of tasks which are dangerous. Although actual physically dangerous jobs have become rare in the modern office-centric work environment, danger can also be political. Some leaders rise through the ranks by never making a mistake. And the best way to avoid mistakes is to either avoid doing anything of substance altogether or, alternatively, to lay the blame for mistakes that do happen on others. The head of a major but failing software project in an American bank, for example, was in the habit of sending his deputy project head to meetings with the corporate board (where he was usually soundly berated) so his own name and face would be less associated with the fiasco.

Obviously, this kind of behavior is bad not just for your relationship with your team but also for your reputation for integrity, and it should thus be avoided.

Mistake 3: Causing subordinates to lose face

Face is a pervasive concept that refers to a person's image and status within a social group (Cardon and Scott, 2003), specifically the respect that results from social achievement and the pride and dignity that come with it (Leung and Chen, 2001). Face is a person's claim to status and social value based on what is important in his or her social group. The feeling that you, the boss, have caused a loss of face for a subordinate can lead to very angry and unpredictable responses and, even if there is no overt reaction, to long-lingering resentment and loss of motivation. While no one likes the boss to angrily shout out their deficiencies in front of everyone in the middle of a team meeting, how severely this loss of face is felt and how long the effects linger depends on a person's personality and is strongly influenced by culture.

The differing importance that cultures attribute to face is demonstrated by two lexicographic studies from the early 1990s that compared the number of expressions related to *face* in samples of Chinese, Japanese, and English dictionaries (Carr, 1992, 1993). The author found that the Chinese dictionaries contained 98, the Japanese 89, and the English 5 such terms. In the former two, expressions indicating 'losing face' and 'saving face' were about equally divided, while in English the majority was for 'saving face'.

How people deal with face and its perceived loss, and by extension, how people from different cultures manage conflict and rapport is the subject of *Face-Negotiation Theory*. Originally developed by Brown and Levinson and initially proposed in 1978[1], it postulates that all people feel threatened by a loss of face in conflict and engage in so-called *facework*, a set of communicative behaviors employed to save or restore face. The exact perception of face and the associated facework is culturally contingent. Face-Negotiation Theory deals with five themes (Ting-Tommey and Gudykunst, 2005):

- face orientation,
- face movements,
- facework interaction strategies,
- conflict communication styles, and
- face content domains.

There are two basic *face orientations*, self-face and other-face. *Self-face* is concern for one's own honor, prestige, and status plus

---

[1] The theory was later repeatedly updated by various authors, with the latest iteration published by Ting-Toomey and Gudykunst in 2005.

the respect that comes with gaining those, while *other-face* is concern for the same in another person. Face as a concept is closely related to the cultural dimensions of power distance and individualism. More individualistic societies also tend to exhibit smaller power distance and be concerned primarily with self-face, while more collectivist societies generally show higher power distance and are more concerned with other-face.

Face movement refers to the options someone has during conflict to save or regain self-face and other-face. Depending on the concern each party has for the two, they may engage in self-face defense, other-face-defense, mutual face protection, or mutual face obliteration. Whether conflict actually breaks out depends on various aspects, such as the existence or lack of trust between the two parties, the importance of the topic for either, and the situational power distance.

Facework interaction strategies are related to Hall's (1959) concept of low versus high context cultures. More individualistic cultures also tend to be more low-context and therefore rely more on explicit verbal or written communication, while more collectivistic cultures tend to be more high-context and thus rely on a much more indirect, context-based communication style. According to Ting-Tommey and Gudykunst (2005), there are three basic facework interaction strategies:

- Dominating, which is aimed at winning the conflict,
- Avoiding, which is aimed at preserving harmony in the relationship, and
- Integrating, which is aimed at content synthesis and maintaining the relationship.

Because of the differences between individualistic and collectivistic societies, in practice this often means that Westerners may try to engage in conflict for self-face defense, while Easterners may try to avoid conflict altogether to save other-face. So, if your Asian team member is refusing to fight with you, it may not be for a lack of courage but out of an implicit, culturally conditioned concern for you. Rather than calling him or her out for this, it should always be your goal as a leader to pursue an integrating facework interaction strategy which considers the arguments of both sides and thus also allows both sides to save face.

In line with these differing facework interaction strategies, people will also engage in differing *conflict communication styles*:

- dominating,
- avoiding,
- obliging,
- compromising, or
- integrating.

The difference between the last two is that a compromising style aims at finding a solution somewhere between the two positions in a step-by-step, give-and-take style more concerned with the outcome than face-saving, while an integrating style shows much higher concern for the face of both parties. As a leader, your goal should always be to follow an integrating style and, if this proves impossible, at least a compromising style. Some people will also employ emotions or a passive-reactive approach to dominate or at least signal conflict. So, if a team member suddenly acts in an uncharacteristic emotional or sarcastic way, it is possible that he or she is engaging in facework and that you should pay attention rather than getting upset.

Finally, *face-content domains* are groups of issues that cause someone to engage in facework in the first place. In other words, they are deep-rooted emotional needs that, when threatened, will make someone react. While these needs depend on the person and the particular communication context and situation, they tend to fall into similar general categories or domains. There are six such domains (Ting-Tommey and Gudykunst, 2005):

- autonomy (i.e. a perceived threat to, among other things, a person's need for independence, privacy, and respect for personal boundaries),
- inclusion (i.e. a perceived threat to a person's need to be a worthy part of something),
- status (i.e. a perceived threat to a person's need to be acknowledged as valuable or even admired),
- competence (i.e. a perceived threat to a person's need to be recognized as capable),
- reliability (i.e. a perceived threat to a person's need to be seen as dependable, loyal, consistent, and trustworthy), and
- morality (i.e. a perceived threat to a person's need to be seen as someone with honor and high integrity).

If a person perceives a threat to any of these, he or she may engage in facework. If you are at odds with a team member but do not know why, ask yourself whether you may have unwittingly violated one or several of these domains. This might have been overt, such as berating a team member in an email to the whole team, or more subtle, such as seating arrangements during a formal event.

Behind all this complicated language, however, is a simple message: do not make someone look bad, particularly in front of others. While this may seem self-evident, making subordinates lose face is a very common leadership mistake caused by a lack of control over emotions, ignorance of the concept and importance of face, and unrecognized or misunderstood cultural differences. Avoiding this requires good self-control and reflection on your part, a solid understanding of what makes each of your followers tick, and a sound conceptual idea of face and culture. Make it a habit to always allow others to save face. This will not just help ensure their implicit or explicit appreciation, or even gratitude and loyalty; it is also good for the team's harmony.

Mistake 4: Inconsistent communication

According to business theorist and former Harvard Business School professor Chris Argyris, inconsistent communication is a common problem in today's corporate world. He sees this as emerging over three stages: one, managers communicate inconsistent messages; two, these managers then act as if the message were consistent; and three, they eventually try to extricate themselves from the mess they made and, in the process, make the issue practically impossible to resolve by declaring it non-discussable (Argyris, 2000). Obviously, this is not good for morale.

Inconsistent communication is not the same as incorrect or inappropriate communication[1]. Communication is inconsistent when leaders habitually contradict their own statements. There are many reasons why this can occur: they may state things they believe their team wants to hear, rather than what they truly think; they may have problems keeping track of what they have said; or they may just not care that much. It is also possible that they are truly oblivious to the inconsistencies.

Regardless of the reasons, inconsistent communication and mixed messages can drive employees crazy. For example, when your boss tells you that you are one of her best employees but then announces that someone else will be promoted to a position you applied for, that is clearly frustrating. Or consider the case of Florian, a member of the global business development team in a fairly large Swiss textile machinery producer. He was planning to enroll on an Executive MBA program to further his professional development. Owing to the company's complex, matrix-style organizational structure at the time, his immediate supervisor sat in China and communicated with him mainly by email and Skype. When Florian initially asked for permission and support, the supervisor said 'no problem'. A week later, however, he sent an email to everyone in the depart-

---

[1] Also see Principle 4 on page 285.

ment announcing without further explanation that, for the time being, no new requests for education support would be entertained. When Florian inquired whether his request of a week ago would fall under this new rule, his supervisor assured him it did not and said he could go ahead. But when Florian logged the request in the company's HR management system the very next day, the supervisor refused to sign off on it. For Florian, this was not just very confusing, it was also highly frustrating and demotivating.

Often, the leader in question is not even aware of the inconsistencies in her or his communicative behavior. This, of course, makes it difficult to fix without outside help. It can also create the problem that the team starts to come to the leader for every little detail, just to make sure conditions and expectations have not changed. In turn, this can simultaneously raise the leader's work load and decrease the team's efficiency and effectiveness. Inconsistent communication should thus clearly be avoided. As a leader, try to frequently reflect on your communications, both verbal and written, with individuals and the whole team alike. Try to put yourself in their shoes and retroactively listen to yourself. Could you make sense of what was said? Is it in line with what was said earlier? If not, was an explanation offered (e.g. that something has changed or that the previous communication was based on incorrect information)?

Consistent communication strengthens your reputation for competence and reliability, increases the trust between you and the team, and reduces your team members' mental stress.

Mistake 5: Refusing to admit mistakes

Bosses who are never wrong in their own minds are found in all organizations. Maybe in your career so far you have also experienced a few leaders like this. Since everyone makes mistakes, however, there really is no possibility that they are correct. So why, then, do some steadfastly refuse to admit even minor errors?

There can be many reasons for such a refusal to own up to mistakes, but the three major ones are

- fear,
- ego, and
- cognitive dissonance.

Some leaders may fear that admitting to any kind of mistake will make them appear weak and/or reduce their status in their subordinates' eyes. Or their egos may not allow them to appear less than perfect in front of others. Or they may actually have convinced themselves that it could not possibly be their fault. This is called cognitive dissonance, and it is particularly common in psychological disorders such as narcissism, where a person's self-image is overinflated and not in line with objective reality[1]. Some bosses even go so far as to blame someone else for their own mistakes. Obviously, leaders are also people and can exhibit the full spectrum of human behavior.

Ironically, not admitting mistakes or, even worse, blaming someone else usually has the opposite effect to the one intended: the team notices and over time takes this boss less and less seriously. It is, of course, possible that an inexperienced boss who makes many mistakes and is constantly apologizing for these can lose respect. But, first of all, admitting and apologizing are not the same thing. Since everyone makes mistakes—and everyone knows this, if they are honest—not every minor mistake warrants an apology. An apology is in order when someone has been disadvantaged as a result of the mistake. Admitting your mistake, on the other hand, is the first step in learning from the mistake and moving on. It shows that you are a mature person of integrity, secure in who you are and what you can

---

[1] Specifically, according to the American Psychiatric Association, narcissists see themselves as superior to others to the extent that they completely disregard the feelings and wishes of others and expect to be treated as superior regardless of their actual achievements or status.

do, and that you do not place yourself above your people[1]. And if it bothers you a lot to admit a mistake, which is nothing wrong, but you do it nonetheless, which you should, see it as a self-motivational technique to make fewer and fewer mistakes as time goes on.

Mistake 6: Creating ethical dilemmas for your subordinates

Ethics has become a hot topic in the workplace. Today, almost all international companies have a code of ethics and/or a code of behavior that details, for example, what kind of gifts someone may accept or how to deal with attempts to solicit bribes. However, not everything can be regulated and as the boss you may create ethical dilemmas for your subordinates that are not covered by these codes, even if your organization has them.

Among common ethical dilemmas created for subordinates are

- demanding clearly unethical or even illegal behavior from them,
- forcing them to choose between two competing superiors,
- confidentially telling them about some secret wrongdoing of yours,
- passing your own ethical dilemma down the line,
- dealing with the harassed rather than the harasser, and
- acting unethically yourself.

Demanding clearly unethical or even illegal behavior from subordinates obviously creates a number of problems for them. Should

---

[1] Despite the often-heard arguments that this is only important in a Western setting with low power distance and that in high-power distance countries this difference would be implicitly accepted, the GLOBE study clearly showed that there is an almost universal, substantial difference between power distance practices and values. In fact, only a single country out of the 62 studied showed higher power distance values than practices (the Czech Republic), and in all cultural clusters the aggregate power distance values were less than 60% of the practices. For the highest power distance countries Morocco, Nigeria, and El Salvador, the value scores were 54%, 45%, and 47% of the practice scores, respectively. In other words, even in countries where power distance is high in practice, the middle managers polled as part of the study across the board wished it to be lower.

they go along with you or refuse and potentially make you angry? Is the relationship with you or the fact that it is clearly wrong more important? Could there be negative consequences for them if this were found out? And so on. For example, if your team is responsible for producing a faulty product and your boss asks you to cover it up, what would you do? Now reverse the roles. Would it be okay to ask your subordinates to cover this up? The answers are clearly no and no.

Equally, forcing subordinates to choose between two competing or fighting superiors creates a conflict of loyalty and thus mental stress for them. This is particularly common in matrix organizations, but that makes it no less wrong.

Confidentially telling subordinates about some wrongdoing of yours also creates an ethical dilemma for them: Should they keep your secret (because you asked them to) or tell someone higher-up (because it might be the right thing to do)? For example, if your own married boss, whose spouse you also know, confidentially tells you about a romantic affair she is having, you may feel torn between protecting her secret and telling her spouse.

Passing your own ethical dilemma down the line essentially eases your own mind to the detriment of the subordinate you pass it to. For example, if your superiors demand that you reduce your team of eight to six by firing two team members, you have several options. You can refuse, and risk being fired yourself; you can resign to avoid having to make the choice, even though this will probably not stop the train; you can go ahead, rationalizing that you had no choice; or you can pawn the task off to someone else, such as your deputy, thereby also evading the choice, but without running the danger of being fired yourself. Weak leaders often choose the last option. As the leader, however, this is their very own difficult choice to make. By passing the task on, they create exactly the same kind of ethical dilemma for their subordinate. This is clearly immoral. In fact, making the choice may be even harder for that leader's deputy, because he or she will quite likely have a closer working relationship with the rest of the team than the boss.

In cases involving workplace harassment, some leaders find it easier to deal with the person harassed rather than the harasser, often appealing to their loyalty or threatening them. In cases of workplace bullying, this may be because they are wary of the bully, while the victim may seem much more approachable. Considering sexual harassment, in most countries the majority of bosses are still male, and since most harassers are also male and most victims are female, there may also be a type of misguided male-to-male loyalty at play. The several very public Silicon Valley cases in 2017 are a case in point. Apart from the fact that victimizing the victim is clearly always wrong, these leaders create further ethical dilemmas for the victims by essentially telling them that they are the problem and that, if they complain to superiors, they will just hurt the team, the company, and in the end also themselves.

Finally, acting unethically yourself can also create an ethical dilemma for others. For example, if you have a second job and are currently very busy with it, you may feel tempted to order a subordinate in your first job to do some of that work for you. This is not just a breach of trust and contract vis-à-vis your first employer; your subordinate may also feel torn between refusing, and thus upholding his or her own ethical standards, and supporting you, thereby essentially becoming complicit in your unethical behavior.

This is by no means a full list. Moral dilemmas lurk in many situations. The important message here is to be careful not to create these kinds of situations for your subordinates. Put yourself in their shoes each time you communicate an expectation or a piece of information. As the leader, it is your job to recognize and avoid ethical dilemmas in advance. Open communication and a culture of trust and honest feedback can contribute significantly to this. For a more expansive treatise on the ethical dimension of leadership, see Schüz (2016).

Mistake 7: Collective punishment

Collective punishment is still a fairly frequently employed leadership technique, particularly in very hierarchical organizations. When the culprit for an offence is not forthcoming and cannot be determined because he or she is protected by the group, you may be tempted to engage in this kind of behavior. The argument for it is usually that this causes the team to actively self-police and gel much more strongly than it otherwise would. The negative effects, however, vastly outweigh any potential benefits.

Proponents usually point to historical examples that supposedly demonstrate its effectiveness. Throughout history, collective punishment has indeed been used to varying effect by both military and civilian leaders to punish or increase in-group self-control.

For example, in the newly unified China under Emperor Qin Shi Huang (221–207 BC), treason, deception, libel, and the study of banned books became punishable by the extermination of the offender's entire extended family, including aunts, uncles, cousins, and even grandchildren[1].

In Ancient Rome's military, the practice of decimation was used as both punishment and deterrent. Offending units were divided into groups of ten. Out of each of these, one soldier was then randomly selected for execution (usually by drawing lots) by the hands of his comrades. This ancient punishment was reportedly revived by Roman consul Marcus Licinius Crassus in 71 BC during the Third Servile War against Spartacus and his slave army and actually used on at least one cohort[2] after the defeat of two legions under the command of his lieutenant Mummius. During the Great Roman Civil War (49–45 BC), Gaius Julius Caesar also threatened to (but never actually did) decimate the 9th Legion.

---

[1] This was called the *nine familial exterminations*.

[2] A Roman cohort at the time consisted of about 500 men.

In medieval Germanic law (used, for example, in what are today Germany, England, and the Netherlands), the term *Sippenhaft* denoted the legal obligation of a family to answer for the crimes of one of its members. This practice was revived by Nazi Germany before and during World War II.

In the 18th century, the British colonial masters passed the Intolerable Acts of 1774 which took away Massachusetts' historic rights and self-government as a form of collective punishment for the Boston Tea Party. Likewise, the Union Army during the American Civil War of 1861–1865, the Prussian Army during the Franco-German War of 1870–1871, the British Army during the Second Anglo-Boer War of 1899–1902, the German Army during World War I, and both the German and the Soviet armies during World War II all used collective punishment against the civilian population, usually in retribution for guerilla-style attacks.

So, historic examples abound. Likewise, almost every modern soldier has a story to tell about how the whole platoon had to clean toilets or a parking lot with a toothbrush because of an individual's infractions. But does this abundance of examples mean that collective punishment is a good idea? The answer is no.

Collective punishment will lead to strong resentment of you as the leader and will considerably diminish trust between you and your subordinates. While it can indeed bring the team closer together, particularly in their hatred of you, it can also have the opposite effect and significantly reduce team integrity if team members start to turn on each other. Studies have also shown that there is no lasting effect of this practice on team effectiveness and in-group enforcement, thus invalidating a chief argument for it (see e.g. Dickson, 2007). And finally, using collective punishment sends strong signals that you are unable to lead your team effectively, that you do not care about your people, and that you lack a sense of fairness— all things that will hamper your success as a leader in the long-run. Although sometimes tempting, collective punishment is thus a clear leadership no-go.

Mistake 8: Breaking promises

Promises should not be made lightly. Once they are made, however, they should be kept at all costs. This is what most people learn as children. In real life, unfortunately, some leaders forget this as soon as they are in a position of power. And, of course, a situation can also change so much that keeping the original promise is no longer possible. In such a case, the person or group the promise was made to should be informed and given an explanation and an apology. For some leaders, this is a problem. Remembering and keeping promises is hard work, and they may not like to work hard. Informing others about something that could potentially make the leader look bad also takes some courage, which she or he may not have. And explaining and, particularly, apologizing is something many people hate doing.

In addition, even well-meaning leaders who take pains not to break promises may occasionally unwittingly do so because what is considered a promise may differ from culture to culture. Confucian-oriented cultures, particularly the Chinese are inclined to consider any official statements as promises, even if to a Western ear no promise has been explicitly voiced.

Keep this fact in mind and make sure you keep your promises, even the ones you did not explicitly voice as such. If you communicate consistently[1], this should be feasible. Keep track of the promises you explicitly make, if necessary by keeping a 'promise journal', and be sensitive to suddenly changing behavior in team members, which often indicates a problem. Keeping your promises strengthens your reputation for integrity and reliability and significantly increases your team members' trust in you.

---

[1] Also see Principle 4 on page 316f.

Illustration 14:   Peter's Unwitting Promise

Peter, a 43-year old partner at the Austrian subsidiary of a large multinational business consulting firm, had a problem with one of his consultants. Yusheng, at 37 slightly younger than he but very experienced, had been acting strangely for the past few weeks. She was the head of the small China Team the firm had stationed in Vienna to serve local companies with ties to the Middle Kingdom and reported directly to him. Originally from Guangzhou, Yusheng was married to an Austrian and had been in Vienna for almost ten years, six of which she had worked for Peter. The two had always had an excellent, if somewhat distant, working relationship.

Recently, however, Yusheng had started to act in what to Peter seemed an odd way. She started to go out of her way to avoid having to speak to him. And when it was unavoidable, there was always a barely noticeable undertone, which Peter picked up but could not really place or understand. Her answers and statements became more and more sarcastic, although always in a very subtle way. This passive-aggressive behavior flummoxed Peter, largely because he could not make sense of it, and after a while, he began to actively push back, becoming more directive and less patient. This, in turn, exacerbated the situation, with Yusheng becoming even more distant and sullen. Finally, Peter had had enough and, remembering their formerly first-rate rapport, started to look for an answer. What could have caused her strange behavior? Trouble at home? Trouble at work? Trouble with him? Something else? But what? Eventually, he stumbled across Lewis' MLR[1] model of culture and read about how people from reactive cultures such as China's may consider even seemingly innocuous statements as promises. Could this be it? But what could she have considered a promise that he then inadvertently broke? Finally, he used the opportunity of the drive home from a management retreat to get to the bottom of the matter. He politely asked Yusheng to ride with him and, after some small talk, cautiously broached the subject. To his surprise, she reacted quite positively and openly. During a management meeting three weeks ago, Peter had relayed the European headquarter's demand that, for budgetary reasons and until further notice, all teams in the Vienna office no longer authorize overhours for administrative staff (because, according to Austrian labor law, these would have to be paid). To Peter's mind, he had merely been a go-between. Yusheng, however, had taken this as an implicit promise that all other teams would act in the same way—something which did not happen. To her mind, she had then lost face with her team because she enforced the rule while other team leaders did not, and she saw it as Peter's responsibility to ensure that they did. While Peter only partly agreed, he accepted that Yusheng could have seen it this way. The two discussed the matter extensively during the 45-minute drive back to the city and slowly started to understand and respect the other's point of view.

Yusheng clearly appreciated Peter's initiative and was also able to reflect on her own reaction. Eventually the two could put this issue behind them and resume their normal working relationship.

[1] *Multi-active–Linear-active–Reactive. For more information, see Chapter 5.27 on page 272f.*

Mistake 9: Disloyalty downwards or upwards

Loyalty is a tricky concept. Most people would probably agree that it is very important on any team, but just as in societal culture, there is often a difference between value and practice. Some leaders will frequently demand loyalty from their team but act in a decidedly disloyal way towards their own superiors, oblivious of the example they set that way. This may be done because they do not get along with their boss and lack self-control, or it may be an attempt to ingratiate themselves with the team if the superior in question is unpopular with them.

For example, a division head in a large French insurance company did not get along with his new boss, a CEO brought in from outside. Each time this division head came back from a one-on-one meeting with the CEO or a corporate management workshop, he would loudly and profanely complain about his boss, without a care for who might hear him. Frequently, he would also use his own management meetings at divisional level or one-on-one meetings with his direct reports to vent his dissatisfaction with his boss. A few times, he even called in one of his subordinate managers specifically to complain about their CEO and to discuss what could and should be done. This did not just make his subordinates very uncomfortable—and created an ethical dilemma for them: whether to tell the CEO or not. They also started to wonder if he spoke similarly about them behind their back. All in all, the divisional head's reputation suffered considerably because of this behavior.

But loyalty also works downwards, of course. Your people have a right to expect that you have their backs, particularly for things you told them to do. If you fail to do so, they will take note of it and either think twice about doing your bidding next time or at least start to resent you. They may also seek your guidance and direction much more frequently than before, so as to avoid mistakes or so that you cannot lay the blame on them for these, and this will increase the demands on your time. While many leaders claim that they do not care about what others think, and in fact, the team's opinion about your personal clothing style or taste in music is irrelevant, it matters very much whether they think you are trustworthy or not.

Your people are not stupid. If you expect loyalty from them but act disloyally, whether towards superiors or subordinates, they will notice the incongruence, and this will diminish both your reputation for integrity and their will to act loyally themselves.

Mistake 10: Stealing credit

Occasionally, when someone on your team has done a good job, you may be tempted to claim this as your own achievement, particularly when you feel that the real achiever will not find out. This kind of behavior is closely related to a person's personality, specifically to a high need for status and low performance orientation, and is not the same as rightfully claiming credit in the name of the entire team.

In some settings, such as in the academic world, this kind of behavior may be explicitly regulated or at least covered by official, widely used guidelines; in others, it may be widely practiced behavior that barely raises an eyebrow. However, it is wrong in either case, both from an ethical and a motivational point of view.

For example, some university professors use doctoral students to do research for them which they then publish under their own name. As long as the doctoral student is named as a co-author, there is nothing particularly wrong with this (although it might be debated whether the PhD candidate should not at least be lead author), but not all academics behave that way. If a student does all the research but the professor is mentioned as the sole author, that is stealing credit.

As another example, a top-level manager at a large Swiss bank owed his career predominantly to the fact that he early on identified a highly promising junior manager and managed to have him transferred to his team. Then, the junior manager produced a series of successes, for which the more senior manager took credit in front of superiors; after all, it was his team, as he put it, and the team's success thus essentially his, in his eyes. The two managed to rise through the ranks together; the senior manager would be promoted for a job well done and then make sure that the junior manager was also promoted and continued to report directly to him at the new, higher level. In this way, both of them eventually made it to the top, although only one of them objectively did valuable work for the company.

Examples like these abound. Obviously, from an organization's point of view, this is undesirable behavior. But it is also in your own interest to avoid this at all costs. Claiming someone else's achievement as your own is unethical however you try to frame it, and it will inevitably come out, even if you try to hide it. This will be bad not just for your reputation for integrity and competence but also for the motivation of your subordinates. Why should they apply themselves if you will swoop in at the last minute to steal credit for a job well done? Give credit where credit is due. This will make your life easier, your people happier, and your leadership more effective in the long run.

6.3 Chapter Recap

TAKEAWAYS

What you should take away from this chapter:

1. There are ten very important leadership principles you should try to apply in your leadership work:
   - understand and respect your leader responsibilities,
   - avoid globally disliked leadership behaviors,
   - conform to implicit leadership expectations in your cultural leader context,
   - declare your expectations clearly,
   - be technically and administratively proficient,
   - be sure of what you say and why you say it,
   - go the extra mile,
   - take care of your people,
   - be present and authentic, and
   - maintain your integrity at all times.

2. There are ten classic leadership mistakes you should try to avoid:
   - setting higher standards for your subordinates than for yourself,
   - persistently delegating tasks that you are unwilling to do yourself,
   - causing subordinates to lose face,
   - inconsistent communication,
   - refusing to admit mistakes,
   - creating ethical dilemmas for your subordinates,
   - collective punishment,
   - breaking promises,
   - disloyalty downwards or upwards, and
   - stealing credit.

CHECK QUESTIONS

Try to answer the questions below. If you need help, check the sample answers in the annex.

1. Which leaders make mistakes?
2. What is a leadership principle?
3. What are the eight behaviors universally considered unacceptable for outstanding leaders?
4. Why is it important for an international leader to understand the relevant cultural context(s)?
5. Why should a leader show uncommon commitment?
6. Apart from ethical considerations, why should you take care of your team members?
7. Why should you lead from the front?
8. What is the importance of integrity for a leader?
9. Why is it a mistake to set higher standards for your subordinates than for yourself?
10. What is face?
11. What are two reasons for the ubiquity of inconsistent leader communication?
12. What are three common reasons for the inability of leaders to admit mistakes?
13. What are common ethical dilemmas created for subordinates?
14. Why should collective punishment be avoided?
15. What should be done if a promise cannot be kept?
16. Why should you not display disloyalty to the company or to your own boss in front of your team?
17. Why is stealing credit from your subordinates particularly bad?

6.4   Exercises

On the following pages, you will find exercises related to the content of this chapter. If you need help, check the sample solutions in the annex.

Exercise 23 Ten Fundamental Leadership Principles

Reflect on the leadership principles introduced in this chapter. Are they relevant for your leadership context? Do you agree with them? Why or why not? In your own cultural and work context, what priority would you assign them (A = highly important, B = fairly important, C = not so important)?

Leadership Principles	Your priority	Your comments
Understand and respect your leader responsibilities		
Avoid globally disliked leadership behaviors		
Conform to implicit leadership expectations in your cultural leader context		
Declare your expectations clearly		
Be technically and administratively proficient		
Be sure of what you say to whom and why you say it		
Go the extra mile		
Take care of your people		
Be present and authentic		
Maintain your integrity at all times		

Exercise 24 Ten Common Leadership Mistakes

Reflect on the leadership mistakes discussed in this chapter. Do you ever commit them? If yes, are these instances exceptions or part of a pattern? What can you do to try and avoid them in the future?

Leadership Mistakes	Frequency with which you commit them				Improvement measures (to reduce or even avoid them in the future)
	Often	Some-times	Rarely	Never	
Setting higher standards for your subordinates than for yourself					
Persistently delegating tasks that you are unwilling to do yourself					
Causing subordinates to lose face					
Inconsistent communication					
Refusing to admit mistakes					
Creating ethical dilemmas for your subordinates					
Collective punishment					
Breaking promises					
Disloyalty downwards or upwards					
Stealing credit					

7 ORGANIZATIONAL LEADERSHIP DEVELOPMENT

LEARNING OUTCOMES

After this chapter, you should be able to

- understand the value of systematic leadership development,
- assess your own leadership development needs and those of subordinates,
- structure and implement leadership development programs, and
- assess the success of leadership development activities.

Leadership development programs (LDP) are found around the world. Their ubiquity and persistence indicates that both organizations and individuals consider them valuable and worthwhile. However, there is no single standard, and the quality of programs differs wildly, with many of them frequently failing to reach their goals (Day and Halpin, 2001).

A leadership development program aims to systematically improve the leadership abilities of leaders and should be based on the needs of the organization as well as those it trains. It should identify development needs based on a range of factors, such as effective leader traits and behaviors, situational awareness, emotional intelligence, and cultural awareness[1]. Its content should be well-balanced and account for both various aspects of leadership and the specific development needs identified. And a good leadership development program will also include impact assessment, because necessary adjustments to the program or the need for further training may not be

---

[1] In today's increasingly globalized workplace, even leaders who work in purely domestic organizations are frequently faced with cultural challenges. Making cultural awareness part of a leadership development program is thus just good common sense.

recognized without it. Does the program deliver on its promise? Does it cover the right aspects? Did participants improve after a specific initiative? These are questions that need to be answered.

Generally speaking, therefore, a leadership development program should have at least three parts:

1. gap and needs analysis,
2. development activities, and
3. feedback loop.

This approach follows the logic of the well-known Deming Cycle[1]. In line with this philosophy, the improvement of your leadership capabilities is continuous and never finished.

7.1   Leadership Gap and Needs Analysis

Every leadership development program should start with a gap and needs analysis. Its starting point should be a comparison of your current profile with the competencies modern leaders must have. As previously explained, key among these are your abilities to

- reliably accomplish tasks and missions,
- effectively lead yourself, the team, and its individuals,
- integrate six leadership key practices and nine leadership key functions into your leadership approach,
- understand and manage cultural differences, and
- recognize development needs and initiate the necessary development measures.

In order to do so, you must also develop

---

[1] The Deming Cycle consists of four steps that are cyclically repeated: plan (ahead for change), do (execute the plan in controlled, incremental steps), check (the results), and act (to standardize or improve the process). It is named after American engineer, professor, and management consultant W. Edwards Deming, who had a large impact on post-World War II Japanese manufacturing and business through his work on continuous improvement and was later a highly successful consultant on quality management in the United States.

- emotional-social intelligence,
- leadership presence,
- resilience,
- international exposure and experience, and
- business and administrative skills.

Additionally, it may be necessary to work on your technical skills. With this skill set in mind, you can now analyze where you stand, where your gaps are, and which of those you want to or need to close. This may be conducted in a variety of ways. Common approaches include

- personal reflection,
- personality tests,
- vignette-based scenarios to establish the leader's preferred reaction to hypothetical situations,
- aptitude tests to determine current ability and compare it to a known standard,
- discussions with education experts, such as business program managers, and
- discussions with and feedback from subordinates, superiors, peers, and/or coaches.

Personal reflection is the easiest and quickest way to think about your deficiencies as a leader. If you are already reasonably experienced and feel you know yourself quite well, you can arrive at a conclusion quickly. The drawback is that you may have blind spots, as most people do, which may mean you miss some important areas that require development. Even if you compile your own development program, therefore, it is a good idea to discuss it with select third persons who have a good understanding of the requirements of leadership and know both you and your job well.

Personality tests, as previously described, may be used to determine a current or potential leader's actual (rather than perceived) behavioral preferences. For example, leaders frequently describe themselves as extravert even if they are not, because they feel subconsciously pressured by the management literature, in which this is often described as a hallmark of good leaders, or role models around them. Over the course of their early careers, they may thus have picked up extravert mannerisms, even if these make them feel uncomfortable. Identifying their true preferences will help them become more authentic as a leader and reduce their psychological stress. This may involve taking one of the widely used personality tests, such as the OPQ32 or the Myers-Briggs Type Indicator.

In *vignette-based scenarios,* leaders are confronted with fictional or real scenarios which require analysis and a decision. This can be done to assess analytical and decision-making capabilities and so identify development needs, or it may be a development activity in itself, for instance by discussing performance, strengths, mistakes made and their ramifications, and so on.

Aptitude tests can help you identify specific areas that require improvement, such as project management, language skills, self-management skills, or specific know-how.

Discussions with education experts can support you or your team by opening your eyes to previously unknown or unconsidered options that might meet a large proportion of your development needs.

Finally, *discussions with and feedback from subordinates, superiors, peers, and/or coaches* can help you to step outside the limitations of your self-view by jointly identifying your strengths and weaknesses and shedding light on the pros and cons of specific activities[1]. If you choose people that know you well, this is the most important element of your gap analysis.

Once your gaps have been identified, you can determine which development activities are necessary.

---

[1] For such discussions, a frame of reference or mental structure such as the *LEAD Model* introduced in Table 4C on page 332 can be helpful.

7.2   Leadership Development Activities

Once the initial analysis has been completed, the development needs that this has identified are structured and put into a written development plan which should include the areas identified, the development activities determined, and the timeframe within which these activities are to be completed. It should also include clear measures of development success: indicators to determine when the goal associated with a particular development activity is reached. Without these, gauging success is difficult.

The specific development activities can take a variety of shapes and forms (see e.g. Day and Halpin, 2001), such as:

- formal training (to foster development of general skills required by the job, such as business and management skills),
- executive coaching (focused one-on-one learning),
- on-the-job training and assignments (to challenge or stretch a person's leadership capabilities),
- mentoring (longer-term developmental relationships,
- networking (connecting to and learning from others),
- reflection (making sense of experiences),
- action learning (project-based work to enhance learning in the context of business settings), and
- outdoor challenges (team-building exercises and problem-solving in an outdoor setting).

Often, leaders are quite enthusiastic when they begin training. As time goes by, however, the twin pressures of work and training, often coupled with the additional demands on their private lives, start taking their toll. Anecdotal evidence from a number of British, German, and Swiss companies indicates that the non-completion rate of leadership development programs is quite high. It is thus worthwhile answering the following questions in advance:

- How can your near- and long-term development needs be fulfilled with optimal efficiency and effectiveness?
- When do your planned development activities need to be finished at the latest?
- When is the best time for you to start?

How your development needs can best be served in the most efficient and effective way possible depends on your personal and professional circumstances. Sometimes this will be a custom program at your company, at other times it may be a standardized program at a business school, and occasionally the best way may be personal coaching. Since development activities depend on the needs identified in stage one, they may differ widely from person to person but usually include an individual, person-specific component and a standardized component for generic skills such as time management. Companies may also try to standardize such development activities further by sending aspiring leaders to an (Executive) MBA program or by introducing an in-house, modular leadership development program as part of a corporate academy. What is important is that these questions and the range of corresponding options are considered in advance.

Another crucial aspect to consider is the starting point. When is the best time? The bad news is that there usually *is* no best time. If you wait for the perfect moment, you may never do it, so if you know you need the development, at one point it will be necessary to close your eyes and just jump, figuratively speaking. Nonetheless, it is still a good idea to compare all the possible not-so-optimal moments in time and decide which one is the least problematic for you.

The third influence factor is why you want the training in the first place. Do you want to get better at leading your current team? Are you angling for a specific promotion? Do you want to prepare generally for the next level of leadership? Your answers to these questions will influence both the type and start of your development activities. All three questions should be considered carefully before you start anything. Table 39 shows an example of how a leadership development plan could be structured.

Table 39: Example Leadership Development Program

Leader Responsibility	Development needs	Goals	Activities	Completed in/by	Success criteria
Achieve tasks and missions	Tactical and strategic thinking	▪ Think beyond boundaries of immediate work ▪ Learn to think in options	▪ Executive MBA	12 months	Feedback, Grades
	Project management	▪ Learn how to structure large tasks into smaller tasks; improve resource planning skills	▪ Executive MBA	12 months	Grades, trainer feedback, team feedback
	Time management	▪ Improve time management skills	▪ Company-internal course	2 months	Team feedback, boss feedback
	…	…	…	…	…
Self-leadership	Self-management	▪ Increase self-awareness & self-discipline ▪ Determine real personal preferences and behavioral style	▪ Discussions with wife, team, and boss ▪ Personality tests (MBTI)	6 months	Feedback from spouse, team, and boss; Coach feedback
	Work-life balance	▪ Reduce stress ▪ Improve family life ▪ Prevent burn-out	▪ Dinner at home 3 times a week	Immediately	Family feedback
	Servant leadership	▪ Understand (and learn from) Greenleaf's *Servant Leadership* model	▪ Self-study ▪ Discussion of book with boss	2 months	Self-assessment
	Resilience	▪ Learning how to deal with and learn from setbacks	▪ Self-study ▪ Peer discussions	3 months	Self-assessment, feedback
	Emotional-social intelligence	▪ Improve emotional social intelligence	▪ EQ personality test		
	…	…	…	…	…

Table 39:   Example Leadership Development Program (cont.)

Leader Responsibility	Development needs	Goals	Activities	Completed by	Success criteria
Team-leader-ship	Building trust	▪ Understand the elements that foster trust in a team	▪ Executive MBA	18 months	Grades, team feedback
	Team-building & development	▪ Be able to build and maintain ef-fective teams	▪ Executive MBA	18 months	Grades, team feedback
	Group problem solving and decision-making	▪ Be able to lead groups through prob-lem-solving and decision-making pro-cesses involv-ing several people to en-tire teams	▪ Executive MBA	12 months	Grades, team feedback
	Situational leadership	▪ Be able to rec-ognize and re-spond to situa-tional de-mands	▪ Executive MBA	12 months	Grades, team feedback
	…	…	…	…	…
Leadership of individuals	Conflict management	▪ Recognize, an-alyze, and solve conflicts with subordi-nates	▪ Executive MBA	12 months	Grades, team feedback
	Culture/ diversity management	▪ Recognize and manage cul-tural differ-ences.	▪ Executive MBA ▪ Additional coaching	18 months	Grades, team feedback, coach feedback
	Effective appraisals	▪ Be able to pro-vide fair, hon-est, and moti-vating feed-backs.	▪ Executive MBA	12 months	Grades, team feedback
	…	…	…	…	…

Source: author.

7.3   Feedback Loop

Recent research (e.g. Kirchner and Akdere, 2014) has stressed the need for impact assessment of leadership development, because without it continuous improvement is not possible. This assessment may include both external and internal elements, such as:

- personal reflection,
- 360° feedback (superiors, peers, subordinates),
- retests (e.g. to check for progress in aptitude tests), and
- self-assessment of progress.

Many organizations have formalized this process, but in the end, you are responsible for the success of your own leadership development. One helpful tool is a development log in which you include the original development plan, any observations made during the various development activities, formal and informal outside feedback, personal insights, additionally identified development needs, and any other pertinent information. This log can also be very useful in assessing the impact of your leadership development.

Based on your reflection, you will be able to identify areas where progress is too slow or nonexistent. The leadership development program can then be updated to reflect these insights, either with more of the same training, if it worked but you need more, or different forms of training, if the original approach did not work.

Leadership development is inherently individual. You should thus be acutely aware of your particular development needs, devise a well-structured program that addresses these needs, and complete this program with drive and ambition. Regularly gauge progress made towards your targets and explicitly welcome outside feedback from superiors, subordinates, and peers, but also friends and family. Keep a personal development log, and do not hesitate to ask for help from more experienced leaders or education experts when necessary. The success of your leadership development will reward you for the effort you put in.

7.4   Chapter Recap

TAKEAWAYS

What you should take away from this chapter:

1. Leadership development programs aim to systematically improve the leadership abilities of a leader.

2. A leadership development program consists of three elements:
   - gap and needs analysis,
   - development activities, and
   - feedback loop.

3. Common approaches in the gap and needs analysis are
   - personal reflection,
   - personality tests,
   - vignette-based scenarios to establish the leader's preferred re-action to hypothetical situations,
   - aptitude tests to determine current ability and compare it to a known standard,
   - discussions with education experts, such as business program managers, and
   - discussions with, and feedback by, superiors, peers, and/or coaches.

4. Three fundamental questions must be answered before embark-ing on a leadership development program:
   - How can your near- and long-term development needs be ful-filled with optimal efficiency and effectiveness?
   - When do your planned development activities need to be fin-ished?
   - When is the best time for you to start?

5. Specific development activities include
    - formal training (to foster development of general skills required by the job, such as business and management skills),
    - executive coaching (focused one-on-one learning),
    - on-the-job training and assignments (to challenge or stretch a person's leadership capabilities),
    - mentoring (longer-term developmental relationships,
    - networking (connecting to and learning from others),
    - reflection (making sense of experiences),
    - action learning (project-based work to enhance learning in the context of business settings), and
    - outdoor challenges (team-building exercises and problem-solving in an outdoor setting).

6. A basic leadership development plan consists of
    - Development needs,
    - Development goals,
    - Development activities,
    - Completion date, and
    - Success criteria.

7. The assessment of a leadership development program's impact can include
    - personal reflection,
    - 360° feedback (from superior, peers, and subordinates),
    - retests (e.g. in the case of aptitude tests to check for progress), and
    - self-assessment of progress.

CHECK QUESTIONS

Try to answer the questions below. If you need help, check the sample answers in the annex.

1. What is the main goal of a leadership development program?
2. Why should a leadership development program also include impact assessment?
3. Why is a needs and gap analysis necessary before you start a leadership development program?
4. What is the drawback of personal reflection for conducting a needs and gap analysis for a leadership development program?
5. What is the most important element of the needs and gap analysis? Why?
6. What should a leadership development plan minimally include?
7. Why is impact assessment of leadership development necessary?

7.5   Exercises

On the following pages, you will find an exercise related to the content of this chapter. If you need help, check the sample solutions in the annex.

Exercise 25 Identifying and Addressing Development Needs

You are called in as a leadership consultant. Consider the information about the leaders below, particularly their personality types and their job prospects.

Aspects	Leader		
	Roger (male)	Amaya (female)	Mira (female)
Personal profile	British (born in Liverpool), Anglican, 32 years of age, 10 years of work experience, 2 years of small team leadership and 6 years of project leadership experience; MSc in Information Management	Sri Lankan (born in Kandy), Theravāda Buddhist, 48 years of age, 24 years of work experience, of which 14 in Germany; 12 years of leadership experience (up to head of department); PhD in Mathematics	Malaysian (born in Malacca), Malay Muslim, 27 years of age; BA in History from UM in Kuala Lumpur; MBA from the University of Michigan, USA; no leadership experience except as student association president
Job environment	IT; has worked for Lanka Bell in Colombo for 2 years; previously 10 years at BT UK in London.	Marketing; has worked for Siemens AG for 26 years, the last 12 of which in Germany, 4 of which at HQ.	Sales; has worked for TV 3 in Kuala Lumpur for 3 years; no prior work experience.
Results of personality test[1]	Typical ISTJ-A personality ('the logistician')	Typical ENFJ-A personality ('the protagonist')	Typical INFJ-T personality ('the advocate')
Results of aptitude tests	Good project management skills; personal time management an issue	Excellent strategic thinker; insufficient detail orientation	Good conceptual and analytical skills Work suffers under pressure
Job prospects	In line for head of IT department (3 teams, 24 people)	In line for division CEO position (12,000 employees)	In line for team leader of a sales team (7 people)

Now consider the three leaders above. What specific development needs can you identify? Why? What development activities would you recommend?

---

[1] For more information about each personality type, see e.g. www.16personalities.com/personality-types.

Leader (who?)	Specific development needs (what?)	Justification (Why?)	Suggested development activities and timeframe (how/when?)
Roger			
Amaya			
Mira			

8 WRAP-UP: INTERPERSONAL LEADERSHIP IN A NUTSHELL

Reaching the end of a book is, one hopes, coupled with a feeling of achievement. Much has been discussed, and if you understood everything and are able to apply it, much has also been achieved. As indicated throughout the book, as an effective leader in today's global economy you must

- reliably accomplish tasks and missions,
- effectively lead yourself, the team, and the individuals on it,
- integrate six leadership key practices and nine leadership key functions into your leadership approach,
- understand and manage cultural differences, and
- recognize development needs and initiate the necessary measures.

As such a leader, you have a sound moral compass and care about those around you. You always set a positive example and are able to heal rifts in relationships and inspire team spirit based on your ability to listen to and read people. You are aware of and address the need for good leadership presence and high levels of emotional-social intelligence and resilience, you make every effort to stay on top of the situation at all times, you stay focused on the big picture and display coolness and clear thinking, thus enabling yourself to make good decisions even under high pressure. You motivate your followers even in difficult situations, and you continuously identify, select, and develop the right people for the right positions. You also adhere to the ten key leadership principles and avoid the ten classic leadership mistakes. Apart from all this, however, many other skills have been discussed during the course of the book.

Table 40 provides an integrative, summary framework of these leader competencies.

Table 40: Integrated Framework of Leader Competencies (LEAD)

L	Lead and manage	Your Team	Individuals	Yourself
		▪ Set and enforce standards ▪ Run productive meetings ▪ Use an appropriate leadership style	▪ Enable, stimulate, and challenge ▪ Show real interest and consideration ▪ Set appropriate leadership rhythm ▪ Use appropriate leadership style	▪ Foster your leadership presence, resilience, and emotional-social intelligence ▪ Structure your work and off-time ▪ Maintain integrity at all times

E	Ener-gize	Your Team		Yourself
		▪ Provide guidance and direction ▪ Motivate and inspire ▪ Set the positive example ▪ Share successes		▪ Ensure appropriate work-life balance ▪ Create regular windows of happiness and relaxation

A	Achieve	Tasks and missions	Personal growth	Situational awareness
		▪ Ensure the right skills (leadership, management, job-related, and conceptual) ▪ Ensure the right attitude (sense of mission; spirit of cooperation; performance, goal, quality, and service orientation) ▪ Ensure the right timing (through realistic and fair time planning)	▪ Set challenging but achievable goals and tasks for yourself and your followers ▪ Periodically assess and discuss your own and your people's development needs	▪ Foster a culture of transparency ▪ Gather and analyze relevant intelligence ▪ Ensure open and direct lines of communication ▪ Communicate frequently and through appropriate channels

D	De-velop	Leaders	Yourself	A positive work climate
		▪ Identify and select the right leaders ▪ Periodically assess and address developmental needs ▪ Support professional and personal growth	▪ Continuously improve your leadership skills ▪ Mentally prepare for unforeseen challenges	▪ Ensure appropriate infrastructure and resources ▪ Ensure strong team cohesion ▪ Encourage and reward initiative

Source: author.

If you remember and understand all this, you are well prepared for the leadership duties ahead of you. Remember, however, that every organization is unique in some ways, and thus yours is likely different from any other. Hence, the theories, principles, and models introduced in this book are simply to help you understand important aspects of leadership and develop your corresponding skills: nothing more and nothing less. In the end, you still need to find your own way.

Best of luck!

ANNEXES

ANNEX 1   REFERENCES

Adair, J. (1973). Action–Centered Leadership, New York: McGraw–Hill.

Adair, J. (1988). Effective Leadership, London: Pan Books.

Arakawa, D., and Greenberg, M. (2007). Optimistic Managers and their Influence on Productivity and Employee Engagement in a Technology Organisation: Implications for Coaching Psychologists, International Coaching Psychology Review, 2(1): 78–89.

Argyris, C. (2000). Flawed Advice and the Management Trap: How Managers Can Know When They're Getting Good Advice and When They're Not, New York: Oxford University Press.

Arvey, R. D. (2009). Why face–to–face business meetings matter, White Paper for the Hilton Group, https://www.vdr–service.de/fileadmin/der–verband/fachthemen/studien/hilton_WhyFace–to–FaceBusinessMeetingsMatter_2009.pdf, retrieved 2017/05/21.

Avolio, B. J., and Bass, B. M. (1991). The Full Range Leadership Development Programs: Basic and Advanced Manuals, Binghamton, NY: Bass, Avolio & Associates.

Avolio, B. J., and Bass, B. M. (2002). Developing Potential across a Full Range of Leadership, Mahwah, NJ: Lawrence Erlbaum Associates.

Banerji, P., and Krishnan, V. R. (2000). Ethical Preferences of Transformational Leaders: An Empirical Investigation, Leadership and Organization Development Journal, 21(8): 405–413.

Barney, J. B. (1986). Organizational Culture: Can it be a Source of Sustained Competitive Advantage?, Academy of Management Review, 11(3): 656–665.

Bar–On, R. M. (1997). The Emotional Quotient Inventory (EQ–i): A Test of Emotional Intelligence, Toronto: Multi–Health Systems.

Bar–On, R. M. (2006). The Bar–On Model of Emotional–Social Intelligence (ESI), Psicothema, 18(1): 13–25.

Baron–Cohen, S., and Wheelwright, S. (2004). The Empathy Quotient: An Investigation Of Adults With Asperger Syndrome Or High Functioning Autism, And Normal Sex Differences, Journal of Autism and Developmental Disorders, 34(2): 163–175.

Bartels, M., Rietveld, M. J., Van Baal, G. C., and Boomsma, D. I. (2002). Heritability of Educational Achievement in 12–Year–Olds and the Overlap with Cognitive Ability, Twin Research and Human Genetics, 5(06): 544–553.

Bass, B. M. (1985). Leadership and Performance beyond Expectations, New York: Free Press.

Bass, B. M., and Stogdill, R. M. (1990). Bass & Stogdill's Handbook of Leadership: Theory, Research, and Managerial Applications, 3. Ed., New York: Free Press.

Beardslee, W. (1989). The Role of Self–Understanding in Resilient Individuals: The Development of a Perspective, American Journal of Orthopsychiatry, 59: 266–278.

Belbin, R. M. (2012). Team Roles at Work, New York: Routledge.

Bennis, W., and Nanus, B. (1985). Leadership: The Strategies for Taking Charge, New York: Harper & Row.

Benyamin, B., Wilson, V., Whalley, L. J., Visscher, P. M., & Deary, I. J. (2005). Large, Consistent Estimates of the Heritability of Cognitive Ability in Two Entire Populations of 11–Year–Old Twins from Scottish Mental Surveys of 1932 and 1947, Behavior Genetics, 35(5): 525–534.

Blake, R., and Mouton, J. (1964). The Managerial Grid: The Key to Leadership Excellence, Houston: Gulf Publishing.

Bouchard, T. J., and McGue, M. (2003). Genetic and Environmental Influences on Human Psychological Differences, Journal of Neurobiology 54(1): 4–45.

Briley, D. A., and Tucker–Drob, E. M. (2013). Explaining the Increasing Heritability of Cognitive Ability Across Development: A Meta–Analysis of Longitudinal Twin and Adoption Studies, Psychological Science, 24(9): 1704–1713.

Brodbeck, F. S., and Frese, M. (2008). Societal Culture and Leadership in Germany, in: Chhokar, J. S., Brodbeck, F. C., and House, R. J. (Eds.), Culture and Leadership Across the World: The GLOBE Book of In–Depth Studies of 25 Societies, New York, NY: Lawrence Erlbaum Associates, 147–214.

Browaeys, M. J., and Price, R. (2008). Understanding Cross–Cultural Management, Essex: Pearson.

Brown, P., and Levinson, S. C. (1978). Universals in Language Usage: Politeness Phenomena, in: Goody, E. (Ed.), Questions and Politeness: Strategies in Social Interaction, Cambridge: Cambridge University Press, 56–310.

Burns, J. M. (1978). Leadership, New York: Harper & Row.

Caplan, G. (1990). Loss, Stress, and Mental Health, Community Mental Health Journal, 26: 27–48.

Cardon, P., and Scott, J. C. (2003). Chinese Business Face: Communication Behaviors and Teaching Approaches, Business Communication Quarterly, 66: 9–22.

Carlyle, T. (1841). On Heroes, Hero–Worship, and The Heroic in History, London: James Frasier.

Carnegie, D. (1936). How to Win Friends and Influence People, New York: Simon and Schuster.

Carr, M. (1992). Chinese "Face" in Japanese and English (Part 1), Review of Liberal Arts, 84: 39–77.

Carr, M. (1993). Chinese "Face" in Japanese and English (Part 2), Review of Liberal Arts, 85: 69–101.

Carroll, G. (1984). Dynamics of Publisher Succession in Newspaper Organizations, Administrative Science Quarterly, 29: 93–113.

Chhokar, J. S., Brodbeck, F. C., and House, R. J. (Eds.) (2008). Culture and Leadership Across the World: The GLOBE Book of In–Depth Studies of 25 Societies, New York, NY: Lawrence Erlbaum Associates.

Cialdini, R. (1984). Influence: The Psychology of Persuasion, New York: William Morrow & Co.

Clark, D. (1998). Leadership Style Survey, http://www.nwlink.com/~donclark/leader/survstyl.html, retrieved 2017/08/05.

Cohen, S., and Wills, T. A. (1985). Stress, Social Support, and the Buffering Hypothesis, Psychological Bulletin, 98(2): 310–357.

Cohen, W. A. (1998). Business is not War, but Leadership is Leadership, Business Forum, 23(3/4): 10–14.

Cotton, K. (1992). Developing Empathy in Children and Youth, Portland: Northwest Regional Educational Laboratory.

Cowley, W H. (1931). The Traits of Face–to–Face Leaders, Journal of Abnormal & Social Psychology. 26(3): 304–313.

Credit Suisse (2016). The Business Plan: A Must for Business Success, 2016 ed., Zurich: Books on Demand.

Daniels, J., Radebaugh, L., and Sullivan, D. (2009). International Business: Environment and Operations, 12th ed., Upper Saddle River, NJ: Prentice Hall.

Davis, J., Millburn, P., Murphy, T, and Woodhouse, M. (1992). Successful Team Building: How to Create Teams that Really Work, London: Kogan Page.

Day, D. V., and Halpin, S. M. (2001). Leadership Development: A Review of Industry Best Practices, U.S. Army Technical Report 1111, http://www.au.af.mil/au/awc/awcgate/army/ tr1111.pdf, retrieved 2015–11–26

De Dreu, C. K., and Weingart, L. R. (2003). Task Versus Relationship Conflict, Team Performance, and Team Member Satisfaction: A Meta–Analysis, Journal of Applied Psychology, 88(4): 741–749.

De Hoogh, A. H., and Den Hartog, D. N. (2008). Ethical and Despotic Leadership, Relationships with Leader's Social Responsibility, Top Management Team Effectiveness and Subordinates' Optimism: A Multi–Method Study, The Leadership Quarterly, 19(3): 297–311.

Den Hartog, D. N., House, R. J., Hanges, P. J., Ruiz–Quintanilla, S. A., Dorfman, and 140 other contributors (1999). Culture Specific and Cross–Culturally Generalizable Implicit Leadership Theories: Are Attributes of Charismatic/Transformational Leadership Universally Endorsed? Leadership Quarterly, 10(2): 219–256.

Deresky, H. (2003). International Management, 4. ed, Upper Saddle River, NJ: Prentice Hall.

Dickson, E. (2007). On the (In)Effectiveness of Collective Punishment: An Experimental Investigation, NYU Working paper, http://www.nyu.edu/gsas/dept/politics/faculty/dickson/dickson_collectivepunishment.pdf, retrieved 2017/07/21.

Dorian, D. McCutcheon, A., Evans, M., MacMillan, K., McGillis, L., Pringle, D., Smith, S., and Valente, A. (2004). Impact of Manager's Span on Leadership and Control, Canadian Health Services Research Foundation.

Drucker, P. (2004). What Makes an Effective Executive, Harvard Business Review, 82(6): 58–36.

EFQM (2012). An Overview of the EFQM Excellence Model, Bruxelles: EFQM.

Elfering, A., Grebner, S., Semmer, N. K., and Kaiser–Freiburghaus, D. (2005). Chronic Job Stressors and Job Control: Effects on Event–Related Coping Success and Well–Being, Journal of Occupational and Organizational Psychology, 78: 237–252.

Elsayed–Elkhouly, S. M. and Lazarus, H. (1997). Why is a third of your time wasted in meetings?, Journal of Management Development, 16(9): 672–676.

Fiedler, F. E. (1967). A Theory of Leadership Effectiveness, New York: McGraw–Hill.

Fiedler, F. E., & Garcia, J. E. (1987). New Approaches to Effective Leadership: Cognitive Resources and Organizational Performance, New York: Wiley.

Fiedler, F.E. Chemers, M.M., and Mahar, L. (1976). Improving Leadership Effectiveness: The Leader Match Concept, New York: Wiley.

Finkel, D., and McGue, M. (1993). The Origins of Individual Differences in Memory Among the Elderly: A Behavior Genetic Analysis, Psychology and Aging, 8: 527–537.

Fisher, S. G., Hunter, T. A., and Macrosson, W. D. K. (1998). The Structure of Belbin's Team Roles, Journal of Occupational and Organizational Psychology, 71(3): 283–288.

Fleishman, E. A. (1953). The Description of Supervisory Behavior, Journal of Applied Psychology, 37(1), 1.

Frederick, H., Mausner, B., and Snyderman, B. (1959). The Motivation to Work, New York: Wiley.

French, J. and Raven, B. (1959). The Bases of Social Power, in: Studies in Social Power, D. Cartwright (ed.), Ann Arbor: Institute for Social Research, 150–167.

Friedman, S. D., and Singh, H. (1989). CEO Succession and Stockholder Reaction: The Influence of Organizational Context and Event Content, Academy of Management Journal, 32/4: 718–744.

Friend, M., and Cook, L. (1992). Interactions: Collaboration Skills for School Professionals, New York: Longman.

Galton, F. (1869). Hereditary Genius. New York: Appleton.

Gardner, H. (1983). Frames of Mind, New York: Basic Books.

Goldratt, E. M. (1997). Critical Chain, Great Barrington: North River Press.

Goleman, D. (1995). Emotional Intelligence, New York: Bantam Books.

Goleman, D. (1998). Working with Emotional Intelligence, New York: Bantam Books.

Goleman, D. (2000). Leadership that Gets Results, Harvard Business Review, March/April: 82–83.

Goleman, D., Boyatzis, R., and McKee, A. (2002) Primal Leadership: Realizing the Power of Emotional Intelligence, Boston: Harvard Business School Press.

Goman, C. K. (2002). Five Reasons People Don't Tell What They Know, Knowledge Management CRM Magazine, February.

Greenleaf, R. K. (2002). Servant Leadership: A Journey into the Nature of Legitimate Power and Greatness, 25th Anniversary Ed., New York: Paulist Press.

Grigorenko, E. L., LaBuda, M. C., and Carter, A. S. (1992). Similarity in General Cognitive Ability, Creativity, and Cognitive Style in a Sample of Adolescent Russian Twins, Acta Geneticae Medicae et Gemellologiae: Twin Research, 41(01): 65–72.

Grusky, O. (1963). Managerial Succession and Organizational Effectiveness, American Journal of Sociology, 69: 21–30.

Halcomb, K. A. (2005). Smoke–Free Nurses: Leading by Example, Workplace Health & Safety, 53(5): 209–212.

Hall, E. T. (1959). The Silent Language, New York: Doubleday.

Hamid, P. N. (1994). Self-Monitoring, Locus of Control, and Social Encounters of Chinese and New Zealand Students, Journal of Cross-Cultural Psychology, 25: 353-68.

Hanges, P. J., and Dickson, M. W. (2004). The Development and Validation of the GLOBE Culture and Leadership Scales, in: House, R. J., Hanges, P. J., and Javidan, M. (Eds.), Culture, Leadership, and Organizations: The GLOBE Study of 62 Societies, New York: SAGE, 122–151.

Hanges, P. J., House, R. J., Ruiz–Quintanilla, S. A., Dickson, M. W., and 170 co–authors (1999). The Development and Validation of Scales to Measure Societal and Organizational Culture, Leadership Quarterly, 10(2): 291–256.

Hartog, D. N., Muijen, J. J., and Koopman, P. L. (1997). Transactional versus Transformational Leadership: An Analysis of the MLQ, Journal of Occupational and Organizational Psychology, 70(1): 19–34.

Hemingway, M. A., and Smith, C. S. (1999). Organizational Climate and Occupational Stressors as Predictors of Withdrawal Behaviours and Injuries in Nurses, Journal of Occupational and Organizational Psychology; 72: 285–299.

Hersey, P. and Blanchard, K. H. (1969). Management of Organizational Behavior – Utilizing Human Resources, New Jersey: Prentice Hall.

Herzberg, F. (1964). The Motivation–Hygiene Concept and Problems of Manpower, Personnel Administrator, 27(1): 3–7.

Herzberg, F. (1968). One More Time: How Do You Motivate Employees, Harvard Business Review, January: 46–57.

Hill, C. W. L. (2002). International Business: Competing in the Global Market Place, 3rd ed., New York: McGraw–Hill.

Hirschhorn, L. (1983). Managing Rumors, in: Hirschhorn, L. (ed.), Cutting Back, San Francisco: Jossey–Bass, 54–56.

Hofstede, G. (1980). Culture's Consequences, Beverly Hills, CA: Sage Publications.

Hofstede, G. (2001). Culture's Consequences: International Differences in Work–Related Values, 2nd ed., Beveryl Hills, CA: Sage Publications.

Hogan, R., Curphy, G. J., and Hogan, J. (1994). What We Know About Leadership: Effectiveness and Personality, American Psychologist, 49: 493–504.

Holt, R. (1982). Occupational Stress, in: Goldberger, L., and Breznitz, S. (Eds.), Handbook of Stress: Theoretical and Clinical Aspects, New York: Free Press, 419–444.

House, R. J. (1971). A Path–Goal Theory of Leader Effectiveness, Administrative Science Quarterly, 16: 321–339.

House, R. J., Hanges, P. J., and Javidan, M. (Eds.) (2004). Culture, Leadership, and Organizations: The GLOBE Study of 62 Societies, New York: SAGE.

Huntington, S. P. (1993). The Clash of Civilizations?, Foreign Affairs, 22–49.

Huntington, S. P. (1997). The Clash of Civilizations and the Remaking of World Order, New York: Penguin.

Inglehart, R. (1997). Modernization and Postmodernization: Cultural, Economic and Political Change in 43 Societies, Princeton, NJ: Princeton University Press.

Inglehart, R., and Baker, W. E. (2000). Modernization, Cultural Change, and The Persistence of Traditional Values, American Sociological Review, 65(1): 19–51.

Ionel, S. (2011). Explicit Teaching of the Pragmatic Concept of Face, Youth on the Move – Teaching Languages for International Study and Career–Building, Bucarest, May 13–14, Conference Proceedings.

Johnson, G. (1992). Managing Strategic Change—Strategy, Culture and Action, Long Range Planning, 25(1): 28–36.

Judge, T. A., and Piccolo, R. F. (2004). Transformational and Transactional Leadership: A Meta–Analytic Test of their Relative Validity, Journal of Applied Psychology, 89(5): 755.

Judge, T. A., Bono, J. E., Ilies, R., and Gerhardt, M. W. (2002). Personality and Leadership: A Qualitative and Quantitative Review, Journal of Applied Psychology, 87(4): 765–780.

Judge, T. A., Locke, E. A., and Durham, C. C. (1997). The Dispositional Causes of Job Satisfaction: A Core Evaluations Approach, Research in Organizational Behavior, 19: 151–188.

Kealey, D. J., Protheroe, D. R., MacDonald, D., and Vulpe, T. (2006). International Projects: Some Lessons on Avoiding Failure and Maximizing Success, Performance Improvement, 45(3): 38–46.

Kemp, C. F., Zaccaro, S. J., Jordan, M., and Flippo, S. (2004). Cognitive, Social, and Dispositional Influences on Leader Adaptability, poster presented at the 19th Annual Meeting of the Society for Industrial and Organizational Psychology in Chicago.

Kenny, D. A., and Zaccaro, S. J. (1983). An Estimate of Variance due to Traits in Leadership, Journal of Applied Psychology, 68(4), 678–685.

Kirchner, M. J., and Akdere, M. (2014). Leadership Development Programs: An Integrated Review Of Literature, The Journal of Knowledge Economy & Knowledge Management, 9: 137–146.

Kirkpatrick, S. A., and Locke, E. A. (1991). Leadership: Do Traits Matter?, Academy of Management Executive, 5, 48–60.

Klimecki, O. M., Leiberg, S., Ricard, M., and Singer, T. (2014). Differential Pattern of Functional Brain Plasticity after Compassion and Empathy Training, Social Cognitive and Affective Neuroscience, 9(6): 873–879.

Kluckhohn, F. R., and Strodtbeck, F. L. (1961). Variations in Value Orientations, Evanston, IL: Row, Peterson.

Kogut, B., and Singh, H. (1988). The Effect Of National Culture On The Choice Of Entry Mode. Journal of International Business Studies, 19(3): 411.

Kossiakoff, A., Sweet, W. N., Seymour, S. J., and Biemer, S. M. (2011). Systems Engineering Principles And Practice, 2nd ed., Hoboken: Wiley.

Kouzes, J. M., and Posner, B. Z. (1987). The Leadership Challenge, Hoboken, NJ: Wiley.

Layous, K., and Lyubomirsky, S. (2014). The How, Who, What, When, and Why of Happiness: Mechanisms Underlying the Success of Positive Interventions, in: Gruber, J., and Moscowitz, J. (Eds.), Positive Emotion: Integrating the Light Sides and Dark Sides. New York: Oxford University Press, 473–495.

Leung, T.K, and Chen, R. (2001). Face, Favor and Positioning – A Chinese Power Game, European Journal of Marketing, 37: 1575–1598.

Lewin, K. (1939). Field Theory and Experiment in Social Psychology, American Journal of Sociology, 44(6): 868–896.

Lewin, K., Lippit, R., and White, R.K. (1939). Patterns of aggressive behavior in experimentally created social climates, Journal of Social Psychology, 10, 271–301.

Lewis, R. D. (1996). When Cultures Collide: Leading across Cultures, London: Nicholas Brealey International.

Lewis, R. D. (2006). When Cultures Collide: Leading across Cultures, 3rd ed., London: Nicholas Brealey International.

Liang, P. J., Rajan, M. V., and Ray, K. (2008). Optimal Team Size and Monitoring in Organizations, Accounting Review, 83(3): 789–822.

Liddel Hart, B. H. (1967). Strategy, 2nd ed., London: Faber & Faber Ltd.

Lieberson, S., and O'Connor, J. F (1972). Leadership and Organizational Performance: A Study of Large Corporations, American Sociological Review, 37: 117–130.

Lientz, B. P., and Rea, K. P. (2003). International Project Management, San Diego: Academic Press.

Locke, E. A. (1976). The Nature and Causes of Job Satisfaction, in: Dun-
nette, M.D. (ed.), Handbook of Industrial and Organizational Psychology, Chicago: Rand McNally, 1297–1349.

Lord, R. G., De Vader, C. L., and Alliger, G. M. (1986). A Meta–Analysis
of the Relation between personality Traits and Leadership Perceptions: An Application of Validity Generalization Procedures, Journal
of Applied Psychology, 71: 402–410.

Luft, J., and Ingham, H. (1950). The Johari Window: A Graphic Model
of Interpersonal Awareness, Proceedings of the Western Training
Laboratory in Group Development.

Luthans, F., Avolio, B. J., Walumbwa, F. and Li, W. (2005). The Psychological Capital of Chinese Workers: Exploring the Relationship with
Performance, Management and Organization Review, 1: 249–271.

Lyubomirsky, S. (2008). The How of Happiness: A New Approach to
Getting the Life you Want, New York: Penguin.

Lyubomirsky, S., Sheldon, K. M., and Schkade, D. (2005). Pursuing Happiness: The Architecture of Sustainable Change, Review of General
Psychology, 9(2): 111.

Madsen, M. T. (2001). Leadership and Management Theories Revisited, DDL Working Paper 4.

Maslow, A. H. (1943). A Theory of Human Motivation, Psychological
Review, 50(4): 370–396.

Mayer, J. D., and Geher, G. (1996). Emotional Intelligence and the
Identification of Emotion, Intelligence, 22: 89–113.

McClearn, G. E., Johansson, B., Berg, S., Pedersen, N. L., Ahern, F., Pe-
trill, S. A., and Plomin, R. (1997). Substantial Genetic Influence on
Cognitive Abilities in Twins 80 or More Years Old, Science,
276(5318): 1560–1563.

McGregor, D.M. (1960). The Human Side of Enterprise, New York:
McGraw–Hill.

McKee, R., and Carlson, B. (1999). The Power to Change, Austin, TX:
Grid International Inc.

Nelke, M. (2012). Strategic Business Development for Information
Centers and Libraries, Oxford: Chandos.

Nicholson, N. (2003). How to Motivate Your Problem People, Harvard
Business Review, January.

Ong, A. D., Bergeman, C. S., Bisconti, T. L., and Wallace, K. A. (2006). Psychological Resilience, Positive Emotions, and Successful Adaptation to Stress in Later Life, Journal of Personality and Social Psychology, 2006, 91(4): 730–749.

Osborne, A. F. (1948). Your Creative Power, New York: Scribner.

O'Shea, P. G., Foti, R.J., Hauenstein, N.M., and Bycio, P. (2009). Are the Best Leaders Both Transformational and Transactional? A Pattern–oriented Analysis, Leadership, 5(2): 237–259.

Pantović–Stefanović, M., Dunjić–Kostić, B., Gligorić, M., Lačković, M., Damjanović, A., and Ivković, M. (2015). Empathy Predicting Career Choice in Future Physicians, Engrami–časopis za kliničku psihijatriju, psihologiju i granične discipline, 37(1): 37–48.

Parry, K. W., and Proctor–Thomson, S. B. (2002). Perceived Integrity of Transformational Leaders in Organisational Settings, Journal of Business Ethics, 35(2): 75–96.

Peterson, S. J., Walumbwa, F. O., Byron, K., Myrowitz, J. (2008). CEO Positive Psychological Traits, Transformational Leadership, and Firm Performance in High–Technology Start–up and Established Firms, Journal of Management, 20(4): 1–21.

Podsakoff, P. M., Todor, W. M., and Skov, R. (1982). Effects of Leader Contingent and Non–contingent Reward and Punishment Behaviors on Subordinate Performance and Satisfaction, Academy of Management Journal, 25(4): 810–821.

Potters, J., Sefton, M., and Vesterlund, L. (2007). Leading–by–Example and Signaling in Voluntary Contribution Games: An Experimental Study, Economic Theory, 33(1): 169–182.

Punnett, B.J., and Withane, S. (1990). Hofstede's Value Survey Module: To Embrace or Abandon? That is the Question, in: Prasad, S.B. (ed.), Advances in International Comparative Management, 5, Greenwich, CT: JAI Press.

Rich, G. A. (1997). The Sales Manager as a Role Model: Effects on Trust, Job Satisfaction, and Performance of Salespeople, Journal of the Academy of Marketing Science, 25(4): 319–328.

Roberts, B., Wood, D., and Caspi, A. (2010). The Development of Personality Traits in Adulthood, in: John, O, Robins, R., and Pervi, L. (Eds.), Handbook of Personality: Theory and Research, 3rd ed., New York: Guilford Press, 375–398.

Rohrbach, B. (1969). Kreativ nach Regen-Methode 635, eine neue Technik zur Lösung von Problemen. Absatzwirtschaft, 12: 73-75.

Rokeach, M. (1979). Understanding Human Values: Individual and Societal, New York: Free Press.

Rooke, D., and Torbert, W. R. (2005). Seven Tranformations of Leadership, Harvard Business Review, April: 66–67.

Rost, J. C. (1993). Leadership for the Twenty–First Century, Westport, CT: Greenwood.

Rotter, J. (1966). Generalized Expectancies for Internal versus External Control of Reinforcement, Psychological Monographs: General & Applied, 80(1): 1–28.

Rowland, K. M., and Gardner, D. M. (1973). The Uses Of Business Gaming In Education And Laboratory Research, Decision Sciences, 4(2): 268–283.

Salancik, G., and Pfeffer, J. (1977). Constraints on Administrative Discretion: The Limited Influence of Mayors on City Budgets, Urban Affairs Quarterly, 12/4: 473–496.

SBA (n.d.). Write Your Business Plan, https://www.sba.gov/ starting-business/write–your–business–plan, retrieved 2017/03/31.

Schein, Edgar H. (1980): Organizational Psychology, Englewood Cliffs, NJ: Prentice–Hall Inc.

Schraeder, M., Tears, R. S., and Jordan, M. H. (2005). Organizational Culture in Public Sector Organizations: Promoting Change through Training and Leading by Example, Leadership & Organization Development Journal, 26(6): 492–502.

Schüz, M. (2016). Angewandte Unternehmensethik: Grundlagen für Studium und Praxis, Hallbergmoos: Pearson.

Schwartz, S. H. (1992). Universals in the Content and Structure of Values: Theoretical Advances, and Empirical Tests in 20 Countries, Advances in Experimental Social Psychology, 25: 1–65.

Schwartz, S. H. (2006). A Theory of Cultural Value Orientations: Explication And Applications, Comparative Sociology, 5(2): 137–182.

Schwartz, S. H. (2008). Cultural Value Orientations: Nature and Implications of National Differences, Moscow: SU HSE.

Scouller, J. (2011). The Three Levels of Leadership: How to Develop Your Leadership Presence, Knowhow and Skill. Cirencester: Management Books 2000.

Seelhofer, D. (2007). New Brooms: the Antecedents and Effects of Foreign CEO Succession, Merenschwand: Edubook.

Seelhofer, D. (2011). The Contingent Importance of Leadership, SML Working Paper.

Seelhofer, D., and Valeri, G. (2017). The Interplay Between Leadership and Team Performance: An Empirical Investigation of Effective Leader Traits and Behaviours in a Major Swiss HR Consulting Firm, Central European Business Review, March.

Seligman, M. (1998). Learned Optimism, New York: Pocket Books.

Shell liveWIRE (2015). Contents of a Business Plan, http://www.shell-livewire.org/business-library/business-plans/business-plan-contents, retrieved 2017/03/31.

Sickafus, E. (1997). Unified structured inventive thinking: How to invent, Grosse Ile, MI: Ntelleck.

Snow, B. R. (1982). Safety Hazards as Occupational Stressors: A Neglected Issue, Occupational Health Nursing; 30(10): 38–42.

Spears, L. (2010). Character and Servant Leadership: Ten Characteristics of Effective, Caring Leaders, Journal of Virtues & Leadership, 1 (1): 25–30.

Spreng, R. N., McKinnon, M. C., Mar, R. A., and Levine, B. (2009). The Toronto Empathy Questionnaire: Scale Development and Initial Validation of a Factor–Analytic Solution to Multiple Empathy Measures, Journal of Personality Assessment, 91(1): 62–71.

Stepien, K. A., and Baernstein, A. (2006). Educating for Empathy, Journal of General Internal Medicine, 21(5): 524–530.

Stogdill, R. M. (1948). Personal Factors Associated with Leadership: A Survey of the Literature, Journal of Psychology, 25, 35–71.

Swiss Army (2004). Operative Führung XXI, Bern: Schweizerische Eidgenossenschaft.

Tannenbaum, R., and Schmidt, W. H. (1958). How to Choose a Leadership Pattern, Harvard Business Review, 36: 95–102.

Thompson, J. D. (1967). Organizations in Action, New York: McGraw-Hill.

Thorndike, E. L. (1920). Intelligence and Its Uses, Harper's Magazine, 140: 227–235.

Ting–Toomey, S. (1988). Intercultural Conflict Styles: A Face Negotiation Theory, in: Kim, Y. and Gudykunst, B. (Eds.), Theories in Intercultural Communication, Newbury Park, CA: Sage, 213–238.

Totan, T., Doğan, T., & Sapmaz, F. (2012). The Toronto Empathy Questionnaire: Evaluation of Psychometric Properties Among Turkish University Students, Egit Arast, 12: 179–98.

Tracey, J. B., and Hinkin, T. R. (1998). Transformational Leadership or Effective Managerial Practices?, Group & Organization Management, 23(3): 220–236.

Trompenaars, F., and Hampden–Turner, C. (1997). Riding the Waves of Culture: Understanding Diversity in Global Business, New York: McGraw–Hill.

Tuckman, B. W. (1965). Developmental Sequence in Small Groups, Psychological Bulletin, 63(6): 384–399.

Tuckman, B. W., and Jensen, M. A. (1977). Stages of Small–Group Development Revisited, Group & Organization Management, 2(4): 419–427.

Tugade, M. M., Fredrickson, B. L., and Feldman Barret, L. (2004). Psychological Resilience and Positive Emotional Granularity: Examining the Benefits of Positive Emotions on Coping and Health, Journal of Personality, 72(6): 1161–1190.

U.S. Army (2006). FM 6–22, Army Leadership (Competent, Confident and Agile), October.

Vroom, V. H., and Jago, A. (1988). The New Leadership: Managing Participation in Organizations, Upper Saddle River, NJ: Prentice–Hall.

Vroom, V. H., and Yetton, P. W. (1973). Leadership and Decision–Making, Pittsburgh, PA: University of Pittsburgh Press.

Wagnild, G. M., and Young, H. M. (1993). Development and Psychometric Evaluation of the Resilience Scale, Journal of Nursing Measurement, 1(2): 165–178.

Waldman, D. A., Balthazard, P. A., and Peterson, S. J. (2011). Leadership and Neuroscience: Can we Revolutionize the Way that Inspirational Leaders are Identified and Developed?, Academy of Management Perspectives, 25(1): 60–74.

Wang, X., and Walker, G. J. (2011). The Effect of Face on University Students' Leisure Travel: A Cross–Cultural Comparison, Journal of Leisure Research, 43(1): 133–147.

Wasserman, N., Nohria, N., and Anand, B. N. (2001). When Does Leadership Matter? The Contingent Opportunities View of CEO Leadership, Harvard Business School Working Paper, No. 01–063.

Way, K. A., Jimmieson, N. L., and Bordia, P. (2016). Shared Perceptions of Supervisor Conflict Management Style: A Cross–Level Moderator of Relationship Conflict and Employee Outcomes, International Journal of Conflict Management, 27(1): 25–49.

Wright, T. A., and Cropanzano, R. (2000). Psychological Well–Being and Job Satisfaction as Predictors of Job Performance, Journal of Occupational Health Psychology, 5(1): 84–94.

Yaffe, T., & Kark, R. (2011). Leading by Example: The Case of Leader OCB, Journal of Applied Psychology, 96(4): 806.

Yammarino, F. J., Dubinsky, A. J., Comer, L. B., and Jolson, M. A. (1997). Women and Transformational and Contingent Reward Leadership: A Multiple–Levels–of–Analysis Perspective, Academy of Management Journal, 40(1): 205–222.

Zaccaro, S. J., Kemp, C., and Bader, P. (2004). Leader Traits and Attributes, in: Antonakis, J., Cianciolo, A. T., and Sternberg, R. J. (Eds.), The Nature of Leadership, Thousand Oaks, CA: Sage, 101–124.

Zicarelli, R. (2000). The Military Advantage: Why Don't More Companies Seize It by Recruiting Veterans?, Across the Board, Jan/Feb: 20–26.

ANNEX 2 INDEX

ANNEX 3   CHAPTER CHECK QUESTION SAMPLE ANSWERS

Chapter 1   Introduction to Leadership

Question		Sample Answer
1	Which aspects are particularly important for interpersonal leadership?	Personality traits, personal skills (e.g. self-awareness and empathy), interpersonal leadership technique
2	What is the number of direct reports called; what is the recommended optimal number; why; and on what does this depend?	Leadership span; 5-8; a higher leadership span leads to higher team fluctuation because the leader spends too much time on personnel management and not enough actually leading, making subordinates feel neglected, which leads to drops in motivation and performance.
3	What is the definition of leadership?	Leadership is making timely decisions, developing workable solutions, motivating and enabling followers to implement them, monitoring the implementation, ensuring the circumstances for success, taking responsibility for direct consequences, and sharing recognition and rewards.
4	What causes uncertainty about a leadership situation?	E.g. incomplete information, organizational factors such as on-going change processes, group dynamics among followers, or factors directly related to the leader's person, such as cognitive style, inside-the-box thinking, ego, ambition, or an inherent resistance to change.
5	What are the Four Factors of Leadership?	The leader; the led (followers); communications; the situation.
6	What must a leader understand about his or her team?	*Individually e.g.* • Personalities and individual histories, • Strengths/weaknesses, and • Response to a particular leadership and communication style. *As a group e.g.* • Group dynamics, and • Group history, rituals, and symbols.

Chapter 2   The Evolution of Leadership Theory

Question		Sample Answer
1	What is the basic premise of the Great Man Theory?	History is shaped by great men; to learn about leadership, the biographies of these great men need to be studied.
2	What are Lewin's basic leadership styles?	Authoritarian, democratic, laissez-faire.
3	What is the view of workers according to McGregor's Theory X?	They are considered to be cogs in a machine that are inherently lazy and try to avoid work, have no ambition, consequently prefer routine tasks, pursue security, and balk at responsibility but are highly receptive to both positive and negative incentives. They must usually be forced to work, supervised very closely, offered rewards for above-average work, and threatened with punishment.
4	What are the two concerns on which the Managerial Grid is based, and what does it present as the optimal leadership style?	Concern for people and concern for production; team leadership, i.e. maximal concern for both.
5	What are the sources of power in French and Raven's Five Points of Power?	Legitimate, reward, coercive, expert, and referent (i.e. charismatic) power.
6	Which forces should a leader consider, according to Tannenbaum and Schmidt's Leadership Continuum, when deciding which leadership style to employ?	Forces in the leader, the subordinates, and the situation.
7	According to Fiedler's Contingency Theory, what is the key determinant of leader effectiveness	Stress.
8	In Hersey and Blanchard's Situational Leadership model, to what do leaders need to adapt their style?	The maturity of followers, as determined by their commitment and competence.
9	In House's Path-Goal Theory, on what does a leader's behavior depend?	The satisfaction, motivation, and performance of followers.
10	Which are the three basic leadership styles in the Vroom-Yetton-Jago Normative Decision Model	Autocratic, consultative, and collaborative.
11	What is full range leadership?	Leadership that incorporates both transactional and transformational aspects.
12	According to Fleishman, on which two aspects do followers base their view and rating of a leader's behavior?	Consideration and initiating structure.

Question		Sample Answer
13	Which are the three main responsibilities of leaders according to Adair's Action-Centered Leadership model?	Achieving tasks, managing the team, and managing individuals.
14	What are Kouzes and Posner's Five Practices of Exemplary Leadership?	Model the way, inspire a shared vision, challenge the process, enable others to act, and encourage the heart.
15	Which are the three levels in Scouller's leadership model and to what do they refer?	Personal level: self-leadership of the leader; private level: leading individuals; public level: leading teams (two or more people).
16	According to Robert Greenleaf, for what does the word 'servant' in Servant Leadership stand?	A desire to help others.
17	What question lies at the center of the Global Leadership School of research?	The cultural transferability of leadership traits, behaviors, and competencies.

Chapter 3   Traits and Behaviors of Effective Leaders

Question		Sample Answer
1	What are the two main strands of leadership research?	Leadership emergence and leadership effectiveness.
2	What is another name for trait research?	Disposition research.
3	What are traits?	Habitual patterns of disposition, thought, and emotion present in a person.
4	Which are the 'Big Five' personality factors?	Openness, conscientiousness, extraversion, agreeableness, and neuroticism.
5	According to Kurt Lewin, what is a laissez-faire leadership style and what is its effect?	The leader offers little or no guidance and leaves decision-making up to group members. This can be effective if group members are highly qualified, but it often leads to poorly defined roles and a subsequent lack of motivation.
6	In Tannenbaum and Schmidt's Leadership Continuum, what is the difference between the consultative I and consultative II styles?	In the consultative I style, the leader presents his ideas to the team and invites questions before making his or her decision, whereas in the consultative II style the decision itself is presented but may change depending on group input.
7	What are the two dimensions that determine a person's leader-ship style in the Blake-Mouton Managerial Grid?	Concern for people and concern for production.
8	According to Fiedler's Contingency Theory, when can it make sense to replace a leader?	If a situation changes significantly, the leader may have to be replaced because, in essence, this is easier than changing the entire team (although that is an alternative option, depending on the specifics).
9	What is the postulated effect of experience in Fiedler's Contingency Theory?	Experience can impair performance under low-stress conditions (because it limits the leader's cognitive horizon and may lead them astray due to false familiarity), although it normally contributes to performance under high-stress conditions.
10	What is the logic behind Fiedler's Least-Preferred Co-worker (LPC) scale?	Fiedler assumed that task-oriented leaders would be less harsh in their judgments about this person than people-oriented leaders, thus leading to a comparatively lower LPC score. Despite its name, therefore, the LPC scale is not really about some least-preferred co-worker. Instead, it captures the leader's emotional reaction to this person.
11	What is a fundamental difference between Fiedler's Contingency Theory and Hersey and Blanchard's Situational Leadership model?	Fiedler sees a leader's leadership as ingrained and therefore more or less fixed, while Hersey and Blanchard assume that good leaders can adjust their leadership style at will to the situation.

Question		Sample Answer
12	What determines the appropriate leadership style in Hersey and Blanchard's Situational Leadership model?	Follower maturity.
13	What are the two fundamental leader behaviors in Hersey and Blanchard's Situational Leadership model?	Directive and supportive.
14	What does the effectiveness of a decision depend on, according to the Vroom-Yetton-Jago Normative Decision Model?	The quality or rationality of the decision; the acceptance or commitment on the part of the subordinates to execute the decision effectively; and the amount of time required to make the decision.
15	In the Vroom-Yetton-Jago Normative Decision Model, which factors determine the level of subordinate involvement necessary in a decision?	Required decision quality (the higher, the more involvement); importance of subordinate acceptance of decision (the more important, the more involvement); and time (the more is available, the more involvement).
16	What basic idea provides the basis for Goleman's Six Emotional Leadership Styles?	Leader's actions and behaviors influence the emotional state of subordinates, which in turn influences performance.
17	Which two of the six leadership styles found around the world by Project GLOBE held universal appeal?	Charismatic/value-based and team-oriented.

Chapter 4   Primary Leader Responsibilities and Competencies

Question		Sample Answer
1	What are your main responsibilities as a leader?	Getting the job done, leading and managing the team, leading and managing the team members, and leading and managing yourself.
2	What are the nine (transactional) leadership functions?	Analyze, decide, plan, initiate, control, support, inform, evaluate, reward and punish.
3	What are the six (transformational) leadership key practices?	Provide guidance and direction; set the positive example; motivate and inspire your team and followers; develop and sustain your leader presence and resilience; show real interest and consideration; enable, stimulate, and challenge.
4	What is the key rationale for thinking in options?	It prevents jumping to conclusions and facilitates consideration of all viable alternatives before making a decision.
5	What is a concept?	A rough idea of how to implement a selected option (i.e. a decision).
6	Why should identifying and allocating the overall net amount of time and person hours available be the first step of time planning when under time pressure?	Because doing this first creates a sense of urgency, while starting with the list of tasks and subtasks to be performed (i.e. the work breakdown) may lead to the list being too detailed (and thus time-consuming) without a sense of the time available for this step.
7	What are buffer times and why are they important?	Bufffer times are small time windows inserted into the time plan that allow for on-going tasks or unforeseen events to take up additional (unplanned) time without jeopardizing the start of the next task
8	How can you develop your leadership presence?	By developing your technical know-how and skills, cultivating the right attitude towards other people, and working on psychological self-mastery.
9	Which four elements contribute to improving your resilience?	Your ability to correctly identify stressors, your ability to realistically assess your own capabilities, your self-confidence based on repeated successful problem solving, and your social support (such as a supportive relationship or a happy family life).
10	What are four key components for motivating team members?	A shared vision; congruence between leader, team, and individual goals; rewards contingent on reaching these goals; and perceived fairness of these rewards.
11	What is the core premise of Herzberg's theory of motivation?	People need to be satisfied before they can be motivated.

Question		Sample Answer
12	When completing a task, which other two factors must be in balance with the demands of this task?	Formal authority and responsibility (for results).
13	Belbin's nine team roles are grouped into three classes of three roles each, based on three differing basic concerns (or orienta-tions). What are these concerns?	Intellectual problem-solving, action, and relationships.
14	What are the five stages in Tuckman's team development model?	Forming, storming, norming, performing, and adjourning.

Chapter 5   Leading Across Borders And Cultures

Question		Sample Answer
1	From a cultural perspective, what needs to be kept in mind regarding the development of modern leadership theory?	Most of it has been developed in a culturally fairly homogeneous, Western setting.
2	Which four factors often cause problems when leading across cultures?	• Communication blunders (both verbal and non-verbal), • Stereotypes and prejudices, • Offense against tradition and religion, and • Offense against deeply held (usually implicit) values and taboos.
3	What are two key factors for becoming cross-culturally proficient?	Emotional-social intelligence and international experience.
4	Why is nationality a problematic proxy for culture?	Because nations are often politically defined and may contain various ethnic groups. Staying at the national evel will then lead to diffuse or even misleading results.
5	Which five types of culture influence a person?	• Societal culture, • Organizational culture, • Generational culture, • Membership group subcultures, and • Reference group subcultures.
6	What is the topic of Edward T. Hall's proxemics concept?	It deals with the culturally contingent need for personal space to feel comfortable.Hall suggested four distance zones (intimate, personal, social, and public) but suggested that differing cultures may have differing space patterns: what is intimate in one culture may be social in another, and so on.
7	Which are the five fundamental questions in Kluckhohn and Strodtbeck's Values Orientation Theory?	• What aspect of time should be our primary focus? • What is our relationship with our natural environment? • How should we relate with others? • What is the prime motivation for our behavior? • What is the nature of human nature? • How do we think about and use space?
8	How can Hofstede's framework be used to identify significant differences between cultures with which someone is not familiar?	By comparing the scores for each dimension in order to find significant gaps/differences which can then be interpreted.
9	Which are the two major value dimensions on which the Inglehart-Welzel Map is based?	• Traditional vs. secular-rational values, and • Survival vs. self-expression values.

Question	Sample Answer
10 Which are the three fundamental questions underlying Schwartz's Theory of Cultural Values Orientation?	▪ What is the nature of the relation between the person and the group, and what are the boundaries between them? ▪ How can the society guarantee that people behave in a responsible manner that preserves the social fabric? ▪ How does the society regulate how people manage their relations to the natural and social world?
11 What is Trompenaars' and Hampden-Turner's cultural dimension internal vs. external control about?	It deals with how someone feels about the forces of nature (and by extensions life): do we (and should we) control them or do they control us? More generally, does life just happen to us or are we the masters of our own destiny? internal vs. external control
12 According to Lewis, what is the cause of cross-cultural problems?	Crossing cultural category (e.g. people from reactive-linear working with people from multi-linear cultures).
13 What is the focus of the cultural dimension time orientation in Browaeys and Price's model of culture?	It captures a culture's attitude vis-à-vis the past, present, and future. What is the influence of traditions and of immediate or potential future situational needs?
14 What is global leadership in the business management sense?	The study and practice of leading across borders and cultures.
15 What is the difference between GLOBE and Hofstede's or Trompenaars' models of culture regarding value orientation?	GLOBE distinguishes between cultural values and practices (which are often contradictory), which the others do not.
16 In the GLOBE framework, what is uncertainty avoidance?	The extent to which a society, organization, or group relies on social norms, rules, and procedures to alleviate the unpredictability of future events.
17 What is the difference between cultural practices and values, according to GLOBE?	Values reflect what *should be*, i.e. the kind of social norms members of that culture generally would like to see in place, while practices reflect *what is*, i.e. how members of that culture actually tend to behave.
18 For an international leader, what is the significance of large gaps between cultural values and practices for a relevant culture?	Large differences between cultural practices and values can indicate potential cross-cultural trouble spots because foreigners will tend to orient themselves along the practices, while the members of that society will tend to be guided by their values when they form implicit leadership expectations, regardless of whether they behave that way themselves or not.

Question	Sample Answer
19	Which are the eight universally (i.e. globally) undesirable leadership attributes identified by GLOBE?	• Asocial, • Dictatorial, • Egocentric, • Irritable, • Loner, • Non-cooperative, • Non-explicit, and • Ruthless.
20	Although cultural models can only be applied at the group level, strictly speaking, what are their potential uses at the individual level?	• They are a useful starting point for reflection when you are trying to make sense of (to you) strange behavior of a foreigner, • They enable you to help that person become aware of their own cultural background and possible differences to yours, and • They allow you to discuss such possible differences in a structured way.

Chapter 6   Common Leadership Principles and Mistakes

Question		Sample Answer
1	Which leaders make mistakes?	All of them.
2	What is a leadership principles?	A general behavioral guideline that can help leaders increase their effectiveness and prevent common leadership mistakes.
3	What are the eight behaviors universally considered inacceptable for outstanding leaders?	Being • dictatorial, • egocentric, • ruthless, • irritable, • asocial, • loner-like, • non-explicit, and • non-cooperative.
4	Why is it important for an international leader to understand the relevant cultural context(s)?	Because the perception of the majority of leader behaviors is culturally contingent, with many behaviors being seen positively in one culture but negatively in another.
5	Why should a leader show uncommon commitment?	Because leaders are the role models for their teams, and if they show uncommon commitment, so will the team.
6	Apart from ethical considerations, why should you take care of your team members?	Because this will increase their motivation and, by extension, their level of engagement.
7	Why should you lead from the front?	This signals to your team members that you share in their efforts and hardships, encourages their hearts and increases their motivation. Additionally, it allows you to make decisions based on an intimate knowledge of the situation.
8	What is the importance of integrity for a leader?	A lack of integrity can reduce the team's trust in that leader and even open him or her up to blackmail. A reputation for maintaining unconditional integrity, on the other hand, will make people follow him or her more willingly.
9	Why is it a mistake to set higher standards for your subordinates than for yourself?	Because this will negatively influence a leader's reputation for integrity and reliability as well as the team's motivation.
10	What is face?	Face is a pervasive concept that refers to a person's image and status within a social group, specifically the respect (and the pride and dignity coming with it) that results from social achievement. *Alternative answer:* A person's claim of status and social value based on what is important in his or her social group

	Question	Sample Answer
11	What are two reasons for the ubiquity of inconsistent leader communication?	Often, leaders will not be aware of the inconsistencies in their communicative behavior. And even if they are, their egos will often not allow them to retract or clarify an earlier communication.
12	What are three common reasons for the inability of leaders to admit mistakes?	▪ Fear, ▪ Ego, and ▪ Cognitive dissonance.
13	What are common ethical dilemmas created for subordinates?	▪ Demanding clearly unethical or even illegal behavior from them, ▪ Forcing them to choose between two competing superiors, ▪ Confidentially telling them about some secret wrongdoing of yours, ▪ Passing your own ethical dilemma down the line, ▪ Deal with the harassed rather than the harasser, and ▪ Acting unethically yourself.
14	Why should collective punishment be avoided?	Collective punishment will lead to strong resentment of you as the leader and will considerably diminish trust between you and your subordinates. It can also significantly reduce team integrity (if team members turn on each other) and it sends a strong signal that you are unable to lead your team effectively, that you do not care about your people, and that you lack a sense of fairness. Finally, counter to the chief argument for this kind of punishment, studies have shown that there is no lasting effect on team effectiveness and in-group enforcement.
15	What should be done if a promise cannot be kept?	The person or group the promise was made to should be informed and provided with an explanation and, if appropriate, an apology.
16	Why should you not display disloyalty to the company or to your own boss in front of your team?	Because it sets a bad example and because you are the role model for your team, whose members will start to wonder if you are also disloyal to them behind their backs.
17	Why is stealing credits from your subordinates particularly bad?	Because this will have a negative effect on your reputation for integrity and competence as well as on the motivation of your subordinates.

Chapter 7 Organizational Leadership Development

Question	Sample Answer
1 What is the main goal of a leadership development program?	To systematically improve the leadership abilities of select leaders.
2 Why should a leadership development program also include impact assessment?	Because without it, necessary adjustments to the program or the need for further training may not be recognized.
3 Why is a needs and gap analysis necessary before you start a leadership development program?	Because without this step the program may be inefficient, training unnecessary aspects while lacking necessary one.
4 What is the drawback of personal reflection for conducting a needs and gap analysis for a leadership development program?	if you have blind spots (which most people do), you may miss some important areas that require development.
5 What is the most important element of the needs and gap analysis? Why?	Discussions with and feedback from subordinates, superiors, peers, and/or coaches, because this can help you to step outside the limitations of your self-view by jointly identifying your strengths and weakness which necessitate development, and shed light on the pros and cons of specific activities.
6 What should a leadership development plan minimally include?	The areas identified that require development, the specific development activities to be completed in order to improve deficiencies or further strengthen existing skills, the timeframe within which these activities are to be completed, and clear measures of development success.
7 Why is impact assessment of leadership development necessary?	Because without this, gauging the success of development activities is difficult.

ANNEX 4   EXERCISE SAMPLE SOLUTIONS

This part of the annex provides assistance regarding the exercises at the end of each chapter. Please note that these are just *sample* solutions.

Exercise 1:   Seeking Solomon
(page 24.)

This is a typical, small, everyday leadership situation. The leader, Liz, might prefer not having to deal with this kind of behavior, yet it is just human nature.

List four realistic options how Liz could proceed, with advantages and disadvantages

Option		Advantages	Disadvantages
1	Cancel the kick-off meeting	▪ No fight between managers in front of chairman	▪ Project delay ▪ Possible loss of face because of postponement
2	Threaten Krish and Peter	▪ Very clear repercussions might keep managers in line	▪ This has not worked in the past
3	Appeal to Krish and Peter's loyalty	▪ Positive incentive, i.e. better for the managers' motivation	▪ This has not worked in the past
4	Brief Bolin in advance	▪ Loss of face might be less severe	▪ Problem itself is not solved ▪ Loss of face could still occur
...	...	...	...

Note: this is not a complete list. Many other solutions are also possible.

Is there a 'fair' way of assigning projects and distributing budgets?

One way Liz could handle this is to have one of the two managers assign appropriate budgets to both projects and then grant the other first pick. This way, neither could claim unfairness.

What is your advice to Liz? How can/should she handle this issue?

Liz should proceed in a measured, unemotional way by calling Krish and Peter in for a pre-meeting in which she explains (again) how the constant fighting creates inefficiencies and takes a toll on her (thus appealing to both reason and emotion). She could then proceed along the lines of the answer to the second question and let one of them assign budgets to the projects while the other gets the first pick. She should also set a clear agenda for the meeting and call the two in again for a debriefing afterwards.

Exercise 2: Analyzing the Four Factors of Leadership
(page 26f.)

This exercise is based on your personal background. Therefore, no sample solution is provided. Refer to the example on page 26.

Exercise 3: Your Preferred Leadership Style According to Lewin
(page 99f.)

The results for this exercise depend on how you answer the questionnaire questions. Just follow the instructions. The highest of the three column scores on the answer sheet will indicate which of Lewin's three styles you normally prefer: autocratic, participative, or laissez-faire.

Exercise 4: Choosing a Style on the Leadership Continuum
(page 102)

Appropriate leadership style based on exercise's case information: Participative

	FORCES IN THE LEADER								
	Value system		Confidence in team			Leadership inclinations		Feelings of security in an uncertain situation		
	More distrusting	More trusting	Low	Moderate	High	More naturally directive	More naturally participative	Low	Moderate	High
A	1	2	1	2	3	1	2	1	2	3
6		1		2			2		1	

	FORCES IN THE FOLLOWERS													
	Need for independence		Readiness for responsibility		Tolerance for ambiguity		Interest in the task		Identification with organization		Skill level		Expectation of participating	
	Low to medium	Medium to high	Low to medium	Medium to high	Low to medium	Medium to high	Low to medium	Medium to high	Low to medium	Medium to high	Low to medium	Medium to high	Low to medium	Medium to high
B	1	2	1	2	1	2	1	2	1	2	1	2	1	2
10		2		1		1		2		1		2		2

	FORCES IN THE SITUATION									
	Type of organization		Group effectiveness			Nature of problem		Time pressure		
	Centralized	Decentralized	Low	Moderate	High	Simple	Complex	Low	Moderate	High
C	1	2	1	2	3	1	2	1	2	3
10		1		2			2		2	

A +B +C	Total						
	15-16	17-18	19-20	21-23	24-27	28-31	32-34
	Authoritarian	Paternalistic	Consultative I	Consultative II	Participative	Democratic	Laissez-faire
	Leader makes decision and informs team.	Leader makes decision and then convinces subordinates of its value.	Leader presents ideas and invites questions before making decision.	Leader presents tentative decision that is subject to change.	Leader presents problem to team and gets suggestions but retains final decision.	Leader defines limits but delegates decision to team.	Leader allows subordinates to function within limits defined by higher instance.

Exercise 5: Your Preferred Position in the Managerial Grid
(page 105f.)

The results for this exercise depend on how you answer the corresponding questionnaire questions. In the end, your preferred position in Blake and Mouton's managerial grid will emerge. Just follow the instructions.

It might be helpful to discuss the three reflection questions with a person that knows you well, ideally a trusted boss, colleague, or team member, but possibly also a spouse or friend. Remember, however, that subordinates may prefer not to give you completely honest answers, and that friends and spouses may not be fully objective and may also not know you in your leadership role.

Exercise 6: Determine your LPC Score
(page 108)

Follow the instructions and select a position on each of the 18 scales for the least-preferred co-worker you have in mind. Scoring interpretation instructions are found at the end.

Exercise 7: The Downturn—Situational Leadership
(page 111)

Questions and Assignments

Reflect on your options. What might be Sarah's issue? What could you do?

Considering her stellar appraisals in the past, the sudden drop in performance and her abruptly unreliable behavior indicate a personal issue. Depression might be possible, as people with clinical depression have a hard time getting up in the morning. Other types of psychological and/or health-related problems, such as an undisclosed illness, either of herself or of a person close to her, might also be possible. Likewise, marital problems (e.g. her having an affair) might explain both her frequent tardiness and her unwillingness to discuss it. A much more likely scenario given her age and history, however, is that she is pregnant and that she feels it is too early to tell people yet. Many women want to wait until the third month of the pregnancy is over before telling anyone, because that is the period in which the most could still go wrong. Some people are very sensitive about this, and many are also worried about how this will influence their relationship with their boss and co-workers. Being pregnant would explain all aspects of the issue: coming in late (e.g. because of morning sickness), offering no convincing explanations (because she is torn between wanting to tell people about her good fortune but not wanting to tell yet because it is too early), and missing meetings (e.g. because of doctor's appointments she does not want to disclose in order to not create a pattern).

Your options are limited. Given her past performance, you likely do not want to lose her, so you will want to tread very carefully. Directly addressing your hunches about what might be behind her behavior is not advisable. Instead, you should call her in for a meeting in a professional but relaxed setting, explaining to her the situation without accusations and without resorting to things like "everyone thinks" or "others are saying". Instead, use phrases like "I have noticed" or questions like "is it possible that...?". Set a clear goal and an agenda for the meeting and steer it towards a clear agreement regarding the way forward. Ideally, she will tell you what the matter is, and the agreement will specifically refer to it. You should not force this, however; if she does not want to, it is better to conclude the meeting with a general agreement rather than a very specific one that makes her feel walked over.

Which of Hersey and Blanchard's leadership styles should be adopted in the case of Sarah? Why?

A coaching style, because of her high competence but currently low commitment. Once the commitment is back up to the usual levels, a delegating style may be better.

Assume you are calling Sarah in for a meeting and are preparing for it. What is your main meeting goal? Create an outline structure of how the meeting ideally will progress. What do you say and how do you act when, how, and why? What can/are you allowed to approach, what not?

Aspect	Examples
Meeting goal:	• Understand what bothers Sarah (relationship-oriented leader), *or* • Get her to show up on time (task-oriented leader), *or* • Both (team-oriented leader, according to Blake and Mouton)
Outline agenda:	• Amicable welcome (offer refreshments like coffee, tea, or water...) • Ask how she is doing (exploratory, open question) • Explain meeting goal(s) • Share your observations • Ask to share her view • Explore (react to what she says; explore carefully where she seems to open up, move away from things she clearly avoids) • Ask her how she proposes to solve the issue • Explain your view (general issue and her proposal for a solution) • Propose and discuss a meeting resolution/agreement • Discuss and agree on next steps • Amicable goodbye
Points to cover:	• The situation as you see it (without accusations; facts only) • The situation as she sees it (without interruptions from your side) • The way forward • ...
Points to avoid:	• Directly asking her if she is pregnant (in some areas this is even illegal) • Highly personal details (spousal infidelity, health, ...) • The view of other people (you can only speak for yourself) • ...

![decorative]

Exercise 8: Situational Leadership—Leading Teams

(page 114)

In this exercise, you use the Hersey and Blanchard Situational Leadership model to recommend a preferred leadership style for each of the situations described.

Situation 1
Recommended leadership style: Delegating (high competence, varying commitment)

Situation 2
Recommended leadership style: Coaching (medium competence, low commitment)

Situation 3
Recommended leadership style: Directing style (low competence, high commitment)

Situation 4
Recommended leadership style: Delegating (high competence, high commitment)

![decorative]

Exercise 9: Situational Leadership—Leading *Your* Team

(page 115f.)

This exercise is based on your personal background. If you are not currently leading a team and have used the team described in Exercise 7 on page 111, a possible solution could be:

Leading the individual team members				Appropriate Style for the individual team members
Team member	**Competence** 1: low; 3: medium; 5: high	**Commitment** 4: low; 6: variable; 8: high	**Maturity** Score (competence x commitment)	
Roger, 42	5	8	40	Delegating
Manoj, 29	1	4	4	Directing
Sonya, 51	3	6	18	Supporting
Sarah, 33	5	4	20	Coaching
Bintang, 44	5	6	30	Delegating
Leading the team				**Appropriate style for overall team**
Average maturity (sum of individual maturity scores divided by number of team members)			(Rounded average score)	(corresponding score in decision matrix on page 81)
			22 (exact: 22.4)	Supporting *or* coaching*

* The exact score of 22.4 indicating the leadership style for the team as a whole is slightly closer to a supporting (24) than to a coaching style in the decision matrix. Both would be possible. As the leader, you will have to decide what makes more sense, considering the specific circumstance.

Exercise 10 Rolf and the Normative Decision Model
(page 117f.)

Based on the information in the exercise's case, the ideal leadership style according to the Vroom-Yetton-Jago Normative Decision Model is Group II: the leader discusses the solution with the group but makes the decision alone.

Decision Question	Decision Tree	Processes
1. Quality requirement: Is there a quality requirement? Is one solution superior for technical or rational reasons?		**A1 (Autocratic):** leader makes decision without subordinate involvement using available information.
2. Commitment requirement: Is acceptance of the decision by subordinates critical?		**A2 (Autocratic II):** leader gets additional information from subordinates before making decision alone; subordinates may or may not be informed.
3. Leader information Do you have sufficient information to make a high-quality decision?		
4. Problem structure Is the problem structured?		**C1 (Consultative I):** leader discusses issue individually with subordinates and asks for input before making decision alone without team meetings.
5. Commitment probability: If you were to make the decision alone, would your subordinates commit to it?		**C2 (Consultative II):** leader discusses problems with team as a group but makes decision alone.
6. Goal congruence Do subordinates share the organizational goals to be attained in solving the problem?		
7. Subordinate conflict Is conflict likely among subordinates over preferred solutions?		**G2 (Group II):** leader discusses problems with team, focuses and directs discussions, and allows group to make decision.
8. Subordinate information: Do subordinates have sufficient information to contribute to a high-quality decision?		

Source: based on Vroom and Jago (1988).

Exercise 11: Shehan's Behavior—Contrasting Leader Styles

(page 120f.)

This is a roleplaying exercise which enables a group to observe specific leader and follower behaviors at first hand. Both leaders should prepare for the meeting by preparing a meeting outline. See the solution to Exercise 7 on page 420 for an example.

Exercise 12: Core Leadership Functions and Responsibilities

(page 229)

Below are examples of possible answers. Note that this is an incomplete list and that other answers are possible. Use logic to decide if your divergent answers make sense or not.

Core functions of leadership	Core leader responsibilities			
	Accomplishing the task	**Managing yourself**	**Managing the team**	**Managing individuals**
Analyzing	• The task	• Time • Resilience	• Overall capabilities • Team spirit	• Strengths/ weaknesses • Motivation
Deciding	• Course of action	• Prioritizing	• Resource allocations	• Division of labor
Planning	• Project charter and plan	• Personal time plan	• Meetings • Highlights	• Workloads • Deadlines
Initiating	• Project kick-off	• Resilience improvements	• Morale maintenance • Leadership rhythm	• Leadership rhythm
Controlling	• Project progress	• Time management	• Resource allocations	• Work progress
Supporting	• Opening doors in the organization	• Take small time-outs to keep up resilience	• Provide necessary access	• Provide additional resources, if necessary
Informing	• Higher-ups	• Reading trade and technical publications	• Decisions of higher-ups	• Work progress
Evaluating	• Attitude of higher-ups	• Leadership presence	• Team performance	• Individual performance
Rewarding	• Third-party contributors	• Yourself	• Team performance	• Individual high-performers

Exercise 13:   Exemplary Leadership Practices

(page 230)

Each of the key leader practices below is supported by a number of leader traits and behaviors. Below are a few examples, along with examples of leaders who reportedly excelled at the respective practice. If you have come up with other traits and behaviors, ask yourself if they really support the specific practice. If you can honestly say yes, the answer is correct. Note that, to ensure maximum recognizability, the leaders below have been taken from history, business, and current politics. Ideally, use your own personal leadership experience, i.e. leaders you have experienced yourself.

Key leader practices	Supporting leader traits & behaviors	Leader examples
Provide guidance and direction	• Communicative • Informed • Motive-arouser • ...	• Winston Churchill • Richard Branson
Set the positive example	• High integrity • Low neuroticism • Honest • ...	• Mahatma Gandhi • Lee Iacocca
Develop and sustain presence and resilience	• Curious • Driven to self-improvement • Relaxed • ...	• John F. Kennedy • Ronald Reagan
Motivate and inspire the team and followers	• Communicative • Motivational • Encouraging • ...	• Martin Luther King • Warren Buffet
Show real interest and consideration	• High empathy • Good communication • Intuitive • ...	• Nelson Mandela • Susan Wojcicki
Enable, stimulate, and challenge.	• Confidence builder • Encouraging • Detail-oriented • ...	• Napoleon Bonaparte • Angela Merkel

Exercise 14:   Personal Leadership and Leadership Presence
(page 231)

This is a personal exercise that you need to conduct for yourself, about yourself. Therefore, no sample solution is provided.

Exercise 15:   Testing Your Personality
(page 232)

Follow the instructions. The internet links provided are just examples of a wide range of personality tests available. Among the most common ones used in business are the Myers-Briggs Type Indicator (MBTI) and the Occupational Personality Questionnaire (OPQ32). Ideally, these are administered by, and then discussed with, a trained, usually licensed professional. Note that all tests, particularly self-completion tests, have their limits. If the results that are not in line with your self-view, discuss them with a person that knows you well, such as trusted colleague or supervisor. Friends and family members may not be objective enough or not know your 'work side'.

Exercise 16:   Measuring Your Resilience
(page 233f.)

Follow the instructions and interpret the score as indicated. The goal is to not just develop but also maintain resilience. Your resilience, like your cell phone, may need to be recharged regularly. For more information on this, see Chapter 4.32 on page 156f.

Exercise 17:   Measuring Your Empathy
(page 236f.)

Follow the instructions and interpret the score as indicated. High levels of empathy are important for a leader, particularly in cross-cultural settings. For more information on this, see Chapter 4.34 on page 162f.

Checking Your Team's Balance

(page 239f.)

This exercise is based on your personal leadership experience. If you are not currently leading a team and have used the team described in Exercise 7 on page 111, the solution is this:

Team Members		Belbin's Team Roles (N=natural role of team member; A=role may be assumed if necessary)								
		Plant	Specialist	Monitor/ Evaluator	Implementer	Shaper	Completer/ Finisher	Teamworker	Coordinator	Resource Investigator
1	Roger, 42				X	X				X
2	Manoj, 29	X								
3	Sonya, 51		X							
4	Sarah, 33			X	X		X			
5	Bintang, 44							X		
Represented? (Yes/Partially/No)		Yes	Yes	Yes	Yes	Yes	Yes	Yes	No	Yes
Take-aways/ comments		All team roles are represented, except for the coordinator (whose role you are currently fulfilling). If a particular skill set is missing, hire another specialist. If you want to continue to coordinate the team's work yourself, the new hire should reinforce one of the team roles that are represented only once. Otherwise, hire someone to fulfill the coordinator role.								

Exercise 19: Checking Your People's Motivation

(page 241f.)

This exercise is based on your leadership experience and team. If you are not currently leading a team and have used the one described in Exercise 7 on page 111, a possible solution is:

Person seems to be overall 2: mostly satisfied 1: somewhat dissatisfied 0: highly dissatisfied	Person seems to be dissatisfied with... A: pay; B: status; C: security; D: working conditions; E: fringe benefits; F: bureaucratic procedures; G: team relations	Person seems to be overall 2: mostly motivated; 1: somewhat unmotivated; 0: highly unmotivated	Person seems to be demotivated by lack of... A: meaningful work, B: challenging tasks; C: recognition; D: sense of achievement; E: increased responsibility; F: opportunities for personal growth

Team Members	Satisfaction	Dissatisfiers	Motivation	Demotivators	Comments
1 Roger, 42	2	F, E	2	B	No action needed
2 Manoj, 29	1	C	1	E	Action required
3 Sonya, 51	0	B, D, G	0	C	Action required
4 Sarah, 33	1	A	1	?	Action required
5 Bintang, 44	2	C	2	F	No action needed
Team overall	1+	Varies	1+	Varies	Action required
Take-aways/ comments	<ul><li>Meetings with Manoj, Sonya, and Sarah are necessary. However, it is always a good idea to regularly 'feel the pulse' of all your team members.</li><li>Manoj should be given clear goals and performance expectations, with the possibility of a permanent contract and more responsibility if his performance goes up appropriately. If not, letting his contract run out should be considered.</li><li>Sonya's constant grumbling and her demotivating effect on her co-workers need to be discussed with her. If there are reasonable opportunities (that are not unfair to the others) to increase her status and/or give her more recognition, these should be considered. If nothing changes within an acceptable amount of time, she might have to be moved to another team or, if all else fails, let go.</li><li>Continuing to give Bintang the necessary flexibility in her working hours will keep her motivation up.</li><li>Sarah's current issues need to explored carefully, without prying, so that she ideally can eventually get back to her former self or, at least, the demotivating effect of her behavior on the rest of the team is resolved.</li></ul>

Note that the assessment of the respective team members' satisfaction and motivation is subject to interpretation. If you interpret them differently, your solution may differ.

Exercise 20: Your Cultural Profile
(page 312f.)

This exercise is based on your personal cultural profile. For an example, see Illustration 13 on page 277.

Exercise 21: Getting Ready for the International Assignment
(page 315f.)

Cultural dimension	Cultural preference		Some key differences to consider
	UK	Sri Lanka	regarding how to manage in Sri Lanka
Power distance	Egalitarian	Hierar-chical	• Dharma or social class and its implications may need to be understood and considered • Subordinates will expect to be told what to do • Ideal boss is less participative and more 'benevolent autocrat' • There will likely be a general tendency towards (and preference for) centralization
	Quite different		
Individual-ism	Highly individualistic	Collecti-vistic	• Face is an incredibly important concept with much stronger implications than in the UK • Leadership style should be group-oriented • Work groups are like a kind of family • Loyalty is paramount
	Quite different		
Masculinity	Masculine	Very feminine	• People will generally not want to stand out from the group • There will likely be a different motivational structure ("working to live") • Conflict resolution will be based on compromise and negotiation
	Quite different		
Uncertainty avoidance	Low	Medium (i.e.no real preference)	• Thinking outside the box is uncommon • There is an emotional need for rules • 'Winging it' may not be accepted • More frequent communication necessary
	Somewhat different		
Long-term orientation	Medium (i.e.no real preference)	Medium (i.e.no real preference)	Likely not a source of cross-cultural conflict
	Very similar		
Indulgence	Indulgent	(No score) Indulgent	• Optimism and a positive attitude are valued • Leisure time and generosity are important
	Fairly similar		

Exercise 22:   The Dysfunctional Cross-Cultural Team

(page 316f.)

This is a fairly complex leadership situation, requiring skills in both interpersonal and organizational leadership. Organizational leadership is covered in book two of this series.

Questions and Assignments

Characterize the legal team. What dynamics are at work? What would you recommend?

The legal team is not really a team but rather a collection of individuals who are not working in concert. The tension stems from a strong sense of competition among its members and a compulsive need for status and recognition of the team's leader. Her autocratic leadership style and the subsequent lack of participation also contribute to the bad team spirit, as does the unruly behavior of some of its members. Tom, the ringleader, will need a stern talking-to from your side (including a verbal warning, if necessary) and, if this does not help, should be removed from the team by either moving him sideways (i.e. to another team, though this might be tricky since there is only one legal team in the organization) or, as a last resort, letting him go. The rest of the team should discuss ways to improve morale and commit to a common goal and common principles of working together. They should also undergo a series of team-building activities. Additionally, you should consider ways to better integrate them into the overall unit, such as joint events with other teams. Claudette, the team's leader, will need to be coached closely by you and, if her behavior persists, replaced.

Explain which of GLOBE's leadership styles Shun exhibits. Is this appropriate, given the team?

Autonomous. It is inappropriate, both because it is a style that is considered one of the least attractive in all cultures studied by GLOBE, and because of the diversity of the team. A charismatic/value-based or team-oriented style would likely be considerably better received.

Describe the problems in the business development team. Which aspects are likely cultural, which individual in origin?

- Shun's autonomous leadership style: personal, although likely culturally influenced; his inability to accept what he considers 'fraternization' is part of this (power distance).
- Practical jokes by Bheka: personal.
- John and Laura's directness: cultural (assertiveness).
- Shun's problem with John: cultural misunderstandings due to differences in their view of relationships (diffuse vs. specific) and power distance (high vs. low).
- John's perceived lack of respect to those higher up in the hierarchy: personal, although probably culturally influenced (power distance, assertiveness).

With regard to individual relationships, which of Goleman's styles would you recommend Shun tries to adopt vis-à-vis each of his team members? Why?

- Laura: coaching, because she shows promise but is inexperienced and needs guidance.
- Bheka: affiliative, because he is emotional and needs to reconnect to you and the team.
- John: democratic, because he will likely have good input but feels undervalued.

Exercise 23: Ten Fundamental Leadership Principles
(page 357f.)

This exercise is based on your personal values and priorities. Therefore, no sample solution is provided.

Exercise 25: Identifying and Addressing Development Needs
(page 374f.)

In this exercise, you try to identify development needs based on limited information. The list below contains examples of what is contained in the exercise text. Some development needs are generic, however, and always a good idea for most leaders. If you have identified these as part of your solution, they are certainly also correct.

Leader (who?)	Specific development needs (what?)	Justification (Why?)	Suggested development activities and timeframe (how/when?)
Roger	Improved emotional-social intelligence	Personality type emphasizes thinking over feeling/sensing	E.g. Executive MBA (asap)
	Improved time management	Identified as part of aptitude tests	
	Organizational leadership	Several teams	
Amaya	Control of empathy	Personality type prone to making others' problems their own	E.g. personal coach (within 6 months)
	Better detail orientation	Identified as part of aptitude tests	
	Strategic thinking	Prospective division CEO	E.g. specialized Executive Program (IMD, INSEAD, etc.) (within 1 year)
Mira	Improved handling of stress	Identified as part of aptitude tests	Stress management training (in-house; within 6 months)
	Better handling of emotions in conflict	Personality type prone to irrational attacks when criticized	E.g. personal coach (asap)
	Gaining initial leadership experience	None so far	On-the-job training as deputy team leader with clear training objectives

ANNEX 5   FORMS AND TEMPLATES

The forms on the following pages are ready to be copied. Just blow them up to the desired format (e.g. A4 or Letter8) and use them for (and at) your convenience.

Form 1   Four Factors of Leadership Analysis

Situation
Possible development paths (scenarios, i.e. how could the situation conceivably progress? What is the worst case, what the best?

Leader	Followers	Communication
Immediate measures to be taken regarding the leader?	*Immediate measures (what needs to be done right now) with regard to followers?*	*Appropriate mix of channels/media, with frequency?*
Leadership development needs?	*Additional measures (for later implementation?)*	

Source: Seelhofer, D. (2017). Interpersonal Leadership: An Applied Guide, Zurich: OGMA Education.

Form 2   Leadership Continuum Style Selection

FORCES IN THE LEADER

	Value system		Confidence in team			Feelings of security in an uncertain situation			Leadership inclinations	
	More distrusting	More trusting	Low	Moderate	High	Low	Moderate	High	More naturally directive	More naturally participative
A	1	2	1	2	3	1	2	3	1	2

FORCES IN THE FOLLOWERS

	Need for independence		Readiness for responsibility		Tolerance for ambiguity		Interest in the task		Identification with organization		Skill level		Expectation to participate	
	Low to medium	Medium to high	Low to medium	Medium to high	Low to medium	Medium to high	Low to medium	Medium to high	Low to medium	Medium to high	Low to medium	Medium to high	Low to medium	Medium to high
B	1	2	1	2	1	2	1	2	1	2	1	2	1	2

FORCES IN THE SITUATION

	Type of organization		Group effectiveness			Nature of problem		Time pressure		
	Centralized	Decentralized	Low	Moderate	High	Simple	Complex	Low	Moderate	High
C	1	2	1	2	3	1	2	1	2	3

Total

A + B + C

15-16	17-18	19-20	21-23	24-27	28-31	32-34
Authoritarian	Paternalistic	Consultative I	Consultative II	Participative	Democratic	Laissez-faire
leader makes decision and informs team.	leader makes decision and then convinces subordinates of its value	leader presents ideas and invites questions before making decision.	leader presents tentative decision that is subject to change.	leader presents problem to team and gets suggestions but retains final decision	leader defines limits but delegates decision to team	leader allows subordinates to function within limits defined by higher instance

Source: Seelhofer, D. (2017). Interpersonal Leadership: An Applied Guide, Zurich: OGMA Education; based on Tannenbaum and Schmidt (1958).

Form 3   Blake and Mouton' s Managerial Grid

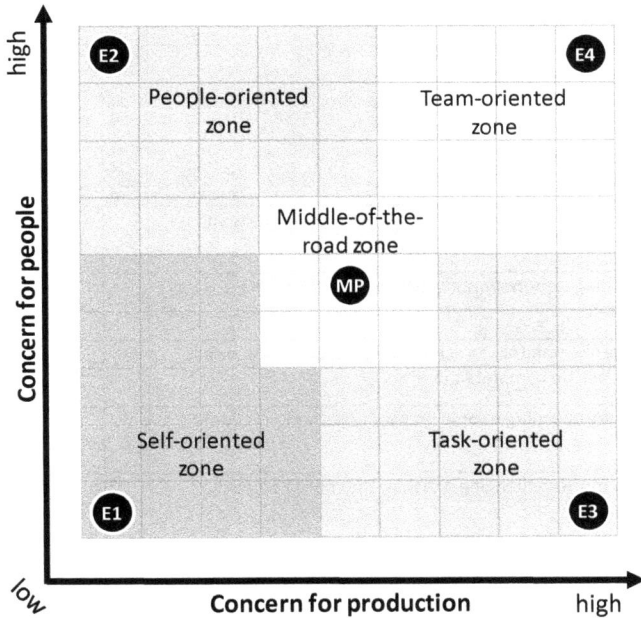

Positions in original Managerial Grid:

- E1: Impoverished style (1/1)
- E2: Country-club management style (1/9)
- MP: Middle-of-the-road style

- E3: Authority-compliance style (9/1)
- E4: Team management style (9/9)

Additional positions in updated Managerial Grid:

- E1, E2, E3, E4, or MP in order to maximize personal benefit: Opportunistic style

- Alternating between E2 and E3: Paternalistic style

Source: adapted from Blake and Mouton (1964) and McKee and Carlson (1999).

Form 4   Your Position in the Managerial Grid

#	Determinant	Your Answer				
		Almost always	Frequently	Occasionally	Rarely	Hardly ever
19	I encourage my team to participate in decisions and I try to implement their suggestions.	5	4	3	2	1
20	Nothing is more important than accomplishing a goal or task.	5	4	3	2	1
21	I closely monitor the schedule to ensure a task or project will be completed in time.	5	4	3	2	1
22	I enjoy coaching people on new tasks and procedures.	5	4	3	2	1
23	The more challenging a task is, the more I enjoy it.	5	4	3	2	1
24	I encourage my employees to be creative about their job.	5	4	3	2	1
25	When seeing a complex task through to completion, I ensure that every detail is accounted for.	5	4	3	2	1
26	I find it easy to carry out several complicated tasks at the same time.	5	4	3	2	1
27	I enjoy reading articles, books, and journals about training, leadership, and psychology; and then putting what I have read into action.	5	4	3	2	1
28	When correcting mistakes, I do not worry about jeopardizing relationships.	5	4	3	2	1
29	I manage my time very efficiently.	5	4	3	2	1
30	I enjoy explaining the intricacies and details of a complex task or project to my employees.	5	4	3	2	1
31	Breaking large projects into small manageable tasks is second nature to me.	5	4	3	2	1
32	Nothing is more important than building a great team.	5	4	3	2	1
33	I enjoy analyzing problems.	5	4	3	2	1

#	Determinant	Your Answer				
		Almost always	Frequently	Occasionally	Rarely	Hardly ever
34	I honor other people's boundaries.	5	4	3	2	1
35	Counselling my employees to improve their performance or behavior is second nature to me.	5	4	3	2	1
36	I enjoy reading articles, books, and trade journals about my profession; and then implementing the new procedures I have learned.	5	4	3	2	1

Now fill in the numeric score of each item on the questionnaire in the list below, and then calculate the total for each column.

Item	Score
1	
4	
6	
9	
10	
12	
14	
16	
17	

Total	
Divide by 5	
X-Position	

Concern for production

Item	Score
2	
3	
5	
7	
8	
11	
13	
15	
18	

Total	
Divide by 5	
Y-Position	

Concern for people

Finally, visualize your result by entering it into the grid below:

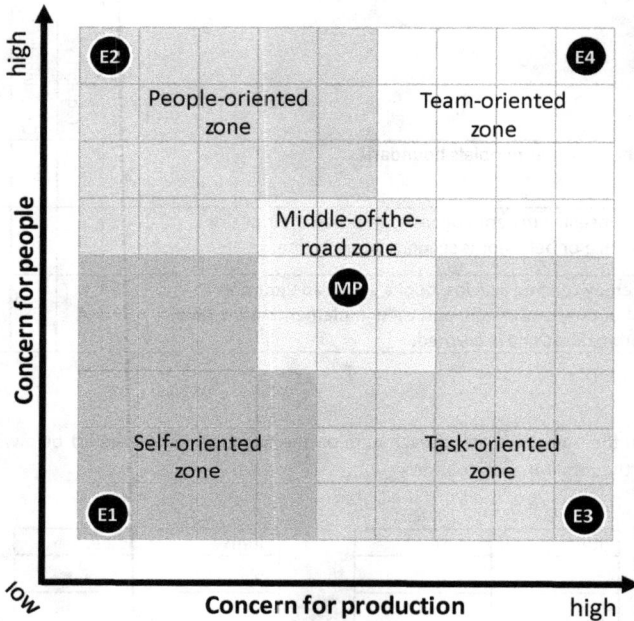

Positions in original Managerial Grid:

- E1: Impoverished style (1/1)
- E2: Country-club management style (1/9)
- MP: Middle-of-the-road style

- E3: Authority-compliance style (9/1)
- E4: Team management style (9/9)

Additional positions in updated Managerial Grid:

- E1, E2, E3, E4, or MP in order to maximize personal benefit: Opportunistic style

- Alternating between E2 and E3: Paternalistic style

Source: adapted from Blake and Mouton (1964) and McKee and Carlson (1999).

Form 5   Contingency Model Leader Type Selection Matrix

Influence factor for situational favorableness			Fiedler's recommendation
Leader/members	**Task**	**Leader power**	
Good relations	Structured	Strong	Task oriented leader
Good relations	Structured	Weak	Task oriented leader
Good relations	Unstructured	Strong	Task oriented leader
Good relations	Unstructured	Weak	People-oriented leader
Poor relations	Structured	Strong	People-oriented leader
Poor relations	Structured	Weak	People-oriented leader
Poor relations	Unstructured	Strong	People-oriented leader
Poor relations	Unstructured	Weak	Task oriented leader

Source: adapted from Fiedler (1967).

Form 6   Situational Leadership Team Portfolio

Leading the individual team members				Appropriate style for the respective team members
Team member	Competence	Commitment	Maturity	
	1: low; 3: medium; 5: high	4: low; 6: variable; 8: high	Score (competence x commitment)	
...	...	...	...	...
...	...	...	...	...
...	...	...	...	...
...	...	...	...	...
...	...	...	...	...
...	...	...	...	...

Leading the team		Appropriate style for the overall team
Average maturity (sum of individual maturity scores divided by number of team members)	(Rounded average score)	(corresponding score in decision matrix* below)
	...	...

To determine the appropriate style, select the score below that is closest to the one above:

* Decision matrix		Commitment		
		Low (4)	Varying (6)	High (8)
Competence	Low (1)	(4) Directing Style (or terminate)	(6) Coaching Style	(8) Directing Style
	Medium (3)	(12) Coaching Style	(18) Supporting Style	(24) Supporting Style
	High (5)	(20) Coaching Style (or switch/enrich job)	(30) Delegating Style	(40) Delegating Style

Source: Seelhofer, D. (2017). Interpersonal Leadership: An Applied Guide, Zurich: OGMA Education; based on Hersey and Blanchard (1969).

Form 7   Vroom-Yetton-Jago Normative Decision Model

Decision Question	Decision Tree	Processes
1. Quality requirement: Is there a quality requirement? Is one solution superior due to technical or rational reasons?		**A1** (Autocratic): leader makes decision without subordinate involvement using available information.
2. Commitment requirement: Is acceptance of the decision by subordinates critical?		**A2** (Autocratic II): leader gets addional info from subordinates before making decision alone; subordinates may or may not be informed.
3. Leader information Do you have sufficient info to make a high-quality decision?		**C1** (Consultative I): leader discusses issue individually with subordinates and asks for input before making decision alone with-out team meetings.
4. Problem structure Is the problem structured?		
5. Commitment probability: If you were to make the decision alone, would your subordinates commit to it?		**C2** (Consultative II): leader discusses problems with team as a group but makes decision alone.
6. Goal congruence Do subordinates share the organizational goals to be attained in solving the problem?		**G2** (Group II): leader discusses problems with team, focuses and directs discussions, and allows group to make decision.
7. Subordinate conflict Is conflict among subordinates over preferred solutions likely?		
8. Subordinate information: Do subordinates have sufficient information to contribute to a high quality decision?		

Source: adapted from Vroom and Jago (1988).

Form 8   Preferred Leadership Style According to Lewin

#	Determinant	Your Answer				
		Almost always	Frequently	Occasionally	Rarely	Hardly ever
1	I always reserve the final decision-making authority on my team for myself	5	4	3	2	1
2	I always try to include one or more employees in determining what to do and how to do it. However, I retain the final decision	5	4	3	2	1
3	My employees and I always vote whenever a major decision has to be made	5	4	3	2	1
4	I do not consider suggestions made by my employees, as I do not have the time	5	4	3	2	1
5	I ask for employee ideas and input on upcoming plans and projects	5	4	3	2	1
6	For a major decision to pass in my department, it must have the approval of each individual or the majority	5	4	3	2	1
7	I tell my employees what has to be done and how to do it	5	4	3	2	1
8	When things go wrong and I need to keep a project or process running on schedule, I call a meeting to get my worker's advice	5	4	3	2	1
9	To get information out, I send it by email, memos, voice mail, or text; rarely is a meeting called. My workers are expected to act upon it.	5	4	3	2	1
10	When someone makes a mistake, I tell him or her not to ever do that again and make a note of it	5	4	3	2	1
11	I want to create an environment where employees take ownership of the project. I allow them to participate in the decision-making process	5	4	3	2	1
12	I allow my employees to determine what needs to be done and how to do it	5	4	3	2	1
13	New hires are not allowed to make any decisions unless approved by me first	5	4	3	2	1
14	I ask employees for their vision of where they see their jobs going and then use their vision where appropriate	5	4	3	2	1
15	My workers know more about their jobs than I do, so I allow them to make their own decisions	5	4	3	2	1

#	Determinant	Almost always	Frequently	Occasionally	Rarely	Hardly ever
		Your Answer				
16	When something goes wrong, I tell my employees that a procedure is not working correctly and I establish a new one	5	4	3	2	1
17	I allow my employees to set priorities with my guidance	5	4	3	2	1
18	I delegate tasks in order to implement a new procedure or process	5	4	3	2	1
19	I closely monitor my employees to ensure they are performing correctly	5	4	3	2	1
20	When there are differences in role expectations, I work with them to resolve the differences	5	4	3	2	1
21	Each individual is responsible for defining their job	5	4	3	2	1
22	I like the power that my leadership position holds over subordinates	5	4	3	2	1
23	I like to use my leadership power to help subordinates grow	5	4	3	2	1
24	I like to share my leadership power with my subordinates	5	4	3	2	1
25	Employees must be directed or threatened with punishment in order to get them to achieve the organizational objectives	5	4	3	2	1
26	Employees will exercise self-direction if they are committed to the objectives	5	4	3	2	1
27	Employees have the right to determine their own organizational objectives	5	4	3	2	1
28	Employees mainly seek security	5	4	3	2	1
29	Employees know how to use creativity and ingenuity to solve organizational problems	5	4	3	2	1
30	My employees can lead themselves just as well as I can	5	4	3	2	1

Now fill in the numeric score of each item on the questionnaire in the list below, and then calculate the total for each column.

Item	Score		Item	Score		Item	Score
1			2			3	
4			5			6	
7			8			9	
10			11			12	
13			14			15	
16			17			18	
19			20			21	
22			23			24	
25			26			27	
28			29			30	
Total			Total			Total	

Authoritarian style   Democratic style   Laissez-faire Style

Your preferred style is indicated by the highest of the three column scores. If it is 40 or more, this is a strong indicator of your preferred style. If a score is 20 or lower, then that would indicate that you really do not feel comfortable with that style. If the difference between the three scores is small, this might indicate that you are not fully aware of your normal operating mode, perhaps because you are new at leading and are still finding your way.

Source: Clark (1998).

Form 9   Leadership Style Preference (Fiedler's LPC)

#	Attribute	Position that best describes LPC								Opposite
19	Open	8	7	6	5	4	3	2	1	Guarded
20	Unfriendly	1	2	3	4	5	6	7	8	Friendly
21	Pleasant	8	7	6	5	4	3	2	1	Unpleasant
22	Rejecting	1	2	3	4	5	6	7	8	Accepting
23	Warm	8	7	6	5	4	3	2	1	Cold
24	Tense	1	2	3	4	5	6	7	8	Relaxed
25	Interesting	8	7	6	5	4	3	2	1	Boring
26	Loyal	8	7	6	5	4	3	2	1	Backbiting
27	Nasty	1	2	3	4	5	6	7	8	Nice
28	Hostile	1	2	3	4	5	6	7	8	Supportive
29	Considerate	8	7	6	5	4	3	2	1	Inconsiderate
30	Insincere	1	2	3	4	5	6	7	8	Sincere
31	Unkind	1	2	3	4	5	6	7	8	Kind
32	Trustworthy	8	7	6	5	4	3	2	1	Untrustworthy
33	Gloomy	1	2	3	4	5	6	7	8	Friendly
34	Peacable	8	7	6	5	4	3	2	1	Quarrelsome
35	Emotionally distant	1	2	3	4	5	6	7	8	Emotionally open/close
36	Supportive	8	7	6	5	4	3	2	1	Hostile

Source: adapted from Fiedler, Chemers, and Mahar (1976).

Now calculate the total sum of all the answers you selected in the questionnaire. Then compare your score with Fiedler's original interpretation below:

57 or less: *low LPC*
You are likely primarily task-oriented. According to Fiedler, these leaders are very effective at completing tasks, while relationship-building is a low priority.

58 to 63: *middle LPC*
You are able to switch between task-oriented and relationship-oriented styles. These leaders may be best suited to fluid situations that frequently change between demands for a task-oriented and relationship-oriented leader.

64 and above: *high LPC*
You are likely primarily relationship-oriented. According to Fiedler, these leaders are good at managing conflict and better able to make complex decisions.

Research suggests that LPC is a stable measure, with high test-retest stability (cf. e.g. Fiedler and Garcia, 1987).

Form 10   Option Evaluation and Recommendation Matrix

Option	ONE	TWO	THREE
Identifier			

Characterization						
Common aspects of all options			
Key aspects of each option			
Strengths/ advantages			
Weaknesses/ disadvantages			

Killer criteria (select 'yes' or 'no' for each criterion and option)						
Feasible regarding resources/constraints	Yes	No	Yes	No	Yes	No
Acceptable in its consequences	Yes	No	Yes	No	Yes	No
Suitable for external/internal situation	Yes	No	Yes	No	Yes	No
Complete regarding critical success factors	Yes	No	Yes	No	Yes	No
Overall	Met	Not met	Met	Not met	Met	Not met

Additional decision criteria (set by the leader or superiors)									
Criteria	**Weight** (1-3)	**Rating** (1-5)	**Score** (Weight x Rating)	**Rating** (1-5)	**Score** (Weight x Rating)	**Rating** (1-5)	**Score** (Weight x Rating)
Overall score (sum)							

Recommendation to decision-maker(s)			

Source: Seelhofer, D. (2017). Interpersonal Leadership: An Applied Guide, Zurich: OGMA Education.

Form 11   Generic Concept Brief (Check-List)

Main item	Comments	Check
Necessary background information	E.g. task or mission received, including rationale and background story; conditions, requirements, and restrictions, including legal; foundational documents, if any; and any other aspects that are relevant to the task or mission	
Concept-related goals and targets	Specific, measurable, attainable, relevant, time-based	
Key influence factors	E.g. stakeholders and environmental change drivers	
Overview of options that were evaluated	Including a justified recommendation	
Actual concept	I.e. the basic idea of what you propose to do, based on the recommended/chosen option	
Rough timeline	Stating in broad strokes what needs to be done by when in order to implement the concept and fulfill the task or mission	
Organizational and administrative aspects	List of workgroup/team membership and structure, with contact information; rough estimate of additional resources and support needed	

Form 12   Attitude Self-Reflection (Check-List)

Attitude element	How you rate yourself			Details	What you want to improve
	Low	Medium	High		
Sense of mission					
Spirit of cooperation					
Goal orientation					
Service orientation					
Quality orientation					
Performance orientation					
Reciprocal trust					

Form 13　　Net Time Calculation Sheet

Net person-hours		Net available time			
Available stretch hours	Available regular hours	Comments	Stretch	Regular	
Total	Total				Date	Day

Form 14   Internal and External Time Plan

Internal time plan (team)	Time-line	Day	Time	External time plan

Form 15   Task and Milestone Management Diagram

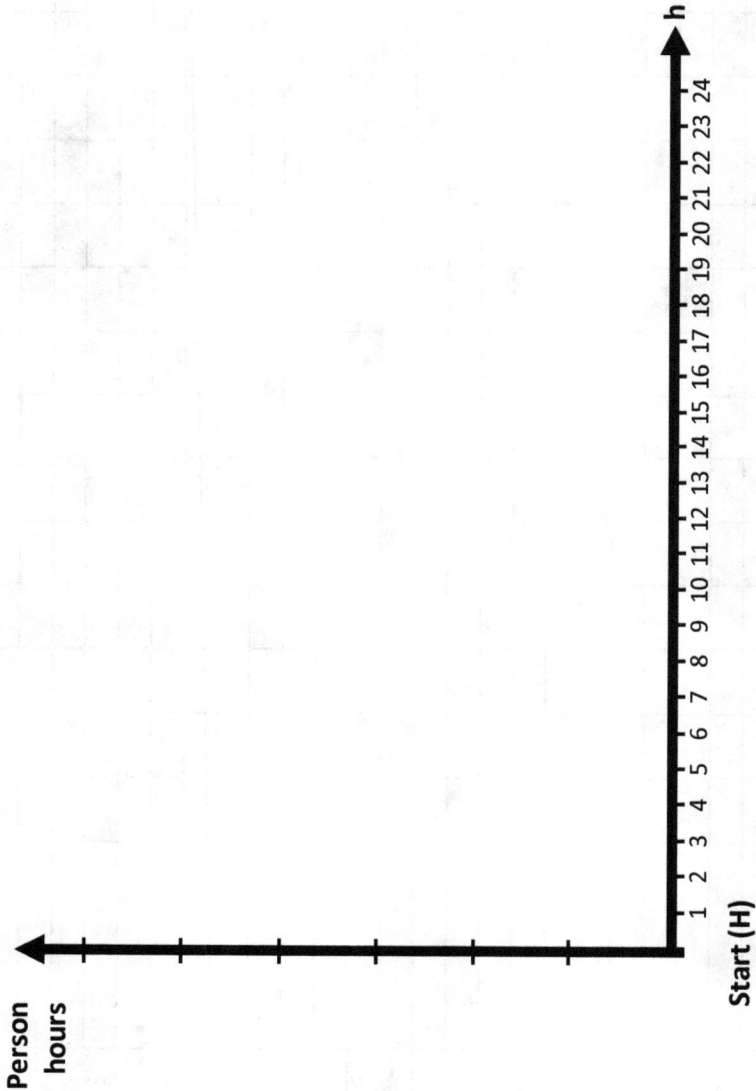

Add team members (Y-axis) and milestones/deadline (X-axis).

Source: Seelhofer, D. (2017). Interpersonal Leadership: An Applied Guide, Zurich: OGMA Education.

Form 16 Week Structure

Week #			Activities			
Date	**Weekday**	**Day's Theme**	**Morning**	**Lunch-time**	**Afternoon**	**Dinner/ Evening**

Source: Seelhofer, D. (2017). Interpersonal Leadership: An Applied Guide, Zurich: OGMA Education.

Form 17   To-Do List

Item #	Task	Created	Assigned	Due	%	Status	Comments

Source: Seelhofer, D. (2017). Interpersonal Leadership: An Applied Guide, Zurich: OGMA Education.

Form 18   Team Leadership Rhythm

Meeting	Participants	Rhythm	Weekday	Time slot	Target week			
					1	2	3	4
Team								
Individuals								

Source: Seelhofer, D. (2017). Interpersonal Leadership: An Applied Guide, Zurich: OGMA Education.

Form 19   Key Elements of Team Leadership (Check-List)

Key team leadership element	How you rate yourself			Details	What you want to improve
	Low	Medium	High		
Building and developing the team					
Selecting and hiring					
Forming and shaping					
Fostering team coherence and collaboration					
Creating highlights					
Providing guidance and direction					
Explaining					
Establishing principles, rituals, and traditions					
Staying on top of things					
Collecting and assessing information					
Adapting, improvising, overcoming					
Setting and enforcing standards					
Setting the standards					
Explaining the standards					
Living the standards					
Checking compliance					
Running productive meetings					
Setting goals					
Defining topics					
Assigning responsibilities					
Managing Time					

Source: Seelhofer, D. (2017). Interpersonal Leadership: An Applied Guide, Zurich: OGMA Education.

Form 20 Key Activities for Staying on Top of Things (Check-List)

Key activity	How you rate yourself			Details	What you want to improve
	Low	Medium	High		
Fostering a culture of transparency					
Declaring your expectations					
Setting the example					
Earning a reputation for integrity					
Being honest					
Keeping your word					
Respecting confidentiality					
Keeping your ear to the ground					
Observing					
Plugging into relevant channels					
Following the grapevine					
Asking pointed questions					
Defining purpose					
Understanding context					
Anticipating answers					
Keeping track					
Taking notes					
Reviewing, interpreting, and updating					

Source: Seelhofer, D. (2017). Interpersonal Leadership: An Applied Guide, Zurich: OGMA Education.

Form 21   General Performance Expectation (GPE)

GPE #	Title:		
Overview			
Task		**Issued**	
Task owner		**Assigned by**	
Task description			
Budget			
Timing (due/milestones)	H (published/sent out): Milestones: 1. 2. 3. 4.		
Expected outcome			
Type		Quantity	
Recipients		CC	
Description			
Assessment criteria			
Quality	Content: Style:		
Additional information and remarks			

Source: Seelhofer, D. (2017). Interpersonal Leadership: An Applied Guide, Zurich: OGMA Education.

Form 22   Team Meeting Agenda

Agenda | Meeting:

Date		Participants	
Time		Excused (reason)	
Pages		Guests (item)	
Inviter (phone)		Enclosures	

Item	Content	Who	From... to (min)
1.	**Welcome/introduction**		
1.1	Overview/goals/duration		
1.2			
2.	**Infos** (hot news, focus of activities, key problems)		
2.1			
2.2			
2.3			
2.4			
3.	**Discussion**		
3.1			
3.2			
3.3			
3.4			
4.	**Summary & conclusions, outlook**		
4.1	Summary of key points and decisions		
4.2	Miscellany/varia		
4.3	Next meeting		

Source: Seelhofer, D. (2017). Interpersonal Leadership: An Applied Guide, Zurich: OGMA Education.

Form 23   Team Meeting Minutes

Minutes | Meeting:

Meeting Date		Participants	
Time		Excused (reason)	
Pages		Guests (item)	
Inviter (phone)		Linked documents	
Compiled by		Date of acceptance	

Item	Content	Content	Decisions and key findings
1.	Welcome/introduction		
1.1	Overview/ goals/ duration		
1.2			
2.	Infos (hot news, focus of activites, key problems)		
2.1			
2.2			
2.3			
2.4			
3.	Discussion		
3.1			
3.2			
3.3			
3.4			
4.	Summary & conclusions, outlook		
4.1	Summary of key points & decisions		
4.2	Miscellany/ varia		
4.3	Next meeting		

Source: Seelhofer, D. (2017). Interpersonal Leadership: An Applied Guide, Zurich: OGMA Education.

Form 24   Meeting Management (Check-List)

Meeting Aspect	Comments	Check
Welcome	Open the meeting by welcoming everyone and thanking them for attending.	
Purpose and goals	Remind everyone of the meeting's purpose and goals.	
Optional: Introductions	Go through a quick introduction round, if not all participants know each other yet. Name tags may also be a good idea in such a case.	
Optional: Minutes of last meeting	If necessary/applicable, review and formally accept the last meeting's minutes and review the team's to-do list.	
Agenda review	Review the agenda. If there is time and you think it is appropriate, ask if there are any additional items that should be discussed at the end of the meeting.	
Core meeting	Go through the agenda items one by one. Provide a short summary of the main points discussed and any decision taken at the end of each item. This will make it easier for the participants to remember them, and it will also make it easier for you or the person taking notes to compile the meeting minutes later on.	
Miscellany/ varia	Briefly deal with additional items requested by participants (see point 4). This part of the meeting is usually listed in the agenda as 'varia' or 'miscellany' and should normally take no more than fifteen minutes. If it turns out that an item will require a full-blown discussion, defer it to a separate meeting.	
Final check	Go around the table, specifically addressing each participant and dealing with any further questions they may have.	
Summary of key outcomes	Summarize the meeting's key outcomes (making sure all participants understand them in the same way), state any new additions to the to-do list, and define the next steps.	
Optional: Next meeting	If necessary, determine the date, time, and location for the next meeting.	
Closing	Close the meeting.	

Source: Seelhofer, D. (2017). Interpersonal Leadership: An Applied Guide, Zurich: OGMA Education.

Form 25   Checking Your Team's Composition

Team Members	Belbin's Team Roles (N=natural role of team member; A=role may be assumed if necessary)								
	Plant	Specialist	Monitor/ Evaluator	Implementer	Shaper	Completer/ Finisher	Teamworker	Coordinator	Resource Investigator
1									
2									
3									
4									
5									
6									
7									
8									
9									
10									
11									
12									
Represented? (Yes/Partially/No)									
Take-aways/ comments	1								

Source: Seelhofer, D. (2017). Interpersonal Leadership: An Applied Guide, Zurich: OGMA Education.

Form 26   Checking Your Team's Motivation

Person seems to be overall	Person seems to be dissatisfied with…	Person seems to be overall	Person seems to be demotivated by lack of…
2: mostly satisfied 1: somewhat dissatisfied 0: highly dissatisfied	A: pay; B: status; C: security; D: working conditions; E: fringe benefits; F: bureaucratic procedures; G: team relations	2: mostly motivated; 1: somewhat unmotivated; 0: highly unmotivated	A: meaningful work, B: challenging tasks; C: recognition; D: sense of achievement; E: increased responsibility; F: opportunities for personal growth

Team Members	Satis-faction	Dissatisfiers	Motiva-tion	Demotivators	Comments
1					
2					
3					
4					
5					
6					
7					
8					
9					
10					
11					
12					
Team overall					
Take-aways/ comments					

Source: Seelhofer, D. (2017). Interpersonal Leadership: An Applied Guide, Zurich: OGMA Education.

Form 27   Culture Profile (Spidergram)

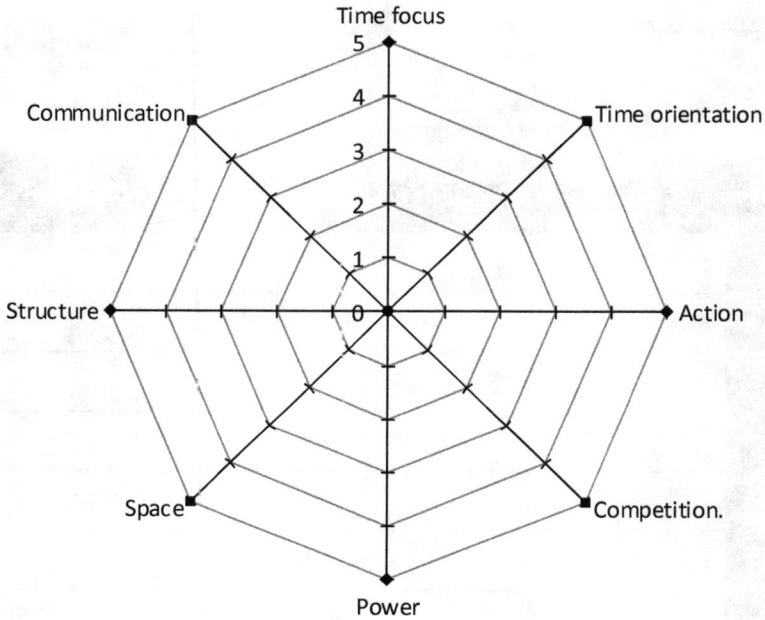

Source: Seelhofer, D. (2017). Interpersonal Leadership: An Applied Guide, Zurich: OGMA Education; based on Browaeys and Price (2008.

Form 28   Cultural Profile (Rubric)

Cultural Aspects	Score				
	1	2	3	4	5
	monochronic ←————————————————→ polychronic				
Time focus	I prefer to concentrate on one thing, finish it, then do the next one. Working on several things simultaneously makes me uncomfortable.	I prefer to work on one thing after another, but I feel comfortable if I have several things on my plate at the same time.	I do not care if I do one thing after another or many at the same time and feel comfortable with both	I prefer to do several things at the same time; having to work on one thing after another frustrates me.	I tend to do many things at the same time and feel comfortable with it.
	individualistic ←————————————————→ collectivistic				
Structure	My priority is to take care of myself and my immediate family	My priority is to take care of myself, my family and friends	Myself, my family, and my social group are equally important	My social group and society at large should come first, but I should not forget myself, either	It is more important to look out for society than for myself
	private ←————————————————→ public				
Space	When talking to someone, if they step closer than a large step, I get uncomfortable; my home is off-limits to new people I meet.	When talking to someone, if they step closer than one regular step, I get uncomfortable; also, I rarely invite someone new to my house.	When talking to someone, it's fine if they step a bit closer than one regular step; I occasionally invite someone new to my house.	I am comfortable if someone talks to me fairly close up; also, I frequently invite someone new to my house.	I am comfortable if someone talks to me very close; also, people constantly come and go at my home.
	being ←————————————————→ doing				
Action	I enjoy life, want to express myself, and live in the moment.	I generally enjoy life, sometimes want to express myself, and often live in the moment.	I primarily want to grow as a person.	I mostly enjoy doing things and achieving personal goals; recognition and promotion are sometimes important to me	I enjoy doing things and achieving personal goals; recognition and promotion are important to me

	past ⟷ future				
Time-orienta-tion	Traditions are very im-portant; we can learn much from the past.	Traditions are fairly important; we can learn some things from the past.	I generally live in the present.	I frequently think about the future.	I am mostly concerned with the future.
	equality ⟷ hierarchy				
Power	I frequently question hier-archy and go outside of channels; I ex-pect my boss to consult me before making any decisions that affect me.	I frequently question hierar-chy and go out-side of chan-nels; I expect my boss to con-sult me before making major decisions that affect me.	I generally ac-cept but occa-sionally ques-tion hierarchy and on rare oc-casions go out-side of chan-nels; I appreci-ate if my boss consults me be-fore making ma-jor decisions that affect me.	I mostly accept hierarchy and hardly ever go outside of chan-nels; I do not ex-pect my boss to consult me be-fore making de-cisions.	I accept hierar-chy without questions and never go out-side of chan-nels; I do not expect my boss to consult me before making decisions.
	low context ⟷ high context				
Communi-cation	I tend to be very explicit when talking or writing and try to include everything the recipient might need to know.	I tend to be fairly explicit when talking or writing and try to include the key points the recipient needs to know.	I include what the recipient need to know when talking or writing, but I don't waste time by repeat-ing stuff that is probably al-ready know	I am normally fairly brief when talking or writ-ing and expect the recipient to understand the rest based on the context without spelling it out in detail.	I am normally very brief when talking or writing and ex-pect the recipi-ent to under-stand the rest based on the context.
	cooperative ⟷ competitive				
Competi-tion	In business, re-lationships and consensus are the most im-portant as-pects	In business, re-lationships and consensus are more important as profit and competition	In business, re-lationships and consensus are as important as profit and com-petition	Competition and achieving profits are quite important in business	Profit and com-petition are the main purpose of business

Source: Seelhofer, D. (2017). Interpersonal Leadership: An Applied Guide, Zurich: OGMA Education.

Form 29   Reflection on Cultural Influences

Person	

Types of culture	Aspect	Characteristics
Societal	Time focus	
	Time orientation	
	Action	
	Competition	
	Power	
	Space	
	Structure	
	Communication	
Organiza-tional	Stories	
	Rituals and routines	
	Symbols	
	Organizational structure	
	Control systems	
	Power structures	
Generational		
Membership group(s)		
Reference group(s)		

Source: Seelhofer, D. (2017). Interpersonal Leadership: An Applied Guide, Zurich: OGMA Education; partly based on Browaeys and Price (2008), and Johnson and Scholes (1992).

Form 30   Universal Leader Attributes

Consider the leader you want to analyze, whether yourself or a subordinate, and indicate for each of the attributes below whether you believe it to represent that person or not. The more universally desirable and the fewer universally undesirable attributes the better. Use this list as the basis for discussions or for your own planning. Remember, however, that any rough assessment like this is always inherently biased.

Attribute	Represents that person		Comments
	Yes	No	
Universally desirable			
Administratively skilled			
Communicative			
Confidence builder			
Coordinator			
Decisive			
Dependable			
Dynamic			
Effective bargainer			
Encouraging			
Excellence-oriented			
Foresightful			
Honest			
Informed			
Intelligent			
Just			
Motivational			
Motive arouser			
Plans ahead			
Positive			
Team builder			
Trustworthy			
Win-win problem solver			
Universally undesirable			
Asocial			
Dictatorial			
Egocentric			
Irritable			
Loner			
Non-cooperative			
Non-explicit			
Ruthless			
What this leader should work on			

Source: Seelhofer, D. (2017). Interpersonal Leadership: An Applied Guide, Zurich: OGMA Education;
based on House, Hanges and Javidan (2004).

Form 31 Ten Fundamental Leadership Principles

Consider the fundamental leadership principles below and indicate to which degree you believe the leader you want to analyze, whether yourself or a subordinate, follows them. The higher the better. Use this list as the basis for discussions or for your own planning. Remember, however, that any rough assessment like this is always inherently biased.

Fundamental Leadership Principle	Leader complies				Comments
	Fully	(Always) partly	Occasionally	Not	
Understand and respect your leader responsibilities					
Avoid globally disliked leadership behaviors					
Conform to implicit leadership expectations in your cultural leader context					
Declare your expectations clearly					
Be technically and administratively proficient					
Be sure of what you say and why you say it					
Go the extra mile					
Take care of your people					
Be present and authentic					
Maintain integrity at all times					
What leader should work on					

Source: Seelhofer, D. (2017). Interpersonal Leadership: An Applied Guide, Zurich: OGMA Education.

Form 32   Ten Classic Leadership Mistakes

Consider the classic leadership mistakes below and indicate to which degree you believe the leader you want to analyze, whether yourself or a subordinate, commits them. The lower the better. Use this list as the basis for discussions or for your own planning. Remember, however, that any rough assessment like this is always inherently biased.

Classic Leadership Mistake	Leader commits				Comments
	Always	(Always) partly	Occasionally	Never	
Setting higher standards for your subordinates than for yourself					
Persistently delegating tasks that you are unwilling to do yourself					
Causing subordinates to lose face					
Inconsistent communication					
Refusing to admit mistakes					
Creating ethical dilemmas for your subordinates					
Collective punishment					
Breaking promises					
Disloyalty downwards or upwards					
Stealing credit					
What leader should work on					

Source: Seelhofer, D. (2017). Interpersonal Leadership: An Applied Guide, Zurich: OGMA Education.

Form 33   Leadership Development Program

Leader Responsibility	Development needs	Goals	Activities	Completed in/by	Success criteria
Achieve tasks and missions					
Self-leadership					
Team-leadership					
Leadership of individuals					

Source: Seelhofer, D. (2017). Interpersonal Leadership: An Applied Guide, Zurich: OGMA Education.

ABOUT THE AUTHOR

Daniel Seelhofer, PhD, is a Professor of International Business at the Zurich University of Applied Sciences' School of Management and Law and a general staff colonel in the Swiss Army. His teaching and research interests revolve around strategy and leadership, particularly in cross-cultural settings.

Dr. Seelhofer was born in 1973 near Berne, Switzerland. He spent most of his childhood in the Upper and Lower Toggenburg regions of Eastern Switzerland, enjoying outdoor activities with his brothers and friends and reading everything that came his way. Starting work as a paper boy at age 11, he bought his first computer that same year and soon taught himself to program in several computer languages. From there on, video games were also among his hobbies, yet as a keen boy scout he still spent a lot of time in the woods. He also began to work part-time for a local small business in an administrative role.

After completing secondary education, he enrolled in a commercial school before moving to the United States, where he earned a high school diploma. After returning to Switzerland for his mandatory military service, he switched back and forth between active and reserve duty, eventually both acquiring a Master's in International Management from the University of St. Gallen (HSG) and becoming a Mustang officer and platoon leader after having served as an infantry squad leader. He then resumed work in the private sector as an IT consultant and software trainer. After graduation, he co-founded a custom software development company and ran it for several years before joining a medium-sized service company in Zurich, Switzerland's commercial center, eventually rising to a board-level position. At the same time, he completed his doctorate in international business after a lengthy and occasionally painful development process of almost six years. During that period, he began to teach part time at a local university and caught the academic bug that would later lead him to enter academia full time.

Continuing his military career in the unique Swiss dual-track system, he served as an infantry company commander and gained experience in security and disaster relief missions. He was selected for the Swiss Army's elite general staff academy after a grueling selection process. Having successfully completed this extremely demanding training, he served in the intelligence section of a divisional staff before assuming command of an infantry battalion with, at the time, over 1,500 soldiers assigned to it. After this intensive but highly rewarding period, he returned to divisional staff, ultimately rising to head the operations section (G3) as a full colonel.

He joined the Zurich University of Applied Science's School of Management and Law as a senior lecturer and later served as Chief of Staff and Vice Dean. After leading his business school's successful effort to achieve AACSB accreditation, he is now the director of the Department of International Business and head of the International Management Institute. A professor of international business, he has taught and worked on projects around the world: in the USA and Canada, Austria, France, Germany, the Netherlands, the Gulf region, Hungary, Turkey, Singapore, Malaysia, Sri Lanka, and Serbia.

He now lives in Winterthur and enjoys spending time with his family, sports (particularly outdoors), reading and writing, and listening to and creating music.